Asian Travel in the Renaissance

T0355531

A Welcome from the Series Editor

With this volume, the Society for Renaissance Studies and Blackwell Publishing are inaugurating an occasional, but regular, series of essay collections on the Renaissance. These are intended to make available in book form selected special numbers of the Society's journal, *Renaissance Studies*. The volumes will be guest edited, and all the material appearing will also have been peer-reviewed in the normal way, and approved by the journal's editorial board.

The board is delighted that Dr Daniel Carey and his contributors are launching this series, and grateful to the Publications Fund of the National University of Ireland, Galway, for its support. As Dr Carey observes in his introduction, the importance of the subject dealt with here – the European encounter with the wider world – was identified by the journal in the special number edited by Professor John Larner in 1992, and it is a pleasure to see it now being taken further.

John E. Law,
Series Editor

This publication was grant-aided by the Publications Fund of the National University of Ireland, Galway.

Asian Travel in the Renaissance

Edited by
Daniel Carey

Preface by
Anthony Reid

**Published on behalf of the
Society for Renaissance Studies**

Blackwell
Publishing

© 2004 by the Society for Renaissance Studies and Blackwell Publishing Ltd

First published as volume 17, number 3 of *Renaissance Studies*

350 Main Street, Malden, MA 02148-5018, USA
108 Cowley Road, Oxford OX4 1JF, UK
550 Swanston Street, Carlton, Victoria 3053, Australia

The right of Daniel Carey to be identified as the Author of the Editorial Material in this Work has been asserted in accordance with the UK Copyright, Designs, and Patents Act 1988.

First published 2004 by Blackwell Publishing Ltd

Library of Congress Cataloging-in-Publication Data has been applied for

ISBN 1-4051-1160-7

A catalogue record for this title is available from the British Library.

Set in 10/12pt New Baskerville by Graphicraft Limited, Hong Kong

For further information on
Blackwell Publishing, visit our website:
http://www.blackwellpublishing.com

Contents

Notes on Contributors

Daniel Carey is a lecturer in English at the National University of Ireland, Galway. His articles on the history of travel, anthropology, and philosophy, have appeared in journals in Britain, America, and Germany. He is the author of *Locke, Shaftesbury, and Hutcheson: Contesting Diversity in the Enlightenment and Beyond*, forthcoming from Cambridge University Press, and *The Paradox of Travel, 1580–1700*, forthcoming from Columbia University Press.

Robert Markley is Professor of English at the University of Illinois. His books include *Fallen Languages: Crises of Representation in Newtonian England, 1660–1740* (1993), and *Fictions of Eurocentrism: The Far East and the European Imagination*, forthcoming from Cambridge.

Malyn Newitt is Charles Boxer Professor of History in the Department of Portuguese and Brazilian Studies at King's College London. He is author of *Portugal in Africa, Portuguese Settlement on the Zambesi, A History of Mozambique*, and most recently *Community and the State in Lusophone Africa*.

Joan-Pau Rubiés is Senior Lecturer in International History at the London School of Economics, and author of *Travel and Ethnology in the Renaissance: South India through European Eyes, 1250–1625 (Cambridge, 2000)*. He is now working on a study of the impact of European travel writing on the origins of the Enlightenment.

Claudia Schnurmann is chair for early modern and modern North American history with its Atlantic and Caribbean perspectives (15th–21th centuries) at the University Hamburg. Her books include *Atlantische Welten: Englaender und Niederlaender im amerikanisch-atlantischen Raum 1648–1713* (1998) and *Vom Inselreich zur Weltmacht: Die Entwicklung des englischen Weltreichs vom Mittelalter bis ins 20. Jahrhundert, Kohlhammer Verlag* (2001).

Nicolas Standaert is Professor of Chinese Studies at the Katholieke Universiteit Leuven (Belgium). He is the author of *Yang Tingyun, Confucian and Christian in Late Ming China* (1988) and the editor of the *Handbook of Christianity in China: Volume I (635–1800)* (2001).

Sven Trakulhun is a research associate at the Forschungszentrum Europäische Aufklärung in Potsdam. He has published numerous articles on the history of

Thailand and is co-editor (with Thomas Fuchs) of a volume on cultural transfer in European history: *Das eine Europa und die Vielfalt der Kulturen* (2003).

M. Antoni J. Üçerler, S.J., is a lecturer in Comparative Intellectual History at Sophia University (Tokyo). He has recently been appointed a full-time Fellow of the Historical Institute of the Society of Jesus (Rome). With Satoru Obara, he published a facsimile edition and introduction to rare manuscripts from the collections of the Vatican Library, Magdalen College Library (Oxford), and the Cabinet Library/National Archives of Japan: *Compendia compiled by Pedro Gómez for the Jesuit College of Japan*, 3 vols (Tokyo: Ozorasha, 1997).

John Villiers is currently a Research Associate in the Department of Portuguese and Brazilian Studies at King's College, London, and general editor of a series of volumes of documents in translation entitled *Portuguese Encounters with the World in the Age of the Discoveries*. His numerous other publications include *East of Malacca: Three Essays on the Portuguese in the Indonesian Archipelago in the Sixteenth and Seventeenth Centuries* (1985) and *Albuquerque: Caesar of the East* (with T. F. Earle) (1990).

Preface

This book appears in an era when the global village and presumptions of ever greater convergence are being challenged by Samuel Huntington's almost self-fulfilling prophecy about a 'clash of civilizations'. Once again fear and ignorance feed on each other, as some of those on each side of the civilizational fault lines demonize many of those on the other.

It is more than usually timely to reflect on another era when some of these civilizations were discovering each other for the first time, without the great burden of inequality which accumulated during the subsequent centuries. The 'Renaissance' of this book, in effect the sixteenth century and much of the seventeenth, was a time of astonishing possibilities. As Europe struggled to come to terms with the impossibility of healing its own profound cleavages between Catholic, Protestant and Orthodox, as well as between the new nationalisms of Spanish, Portuguese, French, Dutch and English, it encountered at the same time totally unfamiliar civilizations from which it had been long separated by the world of Islam.

In this encounter there was no shortage of violence, ignorance, prejudice and fear. As the essays that follow remind us, much of the worst prejudice in Asia was between the Europeans themselves—not simply Protestant against Catholic, but Portuguese against Spanish, Dutch against English, Franciscan against Jesuit. Yet there was also a pervading curiosity, puzzlement and even awe at the different ways in which Asian and European civilizations handled the great questions of ordering human society and connecting to the world beyond.

Concentrating on the intellectual dimensions of the encounter from the European side, and the weighty intellectual baggage that informed European writing and action in relation to Asia, this book dispels the stereotypes about this first stage of the intense encounter of civilizations. The range of ideas is immense, from Jesuits painfully translating Aristotelian texts into Chinese language and neo-Confucian idiom, and Queen Elizabeth saluting 'our loving Brother', the Sultan of Aceh because he had so valiantly fought the Portuguese, to Valignano dismissing India as having 'no learning or scientific knowledge whatsoever', or La Loubère dismissing Siamese history as containing nothing 'worthy of memory'. Europeans were changing and fissuring as never before, and the range of their reactions to the Asian other was so vast as to defy simple categorizations.

Two points do however appear to stand out. Firstly the real heroes for our age, among the many Renaissance European writers and mediators of Asia, were those who spent many years working with Asians in Asia, to the point of hearing them in their own languages. This applied to many of the Jesuits in China and Japan, who had to sit at the feet of Confucian scholars to understand unfamiliar languages and puzzlingly powerful political and social systems. But equally impressive was the careful ethnographic work of Fr Francisco Alzina after three decades in the Visayas (Bisayas). A Dutch merchant like Jeremias van Vliet had different ways of acquiring language and culture, not only in commerce but through his Thai wife, but he too wrote invaluable studies of Siamese history and society. Sadly, however, neither Alzina nor van Vliet were published or appreciated until recently. The most influential accounts of Asia were by those like Bartolomé Leonardo de Argensola or João de Barros, classically educated scholars who wrote beautifully but never set foot in Asia.

Secondly, by the latter part of the seventeenth century European curiosity about Asians and sense of equality with them were fast fading. Asian suspicions of the political ambitions of Europeans also erected barriers from their side. We see this trend in the increasing distrust of Christian missions of all kinds in Japan and China, but we see it too in the lack of interest of later writers such as Turpin about the earlier history of their subjects. The extraordinary moment of open encounters and possibilities was finished after little more than a century. We learn much from revisiting that moment.

The writers in this collection make no secret of the fact that they are writing only about the European side of the encounter. The title might suggest that the genre represented is Travel Literature, but it is much more than that. Each essay is concerned with an intellectual lineage, with the way a particular set of European minds dealt with the challenges of Asia. To that extent it relates rather to the vast enterprise of Donald Lach and Edwin Van Kley, *Asia in the Making of Europe*. While writing about Europeans, the authors are well informed about Asia, to a degree which few scholars emulated even a generation ago.

Another scholar exceptionally well informed about Asia was Charles Boxer, to whose memory this collection might well be dedicated. He was the master storyteller about the European encounter with Asia, who contributed more to illuminating dark corners in elegant prose and balanced judgement than any other single historian of the period. It is fitting that this collection ends with an evaluation of his life and work. May I add my homage to that of Malyn Newitt.

Anthony Reid
National University of Singapore

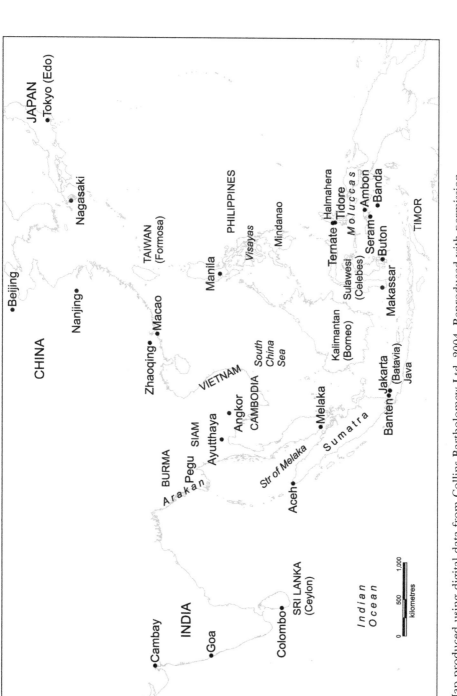

Map produced using digital data from Collins Bartholomew Ltd, 2004. Reproduced with permission.

1
Introduction
Asian Travel in the Renaissance

Perhaps inevitably, the story of European expansion in the early modern period has concentrated to a large extent, both in the public imagination and in academic inquiry, on voyages to the 'New World' and their aftermath. These events resulted in the occupation of a remarkable expanse of territory, and the settlement of European peoples on an unprecedented scale across two continents, in addition to the huge transportation of African slaves. But the consequence of allocating intellectual and narrative resources in this way has been to obscure the range and significance of European activity in Asia where an altogether different set of conditions obtained. Here Europeans encountered the vast empire of China and the problematic cultural interaction in Japan, as well as a geography in Southeast Asia of exceptional political and physical complexity. Yet, quite apart from religious incentives, the wealth that was promised by trade in this region was staggering, and it attracted the efforts of a wide array of European powers, beginning with the Portuguese and joined by the Spanish, English, Dutch, French, Danes and others.

This collection of essays looks at the region afresh, examining Asian travel from a variety of perspectives and integrating the discussion into a wider set of political, economic and cultural networks. The incentive for paying greater attention to Asia stems not only from its historical importance, but also because of its relative neglect by the wider community of Renaissance scholars, despite the excellent work of leading specialists in the region.[1] Yet Dutch enterprise in the region was motivated by attempts to rival the Spanish in the New World, in the midst of a struggle for political independence. (And, as Richard Tuck has recently reminded us, the articulation of modern

---

[1] Among other contributions in English, see writings by Donald F. Lach and Edwin J. Van Kley, Jonathan Spence, Anthony Reid, J. S. Cummins, Leonard Andaya, Dauril Alden, O. H. K. Spate, A. J. R. Russell-Wood, Michael Cooper, and of course C. R. Boxer. See also the edited collections *Vasco da Gama and the Linking of Europe and Asia*, ed. Anthony Disney and Emily Booth (New Delhi, 2000); Francis A. Dutra and João Camilo dos Santos (eds), *The Portuguese and the Pacific I* (Santa Barbara, 1995); Sanjay Subrahmanyam and Kenneth McPherson (eds), 'Special issue: the Portuguese and the Pacific II', *Santa Barbara Portuguese Studies*, 2 (1995); and a special issue of *Renaissance Studies*, edited by John Larner: 'The encounter of two worlds in the Renaissance', 6/3–4 (1992). The history of European interaction with China and to a lesser extent Japan constitute exceptions to this neglect, but they are often seen in isolation, despite the existence of integrated patterns of trade in the region, and important connections through the European presence in Southeast Asia (such as in the Philippines and Indonesia).

natural law theory by Hugo Grotius was one important outcome of these struggles.[2]) At the same time, such economic enterprise created global networks of trade, linking the silver mines of the New World with Europe, which in turn facilitated trade with China and Japan as well as exchanges of Indian finished goods for spices and other commodities in Southeast Asia – exotica that eventually made the journey back to Europe.

In the midst of this activity, a series of religious, political and cultural engagements took place on very different terms to encounters in the New World. In Southeast Asia, for example, systems of elaborate alliance were exploited as Europeans inserted themselves into complex patterns of existing trade. Yet the asymmetrical power relations that scholars have often remarked in New World contexts were reconfigured, where Europeans made contact with civilizations of greater antiquity, sophistication, and wealth than their own. The attempt to participate in these territories, whether as traders, missionaries, or diplomats, required a very different set of procedures and assumptions.

Several shared themes animate the discussion in this book. Issues of historiography predominate in the discussion of narrative resources and traditions available to a range of European writers (Portuguese, Dutch, Spanish, Italian, English and others) who represented Asia in their accounts, some based on personal experience, others culled from witnesses and various printed sources. In untangling these strands, we should of course remember that the East was by no means unknown and that conceptions of it were inevitably filtered through a range of biblical and classical assumptions. The humanist contribution to the study of cultural difference emerges in a number of ways, both from religious and lay figures employed in diverse roles in the Estado da Índia, the Philippines, China and Japan, while representatives of the VOC (Vereenigde Oost-Indische Compagnie) engaged in their own effort to chronicle the history of local states, inspired by different motives and agendas. In these accounts, continual questions of verisimilitude, truth, and fiction arose as individuals attempted to make sense of what they observed as much as of what they read.

As befits an order which dedicated itself so resolutely to the task of missionary work in Asia, the Society of Jesus receives considerable attention here. But this is joined by discussion of the activities of rival religious orders, notably the Franciscans, Dominicans and Augustinians who contributed, for

---

[2] 'Although relations with the very culturally distinct peoples of the New World have caught the eye of most historians, and were indeed strange and dramatic, it is probably true to say that it was the relations with the Asiatic economies which were of greater historical importance. . . . It should not therefore be surprising that it was in a book dealing with the theoretical issues thrown up by Far Eastern trade, Grotius's astonishing *De Indis*, or *De Iure Praedae* that . . . the first truly modern political theory is to be found'. Richard Tuck, *The Rights of War and Peace: Political Thought and the International Order from Grotius to Kant* (Oxford, 1999), 232. See also Martine van Ittersum, 'Profit and Principle: Hugo Grotius, Natural Rights Theories and the Rise of Dutch Power in the East Indies, 1595–1615', Ph.D dissertation, Harvard University (2002).

example, to the Spanish ethnology of Asia. The institutional and inter-institutional conflicts that surfaced in Southeast Asia and the Far East often had their origins in power struggles taking place in Europe. Such struggles were matched, of course, by national conflicts, conspicuously between the Dutch and their Protestant and Catholic rivals, but also between the Portuguese and Spanish themselves, unabated during the sixty-year unification of the crowns (1580–1640).

The essays call attention to the fact that early modern cultural encounter has too often been understood within the terms of a limited paradigm: namely, the instance of individual European travellers who found themselves in unfamiliar environments and attempted to make sense of what they experienced. This model has its merits, and derives, to some extent, from the powerful, originating example of Marco Polo. But it ignores the institutional constraints that defined cultural exchange and the terms in which such encounters took place. Again, the most obvious examples are the Catholic religious orders which not only engaged in vigorous arguments internally but also across rival orders as they competed in overlapping territories in Asia. The same is true for the Dutch chroniclers who examined the East India Company's activities in Siam and elsewhere, just as it is for Spanish historians. Court and company politics intruded on these commissions, circumscribing what might be written and published. Thus it was not a straightforward case of 'representing otherness' on the basis of individual experience but of an intricate set of demands, requiring different rhetorical modes and positionings.

The volume begins with an essay by M. Antoni Üçerler, SJ, who examines the long and eventful career of Alessandro Valignano, beginning with his appointment as Visitor to the Jesuit missions in the Portuguese East Indies in 1573, through his travels east in Africa, India, Malacca (Melaka), Macao, and eventually Japan, where he spent a total of ten years, to his death in 1606. Before embarking on the journey, Valignano's political conflicts had already begun, indicating the difficult negotiation required between the Order and the demands of the Portuguese Jesuits, concerned to protect their interests in territories defined by the *Padroado Real* (the right of the Portuguese crown to govern the church's affairs in lands east of the Cape of Good Hope, as established by a series of papal bulls in the fifteenth and sixteenth centuries). They questioned the authority and decisions of the Italian nobleman who showed a provocative readiness to include numerous Spaniards among his recruits to take part in the mission. These battles did not end in Europe. Similar disputes over jurisdiction later arose in India where Valignano, obliged to resign his responsibilities for the country, had to establish his independence from the new Jesuit Provincial, Francisco Cabral. Ongoing opposition to Valignano stemmed in part from the adventurous stand he took on a number of issues; he introduced several innovative policies, including the establishment of educational institutions for training Japanese youth, the admission of Japanese converts to the Jesuit order, and adaptation to local customs and hierarchies, a point on which he was overruled by the Jesuit General Superior, Claudio Acquaviva, in an anticipation of the rites controversy that later developed famously in China.[3] Thus the struggles associated with missionary work were as much internal to religious orders and institutional as they were matters of negotiating cultural difference.

Despite his recognition that successes in Japan had been overstated before his arrival (thirty years after Francis Xavier established the first Christian community there), Valignano remained convinced of the country's great potential for Christianization. Nor did he refrain from organizing an astute public relations event himself by arranging for four Japanese converts to travel to Europe. The trip was not only designed to impress secular and religious authorities with the Society's progress, but equally to advertise the glories of Christendom to the young men themselves. (He also asked them to return, it may be noted, with a printing press.) On the whole, Valignano believed that Japanese conversions were genuine, based on reason rather than interest, and supported by the native intelligence and application of Japanese students. Yet this project was set against difficult and changing political circumstances in the country. In 1587, the Japanese regent banned all public Christian missionary activity, requiring Valignano, who was then reentering the country, to redefine his status as an ambassador representing the Portuguese viceroy in India, not as Visitor to the Far East, in order to gain readmission. The distinctiveness of Valignano's role is that he combined the task of ethnographer with that of policy-maker; his observations there-fore had a material effect and as he acquired greater knowledge and insight, he revised his missiological strategies accordingly, developing a less ideal-ized account of Japanese society while remaining a devoted supporter of the Christian mission and what he called 'il modo soave' in dealing with the Japanese.

Valignano's contemporary, Matteo Ricci, has attracted greater attention in leading the Jesuit mission in China, an enterprise on which Nicolas Stand-aert focuses in his essay. But Standaert reverses the usual perspective on Ricci and his successors. Rather than concentrating on the conclusions drawn by Jesuits about Chinese culture and tradition, he instead describes the efforts to introduce the literature and thought of the European Renaissance into China. The challenge of creating adequate libraries and disseminating texts beyond Beijing was a huge one, not least because the missionaries were sometimes separated by distances of more than a 1000 kilometers within China itself. In this process of cultural transfer, the book occasionally functioned as a rhetorical device in its own right: the very existence of printed matter,

---

[3] Among other scholarly contributions, see George Minamiki, *The Chinese Rites Controversy from Its Beginnings to Modern Times* (Chicago, 1985); Paul A. Rule, *K'ung-tzu or Confucius? The Jesuit Interpretation of Confucianism* (Sydney, 1986).

expensively bound and elegantly produced, impressed the learned class in China. In general, it was important to locate points of compatibility between China and Europe for purposes of mutual recognition. After varying attempts to assimilate Confucian thought to different classical sources, Ricci came to see it as analogous to Stoicism, regarding Confucius as 'un altro Seneca', which led him in turn to translate the wisdom of Seneca and Epictetus into Chinese, on the assumption that their thought was sympathetic and compatible with indigenous tradition. The long-term project of translating various works, which became more systematic over time, was established in the late sixteenth and seventeenth centuries, ranging from texts of astronomy and mathematics to philosophy, theology, devotional works, medicine and technology. The quantity of non-religious works suggests that this dissemination was intended to achieve a broader cultural prestige, influence and credibility as much as to make specific doctrinal inroads. At the same time, as Ricci noted, there were many ways to draw the Chinese 'into the net of Peter'. These translations had a practical impact in some instances. In the case of astronomy, for example, the Jesuits were instrumental in bringing about a calendar reform in the mid-seventeenth century, based on the Tychonic system, and some of their members joined the ranks of the Astronomical Bureau in the newly established Qing dynasty. Other tasks were less successful, including the attempt to introduce Aristotelian philosophy, which formed so central a part of Jesuit training back home, as the basis of the Chinese educational system.

Conditions in which the Jesuits operated changed considerably over the course of time, but a constant feature was the fact that Europeans faced the challenge of meeting the Chinese predominantly on the lattter's terms. It was essential to acquire the Chinese language, and the insistence on the primacy of Chinese customs required different forms of observance, submitting to the so-called 'cultural imperative'.[4] Given that the Chinese had a well established educational system, there was no occasion for the Jesuits to create new schools as they did elsewhere (notably in Macao) to achieve their ends. As Standaert emphasizes, ultimately the Chinese remained the arbiters of what aspects of Renaissance learning they would adopt and which ones they would ignore.

The historiographical task of describing and comprehending the countries of Asia took different forms in the Renaissance, some humanistic in inspiration, others devoted exclusively to ecclesiastical concerns, and others still inspired by more immediate opportunities for professional advancement or a narrative focus on personal adventure. Initially, the scope for investigating the history of countries in Southeast Asia before the arrival of Europeans was

---

[4] For a comparative account of what this meant for 'foreign' religions in relation to Confucianism, see Erik Zürcher, 'Jesuit Accommodation and the Chinese Cultural Imperative', in D. E. Mungello (ed.), *The Chinese Rites Controversy: Its History and Meaning* (Nettetal, 1994), 31–64.

limited, and relatively little attention was given to the early history or origins of differing peoples. Of course the 'East' was not *terra incognita*, as Sven Trakulhun points out in an essay on contacts with Siam, and efforts to understand this region in an era of expanding exploration and trade inevitably had recourse to classical and biblical traditions with echoes of the 'Golden Chersonese' and the land of Ophir, populated by Judean remnants from King Soloman's time. Nonetheless, some comparative ethnography was broached, at times connecting Siamese Buddhism with religious practices in Japan or establishing ethnic and cultural links by identifying shared customs (as in the sexual anthropology of Siam, Pegu [Lower Burma/Myanmar] and other countries). More commonly the Chinese were credited with a founding role in establishing the Siamese royal dynasties and cultural achievements.

Among historians of the country, the example of Jeremias van Vliet, a Dutch merchant in the employ of the VOC, is remarkable in many respects. Van Vliet, who resided in Ayutthaya from 1633–42, composed a range of works on Thai history, the most significant of which remained unpublished, his 'Cort verhael van 't . . . der Coningen van Siam' (Short history of the Siamese kings), based on an array of indigenous documents and sources. Van Vliet surmounted the linguistic barrier, as few had done, partly aided by a native wife. Yet he also struggled with the question of how to categorize the stories contained in the Thai chronicles, some of which he relegated to the status of fable and others which he seemed to invest with belief. For other commentators, the history they contemplated in Siam was eventless and static, evidence not so much of decline as an eternal present animated by few developments of note. But there is a particular significance attached to these fleeting invocations of Siamese cosmology, legend and tradition since the official records of the country were almost entirely destroyed when the Burmese captured the capital city of Ayutthaya in 1767.

In general the Spanish contribution to the ethnology of Asia has not been as widely appreciated as the Portuguese and Dutch material from the same period, and remains overshadowed by New World narratives (with the possible exception of certain writings devoted to China). Yet a substantial literature, examined by Joan-Pau Rubiés, developed as a result of the Spanish conquest of the Philippines in the 1560s. The colony in fact became the most extensive territory in the East ruled directly by a European power. Furthermore, from this base, Spaniards journeyed in various capacities throughout Southeast Asia and the Far East – indeed it made possible a number of prospective activities of conquest, including a failed mission in Cambodia or schemes to capture China or retake Malacca (Melaka) which were actively contemplated but (no doubt wisely) abandoned. The circumstances in which such work was produced requires careful attention not merely to distinctions between lay and religious writers and their respective orders, whether Augustinian, Jesuit, Dominican or Franciscan, but more broadly to the institutional constraints that were imposed on the varying participants in evangelization, trade, and military conflict. It was rare for anyone to travel in an independent capacity; the norm was to receive royal, ecclesiastical, or aristocratic patronage which established ideological limits on the expression of these accounts. What is more, the ongoing conflict between Spanish (or rather Castilian) and Portuguese interests, intensified during the union of the crowns. As Rubiés points out, the amalgamation in 1580 entailed the sharing of a sovereign, not an imperial system. Jealousies continued, despite the need for a more integrated vision of national purpose in the East in the light of Dutch and English incursions after 1600.

The literary production that resulted was informed by a number of traditions and composed in a variety of genres and sub-generic forms: 'relations', reports, letters, histories and cosmographies. Texts by Antonio de Morga (1609), Pedro Chirino (1604) and Francisco Alzina (completed 1668), for example, describing the Tagalog and Bisayas (Visayas) people in the Philippines, are notable in different ways for their comprehensiveness, relying on empirical sources and classical comparison to create an ethnography of some depth, with a humanist inflection in the case of Chirino and Alzina. They varied in their degree of tolerance or warmth for native practices, but were certainly capable of giving praise for local languages, as part of a broader and serious engagement with the phenomenon of human (and natural) diversity.

John Villiers describes an intriguing example of this Spanish historiographical tradition – the Aragonese priest, poet, historian (and friend of Cervantes), Bartolomé Leonardo de Argensola, whose account of the Spanish capture of the Moluccan spice island of Ternate appeared in 1609. The *Conquista* chronicled the victory of Don Pedro de Acuña, governor of the Philippines, which took place three years earlier. Argensola positioned the Spanish achievement as a breakthrough in the struggle not so much to achieve a direct participation in the spice trade but against the pernicious advance of the Dutch, whose Protestantism was the principal threat (only a year before, the Dutch had forced the Portuguese out of the neighbouring islands of Tidore and Ambon). In part this work of justification was necessary because the Moluccas fell within the purview of the Portuguese under the terms of the *Padroado Real*, although they had been driven from the clove-producing island of Ternate in 1575 by its Muslim ruler. The religious sensibility and Catholic ideology that informed his writing led Argensola to celebrate a military triumph that ostensibly halted the relentless Dutch progress in the region, securing the islands for the true Faith against the incursion of heresy and raising the prospect of a harvest of 200,000 souls.

Villiers vividly describes the narrative predicament of Argensola. With no personal experience of Indonesia, Argensola relied on numerous sources of testimony to create a heroic narrative that married the objective of a *historia verdadera* with a consistent moral and spiritual purpose, at the same time as he refused to gloss over the bloody nature of conflict there. The resulting chronicle contained a mixture of authentic material and other passages demonstrating his occasional credulity and appetite for marvels or monsters. On Southeast Asian kingship Argensola had some feeling for the need of native rulers to establish their legitimacy by securing a genealogical foundation in myth, as well as the distinctive combination of Islam with pre-Islamic religious practices in the Moluccas. Elsewhere he made the unfortunate mistake of confusing Cambodia with Cambay in Gujarat, India, even as he compiled a surprisingly accurate picture of the abandoned former Khmer capital of Cambodia, Angkor Thom. Nor was his history free from engaging with ongoing disputes between Spanish and Portuguese rights under the *Padroado* (or in the Spanish case *Patronato*) *Real,* despite being composed during the union of the crowns. The cosmological arguments over the dividing line between East and West focused to some extent on the Moluccas. And – although he did not ignore Spanish abuses – he was willing to retail stories of Portuguese outrages that complemented the *leyenda negra* or Black Legend that accompanied the Spanish in the New World.

Spanish triumphs in the Moluccas did not of course inhibit the Dutch for long, who established themselves as the premier European trading nation with interests in Southeast Asia, China and Japan. Responding to English developments in organizing an effective joint-stock company, the Dutch followed suit in 1602 by integrating disparate trading operations in order to form the VOC. In 1621 they pursued a similar plan in creating the West India Company (WIC), dividing territorial operations along similar lines to the separation between Portuguese and Spanish spheres of activity. Both companies enjoyed the right to engage in war, make treaties, capture foreign ships, and to attack Iberian territories – in effect a considerable measure of sovereign power. Claudia Schnurmann explores the relative fortunes of these Dutch companies in her essay. While they sprang from a single culture dominated by merchants and a desire to frustrate Spanish and Portuguese enterprise in Asia, Africa, the Caribbean, Brazil, and the rest of South America, the Dutch companies encountered very different conditions in Asia and the New World which throw the challenge of colonial and economic expansion into relief. The two ventures formed part of an unfolding global system of commerce, yet they were established with different forms of settlement pattern, different markets, and sources of labour supply. In Asia, the Dutch mastered their European competitors, in part by imitating them. With the exception of Batavia in Java, from which they directed their trading operation, they refrained from pursuing a policy of territorial rulership. In the New World, by contrast, they were competing with settler colonies on a vast scale. The successful capture of Brazil was only shortlived, while the first and second Anglo-Dutch wars had a significant bearing on their ability to retain not only Brazil but also the colony of Nieuw Nederland (New York), although they did acquire Surinam in the process. To some extent the WIC tried to emulate the control over disparate trading centres enjoyed by Batavia by placing Recife in Brazil on a similar footing (Dutch ships coming and going were required to call there), but the arrangement of course did not last. And while monopolies had been enforced successfully in Asia, they crumbled in the case of the Caribbean, particularly in Surinam. Once confined to producing sugar solely for the Netherlands, and relying in turn exclusively on Dutch imports, the Surinam colonists eventually created their own inter-colonial trade network, in part to acquire sufficient slave labour. The tendency to 'celebrate' the VOC's successes is thus somewhat naïve, at least as they contrasted with alleged 'failures' in the New World. Both had their breakthroughs, periods of decline, and long-term impact.

The challenge of comprehending the host of opportunities presented by commerce in Southeast Asia and the Far East was not confined to merchants in the great trading companies, of course, but remained a preoccupation of cosmographers as well, attempting to situate their respective countries' place in the world of trade. The example of Peter Heylyn, discussed by Robert Markley, indicates the struggle this entailed for an English author, as a series of triangular relationships emerged among European rivals and local states. Attempting to exploit dissatisfactions with the Portuguese, Spanish and Dutch, the English sought connections from Aceh to Japan,[5] not only as a prospective market for English goods but as a place of exchange where silver would obtain valuable commodities like nutmeg, mace, and cloves that the Dutch progressively monopolized. In a world providentially organized by God in such a way that no country was sufficient in itself, trade and Christian theology cooperated in validating eastern voyages. At the same time, a figure like Heylyn mapped on to the ethnographic function of travel and cosmography a bias in favour of established trading relations and hoped-for alliances in the region. It is striking that, in terms of social customs, what could be forgiven in one context (on the basis of such commercial ties) was elsewhere condemned as savagery or perfidy.

The Japanese in this respect represented a difficult cultural conundrum; the civility, good government, and refinement of the Japanese continually impressed European visitors, but Christian missions had been extirpated there, even if they were led by Catholic orders. However, the country constituted an enticing market for English cloth given its northerly latitude, not to mention a valuable source of prospective silver in its own right. Heylyn's rhetoric struck a careful, if not entirely consistent balance, finding much to praise but chiding the rigidity and self-denial that made the Japanese come across, in his eyes, as eastern Puritans. In the end, the English had to confront the fact that they were marginal players despite perpetual ambitions to improve their stakes. This tale of disappointed expectations reminds us more generally that Asia enjoyed economic superiority in the period and that later

---

[5] On Aceh, see Anthony Reid, 'Trade and the Problem of Royal Power in Aceh', in Anthony Reid and Lance Castles (eds), *Pre-Colonial State Systems in Southeast Asia* (1975; reprinted Kuala Lumpur, 1979), 45–55.

developments in trade and production distort our understanding of the state of play in the sixteenth and seventeenth centuries.

The final piece in the collection continues many of these themes arising in the earlier essays: problems of political economy in European competition in Asia, the ethnography and historiography of Indonesia, and the narrative resources available to European writers in describing an unfamiliar environment. In this instance, Daniel Carey focuses on Makassar poison, which was used by warriors in the eastern Indonesian sultinate of Makassar in their battles with Dutch forces. This pernicious substance became the subject of numerous travel accounts and reports as foreign observers struggled to understand its hidden properties and antidotes. The mixture of the factual and fantastic in these relations (by Portuguese, Spanish, Dutch and English authors) created an aura of decided mystery around Makassarese 'arts' in cultivating and employing the poison. The country's rulers added to the effect by staging public executions in which convicts were dispatched, in theatrical fashion, by being struck with poisoned darts.

Such was the fascination generated by these stories that the newly founded Royal Society of London sought out samples with which to conduct experiments in the 1660s. Naturalists actively pursued further understanding of its operation experimentally but despite their persistence they did not meet with success. On the one hand they could not be sure they had obtained the correct material, and on the other they were unable to standardize dosages. But most importantly, they could not ensure that their samples arrived in England with sufficient swiftness or were handled with proper care during the long ocean journey back. For this reason they relied heavily on narrative accounts from different sources, including published documents and commissioned inquiries from various correspondents. These activities occurred during the period leading up to and during the second Anglo-Dutch war (1664–67), suggesting that natural knowledge was not a disinterested activity but one deeply implicated in the political economy of trade and colonization. The Dutch were unable to counteract the poison effectively, making information on its toxicity of considerable value. Equally, any breakthroughs in identifying antidotes would have assisted the English if they in turn – as they fervently hoped – supplanted their rivals and gained the upper hand in the spice trade through the key entrepôt of Makassar.

Collectively the essays break down the conception of Asia and the 'East' as a monolithic entity, showing the highly particular and diverse locations in which Europeans interacted with various polities as traders, colonial agents, missionaries, soldiers and diplomats. Although English experience receives considerable attention, the essays devote greater space to the Dutch, Italians, Portuguese, Spanish and French. The geographical focus falls on Southeast Asia and the Far East, rather than transactions in South Asia, which have received much more attention in English-language scholarship. Asia generally was a domain of mixed fortunes, a place in which Europeans in some cases had a huge impact in the period (especially Indonesia and the Philippines) while elsewhere they were stymied despite their commercial ambitions. These cultural and economic exchanges formed a vital part of Renaissance history, both at the level of aspiration and reality.

This volume took shape after the death of Charles Boxer, who more than any other scholar integrated the study of travel, colonialism, and empire in Asia and the Americas. His remarkable life and career, considered by Malyn Newitt as a sequel to the essays published here, remind us of the challenges and opportunities for combining the study of the Renaissance with the intricate dealings of Europeans in Asia.

For their invaluable assistance and advice in bringing about this volume, I am indebted to various friends and colleagues: John Law, Kevry Sinanan, Ceri Sullivan, and especially John Villiers. At Blackwells this project has had crucial support throughout from Philip Joseph. My thanks to Cee Pike, Jacqueline Scott, and Jackie Tate for their work on the production, and to Nigel James for help in producing the map: The Publications fund of the National University of Ireland, Galway, supported this volume with a grant, for which I am very grateful.

2

Alessandro Valignano: man, missionary, and writer

M. ANTONI J. ÜÇERLER, SJ

THE FIRST YEARS

The son of Giambattista Valignano and Isabella de Sangro, Alessandro was born in February 1539 into a noble family in Chieti, a city in the Abruzzi region of central Italy and part of the kingdom of Naples under Spanish domination.[1] Very little is known about his early years as a boy in Chieti, except that 'during his upbringing he was engaged . . . in the study of Latin and exercises of chivalry'.[2] The first significant fact in his life as a young man

---

[1] For more complete biographical information on Valignano as well as a description of his activities in Asia, see Daniello Bartoli, *Del Giappone* (3 vols, Turin, 1825), I (= vol. x), 136–69, 248–78, 347–86; II (vol. XI), 137–45; III (vol. XII), 134–55. This work was originally published as *Dell'Historia della Compagnia di Giesù: Il Giappone. Seconda Parte Dell'Asia* (Rome, 1660); Matteo Ricci, *Storia dell'Introduzione del Cristianesimo in Cina* in *Fonti Ricciane: Documenti originali concernenti Matteo Ricci e la storia delle prime relazioni tra l'Europa e la Cina (1579–1615)*, ed. Pasquale M. D'Elia (3 vols, Rome, 1942–9), I, 140–8, 221–3; II, 362–7; Luis de Guzmán, *Historia de las missiones que han hecho los religiosos de la Compañía de Jesús para predicar el Sancto Evangelio en la India Oriental y en los reynos de la China y Japón* (2 vols, Alcalá, 1601); Ferrante Valignani, *Vita del Padre Alessandro Valignani della Compagnia di Giesù* (Rome, 1698). Among contemporary writers, the following are of special value: Josef Franz Schütte, *Valignano's Mission Principles for Japan, Volume I/1. From His Appointment as Visitor until His First Departure from Japan. Part I. The Problem (1573–1580); Volume I/2. Part II. The Solution (1580–1582)*, trans. John J. Coyne (2 vols, Gujarat Sahitya Prakash, 1980–81) [this English edition is henceforth referred to as *VMJ-E*; the German version is *VMJ-G*]; Alessandro Valignano, *Sumario de las cosas de Japón (1583). Adiciones del sumario de Japón (1592)*, ed. José Luis Alvarez-Taladriz (Tokyo, 1954); see the introduction, 1*–205* (1*–17*); Alessandro Valignano, *Historia del principio y progresso de la Compañía de Jesús en las Indias Orientales (1542–1564)*, ed. Josef Wicki (Rome, 1944); see the introduction, 1*–108* (42*–9*); Pietro Tacchi-Venturi, 'Valignani (Valignano), Alessandro', in *Enciclopedia Italiana di Scienze, Lettere ed Arti* (44 vols, Rome, 1929–81), XXXIV (1937), 923; J. F. Moran, *The Japanese and the Jesuits. Alessandro Valignano in Sixteenth-Century Japan* (London, 1993), 20–8. See also the chapter entitled 'Alessandro Valignano' in Andrew C. Ross, *A Vision Betrayed. The Jesuits in Japan and China, 1542–1742* (Edinburgh, 1994), 32–46; and Joseph B. Mühlberger, *Glaube in Japan. Alexandro Valignanos Katechismus, seine moralteologischen Aussagen im japanischen Kontext* (Rome, 1994), 129–38. This is by no means a complete list of primary and secondary sources related to Valignano. A wealth of unpublished manuscript material regarding his activities in East Asia can be found in the Jesuit Archives in Rome (Archivum Romanum Societatis Iesu, henceforth referred to as ARSI) and especially in the *Iaponica–Sinica* collection (henceforth referred to as *Iap.-Sin.* For published manuscript material from ARSI (mainly from the *Goa* collection), see Josef Wicki (ed.), *Documenta Indica* (18 vols, Rome, 1948–88); henceforth these volumes are referred to as *DI*, followed by the date of publication of the volume in parentheses. Despite some minor lacunae, the most comprehensive list to date of manuscripts of Valignano's writings is that of Josef Franz Schütte in *VMJ-E*, I/1, 402–28.

[2] See Valignani, *Vita del Padre Alessandro Valignani della Compagnia di Giesù*, 2. All translations are my own unless otherwise stated.

that we know for certain is that he was a student of law *in utroque iure* at the university of Padua, a renowned centre of Renaissance learning and the principal university of the Republic of Venice. It was at the *studio di Padova* that he was awarded the title of doctor of civil law in 1557.[3] Having completed his studies, he returned briefly to Chieti and received the tonsure before departing for the Eternal City, where he hoped to take advantage of his family connections at the papal court and gain promotion in the world. While in Rome, he spent several years under the patronage of two powerful men, Pope Paul IV (Gianpietro Carafa), who had been a good friend of Valignano's father whilst archbishop of Chieti, and Cardinal Sittich von Hohenems (d'Altemps), nephew of Pope Pius IV.

Unfortunately, we know little or nothing regarding the activities of the young Valignano during this first Roman sojourn. In 1562 he returned to Padua, where on the night of 28 November, brandishing a knife, he is alleged to have slashed the face of Franceschina Trona, a young woman with whom he had presumably had a violent altercation. This accusation, to which Valignano later pleaded innocent in court, landed him in prison in Venice, where he languished for over a year-and-a-half until March 1564. Were it not for his rapidly deteriorating health, his status as a nobleman, and, above all, the intervention with the magistrates by powerful acquaintances on his behalf, such as Carlo Borromeo and the papal nuncio in Venice, his enforced sojourn in the *Serenissima* would have undoubtedly brought his career to an abrupt end. Having regained his freedom after payment of a substantial fine and on condition that he accept banishment from the Republic for four years, he journeyed once again to Rome, where he made the decision that was to change his life definitively: he asked for admission into the Society of Jesus. His request was granted by the third General Superior of the newly founded order, Francisco Borja, former duke of Gandía, and Valignano entered the novitiate at the Sant'Andrea al Quirinale Professed House on 27 May 1566. After a year of initial formation as a novice, he took his religious vows and moved on 10 May 1567 to the Roman College, where he spent three years studying philosophy and theology. He made his solemn religious profession of three vows on 12 February 1570 and was ordained a priest at the Lateran in Rome by William Chisholm II, Roman Catholic bishop of Dunblane, on 25 March 1571, during his second year of theological studies. What followed was a short period as master of novices at the Quirinale, where Matteo Ricci had just entered the Society, and a four-month trip to the Abruzzi region with the purpose of exploring the possibility of founding a Jesuit college in his native city of Chieti. Upon his return, he resumed his study of theology at the Collegio Romano until 1572, when he was appointed rector of the Jesuit College in Macerata.

---

[3] Unfortunately, the list of doctorates in law for the years 1545–79 has gone missing from the university archives. See Schütte, *VMJ-E,* 1/1, 32, note 101.

Like many of his brethren, Valignano had written to the General Superior manifesting a desire to be sent to the 'Indies' as a missionary. Little did he know that, the following year in August, the new General Superior of the order, Everard Mercurian, would take one of the most important decisions of his time in office and appoint him *Visitador* (personal delegate), to all Jesuit missions in the *Índias Orientais*, which at the time included places as diverse and distant from each other as Mozambique, Malacca (Melaka), India, Macao, and Japan.[4] On 8 September 1573 Valignano took his solemn religious profession of four vows. Less than two weeks later he departed for Genoa, whence he continued his voyage soon afterwards for Alicante. As he had been authorized by Mercurian to gather a group of suitable candidates for the Asian missions before his departure for India, he spent nearly two months in Spain visiting many cities, including Toledo, Cuenca, Alcalá, and Madrid, and conferring with the Jesuit provincial superiors of Toledo, Aragón, and Castile. By the time he crossed the border into Portugal in late December, he had already assembled a group of over twenty Spanish Jesuits, who accompanied him on the journey through Evora and on to Lisbon.[5] After Christmas, Valignano presented himself at court in Almeirim, where the young King Sebastian (Dom Sebastião) granted him an audience on New Year's day, 1574. The meeting between monarch and missionary could not have been more successful, with the king graciously agreeing to all of Valignano's requests for financial support to cover the expenses of the missionaries' passage to India. The king also made further generous grants with which to support the Jesuit missions in Malacca and Japan.[6]

Besides moments of diplomatic success, his time in Portugal was also marked by conflict and divisions within the Society that had a direct bearing on his new mission. His numerous meetings with the three most important men of the Portuguese Jesuit province, Jorge Serrão, Leão Henriques, and Luís Gonçalves da Câmara, before and after his audience with the king, proved in fact to be very difficult and ended in open confrontation. Curiously, whilst the court had not raised any major objections to the Visitor's plans, his fellow Jesuits displayed much zeal in their attempt to dispel what they viewed

---

[4] The official letter of appointment is dated 24 Spetember 1573 (ARSI, *Historia Societatis*, 61, fol. 3') reproduced in *DI*, ix (1966), 1–2.

[5] See Valignano, *Sumario*, 11*–17*.

[6] On Valignano's meeting with King Sebastian (Dom Sebastião) and Cardinal Henry (Infante, Dom Henrique), see the following letters, all written from Almeirim to the General Superior: Jerónimo Costa (31 December 1573) (ARSI, *Lusitania*, 65, fol. 304') in *DI*, ix (1966), 48; Alessandro Valignano (6 Janaury 1574) (ARSI, *Iap. Sin.*, 7 iii, fol. 174') in *ibid.* 55; Valignano gives a detailed list of 'Le cose che si sono dimandate al Re et si sono state concesse' ('the requests that we put to the King which were granted') in his letter of 7 Janaury 1574 (ARSI, *Iap.-Sin.*, 7 iii, fol. 176') in *ibid.* 60–1; Jorge Serrão (9 Janaury 1573) (ARSI, *Lusitania*, 65, fol. 115') in *ibid.* 71. The king made even more generous provisions the following month. In a letter to Mercurian (Lisbon, 8 February 1574) (ARSI, *Iap.-Sin.*, 7 ii, 194', 195') in *ibid.* 153, 156, he informs the General Superior that he has enough money for thirty-five men to go to India.

as a threat to the prerogatives of the *Padroado Real*, which, as various papal bulls had previously stipulated, gave the Portuguese crown exclusive rights to govern the affairs of the Church in all the lands belonging to their *conquista* – those east of the Cape of Good Hope.[7] Moreover, perhaps even more important for these men was the fact that Portugal had been the first country to have an independent Jesuit province established by the founder of the order, Ignatius of Loyola, as early as 1546.[8] Another closely related factor that contributed to their sceptical attitude was the moral and spiritual authority enjoyed by Valignano's main detractor, Gonçalves da Câmara, who had been a close personal acquaintance of Ignatius and is best known for having recorded the founder's autobiography for posterity.[9] He had also been a royal tutor to King Sebastian, who came to depend – some would say to an unhealthy degree – on his Jesuit mentor. Thus, it is not surprising that such a man, endowed with exceptional intellectual gifts, spiritual authority, and influence at court, resisted what he perceived as concerted attempts by Valignano to undermine the position of predominance that his fellow countrymen enjoyed in missions to the Indies. He was certainly not accustomed to being contradicted – as he repeatedly was – by a young and brash foreigner, who was obviously lacking in experience of government within the Order.[10]

One cannot gauge the intensity of this disagreement without a proper understanding of what the office of Visitor entailed within a religious order as centralized as the Society of Jesus. As Mercurian's personal delegate in the Indies, Valignano had, in fact, been granted an extraordinarily wide range of powers to oversee and govern the mission as he saw fit.[11] This meant that, within his area of jurisdiction, the young Visitor had the authority to accept and dismiss members from the Society, send any member to any place where he judged that a man might be of use for a particular mission, change local superiors, and implement new mission policies whenever and wherever he

---

[7] For an account of the *Padroado* and its workings, see C. R. Boxer, *The Portuguese Seaborne Empire, 1415–1825* [1969] (Manchester, 1997), 228–48; see also Emma Falque, 'Bulas alejandrinas de 1493. Texto y traducción', in Juan Gil and José Maria Maestre (eds), *Humanismo latino y descubrimiento* (Cadiz and Seville, 1992), 11–35.

[8] For an account of the missionary enterprises of the Portuguese Jesuits, see the monumental work by Dauril Alden, *The Making of an Enterprise. The Society of Jesus in Portugal, Its Empire, and Beyond, 1540–1750* (Stanford, 1996), 24–38.

[9] For a fascinating revisionist account of Câmara's 'transcription' of Ignatius of Loyola's 'autobiography', see Marjorie O'Rourke Boyle, *Loyola's Acts. The Rhetoric of the Self* (Berkeley, 1997).

[10] For details of this conflict, see Schütte, *VMJ-E*, I/1, 64–91, and Ross, *A Vision Betrayed*. 37–40.

[11] The original document containing the faculties or special powers granted by Mercurian (25 September 1573) appears to have been lost; see Schütte, *VMJ-E*, I/1, 5–12, 48, 52. I have, however, discovered a partial eighteenth-century apograph copy produced in Macao in the Biblioteca da Ajuda, Lisbon, *Jesuítas na Ásia*, 49-IV-56, fols 203ᵛ and 193ʳ, that lists twenty (out of a total of thirty-two?) of the Visitor's faculties. Valignano suggested emendations to this list sometime before 25 October 1573 whilst still in Genoa; see ARSI, *Goa*, 24 I, fols 76ʳ⁻ˢ in *DI*, IX (1966), 5–8. He acknowledges receipt of the emended list of faculties on 6 February 1574; see Schütte, *VMJ-E*, I/1, 48–55.

deemed it necessary. He was not, however, under any obligation to heed the counsel of the Portuguese provincial. In places like Japan, the furthest missionary outpost of the *Padroado*, and where until 1596 there was no bishop in residence, this amounted to virtually complete control of the activities of the Church. He was bound, nevertheless, to give the authorities in Rome and Portugal a detailed account of his activities and policies, and the General Superior could always overrule any of his decisions. In view of the immense distances between Asia and Europe, and the uncertainties of epistolary communication, the system remained remarkably flexible.[12] In fact, on occasion even the General Superior found himself overruled by the Visitor, when the latter judged that a decision that had been taken in Rome two years before could no longer be implemented in light of new circumstances in Asia without serious detriment to the mission.[13] Such boldness on the part of Valignano can be explained by the confidence he had in the trust placed in him by Mercurian and his successor, Claudio Aquaviva, who had been a close friend since their time together as fellow students at the Roman College. It also serves to highlight how much power Valignano wielded in the day-to-day running of the ecclesiastical affairs of the East Indies.

At a practical level, the clash between the Portuguese Jesuit leadership on the one hand and Valignano on the other centred around three sensitive issues: first, the way the new Visitor should carry out his duties in India, *citra* and *ultra Gangem* (to the West and East of the Ganges), and the extent to which he should rely for guidance on the Portuguese province; secondly, the spirit that should inform religious life in the newly founded Society of Jesus; and thirdly, Valignano's determination to take so many Spaniards with him to the East despite the protests of the Portuguese.

From the outset, Valignano made it clear that, having received clear instructions from Mercurian, he did not intend to allow the Portuguese Jesuits to dictate to him how he should run the mission. Valignano interpreted the authority invested in him as an attempt by the General Superior to release the Indian mission from the stranglehold of the Portuguese province and bring it under the more direct control of Rome. He did not ignore the

[12] It may be appropriate at this point to note briefly the chief languages in which Valignano conducted his copious correspondence. Rarely if ever writing in Latin, of which he claimed not to possess the appropriate literary style, he employed Italian, his native tongue, only on occasion when writing to Everard Mercurian or a small number of fellow Italians, the most prominent of whom was Claudio Aquaviva. Otherwise, he composed the vast majority of his letters and reports either in Portuguese or in Spanish, the two languages of government of the East Indies. All English translations from the original texts are mine unless otherwise indicated.

[13] An example of Valignano overruling an important order issued by Aquaviva is the former's suspension of the General Superior's appointment on 10 April 1597 of Francesco Pasio to replace the ailing Vice-provincial, Pedro Gómez. In a letter to Aquaviva (Nagasaki, 20 February 1599) (ARSI, *Iap.-Sin.*, 13 ii, fol. 255′) the Visitor notes that the governor of Nagasaki, Terazawa, favours Gómez; he also expresses his fear that the appointment of yet another Italian superior in Japan would be an intolerable affront to Portuguese pride. For Valignano's letter, see José Álvarez-Taladriz, 'Cinco cartas de religiosos de la Compañía de Jesús misioneros en Japón (1594–1599)', *Sapientia. The Eichi University Review*, 7 (1973), 73–105, at 95–6.

fact that his independence represented a direct threat to the *status quo* in Lisbon.[14] He notes with irony how the leaders of the Portuguese province

> had attempted to 'catechize' and indoctrinate me in their way of thinking in order that I should govern India in the same spirit that they do here; nevertheless, they revealed so many things to me that as a result they were the ones who ended up being 'catechized'.[15]

Thus, the fundamental point of contention was the spirit in which the Society of Jesus was to be governed. Again, Valignano expressed his reservations over the way of proceeding among the Jesuits in Portugal and made it clear that he did not share his brethren's views. He repeatedly complained to Mercurian about the unreasonably harsh and rigorous regime, characterized by a spirit of fear, that the Portuguese Jesuit leadership had imposed on its members, and which, in his opinion, painfully contradicted the 'spirito soave della Compagnia'.[16] To compound the problem, it was public knowledge that some of the superiors had even gone so far as to accuse openly the Jesuits in Rome of having abandoned the true spirit of the order. Valignano scarcely hid his frustration and impatience as he related how, in governing the province,

> The first criterion whereby they judge us is by claiming that the way of governing in Rome is not good and that the spirit of the Society has been all but destroyed in Italy. Not only did Father Luis Gonzalez insinuate this repeatedly in conversations with me, but they [the Portuguese Jesuits] even have a common saying among themselves that 'Ours in Italy adhere only to the "essentials" but pay no attention to the "accidentals" [i.e. details]'.[17]

Thirdly, with regard to Valignano's concrete preparations for the mission, their objections had concentrated on the question of personnel, in terms of both recruitment and assignment. Valignano intended to travel with forty missionaries; the king, they claimed, would never agree to finance such a large group, especially as the majority were Spaniards.[18] Furthermore, many

---

[14] See Valignano to Mercurian (Lisbon, 8 February 1574): '. . . I discovered that the way in which I had made my own plans for the journey – independently of them – and the authority that I had been given displeased them very greatly . . . plainly put, they just could not come to terms with the fact that the *governance of the Indies has thus been taken out of their hands* [my italics]'. For the original Italian text, see ARSI, *Iap.-Sin.*, 7 ii, 196' in *DI*, ix (1966), 162.

[15] Lisbon, 28 January 1574. For the original Italian, see ARSI, *Iap.-Sin.*, 7 iii, fol. 186', in *DI*, ix (1966), 110–11.

[16] See Valignano's two letters from Lisbon to the General Superior: 12 January 1574 (ARSI, *Iap.-Sin.*, 7 iii, fols 179ʳ⁻ᵛ) in *DI*, ix (1966), 83–8; and 28 January 1574 (ARSI, *Iap.-Sin.*, 7 iii, fols 186'–187') in *ibid.* 111–15. For the above cited expression used frequently by Valignano, see the second letter in *ibid.* 110.

[17] See Valignano to the General Superior, 28 January 1574 (ARSI, *Iap.-Sin.*, 7 iii, fol. 186'), in *DI*, ix (1966), 111.

[18] For a list of objections and criticisms of Valignano's way of proceeding, see the letter of the Portuguese Provincial, Jorge Serrão, to Everard Mercurian (Lisbon, 11 February 1574) (ARSI, *Lusitania*, 66, fols 55'–58') in *DI*, ix (1966), 178–85; he specifically mentions the question of Spaniards on fol. 58' (183–4).

of the men chosen by the Visitor were 'new Christians', or *confessi*. Such a decision, they were convinced, would not be acceptable either to the court or to the Portuguese in India. Moreover, all of the recruits had been destined for India, whereas the General Superior had promised them that a group would also be sent to Brazil.[19] To the accusation that he was inconsiderate towards his patrons in that he appeared to favour the Spaniards at every turn, he bluntly retorts: 'I am an Italian; and between Castilians and Italians there is naturally a greater antipathy than between Castilians and Portuguese.'[20] In another letter he writes to the General Superior about how, at the height of the conflict, he was forced to threaten them with public scandal, telling them that

> if in one way or another they continued to obstruct me, I would take all my men back to Italy . . . for I was always very firm in stating that, if the King hindered me or did not provide me with what was necessary for the passage [to India], I would blame it on them and make it known to the whole Society, including Your Paternity.[21]

As neither King Sebastian nor Cardinal Henry had seriously challenged any of the Visitor's plans, and as he continued to enjoy Mercurian's full support, Valignano ultimately prevailed, and the Portuguese leadership was left with no choice but to give in, at least temporarily, to his demands. The final blow, however, was delivered when the Visitor, in accordance with written orders he had received from Mercurian, announced the nomination of Alessandro Vallareggio, another Italian, to the office of Jesuit Procurator of the Indian mission in Lisbon. His main task was to act as a liaison between Europe and India, and, among his other duties, he was to ensure that the correspondence to and from the missionaries in India was not tampered with by the Portuguese, who had previously reserved for themselves the right to open all letters. Understandably, more objections were forthcoming from the Jesuits in Lisbon, but to no avail.[22] By the time Valignano set sail for Mozambique on 21 March 1574 together with his forty-one

---

[19] Valignano writes to Mercurian about the objections voiced by the Portuguese regarding his choice of men in several letters from Lisbon: 28 January 1574 (ARSI, *Iap.-Sin.*, 7 III fols 188ᵛ–189ʳ) in *DI*, IX (1966), 118–19; and 8 February 1574 (ARSI, *Iap.-Sin.*, 7 II, 195ʳ) in *ibid.* 156. He also relates with much anguish the situation regarding the *confessi*; see 12 January 1574 (ARSI, *Iap.-Sin.*, 7 III, fols 108ʳ and 181ʳ) in *ibid.* 90–3; and 28 January 1574, in *ibid.* 117–18.

[20] Cited in English translation in *VMJ-E*, 1/1, 90, note 171; for the original letter, see Valignano to Mercurian (Chorão, 30 October 1576) (ARSI, *Iap.-Sin.*, 8 I, fols 37ᵛ–38ʳ) in *DI*, IX (1966), 577. These remarks were made in response to a vitriolic letter by Pedro da Fonseca, Portuguese Assistant in Rome, in which the latter berates the Visitor for stubbornly persisting in his 'anti-Portuguese' stance and having grossly overstepped the bounds of his authority; see Fonseca to Valignano (Rome, 7 January 1575) (ARSI, *Goa*, 12 I, fols 268ᵛ–270ʳ) in *DI*, IX (1966), 574–8.

[21] Lisbon: 8 February 1574 (ARSI, *Iap.-Sin.*, 7 II, fol. 195ʳ) in *DI*, IX (1966), 157.

[22] Valignano discusses Gonçalves da Câmara's objections in the letter cited above (ARSI, *Iap.-Sin.*, 7 II, fols 195ʳ–96ʳ) in *ibid.* 158–62.

recruits,[23] whom he had put through an intense programme of preparation at the Jesuit Residence of São Roque in Lisbon, effective control of the Jesuit enterprise in the *Indias Orientales* by the powerful conservative faction of the Portuguese Jesuit province, led by Gonçalves da Câmara, had been significantly reduced.

In order not to overdramatize the conflict between the new Visitor and some of his Jesuit brethren in Portugal, it must be remarked that Valignano continued to rely heavily on Lisbon for both manpower and for a significant part of his funds, and, all told, was far from being anti-Portuguese. In fact, despite his stinging criticisms of the *modus gubernandi* of the Jesuits in Portugal and the Lusitanian administration in India, he always strove to maintain friendly relations with his patrons, both on the Iberian peninsula and in India, Malacca, and Macao. Both his writings and those of others clearly show that he never faltered in his efforts to uphold the Society's firm support for Portugal's exclusive right to govern the East Indian missions.

Surprisingly, even after the unification of the two Iberian crowns under Philip II in 1580, he was adamant that Spanish missionaries be admitted to the territories of the *Padroado Real* only with the explicit permission of Lisbon. He was thus opposed to any direct contact between Japan, New Spain, and the Philippines. The Visitor did not, however, reject the recruitment of Spaniards as such, as long as they respected the terms agreed to at the Union of Tomar in 1581, which upheld the principle of separate administration for the territories of the two crowns. Nevertheless, Valignano's compromise remained an unsatisfactory solution for the Portuguese, who proved unrelenting in their efforts to halt Spaniards from being sent to the East Indies altogether. As a result of such pressure, the General Superior complied, and no more Jesuits from Spain left for India during the years 1575–8. Mercurian even went as far as trying to recall all Spanish Jesuits working in the Indies *ultra Gangem* (Malacca, Macao, and Japan).[24] The king himself had written to Mercurian asking him to ponder carefully the disadvantages or difficulties ('inconvenientes') related to 'os Padres da Companhia de Jesu estrangeiros que vão às partes da Índia'.[25]

---

[23] In the end, Valignano's *équipe* consisted of seven Italians (besides himself), twenty-four Spaniards, and ten Portuguese. For a complete list of these men, see *Catálogo dos Padres e Irmãos* (*Catalogue of the Fathers and Brothers*) (Lisbon, 1574) (ARSI, *Goa*, 24 I, fols 73ʳ⁻ᵛ) in *DI*, IX (1966), 237–44 and Alessandro Vallareggio to Mercurian (Lisbon, 23 March 1574) (ARSI, *Lusitania*, 66, fols 91ʳ–93ᵛ) in *DI*, IX (1966), 245–50.

[24] Mercurian's original instruction has not survived. Valignano acknowledges having received such an order, dated 28 October 1575 at the beginning of his letter to Mercurian (Chorão, 30 October 1576) (ARSI, *Iap.-Sin.*, 8 I, fol. 36ʳ) in *DI*, x (1968), 569.

[25] See King Sebastian (Dom Sebastião) to Mercurian (Almada, 21 July 1575) (ARSI, *Epp. Ext.*, 27, fol. 301ʳ) in *DI*, IX (1966), 660. The new Portuguese Provincial, Manuel Rodrigues, mentions in two letters to Mercurian that neither King Sebastian nor Cardinal Henry (Henrique) think it wise that Spaniards be sent to the East Indies: Coimbra, 8 August 1575 (ARSI, *Lusitania*, 7, fol. 160ʳ) in *DI*, IX (1966), 670–1 and Braga, 27 September 1575 (ARSI, *Lusitania*, 7, fol. 202ᵛ) in *ibid*. 688–9. Of much the same opinion as Rodrigues is Francisco Porres, procurator at the court of Philip II, in his letter to Mercurian, in which he mentions that the Portuguese ambassador in Madrid, Eduardo Castelo-Branco 'has said that it is not a good idea that Castilian Fathers be sent to the Portuguese Indies . . . because Castilians cannot help but favour other Castilians'. For the original Spanish, see Madrid, 1 June 1575 (ARSI, *Hispania*, 124, fol. 103ʳ) in *ibid*. 645.

The court was particularly concerned about Spanish Jesuits providing Madrid with information about China and endangering Portuguese interests in that region, as the two crowns were at odds at the time over the line of demarcation of their respective spheres of influence.[26]

In response to the whole controversy, in a long and very detailed letter to Mercurian, written from Chorão on 30 October 1576, Valignano argues that the General Superior should seriously reconsider his decision to recall the 'castigliani' from the East and revoke his order in view of the sheer impracticality of such a move, the damage it would inflict on missionary work, and the fact that these men – in the Visitor's opinion – did not pose any threat to the national interests of Portugal.[27] Most telling is his argument that none of this makes any difference whatsoever in the case of Japan, which

> neither the King of Portugal nor the King of Spain have the power to conquer, even if they were to join forces . . . for their people [the Japanese] are very warlike and constantly undergoing training in arms . . . and they are quite unlike any other people of these Indies; therefore it matters little whether the Fathers who are in Japan are Portuguese or Castilian.[28]

He wryly adds that even if one of the two Iberian empires had the power to conquer Japan, it would still be of no consequence to the national interests of either country whether the Jesuits there were Portuguese or Spanish, as such affairs are settled with soldiers and arms, and 'not with the art of persuasion of the Fathers, who are so "powerful" in Japan that they have literally to run for their lives on a daily basis'.[29] Times and circumstances change and, as we shall see, Valignano was later to make every effort to prevent Spanish Jesuits from New Spain and the Philippines from coming to Japan.[30]

I have purposely dwelt at length on Valignano's initial confrontation with his Portuguese brethren and its wider political implications, since the way he handled the situation reveals a great deal about the man and his convictions. Not only does it throw light on his strong character and at times obdurate temperament in the face of opposition, it equally serves as a basis for interpreting his complex relations with the Portuguese and the Spanish, in both the secular and ecclesiastical spheres. The 'Iberian problem' was possibly the

---

[26] See above, Francisco Rodrigues to Mercurian (Coimbra, 8 August 1575) (ARSI, *Lusitania*, 67, fol. 160ᵛ in *DI*, ɪx (1966), 670, and Alessandro Vallareggio to Mercurian (Lisbon, 22 July 1575) (ARSI, *Lusitania*, 67, fols 136ᵛ–37ʳ) in *ibid.* 661–64.

[27] See ARSI, *Iap.-Sin.*, 8 ɪ, fols 36ᵛ–39ᵛ, in *DI*, x (1968), 571–84. He deals with the same issues in a previous letter to the General Superior (at sea between Cochin and Goa, 4 December 1575) (ARSI, *Goa*, 47, fols 42ᵛ–43ʳ) in *ibid.* 149–52.

[28] See Valignano to the General Superior, Everard Mercurian (Chorão, 30 October 1576) (ARSI, *Iap.-Sin.*, 8 ɪ, fol. 37ʳ) in *DI*, x (1968), 573.

[29] For the original Italian text, see *DI*, x (1968), 573–4.

[30] See two letters written by Valignano from Goa; one to the General Superior, Claudio Aquaviva (1 April 1585) (ARSI, *Iap.-Sin.*, 10 ɪ, fols 25ᵛ–26ʳ) in *DI*, XIV (1979), 10–11; and the other (8 April 1585) to the Rector of the Jesuit Mission in the Philippines, Antonio Sedeño (ARSI, *Iap.-Sin.*, 10 ɪ, fol. 28ʳ) in *ibid.* 21–22.

greatest single hindrance the Visitor faced in carrying out his reforms of the missions in the East, and it continued to engender much hostile controversy and haunt Valignano throughout the thirty-two years he spent in Asia. Finally, his stance in the face of opposition in Lisbon serves to highlight his pragmatism, independence, and willingness to challenge the ultra-conservative understanding of religious life that he encountered in the 'home country', whose Jesuit missions he was to govern.

VALIGNANO'S VOYAGES AND ACTIVITIES: AN OVERVIEW

After a successful journey of nearly four months, with a short stop-over in the Canary Islands and another fortnight in Guinea, Valignano reached Mozambique on 14 July 1574.[31] On 9 August he was back on board the flagship, the *Chagas* or *Constantina*, which, after an uneventful journey, sailed into the port of Goa on 6 September.[32] He spent the next three years travelling to the various cities and outposts in India where the Jesuits were engaged in everything from the running of colleges to preaching among the people of the Fishery Coast. Having concluded his visit to India, and taking advantage of the monsoon, he left Goa on 20 September 1577 and journeyed further east to Malacca, where he arrived a month later. He remained there for approximately nine months before continuing his journey to Macao, which he reached at the beginning of September 1578. His stay in the Portuguese port known as the 'Cidade da Madre de Deus' on the south China coast lasted another nine months. It was from there that he finally embarked for Japan, landing safely at the small port of Kuchinotsu on the island of Kyushu on 25 July 1579 after a journey of eighteen days. Exactly thirty years had passed since the arrival of Francis Xavier, who had established the first Christian community in Japan in 1549.[33] His first, long-awaited visitation to the country that he had always considered the most important enterprise of the Society in the Orient was to last for nearly two-and-a-half years. During this time he was to devote himself to a complete reorganization of the mission. He was greatly dismayed to find, however, that the reality of the mission in Japan did not conform to his expectations, and he was beset with many doubts over the best way to proceed in view of the disconcerting circumstances. It was only at the end of his stay that he regained a sense of self-confidence and issued a series of *Instructions* (*Regimentos*) for the Jesuits in Japan that were to change the very nature of the missionary enterprise in that country.

---

[31] See Valignano to Antonio Possevino (Mozambique, 4 August 1574) (ARSI, *Iap.-Sin.*, 7 III, fol. 219ʳ) in *DI*, IX (1966), 375.

[32] See Valignano to Mercurian (Goa, 25 December 1574) (ARSI, *Iap.-Sin.*, 7 I, fol. 295ʳ) in *DI*, IX (1966), 483.

[33] Altogether Valignano spent a total of approximately ten years in Japan. His first sojourn (25 July 1579–20 February 1582) coincided with the reign of Oda Nobunaga; his second (21 July 1590–9 October 1592) with the reign of Toyotomi Hideyoshi; and his third and last stay (5 August 1598–15 January 1603) with the reign of Tokugawa Ieyasu.

When he finally set sail from Japan in February 1582, he did not leave alone. Before his departure, he had arranged for four Japanese youths to accompany him in what was to be the first diplomatic expedition ever from Japan to Europe. The Japanese were to represent the Christian feudal lords, Ōmura Sumitada, Ōtomo Yoshishige (Sōrin), and Arima Harunobu, at the papal court in Rome, as well as at the royal courts in Madrid and Portugal. The boys who were chosen were Martinho Hara, Julião Nakaura, Mancio Itō, and Miguel Chijiwa.[34]

Many reasons were cited for sending the embassy, but they can be summarized as a carefully concerted effort on the part of the Visitor to organize on a grand scale a 'public relations' event that would be played out on both the secular and ecclesiastical stages of Europe. Put simply, his purpose was to impress Europe with the tangible successes of Jesuit efforts in Japan by presenting them with living examples of noble and pious youth from that country. He was equally keen to impress the Japanese youth with the glories of European Christendom so that they in turn might influence the views of their fellow countrymen to whom they would recount their experiences upon their return.[35] Valignano was painfully aware that since the very beginning both the Japanese and the Europeans had heard conflicting and even false reports about the true character of each other's peoples. This embassy is of particular significance, as it illustrates the extent to which the Visitor was convinced of the importance of persuading his audience that the Jesuit way was the 'right' way of proceeding.

After nine more months in Macao, Valignano returned with the young ambassadors to India. The party arrived in the port of Cochin on 7 April 1583. Six months later the Visitor received a letter from the new General Superior, Claudio Aquaviva, appointing him Provincial of India and confirming his position as Visitor to the East Indies. In practice, this decision meant he would not be continuing the voyage to Europe with the Japanese embassy. Valignano thus had no choice but to remain in India, where for four years he awaited their return. At the insistence of the Portuguese court and as a result of the embassy, which to Valignano's chagrin had given the authorities

---

[34] For a brief account of the embassy, see Schütte, *VMJ-E*, 1/2, 257–66. See also Valignano's description of the backgrounds of the four boys in his *Apología en al qual se responde a diversas calumnias que se escrivieron contra los Padres de la Compañía de Jesús de Jappón y de la China. Hecha por el Padre Alexandre Valignano de la misma Compañía en el Collegio de Machao en Henero del año 1598. Y después revista y acrecentada en Jappón por el mismo Padre en Octubre del mismo año* [*Apologia in which responses are given to various calumnies written against the Fathers of the Society of Jesus in Japan and China. Compiled by Father Alessandro Valignano, of the same Society, in the College of Macao in January, 1598. Revised in Japan with further additions by the aforementioned Father in October of the same year*]. This work has been edited by José Álvarez-Taladriz: *Apología de la Compañía de Jesús de Japón y China* [1598] (Osaka, 1998). As this printed edition is not widely available, in all references to the *Apología*, besides the page number in Álvarez-Taladriz's edition, I also give the folio number in ARSI (*Iap.-Sin.*, 41). Álvarez-Taladriz used this manuscript as his 'base-text' and reproduced its folio numbering in his own text. For the above reference, see 56–7 (ARSI, *Iap.-Sin.*, 41, fols 20ʳ–21ʳ).

[35] Valignano says that there were 'three principal reasons' for sending the embassy; see his *Apología* (1598), 53–6 (ARSI, *Iap.-Sin.*, 41, fols 20ʳ⁻ᵛ).

in Europe the impression that Japan was well on its way to becoming a land dominated by Christians, the first Japanese bishopric was created by papal bull on 19 February 1588 in the city of Funai (Bungo). The new see was dependent on the archdiocese of Goa and thus fully part of the Portuguese *Padroado*.[36]

Valignano had long reflected upon the possibility of a bishop being appointed for Japan but had ultimately come to oppose the idea. Nevertheless, the embassy's success ironically led Rome to take decisions regarding the ecclesiastical administration of Japan that were least in accord with Valignano's overall plans for the Japanese church. Had Valignano been allowed to travel to Rome and make use of his powers of persuasion instead of remaining in far-away India, things might have taken a different turn.

In the spring of 1588 he left Goa together with the young Japanese ambassadors for Macao. On board was a printing press with moveable type that Valignano had instructed his fellow Jesuits to bring from Europe so that books could be printed in China and Japan. What came to be known as the Jesuit Mission Press was first put to use whilst still in Goa to print an oration delivered by Martinho Hara in Latin about their trip to Europe.[37] In 1590 in Macao, another work commemorating the embassy's voyages and experiences in Europe was printed in Latin. The book was entitled *De missione legatorum Iaponensium ad Romanam curiam, rebusque in Europa, ac toto itinere animadversis dialogus*. The carefully crafted text was first composed in Castilian prose, most probably by Valignano himself, and subsequently recast into Latin dialogue form by the Portuguese Jesuit and Latinist, Duarte de Sande. Not only was it to serve as a textbook for Latin education in Japan, it was also a brilliant work of humanist-style rhetoric recounting the adventures of the four boys in the context of an elaborate comparison of the cultures of Europe and Japan.

The exuberant mood of the delegation in Macao was nevertheless overshadowed by the precarious political situation and gloomy prospects of the Christians in Japan. When Valignano left India he was no longer formally travelling as a missionary but rather in his official capacity as ambassador of the Portuguese viceroy in India, Duarte de Meneses. The Japanese regent, Toyotomi Hideyoshi, had formally banned all public Christian missionary activity in the country in July 1587. Hence, regardless of his role as mentor

---

[36] On the creation of a diocese in Japan and the appointment of a bishop, see Hubert Cieslik, 'Zur Geschichte der kirchlichen Hierarchie in der alten Japanmission', *Neue Zeitschrift für Missionswissenschaft*, 18 (1962), 42–58, 81–107, 177–95. See also João Paulo Oliveira e Costa, 'Em torno da criação do Bispado do Japão', in Artur Teodoro de Matos and Luís Filipe F. Reis Thomaz (eds), *As relações entre a Índia portuguesa, a Ásia do sueste e o Extremo Oriente: Actas do VI seminário internacional de história indo-portuguesa (Macau, 22 a 26 de outubro de 1991)* (Macao and Lisbon, 1993), 141–71, at 141–2, 167–71; and Jesús López-Gay, 'Don Pedro Martins, SJ (1542–1598), primer obispo portugués que visitó el Japón', in Roberto Carneiro and A. Teodoro de Matos (eds), *O século cristão do Japão: Actas do colóquio internacional comemorativo dos 450 anos de amizade Portugal-Japão (1543–1993) (Lisboa, 2 a 5 de Novembro de 1993)* (Lisbon, 1994), 79–94.

[37] See *Oratio habita a Fara D. Martino Iaponio* [*Oration Delivered by Dom Martin Hara, of Japan*] (Goa, 1588).

and guardian to the four Japanese youths, the Visitor would not have been able to re-enter the country without this diplomatic pretext. Even with his credentials, the Visitor and his company were forced to postpone their trip to Japan until June 1590, when a ship became available and Asano Nagamasa, an influential *daimyō*, wrote to Valignano informing him that it was finally safe to undertake the journey. Needless to say, the single most important task the Visitor had to attend to as he began his second visitation of Japan was his audience with Hideyoshi, which took place at the regent's magnificent Juraku-dai palace in Miyako on 3 March 1591.[38] The Taikō was in an exceptionally good mood that day, and appeared to be both delighted with and proud of the apparent success of the Japanese embassy to Europe. The four youths even went so far as to perform a quartet on Western musical instruments in his honour. Despite the cordiality and good humour he displayed on that memorable occasion, the regent continued to harbour strong suspicions as to the ultimate purpose of the Visitor's diplomatic mission to Japan and had no intention of abrogating his previous anti-Christian decree. He simply chose not to enforce it with vigour for the time being, a strategic move that suited his political purposes insofar as it enabled him to keep the Europeans, both missionary and merchant, off balance and under control. Six months later, the Portuguese Jesuit João Rodrigues 'Tçuzzu' (=Tsūji) [Interpreter] was summoned to court to assure Hideyoshi yet again that the Valignano's embassy had been genuine. As a consequence, Valignano was left with very little room for manoeuvre and had to act with utmost caution during the two years he remained in the country lest he provoke the wrath of the unpredictable *Kampaku*.

At the end of October 1592 the Visitor finally returned to Macao, where he remained until the autumn of 1594. Before continuing his voyage to India in November of that year, he succeeded, albeit with great difficulty and amidst much opposition from his Portuguese brethren, in establishing a college for the training of Japanese students in the Chinese port. Valignano reports that the Portuguese, among other things, especially feared that the new college would undermine the position of the College of St Paul in Goa, and that it would become an excuse for Spaniards from New Spain to bypass India in order to study in Macao, whence they could easily gain access to Japan and China.[39] As usual, Valignano was determined to see his project through to completion, and on 1 December 1594, shortly after his departure for India, the newly built 'Colégio de São Paulo' began its academic activities; within three years it was conferring its first degrees in the arts and theology. It thus effectively came to be the first university college organized

---

[38] See Michael Cooper, *Rodrigues the Interpreter. An Early Jesuit in Japan and China* [1974] (New York and Tokyo, 1994), 75–82. For Rodrigues's historical account of Japan, see also *João Rodrigues's Account of Sixteenth-Century Japan*, ed. Michael Cooper (London, 2002).

[39] See his letter to Aquaviva (Macao, 27 November 1595) (ARSI, *Iap.-Sin.*, 12 II, fol. 321') in *DI*, XVII (1988), 324–5.

according to a European model in East Asia, where for decades to come many Japanese were to study.[40]

Meanwhile, Valignano's detractors continued to write letters to Rome asking that he be relieved of his responsibilities as Visitor to India. One of their most urgent complaints was that he was taking away too many able men from India and sending them all to Japan. These and other complaints notwithstanding, Aquaviva continued to have confidence in his old friend but decided that it would be best for Valignano to relinquish his responsibilities *vis-à-vis* the Indian province. Upon reaching Goa in the spring of 1595, Valignano officially resigned from his post of Visitor to India in the presence of Francisco Cabral. The latter, who disagreed profoundly with Valignano's policies in general and his running of the Indian province in particular, had been mission superior of Japan until 1583, when he asked to be relieved of his responsibilities and returned soon thereafter to Macao. After Valignano left office as Visitor to India, Cabral became Provincial of India and Nicolao Pimenta was subsequently appointed as the new Visitor. With these changes, some confusion arose as to Valignano's official position, and a heated debate ensued between Valignano and Cabral as to whether the former had been appointed vice-provincial of Japan, and hence subject to the new Provincial of India (Cabral), or whether Valignano was to stay on in a new capacity as 'Visitor to Japan and China', and hence independent of the Indian Province.[41] They finally agreed that a committee (*consulta*) of 'experts' from among the fathers in Goa should clarify the issue regarding their respective authority and status. As a result, it was established that, according to the correspondence that had come from Rome, the General Superior did in fact intend Valignano to continue his work as Visitor to Japan and China. Moreover, in their view, he was not vice-provincial, and therefore was not subject to Cabral.[42] Valignano was thus free to carry out his duties as Visitor in accordance with the new terms restricting his authority to the Far East, an office he held until his death nine years later.

In April 1597 he left India and travelled via Cochin, Malacca, and Macao to Japan for the third time. In Macao he was informed of the crucifixion of the twenty-six Christians in Nagasaki by order of Hideyoshi two months before. Among those executed were six Franciscan friars from the Philippines, seventeen Japanese lay Christians, and three Japanese Jesuit *irmãos* (= brothers). It was also brought to his attention that various Franciscans in Japan, including Fray Martín Aguirre de la Ascensión, who was among those

[40] For a brief history of this foundation, see Domingos Maurício Gomes dos Santos, 'Macao: the first Western university in the Far East', *Review of Culture (Instituto Cultural de Macau)*, 21, 2nd ser. (1994), 5–25.

[41] Valignano colourfully describes this debate in his twelfth letter to Aquaviva (Goa, 27 November 1595) (ARSI, *Iap.-Sin.*, 12 II, fols 323ʳ–24ᵛ) in *DI*, XVII (1988), 329–38.

[42] See (Goa, 31 October 1595) (ARSI, *Goa*, 32, fols 559ʳ–60ᵛ) in *DI*, XVII (1988), 97–100. The 'consulta' refers to two letters by Aquaviva that had initially engendered the misunderstanding: the first to Francisco Monclaro (Rome, 14 January 1595) (ARSI, *Gall.*, 44, fols 25ᵛ–26ʳ) in *ibid*. 30–1, and the second to Francisco Cabral (Rome, 17 January 1595) (ARSI, *Goa*, 32, fol. 559ʳ) in *ibid*. 41–2.

executed, had compiled various *relaciones* in which they accused the Jesuits in Japan of hindering the missionary efforts of the friars in order to conceal their own scandalous lifestyle and unorthodox religious behaviour. These and other writings occasioned a lengthy response by Valignano in the form of an *Apología*, which he started to compose in Macao but only found the time to complete the following year, in October 1598.[43]

Soon thereafter, Valignano carried out his last visitation of the Jesuit mission in Japan, which began with his arrival on 5 August 1598 and lasted for four-and-a-half years. Hideyoshi had died a few months earlier and the mood among the missionaries was one of relief, if not cautious optimism. After Tokugawa Ieyasu emerged as the new leader at the battle of Sekigahara in 1600, the Christian community and the Jesuits were plunged into uncertainty yet again, as some of the Christian lords had backed the unsuccessful side in the dispute between Ieyasu and his chief opponent, Ishida Mitsunari. The Christian lord, Konishi Yukinaga, also known as Don Augustino, a bene-factor and protector of the Jesuits, was one of those singled out for public execution (as he refused to commit ritual suicide, *seppuku*).[44] Although his death dealt a severe blow to the mission in general and to the Jesuits in particular, Ieyasu decided that it was politically expedient to remain on friendly terms with the Jesuit missionaries and gave them limited freedom to preach openly for the first time since 1587. He was, in fact, anxious to maintain good trade relations with both the Portuguese and the Spaniards, and suspected that the missionaries might still be needed as mediators. This was to change only several years later when the Portuguese Jesuit, João Rodrigues, was replaced as official interpreter at court by Will Adams, the first Englishman to set foot in Japan when he arrived in 1600 aboard the Dutch ship, *De Liefde*.

Regarding the circumstances of the mission at the turn of the century, a perusal of Valignano's correspondence from this period shows that he was relatively pleased with the new developments following the demise of the Taikō, and was counting on a more tolerant stance from Ieyasu.[45] His letter to Robert Bellarmine in Rome, written from Nagasaki on 16 October 1601, is of special interest with regard to this period. His aim was to inform the cardinal as to the latest vicissitudes of the Japanese Church in the hope of stimulating both interest and support for the affairs of the Far East. Some of the statistics provided in the letter are especially valuable. The Visitor lists the following figures: 107 Jesuits in Japan besides the Jesuit bishop, Luis Cerqueira; 23 houses and residences of the Society; 250 Japanese lay assist-ants or *dōjuku*; 300,000 Christians, of which 150,000 are in the kingdoms of Arima and Ōmura and 80,000 reside in the kingdom of Higo. Besides these

---

[43] For the full title of this work and its recent edition, see note 34 above.
[44] See Cooper, *Rodrigues the Interpreter*, 193–4.
[45] See his numerous letters in ARSI, *Iap.-Sin.*, 14 i.

numbers, he also mentions another important and historic event in the history of Christianity in Japan, the ordinations to the priesthood of the first two Japanese Jesuits, Sebastião Kimura and Luis Niabara, in Nagasaki in September 1601.[46] Two years later, on 15 January 1603, Valignano left Japan for the last time and spent the final three years of his life in Macao, where, among other occupations, he set about revising his *Principio y progresso de la religión Christiana en Jappón* (*Beginnings and Progress of the Christian Religion in Japan*), a history of the Japanese Church which was his last word on things Japanese. The first draft had been written while he was still in Nagasaki in the spring of 1601; it was later revised in Macao in 1603.[47] Death finally caught up with the Italian missionary and nobleman on 20 January 1606; he died at the age of sixty-seven, an old man for his day.[48]

AFRICA AND ASIA SEEN THROUGH THE EYES OF AN ITALIAN

Wherever he travelled beyond the boundaries of Europe, Valignano, like many others before him, was confronted with new peoples, unknown and exotic customs, and complex social, political, and religious circumstances. Fortunately, the Visitor's intellectual struggle to come to terms with these experiences is well recorded in his copious and detailed reports, including his final reflections in the *Principio y progresso*. What made his interpretation of what he saw so significant in terms of the missionary enterprise as a whole in the East was the close link between his assessment of the situation and the policies he subsequently devised in response to his positive or negative evaluation, since he had the authority to implement the necessary changes on the basis of those perceptions. Japan is certainly the most notable case in this regard.

Although Valignano was usually quick to form a judgement, his views often underwent radical change over the years as he gradually grew more knowledgeable about his environment. In some cases, he even came to reverse completely or at least revise his previous assessments, and this is especially true with regard to his interpretation of people and events in Japan and China. However, some of the opinions he formed on the basis of his first impressions outside of Europe, such as those regarding Africa, remained unaltered till the very end of his life because of his lack of a prolonged experience in that region.

---

[46] See Valignano to Bellarmine (Nagasaki, 16 October 1601) in ARSI, *Iap.-Sin.*, 14 i, fols 81ʳ–82ᵛ.

[47] There are three extant manuscripts of this work: British Library Additional MS, 9857; Biblioteca da Ajuda, Lisbon, *Jesuítas na Ásia*, 49-iv-53; and Tokyo, Private Collection (previously, Phillipps MS, 3065). At present I am completing a full critical edition of this work, based on a collation of the three manuscripts, which will be published in electronic form on CD-ROM.

[48] For an interesting anonymous panegyric of the Visitor's life, see Biblioteca da Ajuda, Lisbon, *Jesuítas na Ásia*, 49-v-5, fols 67ʳ–70ᵛ and 49-vi-8, fols 85ʳ–88ʳ. For an English translation with commentary, based on the first of these two MSS, see J. M. Braga, 'The panegyric of Alexander Valignano, S. J. (reproduced from an old Portuguese codex) with an introduction and notes', *Monumenta Nipponica*, 5 (1942), 523–35.

During his brief interlude in Mozambique, his first encounter with a non-Caucasian people, Valignano writes to Mercurian describing the Monomotapa tribes but can scarcely find anything to say to commend them:

> This people of Monomotapa . . . are of very limited ability . . . I am told, in fact, that they are completely incapable of grasping our Holy Law and customs . . . which can be accounted for not only by the naturally inferior capacity of their intellect . . . but also by their savage conduct and the vices which plague them, for they do live like brute beasts.[49]

Valignano's main concern is to underline their lack of rational ability. Without a natural aptitude to assent to the faith, he is convinced that the prospects of missionary work among them are indeed bleak. Augustinian overtones dominate the argument he employs to resolve the issue. He concludes that such fundamental deficiencies manifest an inevitable and particular expression of divine providence, whereby that land

> by the just and yet mysterious judgement of our Lord has been abandoned in this state of 'semi-paralysis' as a sterile and reprobate land, from which for a long time to come no fruit can be hoped for.[50]

Consequently, he feels that it will be more fruitful to concentrate missionary efforts in India and further East. His reflections on the African tribes are well summarized in his first *Historia* of the Indies, written in 1583. Having already visited India, Malacca, Macao, and Japan by that time, he is in a position to make comparisons and concludes that the natives of Mozambique 'are a people . . . of such strange and barbarous customs that they are deemed to be of the least ability and understanding of all the peoples that we find here in the Orient'.[51]

With regard to India, his appraisal is slightly more positive, although he seemingly contradicts himself when, in speaking of the low level of learning among the people of the subcontinent, he affirms that

> they are all ignorant, as is the case with all those who have no learning or scientific knowledge whatsoever, although it is common for all these nations [*naciones*] to know at least how to read and write in their respective languages. And they write on palm leaves which are used to make books.[52]

---

[49] For the original Italian text, see Valignano to Mercurian (Mozambique, 7 August 1574) (ARSI, *Goa*, 12 i, fol. 197') in *DI*, ix (1966), 402.

[50] For the original Italian, see Valignano to Mercurian (Mozambique, 7 August 1574) (ARSI, *Goa*, 12 i, fol. 197') in *DI*, ix (1966), 404. Valignano is here echoing Augustine's words; see his *Sermo*, 301, ch. 3 in *PL*, xxxviii, 1481 (cited in *ibid.* 404, note 31).

[51] For the original Portuguese, see Valignano, *Historia (1542–64)*, 394.

[52] For the original Spanish, see Valignano's *Sumario índico*, ii (Shimo, 1580) (ARSI, Goa, 6, fol. 5'–6') in *DI*, xiii (1975), 146.

It would at first appear difficult to reconcile the Visitor's remarks on 'ninguna suerte de letras' (no learning whatsoever) with his claim that there is a widely diffused ability to read and write, and his acknowledgement of the existence of books in the various regional languages. An explanation may perhaps be found in his humanist conception of 'letras' as a higher form of literary culture that transcends the basic levels of literacy. Obviously, he was unaware of the vast corpus of Indian literary and philosophical works when writing these words. As with the African tribes, he reflects on the aptitude of the Indians to become Christians. He fears that the task will be exceedingly difficult:

> And as they are not motivated in their behaviour by reason, they are very difficult to convert . . . and commonly none of them converts on account of an *interior motion* of the Spirit or of *reason* [my italics].[53]

An evaluation presented in such terms would seem to allow us to speak here literally of a *preiudicium* in Valignano's mind, and which is repeated time and time again in his writings regarding the peoples *citra Gangem*, in that he never fails to contrast their shortcomings with the extraordinary potential of the 'white people' *ultra Gangem* (of Japan and China). In view of his rather disappointing experiences, this would be relatively unremarkable were it not for the fact that he was singing the praises of Japan and China even *before* having sailed east of Malacca. This is plainly illustrated in his comparison of the peoples of Asia written two years before first setting foot on Japanese soil:

> It is common for these people (I do not speak here either of China or of Japan, whose people are white), to be of little spirit and ability or rather (as Aristotle says) to be born *by nature* to serve rather than to govern and to lead [my italics].[54]

In his attempt to distinguish the civilized man from the barbarian and the respective roles assigned to each by virtue of nature, Valignano falls back on the criteria set forth in Aristotle's *Politics*:

> Authority and subordination [*archein to archesthai*] are conditions not only inevitable but also expedient; in some cases things are marked out from the moment of birth to rule or to be ruled.[55]

> For he is by nature a slave . . . who participates in reason so far as to apprehend it but not to possess it.[56]

---

[53] For the original Spanish, see *ibid.* 146.

[54] For the original Italian, see *ibid.* 144.

[55] See *Politics*, 1254a22 in *Aristotle*, xxi [1932], trans. H. Rackham (Cambridge, MA, 1990).

[56] *Politics*, 1254b21–3.

It is manifest therefore that there are cases of people of whom some are freemen and the others slaves by nature [*fusei*].[57]

Such are the considerations that informed Valignano's initial assessment of the Indies. The above descriptions are taken from his first systematic attempt to write a work on the state of affairs in the Indies of the Portuguese *Padroado* for the benefit of the General Superior in Rome. He composed the first draft of this work over a period of several weeks (22 October–8 December 1577) during his stay in the port of Malacca. His principal aim was to explain in far greater detail than in his previous letters the present circumstances of the Indian Province. Originally divided into thirty-four chapters, the work is called the *Sumario de las cosas que pertenecen a la Provincia de la India Oriental y al govierno della* (*Compendium related to the Province of the East Indies and its Governance*), and is also often referred to simply as the *Sumario índico* (*Indian Compendium*). The 'compendium' or 'summary' underwent several subsequent revisions, the most important of which was that of 1580, which coincides with his first visitation of Japan. In this later version of the *Sumario índico* several new chapters were added: one on China, three on Japan, and another on Ethiopia. What is characteristic of the *Sumario índico*, as well as of his later *Sumario de las cosas de Japón* (*Compendium on Things Japanese*), is the way in which he combines detailed descriptions with numerous recommendations as to how to improve the administration of the Jesuit enterprise in the region. In rhetorical terms, the vast majority of his writings thus display a *deliberative* function, linked invariably to the pursuit of proper government. The questions, *quid faciendum* (what should be done) and *quomodo faciendum* (how it should be achieved), inform his style of argumentation throughout.

In spite of his initial pessimism at the sad state in which he found the Indian mission, writing in 1583 he came to modify considerably his views on the natural ability of the people in India:

They are generally people of little understanding, as they are uneducated and do not possess any manner of scientific knowledge . . . however, there are many among them who know a great deal and are gifted with a very subtle intellect . . . there are also others who know something of astrology and medicine and can predict eclipses as well as we can. Most of them know how to write and they compose their books of history and ballads in prose and verse; finally, though these people, in comparison to the nations of Europe, are mean and base, nevertheless *they are rational beings* . . . and they have their own manner of knowledge and good-breeding; and after they become Christians, if their abilities are properly cultivated, *they are capable of learning and of grasping* [Christian] *doctrine.*[58]

---

[57] *Politics*, 1255a1.
[58] For the original Spanish, see his *Historia (1542–64)*, 30.

Consequently, he was determined to promote the formation of a local clergy, which he believed to be an essential condition for the development of the Church in that country. The first step was the establishment of 'seminarios' for children and 'colegios' where the future clergy could study the liberal arts and theology. In his *Sumario índico*, ch. 35, he lists three principal reasons for this policy. Besides the two practical reasons, namely the inability of the Society to sustain the whole mission on its own and the general shortage of clergy, he gives another, more compelling reason, which reflects the more fundamental issue of the assimilation of the faith by the natives:

> Until the natives become clerics, acquaint themselves with the Divine Cult, and acquire through proper learning the elements of our Faith, in all these regions Christianity will remain suspended on a thread and without any foundation, interior roots, or the ability to survive by itself for very long.[59]

Once again the rational and free act of faith, based on a solid foundation of doctrinal knowledge, is, in Valignano's view, the only guarantee of true assimilation of Christianity. What is new is his belief that the Indians will be able to take on this arduous task of constructing a local Church by themselves, provided that they receive the necessary training.

In contrast with the 'deficiency' in natural potential to become good Christians among the inhabitants of Africa, and the serious limitations he perceived in the peoples of India *citra Gangem*, the Japanese are placed in a completely different category. The reason for this enthusiastic interest in Japan emerges from his observations on the national character and religious inclinations of the Japanese. Among the numerous reports he compiled, the *Sumario de las cosas de Japón*, written in 1583, is particularly significant, as it provides both a summary of his assessment of the situation of the Japanese and the Church there at the end of his first visitation, as well as detailed proposals for resolving the major problems he encountered in the administration of the mission. From this point of view, the Japanese *Sumario* is undoubtedly one of the most original works, if not the most important one, he ever wrote. In ch. 6, entitled 'De la importancia de esta empresa y del grande provecho que se hace y está para hacer en Japón' ('On the importance of this enterprise and the great harvest that is being reaped and is about to be reaped in Japan'), he confidently states that

> of all the peoples of the Orient, we see that only the Japanese are motivated to become Christians of their own *free will* [*libre voluntad*], convinced by *reason*, and with the *desire* for salvation. It is common among all other

---

[59] See Valignano, *Sumario índico* (ARSI, *Goa*, 6, fol. 49ʳ) in *DI*, xiii (1975), 290. See also his remarks in the first draft of the *Sumario* (Malacca, 22 November–8 December 1577) (ARSI, *Goa*, 31, fol. 375ʳ) in *ibid.* 115.

peoples of the Orient, on the other hand, to be motivated to accept the
Faith for the sake of personal convenience and other human interests;
from this it is evident that the Japanese accept our Doctrine more whole-
heartedly and make the necessary effort to prepare themselves in a very
short time to receive the sacraments . . .[60]

Regarding the question of 'religious inclinations', writing almost twenty years
later, in *Principio y progresso*, ch. 8, he is inspired to compare Japanese religion
with that of the ancient Romans. This is of particular interest inasmuch as it
shows his concern for classical models, a central topos in humanist thought.[61]
In the following text, a rare instance in which he comments on Buddhism in
Principio y progresso, Valignano defends some of the teachings of the Bonzes
with whom he elsewhere constantly takes issue:

> But it can be truly said that no pagan people (including the Romans when
> they were pagans) were ever so modest and decent as the Japanese. For
> although there are indeed many sins among them, there is not the public
> and authorized immorality that there has always been among other pagan
> nations . . . For the sects of the bonzes do not tell any such stories of their
> buddhas as the immoral stories of Jupiter and Venus, and of Cupid, and of
> other very immoral gods whom even the Romans adored. They do indeed
> tell many fables about them, but they are all stories of virtue and morality,
> and in their sects they are emphatic in urging a rejection of sensuality and
> a turning away from the things of this world, and they also provide excel-
> lent moral precepts . . .[62]

Valignano is quite explicit in stating that he believes that there are aspects of
Japanese religion that are equal to or even superior to their European classical counterparts. Although the Visitor did not attempt to engage in what
today would be called 'inter-faith dialogue', he acknowledged the importance of studying Buddhist doctrine in order to acquire the skills necessary
to participate in philosophical and theological disputations with the Bonzes
and other learned men of Japan.[63] Thus, the Visitor's approach to Japan's
native religions, though critical, is not one of total rejection or disapproval.

---

[60] For the original Spanish, see Valignano, *Sumario*, 132.

[61] For the importance of classical models in a Europe struggling intellectually to come to terms with the
unfamiliar peoples of America, see Sabine MacCormack, 'Limits of understanding: perceptions of Greco-
Roman and Amerindian paganism in early modern Europe', in Karen Ordahl Kupperman (ed.), *America in
European Consciousness, 1493–1750* (Chapel Hill, 1995), 79–129.

[62] See *Principio*, 8, fols 36ʳ–37ʳ. The present translation is reproduced by kind permission from Moran, *The
Japanese and the Jesuits*, 99–100.

[63] Although he regarded Japanese religions as distortions of the truth, he did acknowledge positive elements in them. Furthermore, and of greater significance, was his willingness to engage in an intellectual
dispute with Shintoist and Buddhist doctrines. For this purpose he composed the following work: *Catechismus
christianae fidei, in quo veritas nostrae religionis ostenditur, et sectae Iaponenses confutantur* (2 vols, Lisbon, 1586).

At the same time, Valignano was not blind to what he perceived as the defects in character of the Japanese. These are spelt out in full in European correspondence during his first stay in the country, and in particular in the above-mentioned *Sumario de las cosas de Japón* and in his first history of the Jesuit missions in the Indies, the *Historia del principio y progresso de la Compañía de Jesús en las Indias Orientales* (*History of the Beginnings and Progress of the Society of Jesus in the East Indies*), both composed in 1583. Whereas his initial assessments tended to be harsh as a result of having taken the *costumbres de Japón* (customs of Japan) at face value, he goes to great lengths in his later works, and especially in *Principio y progresso*, to adopt a more subtle and even apologetic approach towards customs he had previously condemned. An intermediate phase between the *Sumario*, his first *Historia*, and *Principio y progresso* is represented by the *Adiciones del Sumario de Japón* (*Additions to the Compendium of Japan*), which he penned in 1592 with the purpose of bringing up to date some of the descriptions of Japan and the policy recommendations found in his *Sumario*. The change of tone in his writing over the years is evident in that he often shifts from a severe judgement to a more moderate interpretation of the same phenomenon. This tendency is eloquently illustrated in his comments concerning the natural cruelty of the Japanese and their widespread practice of infanticide and abortion:[64]

> The fourth [negative] quality of their [the Japanese] character is that they are very cruel and very quick to kill . . . for the smallest perceived grievance they kill their subjects and think nothing of cutting a man in half as if he were but a dog (or a pig). And what is even crueler and against all natural order is that even mothers often kill their own children, either while they are still in the womb by taking means to abort them, or, by placing their feet on their throats and smothering them to death.[65]

These earlier remarks from the 1580s are tempered by his final statement in his *Principio y progresso* of 1601–3, where, though he does not justify these apparent acts of cruelty, he at least attempts to explain fair-handedly why they occur so frequently. It is interesting to note how he remarks that, despite the frequent killings, the Japanese are neither 'barbarous or cruel' by nature and that when they do kill their newborn children it is almost always on account of the poverty of the parents who 'think it less cruel to end the lives of their children than to subject them to constant misery and poverty'.[66]

---

[64] See also Moran, *The Japanese and the Jesuits*, 95–101.

[65] For the original Spanish, see both Valignano, *Historia (1542–64)*, 140–1, and his *Sumario*, 30–1. The two texts have slightly different wording, from which I have collated and translated the above quotation.

[66] For the original Spanish text in *Principio y progresso*, see British Library, Add. MS 9857, fols 37ʳ–38ʳ. A partial English translation of these comments by Valignano can be found in Moran, *The Japanese and the Jesuits*, 100–1.

Conversely, there were also positive qualities of the Japanese, such as their alleged ability to learn to read and write more easily than Europeans, and their general level of intelligence, that Valignano realized he had exaggerated. Whereas in the *Sumario de Japón* he extols the extraordinary talents of Japanese children, in *Principio y progresso* he takes a more moderate view and admits that, although it is true that they are in fact very industrious and clever, such comparisons are generally misleading and are best avoided.[67]

What these limited examples reveal is that, for the most part, with some notable exceptions, the Visitor succeeded in keeping an open mind, and was willing to modify his judgements and decisions when experience taught him that his previous assessment of the situation had simply been wrong. This was certainly true in the case of India and Japan. Unfortunately, we shall never know whether a prolonged stay among the people of Monomotapa would have compelled him to find positive and redeemable elements in a culture that he had found deficient in almost every respect.

THE QUESTION OF MISSIONARY METHOD: ACCOMMODATION AND EDUCATION

We now turn to the central issue of how Valignano's numerous experiences were reflected in concrete policies through which he attempted to reorganize the mission in Japan. Soon after landing in the small port of Kuchinotsu, near Nagasaki, at the beginning of his first visit to Japan in July 1579, one of Valignano's first official acts was to convoke a 'consulta', the principal forum for discussion among the missionaries.[68] Its purpose was to provide the mission superior with a clear and detailed picture of the situation so that he could make the necessary decisions concerning the work of individuals as well as the objectives the Jesuits needed to pursue as a group. The consultation took place at three different venues over a period of two years. The first group assembled in Usuki (Bungo) in October 1580. The second gathering took place in Azuchi (Gokinai) in July 1581. The final assembly, which reconsidered some of the questions discussed during the previous two meetings, was held in Nagasaki in December 1581. The whole process was thus prolonged, 'since the Fathers had [previously] not been able to assemble altogether in one place in order to hold this consultation'.[69] Before his departure from the country on 20 February 1582, he officially endorsed the decisions which he had taken as a result of the two-year consultation and

---

[67] See Valignano, *Sumario* (1583), 5, and contrast them with his remarks in *Principio y Progresso*, fol. 32ʳ. For partial translations of these texts, see Moran, *The Japanese and the Jesuits*, 151–2.

[68] Several manuscript copies of the deliberations of the Consult have survived: see ARSI, *Iap.-Sin.*, 2, fols 42ʳ–69ʳ (1ª vía); Rome: Biblioteca Nazionale Centrale Vittorio Emmanuele, *Fondo Gesuitico*, MS 1482/3611/no. 29 (2ª vía); and ARSI, *Iap.-Sin.*, 2, fols 4ʳ–34ʳ (3ª vía). This third and definitive version has the following title: *Consulta feita em Bungo pollo P.ᵉ Alexandro Valignano Visitador da Ýndia no mês d'outubro de anno 1580 acerca das cousas de Japão* (*Consultation held in Bungo by Fr. Alessandro Valignano, Visitor of India, in the month of October, 1580 regarding* [various] *issues in Japan*). For a complete list of MSS, see *VMJ-E*, 1/1, 407, 409.

[69] For the original Portuguese text of the acts of the *Consulta*, see ARSI, *Iap.-Sin.*, 2, fol. 3ʳ.

which were called the 'resolutions' (*resoluções*) of the Visitor.[70] The two most significant events during this first visitation were the establishment of colleges for the education of Japanese youth in Funai in 1580, an outcome of the *consultas*, and the donation of the port of Nagasaki to the Society of Jesus by the Christian lord Ōmura Sumitada in the same year.[71]

Despite the bold policies that the Visitor was to implement as a result of these meetings, the consultations were a particularly difficult time for Valignano, whose first visit to Japan was marked from beginning to end by much uncertainty and disappointment. His initial experiences left him painfully disillusioned, and shattered the image he had previously formed of a flourishing mission in Japan. He openly vents his frustration in a letter to the General Superior in which he complains about the misleading and uncritical reports that had led him to idealize the situation of the Church in Japan:

> I can truthfully confess to Your Paternity that the difference between what I have found here in Japan from personal experience and the information about this country that they gave me in India and even in China [in Macao] is as stark as the difference between black and white.[72]

While he was relieved to see that the Japanese were truly a capable people, he felt forced to acknowledge that he had grave misgivings about some of their moral qualities. Unable to reconcile the reality with his perhaps unrealistically high expectations of the people whom Xavier had referred to as 'the best that have as yet been discovered', Valignano became depressed and was overwhelmed with feelings of anxiety about what he should do to improve the situation.[73] Despite his initial pessimism, by the time the *consulta* began the following year, Valignano had recovered his sense of balance and was able to judge the situation with greater clarity. He concluded that much of the blame for what he perceived as the sadly inadequate state of the Jesuit mission lay with the methods adopted by Francisco Cabral, a zealous preacher and ex-soldier who had been sent to Japan in 1570 to succeed Cosme de Torres as superior of the mission.

Writing to Aquaviva almost twenty years after his first visit to Japan, Valignano looks back at his own decisions and contrasts them at length with the detrimental policies of Cabral. The Visitor identifies seven 'principles' (*principios*) that Cabral had followed in his dealings with the Japanese and which he is convinced were at the root of the problem: first, Cabral's adherence to strict disciplinarian methods, based on the belief that the Japanese brothers should be treated

---

[70] The Visitor signed the 'Resolutions' on 6 January 1582. For the text of the Resolutions there are several extant copies; see, for example, ARSI, *Iap.-Sin.*, 2, fols 70ʳ–86ᵛ and 49, 223ʳ–238ᵛ. For a list of other MS copies, see *VMJ-E*, 1/1, 409.

[71] For more on the donation of Nagasaki, see Diego Pacheco [=Yūki Ryōgo], *The Founding of the Port of Nagasaki* (Macao, 1989), 29–45.

[72] For the original Spanish, see Valignano to Mercurian (Kuchinotsu, 5 December 1579) (ARSI, *Iap.-Sin.*, 8 I, fol. 242ᵛ), cited in *Sumario*, 65*.

[73] See *VMJ-E*, 1/1, 271–80.

harshly, 'with an iron hand with blows and harsh words' ('in virga ferrea con açotes y palabras duras'); secondly, his belief that the Japanese and the Portuguese should always be treated differently; thirdly, his insistence that the Japanese should accommodate themselves to the foreigners and not vice versa; fourthly, Cabral's continuous criticism of Japanese customs; fifthly, his conviction that, in order to ensure that the Japanese should not lose respect for their European superiors, they should not be taught either Latin or Portuguese or any other academic disciplines; sixthly, his refusal to establish seminaries or colleges where the Japanese could be trained for the priesthood; and finally, his opinion that the missionaries need not waste time learning the Japanese language except for the bare rudiments required for survival in the country.[74]

In an earlier communication to Mercurian, composed at the time of the first session of the consult in 1580, Valignano reports how Cabral's attitude had created profound 'resentment, disunity, and aversion' ('grandísima desunión y aversión') between the Japanese *dōjuku* and the European missionaries. Valignano, on the other hand, insists that the only way to undo the damage is to adopt exactly the opposite attitude and treat the Japanese as equals and with respect. Time and time again he speaks of adopting a 'kind manner' ('il modo soave') when dealing with others.[75] Moreover, he notes that those engaged as lay assistant catechists had been given little or no support in their religious life and practically no intellectual formation. Valignano points out the inherent contradiction in expecting them to be 'preachers and teachers (predicadores y doctores)' to their own people, while at the same time denying them the means to prepare themselves for the task through proper studies ('no havían de tener ni saber ni sciencia').[76]

What is strange about this controversy is that it was Cabral who had first made a case several years before Valignano's arrival in Japan in favour of the admission of Japanese into the order and the creation of a centre where they could be trained to carry out their duties.[77] Upon receiving Cabral's requests, Valignano despatched a letter from India instructing him to hold a discussion on various matters pertaining to the government of the mission, including the status of the Japanese. A consultation of Jesuits working in the Ōmura and Arima districts was convened sometime in the latter part of 1576. Most participants agreed to forward proposals to the Visitor in favour of incorporating some of the *dōjuku* into the Society.[78] Their plans were temporarily put on hold, however, by Valignano and others in India, who felt that more information and consultation was needed before any decisions could

---

[74] See Valignano to Aquaviva (Goa, 23 November 1595) (ARSI, *Iap.-Sin.*, 12 ɪɪ, fols 315ʳ⁻ᵛ) in *DI*, xvɪɪ (1988), 261–4.

[75] Valignano speaks of the importance of 'il governo soave' in many letters. See, for example, Valignano to Mercurian (at sea between Cochin and Goa, 4 December 1575) (ARSI, *Goa*, 47, fol. 42ʳ) in *DI*, x (1968), 147.

[76] See Valignano to Mercurian (Usuki, 27 October 1580) (ARSI, *Iap.-Sin.*, 8 ɪ, fols 298ʳ⁻ᵛ) in *VMJ-G*, ɪ/2, 488–90.

[77] See *VMJ-E*, ɪ/1, 221–2, 230–8.

[78] For Cabral's report to Valignano on the consultation held in the port of Kuchinotsu, see ARSI, *Iap.-Sin.*, 8 ɪɪ, 13a–d, cited in *VMJ-E*, ɪ/1, 231, note 192.

be prudently reached on such an important matter.[79] It therefore remains unclear what ultimately prompted Cabral to change his mind and oppose so vehemently less than five years later Valignano's plans, which were in part based on some of his own recommendations. Schütte notes that from the outset Cabral's proposals had, in fact, cautiously sidestepped the issue of allowing the Japanese brothers to be promoted to the study of humanities and philosophy.[80] Whilst acknowledging the necessity of working together with the Japanese, it would seem that Cabral had had a much less daring scheme in mind, and certainly had never intended for the Japanese *irmãos* to be afforded an equal standing within the Order.[81]

Valignano soon came to the conclusion that a solid religious formation and education in the humanities for the native Japanese *irmãos* held the key to overcoming what he saw as a crisis which he feared would otherwise lead to the imminent 'ruin of the Society of Jesus'.[82] One recalls how he had proposed an almost identical solution to the development of the Church in India in spite of certain misgivings about the intellectual and moral aptitude of the native populations of the subcontinent. Unlike India, however, he strongly advocated the admission of Japanese into the Society of Jesus. In a report to the General Superior written on 27 October 1580, Valignano justifies this historic decision by reiterating his conviction that

If the Japanese are treated properly, go through the novitiate experiments, and acquire the requisite learning, we may confidently hope they will become able workers in no whit inferior to European subjects. They are in reality a very capable people endowed with talents of a high order ... They are very courageous and patient in meeting adversity and hardship, and persevering and meticulous in their studies.[83]

In fact, both he and those who attended the *consultas* were convinced that this was the only viable way of ensuring the continuity of the mission ('éste era único y verdadero remedio para la conversión y conservación de Japón').[84] As a result,

[79] See 'Question 44: Whether a college is to be established in Malacca, China, or Japan' of the Indian Mission Consult (Chorão, 6–18 December 1575) (ARSI, *Goa*, 47, fols 29ʳ–30ʳ) in *DI*, x (1968), 292–3.

[80] See *VMJ-E*, 1/1, 237.

[81] See Cabral's bitter denunciation of Valignano's admission of too many Japanese into the Order and the imminent disaster he foresees as a result in his letter to the Portuguese Assistant, João Álvares (Goa, 10 December 1596) (ARSI, *Goa*, 32, fols 585ʳ and 586ʳ) in *DI*, xviii (1988), 610–11, 613–14.

[82] See Valignano to the General Superior (Usuki, 27 October 1580) in ARSI, *Iap.-Sin.*, 8 1, fol. 298ʳ, published in *VMJ-G*, 1/2, 487.

[83] See *ibid.* fol. 299ʳ, in *VMJ-G*, 1/2, 492; the English translation can be found in *VMJ-E*, 1/2, 60.

[84] See especially the following questions (*preguntas*) discussed at the *consulta*: 'Question 5: Whether schools (*seminarios*) should be established for the native Japanese' (see Valignano, *Sumario*, 172 for the above citation); 'Question 8: Whether it would be good to establish several houses as colleges [*collegio(s)*] where Ours [the Jesuits] should live [and study] together'; 'Question 10: If Japanese should be accepted into the Society [of Jesus]' (ARSI, *Iap.-Sin.*, 2, fols 49ʳ–50ʳ, 54ʳ–56ʳ, and 57ʳ–58ʳ), published respectively in Valignano, *Sumario*, 172–4, 106–10, and 181–3. These decisions were subsequently incorporated into chs 12–14 of Valignano's *Sumario de las cosas de Japón*, in which he discusses the same issues at greater length.

a 'seminario' (a preparatory school for boys aged 12–18) was set up in Arima in
the spring of 1580. Around the same time, another such school ('seminario')
was founded in the Gokinai region (Azuchi) on a plot of land donated by
Nobunaga himself. The establishment of a 'collegio' (a college of higher
studies) in Funai followed in October, and the novitiate was inaugurated on
Christmas Eve of the same year. Whereas the novitiate was to initiate suitable
candidates into the religious life, the purpose of the 'seminarios' was to provide
a general education in the 'humanities and other sciences' ('humanidad y
más sciencias'). This included learning to read and write in Latin and Japanese,
'proper behaviour' ('buenas costumbres'), and the 'etiquette, customs, and ceremonies' ('cortesías, costumbres, y ceremonías') proper to Japan. The entire
programme was to be informed by a pursuit of virtue and 'sound doctrine'
('buena doctrina').[85] The college, on the other hand, was to provide higher-
level studies in both European and Japanese humanities. Although a further
discussion of the vicissitudes of the Japanese colleges exceeds the scope of
the present study, it is important to note that education was one of the
cornerstones on which Valignano chose to build his missionary policy.[86]

This went hand in hand with another equally important strategy, namely
the Visitor's determination to avoid presenting the Christian message in an
exclusively European cultural format. Although he had already rejected such
tendencies in Cabral's methods and mentality, the Visitor was still in search
of practical and viable alternatives. It was at this time that he came into
contact with several Japanese Christian noblemen, namely Ōmura Sumitada
(Don Bartolomeu), Arima Harunobu (Don Protásio), and Ōtomo Yoshishige
(Don Francisco). These were the most prominent figures of the Japanese
Church, without whose continued support the very existence of Christianity
in Japan would have been virtually impossible. And thus, when Valignano saw
that they agreed in their criticisms of the behaviour of the missionaries, he
knew he would have to take their grievances seriously and find an acceptable
solution. The Japanese noblemen seem to have been unanimous in their
insistence that, if the Jesuits were going to succeed at all in bringing the faith
to the people of Japan, they would have to adopt the customs and etiquette
of their host county.[87] Don Francisco, in particular, impressed the Visitor with
his sophisticated artistic and literary tastes, as well as his skills in local government, and convinced him that Japanese formality had to be respected lest
the missionaries become the laughing stock of the samurai class and end up
damaging their cause even further. Ōtomo also did not hesitate to remind
Valignano that he had personally heard Cosme de Torres say that Xavier had

---

[85] See Valignano, *Sumario*, 170–5.

[86] For a more detailed exposition, see my 'Jesuit humanist education in sixteenth-century Japan: the Latin
and Japanese MSS of Pedro Gómez's 'Compendia' on astronomy, philosophy, and theology (1593–95)', in
Kirishitan Bunko (ed.), *The Latin and Japanese MSS of Pedro Gómez's Compendia* (3 vols, Tokyo, 1997), III, 11–60.

[87] Valignano quotes what these three lords told him in a letter to Aquaviva (Goa, 23 November 1595)
(ARSI, *Iap.-Sin.*, 12 II, fols 315ʳ–316ʳ) in *DI*, XVII (1988), 266–8.

always enjoined the missionaries to accommodate themselves insofar as possible to the ways of the Japanese.[88] Thus, it is not implausible to say that Ōtomo's influence was decisive in what the Visitor did next. Persuaded by the arguments he had heard from both the Japanese and his fellow Jesuits, he decided to compose a set of guidelines that would carefully regulate the way the Jesuits behaved, both within their own houses of residence among themselves and in their dealings with others.

An area of special concern was the proper observance of etiquette when receiving guests and paying visits to the houses of the Japanese. Every effort was to be made to respect local customs or *katagi* (from which the term *catangues* was coined), especially with regard to forms of courtesy. These norms, composed in Bungo in October 1581, were entitled *Advertimentos e avisos acerca dos costumes e catangues de Jappão* (*Observations on the Habits and Particular Customs of Japan*). The work is extremely detailed and offers a practical guide to everyday life, including dress, food, table manners, cleanliness, and the use of honorific forms when addressing people of a different rank from one's own. Not only does it reflect a detailed knowledge of Japanese life, it also advocates the imitation within the Society of Jesus of the social organization and structure of the leading Zen temple in Kyoto, the Nanzenji.[89] Although these rules were formulated as a result of the discussions of the *consulta* of 1580, which had expressed the need for greater adaptation to local circumstances, it is unlikely that the Fathers were prepared for what Valignano finally presented them with.[90] When Aquaviva in Rome read a copy of the *Advertimentos e avisos*, he was not altogether pleased with some of the more creative aspects of Valignano's guidelines, such as the close adherence to Buddhist temple ranks. As a result, on Christmas Eve, 1585 he sent a long letter to the Visitor expressing some of his more serious doubts with regard to the *Advertimentos e avisos* and the potentially negative impact they might have on religious life in the Society. The first chapter of the treatise proved to be, in effect, the most controversial and was subsequently redrafted by Valignano. It carries the title 'Do modo que se ha de ter pera aquirir e conservar autoridade tratando com os Jappoens', and is centred around the careful consideration of one's own dignity ('dignidade') and rank *vis-à-vis* the Bonzes. The General Superior reminds the Visitor that it is not honour but rather the simplicity and poverty of Christ crucified that should inform the Jesuit way of proceeding, especially when preaching the Gospel among non-Christians.[91]

---

[88] See Valignano, *Sumario*, 130*.

[89] This work has been edited and translated into Italian by Josef Franz Schütte, as *Il Cerimoniale per i missionari del Giappone* (Rome, 1946). This bilingual edition provides the original Portuguese text. For more on this work, see Schütte's introduction, 1–115, and his description of this work in *VMJ-E*, 1/2, 155–90.

[90] See Questions 17–19, published in Valignano, *Sumario*, 241–8 and ch. 23 of the *Sumario de las cosas de Japón* (1583): 'The way in which the Fathers are to comport themselves both in the houses and outside of them', in *Sumario*, 230–49.

[91] See Schütte, *Il Cerimoniale*, 37–41.

Valignano promptly wrote back and tried to justify some of the more problematic passages by reassuring the General Superior that the guidelines he had drafted were not meant to contradict the fundamental values of religious humility and poverty. A long period of revisions and adjustments followed until finally, in 1592, at the end of the first Provincial Congregation of the Jesuits in Japan, the *Advertimentos e avisos* were superseded by a new set of norms that covered similar ground but dropped completely the conformity to Buddhist ranks and the pursuit of 'dignities and honours'.[92] Valignano's original and bold attempt to redefine the very framework within which religious life functioned by giving precedence to structures and institutions alien to traditional Western Christianity had certainly alarmed Rome, and thus his experiment was ultimately abandoned. Undoubtedly, Valignano's initiatives in Japan, such as that of the *Advertimentos e avisos*, also gave impetus to developments in China. From the outset he had encouraged Matteo Ricci to study the language and etiquette of the mandarins and become fluent in their classics. Ricci acknowledges the authorship of this novel approach, to which he was to lend his own personal genius, when he refers to the Visitor as 'the first founder of this enterprise of China'.[93]

In more general terms, we may ask what all this tells us about Valignano and his impact on the development of the mission in Japan. The conscious choice by the Visitor to implement a policy of cultural accommodation and adaptation to Japanese culture and customs may very well be taken for granted today and deemed relatively unremarkable, but such an approach was nevertheless quite pioneering and even revolutionary for his time. In this regard, it seems safe to say that Cabral's 'intransigent' attitude and his apparent unwillingness to compromise, far from being unusual, represented the norm among European missionaries in Asia during the sixteenth century. It has been pointed out how by that time 'Europeanism' had become 'so deeply entrenched and the principle of accommodation so little understood' that 'the identity of Christianity and European cultural forms and social customs was taken for granted'. In such an intellectual milieu, 'slight concessions to non-European usages or attitudes ran the risk of being regarded as a betrayal of the faith'.[94]

CONCLUSION

This overview of Valignano's life and thought has brought together what might seem like an unlikely mix of people, events, and writings. Although

[92] For the original Portuguese, see the *Regulae Provinciae Iaponiae* in ARSI, *Iap.-Sin.*, 2, fols 88'–148'.

[93] See Matteo Ricci, *Storia dell'introduzione del cristianesimo in Cina*, II, 362, no. 774, line 4. See also *ibid.* I, 221, no. 275, lines 19–20, where he calls Valignano 'il primo autore di questa missione'. For the full bibliographical reference, see note 1 above.

[94] See G. H. Dunne, *Generation of Giants. The First Jesuits in China* (Notre Dame, IN, 1962), 228. See also Ross, *A Vision Betrayed*, xv.

the character sketch that emerges remains incomplete, it has hopefully helped to identify some of the more salient features of the personage. Perhaps the most important of these is the apparently discordant coexistence of conservative ideas with a vigorous determination to carry forward the missionary enterprise along new and uncharted paths. In the Visitor's career moments of uncertainty alternate with somewhat unusual expressions of self-confidence, persistence, and even authoritarianism. Hence, it was perhaps inevitable that Valignano's strong views and original experiments did not go unchallenged for long. A number of events in Europe and Asia came to alter completely the carefully devised mission strategies and policies of previous years. The criticisms of the Jesuit way of proceeding that emerged as a result of major political changes and upheavals in both the secular and ecclesiastical spheres in the 1580s and 1590s had an impact on Valignano's later writings, and especially on his interpretation of history. These and other aspects of the Visitor's career require further study but cannot be adequately developed within the limited scope of the present essay. Nevertheless, this brief introduction will hopefully have helped the reader to gain some insight into the unique and tumultuous encounter between Europe and Japan at the close of the sixteenth century – an encounter which was in part shaped by a stubborn yet brilliant Italian nobleman and missionary, Alessandro Valignano.

3

The transmission of Renaissance culture in seventeenth-century China

NICOLAS STANDAERT

When in 1613 Niccolò Longobardo, the superior of the Jesuit mission in China, sent Nicolas Trigault, a talented young Jesuit who had been in China for only about two-and-a-half years, back to Europe, he took a great risk. Would Trigault ever reach Europe or would he die as a result of shipwreck or illness during the journey? And, if his mission were successful, would he ever manage to return to China? Longobardo had commissioned Trigault with several tasks: the settlement of the institutional reorganization of the China mission within the Society of Jesus, negotiations with the Holy See concerning the recognition of Chinese as a liturgical language, recruitment of new missionaries, financial support for the mission, and the assembling of a library for Beijing (Peking) and other places. The latter activity would become one of the most successful aspects of Trigault's three-and-a-half year stay in Europe. He returned to China with a large collection of books in 1620. Because of its importance and later influence, this library provides a fruitful starting point for our knowledge about the spread of Renaissance culture in China in the seventeenth century.

Trigault, however, was not the first to have introduced Renaissance culture in China. Among others, he was preceded by Matteo Ricci, the most prominent of these figures, who had arrived in China forty years earlier in 1582. If one considers the Renaissance to have lasted until the seventeenth century, then the transmission of this culture to China can be divided into approximately three phases. The first period, corresponding to the initial thirty years (1582–1610), is characterized by a spontaneous transmission primarily through the person of Ricci. In the second phase, under the initiative of Longobardo, this transmission became a more systematic project which included the translation of books brought by Trigault (c. 1620–c. 1630s). This was mainly carried out by missionaries from various European countries who had accompanied Trigault on his return to China. The third phase is only an aftermath: following the turbulent years of dynastic transition in China (1640s) and repositioning of the Jesuits at the Chinese court, the Jesuits made a (failed) attempt to have Aristotelian philosophy introduced as the basis of the Chinese educational system (1678–83).

This article will take the three phases as a chronological division. While selecting only a few themes among the various philosophical, theological, scientific, or artistic aspects of Renaissance culture that were transmitted, it will attempt to integrate some analysis of the transmission process itself. Since Dominicans and Franciscans arrived in China only in the 1630s, the role of the Jesuits as transmitters will be the main focus.

SPONTANEOUS DIFFUSION (1582–1610)

General context

In order to understand some of the dynamics of cultural transmission, one needs to start with some very basic facts. When people travel to a culture on the other side of the world, they carry with them some 'luggage'. This freight is constituted on a triple basis: the resources available in one's culture of origin, the mobility and amount of material that one can carry, and one's imagination of the climate and culture on the other side, generated by the available information about that other culture. The luggage, however, is not only material, but also consists of the cultural, intellectual, and educational background in which one was enculturated in one's place of origin. This mental framework and the memory of the culture one has left behind become the glasses through which one will observe and analyse the other culture.

The first Jesuit missionaries who left for China departed with this kind of 'baggage'. However, they had hardly any information about the culture where they would spend the rest of their lives. Most of the information that circulated about other cultures concerned the predominantly unlettered and supposedly 'superstitious' peoples of Latin America and the Indies. Moreover, explorers provided little information about the higher forms of knowledge or culture of these regions. As a result, the missionary adventure in which the Jesuits engaged presupposed the need of spreading a solid faith more than transmitting advanced knowledge sustained by books.

When the first Jesuit missionaries, after many attempts, finally managed to enter into China in 1583, they discovered a country, or rather a continent, that was quite different from what most Europeans could imagine at that time. At the end of the sixteenth century, the Ming dynasty seemed at the height of its glory; it would decline only in the 1620s and fall in 1644.[1] Its achievements in culture and the arts were remarkable, urban and commercial life were spreading new levels of prosperity, while the manufacture of porcelain and silk exceeded anything that could be found in Europe at that

---

[1] For a short description of the 'glory of the Ming', see Jonathan D. Spence, *The Search for Modern China* (New York, 1990), ch. 1; see also Jonathan D. Spence, *The Memory Palace of Matteo Ricci* (London, 1985).

time. With a population more than double that of Europe – *c.* 150 million inhabitants versus 60 million in 1600 – China was not divided into multiple states like Europe, but was a united country with an efficient bureaucratic system bonded by an immense body of statutory laws and provisions. One segment of this bureaucracy lived in Beijing, serving the emperor in an elaborate hierarchy that divided the country's business among six ministries, dealing respectively with finance, personnel, rituals, laws, military affairs, and public works. The other segment of the Chinese bureaucracy consisted of those assigned to posts in the fifteen major provinces, which were further divided into prefectures and counties. Officials were selected by an examination system which started at the county level and culminated in the three-year Metropolitan Examination in which *c.* 300 new officials were selected for the highest positions. These aspects went beyond the missionaries' original imagination, as appears from one of the bestsellers at that time: Nicolas Trigault's Latin translation of Matteo Ricci's account of the Christian mission in China, *De Christiana expeditione apud Sinas, suscepta ab Societate Iesu, ex P. Matthaei Ricii eiusdem Societatis Commentariis, libri V, in quibus Sinensis regni mores, leges atque instituta et novae illius Ecclesiae difficillima primordia accurate et summa fide describuntur* (Augsburg, 1615).[2] The first part of the book describes the cultural, scientific, geographical, and political setting of China in detail. Thus, Ricci and Trigault were not only transmitters of Renaissance culture to China, but, conversely, also among the first to introduce Chinese culture to late Renaissance Europe.

This general cultural and intellectual setting is important for the transmission of Renaissance culture to China in several respects, making this experience, at least from the European perspective, very different from encounters in other countries at that time. In China, the Jesuits encountered a culture that was relatively similar to their own as regards cultural, economic, institutional, intellectual, and material complexity. In contrast with types of transmission involving cultures with a different complexity, in China the means of reproduction of knowledge were more or less similar, and to a certain

[2] This work is the Latin translation of the original Italian text which was only published in the twentieth century: first by Pietro Tacchi Venturi, *Opere Storiche del P. Matteo Ricci S. I.*, vol. 1. I *Commentari della Cina* (Macerata, 1911); next by Pasquale M. d'Elia (ed.), *Fonti Ricciane* (3 vols, Rome, 1942–9). The second volume of Tacchi Venturi contains Ricci's letters: *Le Lettere dalla Cina (1580–1610), con appendice di documenti inediti* (1913). The Latin version was also translated and published in French (1616), German (1617), Spanish (1621), Italian (1622), and partly in English (1625). For a modern English translation, see Matteo Ricci and Nicolas Trigault, *China in the Sixteenth Century: The Journals of Matthew Ricci, 1583–1610*, trans. Louis J. Gallagher (New York, 1953). It is well known that Trigault made several changes and additions to Ricci's *Storia* for propagandistic purposes. See Joseph Shih, 'Introduction', in M. Ricci and N. Trigault, *Histoire de l'expédition chrétienne au royaume de la Chine (1582–1610)* (Paris, 1978), 11–59; see also Theodore N. Foss, 'Nicholas Trigault, S. J. – amanuensis or propagandist? The rôle of the editor of *Della entrata della Compagnia di Giesù e Christianità nella Cina*', addendum to Lo Kuang (ed.), *International Symposium on Chinese–Western Cultural Interchange in Commemoration of the 400th Anniversary of the Arrival of Matteo Ricci, S.J. in China* (Taipei, 1983); on the sixteenth-century texts about China by European authors which Ricci used as a source, see G. Ricciardolo, 'Il *Libro Primo* dei commentari del Ricci e gli scritti europei del XVI secolo sulla Cina: La loro natura e la loro relazione', *Mondo Cinese*, 26/1 (1998), 25–37.

extent even more developed than in Europe. As a result, aspects that usually would be considered essential components of the spread of Renaissance culture in Europe were not introduced in China. For instance, unlike in other countries, the missionaries did not introduce the printing press in China since there was already a widely available printing system. Moreover, the Jesuits, known for having set up schools in Europe and other continents, found in China a very good and well established educational system which made it impossible for them to create new schools. To a large extent, the Chinese side occupied the dominant position in the exchange, since the Chinese received the foreigners in their own habitat, and because of their strategy of 'cultural imperative', which obliged the foreigner to accommodate to the native culture.[3] The most important aspect is the predominance of the Chinese language in the exchange, because before Renaissance ideas could evoke any response, 'they had to be communicated, and they could be communicated only by being filtered through Chinese language and thought patterns'.[4] Contrary to the interaction in Japan, where the Japanese learned Portuguese or Latin, or to modern interactions, where many Chinese have to learn a foreign language in order to participate in cultural transfer, in the seventeenth and eighteenth centuries, except for a very small number of Chinese educated for the priesthood, no Chinese involved in the interaction learned a foreign language. An imperative therefore existed for foreign missionaries to learn Chinese.

Books as the first pole of attraction

The first important transmitter of Renaissance culture to China was the Italian Jesuit Matteo Ricci (1562–1610). The culture that he brought to China was essentially that body of knowledge he acquired during his education. Ricci came from Macerata in the Papal States, had been a student of the Jesuit College there, and was studying law in Rome when he decided to join the Society in 1571. After half a year at the Jesuit college in Florence, he studied at the faculty of arts in the Roman college between late 1573 and 1577. There he followed courses in rhetoric, philosophy, and mathematics, the last under the famous Christophorus Clavius (1538–1612), a noted astronomer and author of the Gregorian calendar reform.[5] His education was in the best Jesuit humanist tradition.[6]

---

[3] Erik Zürcher, 'Jesuit accommodation and the Chinese cultural imperative', in David E. Mungello (ed.), *The Chinese Rites Controversy: Its History and Meaning* (Nettetal, 1994), 40–1.

[4] Paul A. Cohen, *Discovering History in China: American Historical Writing on the Recent Chinese Past* (New York, 1984), 14.

[5] For the Roman College at Ricci's time, see Peter M. Engelfriet, *Euclid in China: The Genesis of the First Translation of Euclid's Elements in 1607 and Its Reception up to 1723* (Leiden, 1998), 23–42. For the scientific curriculum at the Roman College, see Ugo Baldini, *Legem Impone Subactis: Studi su filosofia e scienza dei Gesuiti in Italia, 1540–1632* (Rome, 1992). See also Mario Fois, 'Il Collegio Romano ai tempi degli studi del P. Matteo Ricci', in Maria Cigliano (ed.), *Atti del convegno internazionale di studi ricciani* (Macerata, 1984), 203–28.

[6] Paul Rule, *K'ung-tzu or Confucius? The Jesuit Interpretation of Confucianism* (Sydney, 1987), 12; d'Elia, *Fonti Ricciane*, iii, 20–1.

It is not known what books or objects Ricci himself had carried with him on his way to China. At any rate, in Macao, where the Jesuits had established a college, Western books were available for their personal use.[7] When the first missionaries managed to set up a house on mainland China in Zhaoqing, west of Canton, they brought a personal library with them. These books, material exponents of Renaissance culture, became one of the most effective ways of gaining recognition from Chinese *literati*. Ricci and Trigault reported on it in the following way:

> The high esteem acquired by the Christian religion, from its seemingly futile beginnings, was built up not only by the truth of its doctrine and the holy lives of its missionaries, but at times from little things which in themselves were quite insignificant. For example, among the many books in the mission library there were two large volumes of Canon Law, which were greatly admired by the learned Chinese for their exquisite printing and also for the excellent workmanship of the covers, which were ornamented in gold. The Chinese could neither read these books nor did they have any idea of what they treated, and yet they judged that the content of such volumes must be of major importance, when no expense was spared on their binding. Moreover, they concluded that letters and science must be held in high esteem in Europe, and that in this respect the Europeans, with such books, must surpass not only the other nations but even China itself. This indeed was an admission that they would never have made without seeing evidence of it with their own eyes. They noticed also that the Fathers, not satisfied with a knowledge of European science, were continually, day and night, delving into Chinese scientific tomes. In fact, they had hired a Chinese scholar of high reputation, and at good wages to live at the house with them as an instructor, and their library was well stocked with Chinese books. There was no doubt among the educated Chinese that these Europeans had a reputation for doctrine and learning. It was this reputation that accounted for the fact that some of the highly lettered class requested a fuller explanation of the precepts of Christianity than was contained in a copy of the Commandments which they were accustomed to carry about with them.[8]

This passage, which tells the story from the point of view of the missionary, contains some considerations that are significant for our subject. An essential characteristic of transmission is that during the first phase a given culture accepts only those elements of the other culture that in one way or another are suited to its pre-existing pattern. In this passage one can notice that there

---

[7] On the presence of books in Jesuit East-Asian missions, see Henri Bernard-Maître, *Le Père Matthieu Ricci et la société chinoise de son temps (1522–1610)* (2 vols, Tientsin, 1937), I, 109–11.

[8] Ricci and Trigault, *Journals*, 157–8; compare with d'Elia, *Fonti Ricciane*, I, 196–7 (Trigault added the reference to 'Europeans').

was a prior interest among the Chinese *literati* in books, even in books they could not read, but which represented a corpus of knowledge that made the missionaries suitable partners in dialogue. In this respect, one should also add that the late Ming context constituted a favourable time, in the sense that the doubts about traditional values and an openness to other traditions facilitated contacts with people from other cultures.[9] Moreover, this intellectual environment encouraged the missionaries, who came from a strong humanistic background, to pursue their own search for knowledge and to learn from China by hiring a Chinese scholar. Thus, encounter was a two-way process.

Cartography, mathematics, astronomy

Besides books, there were other Renaissance objects in which Chinese became interested, like prisms, clocks, astronomical instruments, and religious objects, as well as a world map.

> Hanging on the wall of the reception room in the Mission House [in Zhaoqing] there was a cosmographical chart of the universe, done with European lettering. The more learned among the Chinese admired it very much and, when they were told that it was both a view and a description of the entire world, they became greatly interested in seeing the same thing done in Chinese. Of all the great nations, the Chinese have had the least commerce, indeed, one might say that they have had practically no contact whatever, with outside nations, and consequently they are grossly ignorant of what the world in general is like. . . . When they learned that China was only a part of the great east, they considered such an idea, so unlike their own, to be something utterly impossible, and they wanted to be able to read about it, in order to form a better judgment. So the Governor consulted with Father Matteo Ricci and asked him, as he expressed it, if he, with the help of his interpreter, would make his map speak Chinese, assuring him that such a work would bring him great credit and favour with everyone. Ricci had had considerable training in mathematics, which he studied for several years at Rome under Father Christophorus Clavius, Doctor of Science and Prince of Mathematicians of his day. In answer to the Governor's request, he went to work immediately at this task, which was not at all out of keeping with his ideas of preaching the Gospel. According to the disposition of Divine Providence, various ways have been employed at different times, and with different races, to interest people in Christianity.

[9] John E. Wills Jr, 'Relations with maritime Europeans, 1514–1662', in D. Twitchett and F. W. Mote (eds), *The Cambridge History of China: Vol. 8. The Ming Dynasty, 1368–1644, Part 2* (Cambridge, 1998), 364–5; Ad Dudink, '2.6.1. sympathising *literati* and officials', in N. Standaert (ed.), *Handbook of Christianity in China: Volume One (635–1800)* (Leiden, 2000), 476–7.

In fact this very attraction was to draw many of the Chinese into the net of Peter.[10]

We do not know which map Ricci had hanging in his room, and no copy of Ricci's first Chinese map is known to exist. The Chinese interest in Western maps, however, led to the relatively rapid transmission of the latest Renaissance knowledge about cartography, astronomy, and mathematics. Due to the observation of lunar eclipses, Ricci succeeded in determining the longitude of China and subsequently published *Kunyu wanguo quantu* (*Complete Map of all Nations on Earth*; earliest extant version, 1602).[11] In addition to personal observation, it integrated world maps by European cartographers such as Gerard Mercator (1512–94) and Abraham Ortelius (1527–98),[12] and also local maps of China, which corrected European ones considerably. Ricci's world map proved to be an important device for arousing the interest of Chinese *literati* in his scientific and religious work.[13] In addition, he translated mathematical and astronomical writings with the help of Chinese scholars.[14]

Between 1607 and 1614, four books in the field of mathematics were published as a result of translation work done by Matteo Ricci – two in collaboration with the Chinese scholar Xu Guangqi (1562–1633), *Jihe yuanben* (*Elements of Geometry*, 1607)[15] and *Celiang fayi* (*The Meaning of Measurement Methods*, 1608), and two in collaboration with another Chinese scholar Li Zhizao (1565–1630), *Tongwen suanzhi* (*Rules of Arithmetic Common to Cultures*, 1614) and a work on isoperimetric figures, *Yuanrong jiaoyi* (*The Meaning of Compared [Figures] Inscribed in a Circle*, 1614). As for the astronomical writings translated into Chinese by Ricci in collaboration with Li Zhizao, they consisted of *Qiankun tiyi* (*On the Structure of the Heaven and Earth, c.* 1608), and *Hungai tongxian tushuo* (*Illustrated Explanation of Cosmological Patterns*, 1607). All these translations were based on works by Clavius,[16] with whom Ricci had studied at the Roman College, and most of these books must have arrived while Ricci was already in China. As appears from a letter written on 24 November 1585, Ricci reported that he only had Clavius's *In Sphaeram* and one book by Alessandro Piccolomini (1508–78) (*De la Sfera del mundo*) in

---

[10] Ricci and Trigault, *Journals*, 165–6; compare with d'Elia, *Fonti Ricciane*, I, 207–8.

[11] Kiyosi Yabuuti, *Une histoire des mathématiques chinoises* (Paris, 2000), 124.

[12] Ricci presented Ortelius's *Theatrum Orbis Terrarum* to the Emperor when he was in Beijing in 1601: d'Elia, *Fonti Ricciane*, II, 114.

[13] For an overview and relevant bibliography, see Theodore N. Foss, '4.2.4. Cartography' in Standaert, *Handbook of Christianity in China*, 752–70.

[14] For a succinct overview, see Keizo Hashomoto and Nicole Halsberghe, '4.2.2. Astronomy' and Catherine Jami, '4.2.3. Mathematics' in Standaert, *Handbook of Christianity in China*, 711–37, 738–51.

[15] For an extensive study, see Engelfriet, *Euclid in China*.

[16] Respectively: *Euclidis Elementorum Libri XV Accessit XVI de Solidorum Regularium Cuiuslibet Intra Quodlibet Comparatione, Omnes Perspicuis Demonstrationibus, Accuratisque Scholiis Illustrati, ac Multarum Rerum Accessione Locupletati* (Rome, 1574); *Geometria Practica* (Rome, 1604); *Epitome Arithmeticae Practicae* (Rome, 1583); *In Sphaeram Ioannis de Sacro Bosco commentarius* (Rome, 1570); *Astrolabium* (Rome, 1593).

his possession.[17] In his correspondence with Europe he regularly asked for books.[18] The present-day Beitang library in Beijing includes no more than ten books which can be related with certainty to the Ricci collection, among them Clavius's *Astrolabium*, with a dedicatory inscription by the author to his former pupil.[19]

From this small number of books, one can still notice the relatively rapid transmission from Europe to China. Moreover, the master–disciple relationship that had existed between Clavius and Ricci confirms a phenomenon that appears commonly in transmission of knowledge: one first transmits the knowledge that one has received from one's own teacher. Furthermore, in a context where one is devoid of specific resources, one will first seek further knowledge from one's master. It was quite fortunate that Ricci had studied under Clavius. As such, Ricci became the right person at the right time because in his person converged the demand by the Chinese for mathematical knowledge and the possibility to respond to it.

Confucianism and Stoicism

The Renaissance culture that Ricci brought to China included knowledge not only of the books that he translated for the Chinese (having acquired a proficienty in the language), but also of the general humanistic background which provided him with a framework for interpreting Chinese society. This appears in another aspect of his activities: his attitude to Chinese religions.

As Paul Rule has shown,[20] Ricci gave his assessment of the major religious traditions of China in his earliest surviving letter from China, written on 13 September 1584. Among them, he preferred the 'sect of the *literati*', as he called scholars from the Confucian tradition. Although 'commonly they do not believe in the immortality of the soul', they reject the superstitions of the Buddhist and Taoist traditions, and practise an austere cult of heaven and earth.[21] A year later, writing to Claudio Acquaviva (1543–1615), the Jesuit General, he again favourably compares the Confucians, whom he describes as 'a sect of Epicureans, not in name, but in their laws and opinions', with

[17] Tacchi Venturi, *Opere Storiche*, II, 72; d'Elia, *Fonti Ricciane*, I, 207 note 1.

[18] Cf. H. Bernard-Maître, *Le Père Matthieu Ricci*, I, 111, note 5: Tacchi Venturi, *Opere Storiche*, II, 60 (20 October 1585: Ricci complains about not having books to construct a celestial globe); Tacchi Venturi, *Opere Storiche*, II, 217 (12 October 1596: he hopes to receive the books he ordered from Europe); Tacchi Venturi, *Opere Storiche*, II, 284–5 (12 May 1605: books about geometry, clocks and astrolabes are sufficiently available, but others are still missing); Tacchi Venturi, *Opere Storiche*, II, 336 (6 March 1608: because of lack of books, most of the things that Ricci is printing are things that he has been holding in his memory); see also Tacchi Venturi, *Opere Storiche*, II, 260 (15 August 1599: Book of Nadal and the Plantin bible), 354, 388.

[19] Hubert Verhaeren, *Catalogue de la Bibliothèque du Pé-T'ang* (Beijing, 1949; repr. Paris, 1969), vii, no. 1291; on 25 December 1597, Ricci wrote to Clavius thanking him for having sent this book (Tacchi Venturi, *Opere Storiche*, II, 241–2).

[20] Rule, *K'ung-tzu*, 28–9.

[21] Tacchi Venturi, *Opere Storiche*, II, 48–9 (*[seta] de los letrados*); Rule, *K'ung-tzu*, 28.

the Buddhists, who are 'Pythagoreans'.[22] By 1593, again writing to Acquaviva, and describing his translation of the Confucian *Four Books*, he finds a more favourable comparison for Confucius (552–479 BC). The Sage is now 'un altro Seneca' and the *Four Books* are 'buoni documenti morali'.[23] In other words, Ricci was first attracted to Confucianism not by the religious values he saw in it, but by what he saw as its non-religious character, its ethical and social values. Moreover, as time passed, Ricci also became aware of the divergences between the twelfth-century commentaries and the basic sources of Confucianism which date from the period BC. He wrote to his old friend, Lelio Passionei, in 1597:

> At the very time when, if I calculate correctly, Plato and Aristotle flourished amongst us, there also flourished amongst [the Chinese] certain literati of good life who produced books dealing with moral matters, not in a scientific way, but in the form of maxims. The chief of these wrote four books which are most highly esteemed, and read day and night. In volume they do not exceed the size of letters of Marcus Tullius, but the commentaries and glosses, and the commentaries on the commentaries, and further treatises and discourses upon them by this time are infinite.[24]

As we can see, Ricci compared Chinese traditions with frameworks that were familiar to his European audience, who had received the same humanistic grounding as he had. Noteworthy is his conviction of an affinity between Confucius and the Stoics. This seems to be the impulse for other humanistic writings by Ricci which proclaimed wisdom from the West on the basis of sayings by 'ancient saints and sages' and which were explicitly written for a general, non-Christian readership.[25] His *Jiaoyou lun* or *De Amicitia* (*On Friendship*, 1595) is based upon Andreas Eborensis's *Sententiae et Exempla, ex probatissimis quibusque scriptoribus collecta et per locos communes digesta*, a collection of edifying aphorisms borrowed from Cicero, Seneca, and many other classical authors, five editions of which are known to exist (1569, 1572, 1575, 1585, 1590).[26] Andreas Eborensis (original name: Andrea de Rèsende; 1498–1573), born in Ebora, was a well-known Portuguese Latinist who had studied at different European universities and taught at Lisbon and Coimbra. He had been a Dominican, but apparently, due to his frequent travels and commitments to study, he was unable to lead a life in accordance with monastic regularity and was allowed to return to the secular state.

---

[22] Tacchi Venturi, *Opere Storiche*, II, 57 (20 October 1585: *setta epicurea; pitagorici*); Rule, *K'ung-tzu*, 28.

[23] Tacchi Venturi, *Opere Storiche*, II, 117; Rule, *K'ung-tzu*, 29.

[24] Tacchi Venturi, *Opere Storiche*, II, 237 (9 September 1597); Rule, *K'ung-tzu*, 29.

[25] See Ad Dudink and Nicolas Standaert, '4.1.2. Apostolate through books', in Standaert, *Handbook of Christianity in China*, 604–5.

[26] Pasquale M. d'Elia, 'Il Trattato sull'Amicizia: Primo Libro scritto in cinese da Matteo Ricci S. I. (1595). Testo cinese, Traduzione antica (Ricci) e moderna (D'Elia), Fonti, Introduzione e Note', *Studia Missionalia*, 7 (1952), 425–515.

Ricci's *Ershiwu yan* (*Twenty-Five Sayings*, 1605) is basically a translation of a Latin version of Epictetus's *Encheiridion*, although he did not strictly follow Epictetus's text. He seems to have rearranged various elements to suit his missiological purposes. Some parts he translated, some he paraphrased, some were abbreviated, others were expanded, with modifications to adapt to Confucian or Christian thought.[27] Sayings from ancient Western sages were also an important component of Ricci's *Jiren shipian* (*Ten Discourses by a Paradoxical Man*, 1608), which contained some of Aesop's fables, along with extensive paraphrases of Epictetus. Finally, in a collection of songs that Ricci was ordered to compose by the Wanli emperor in 1601 (*Xiqin quyi*, now lost except for eight songs), so that the eunuchs could have something to sing as they played on the harpsichord that Ricci had presented to the court, Ricci cleverly wove together poems by Horace and essays by Seneca and Petrarch.[28]

In these writings Ricci used the most traditional of humanistic assumptions and techniques to make the Western classics come alive in China.[29] From the patristic era, Stoicism had been perceived as fundamentally compatible with Christianity. Many Stoic ethical doctrines were adopted by Christian writers, and although Renaissance authors were aware of the important distinctions between Stoicism and Christianity, many of them managed to combine the two ethical systems by focusing on areas of agreement and avoiding issues where conflict was inevitable.[30] In a similar manner, Ricci selected passages from Stoic authors that were compatible with Christianity, and also in his dialogue with Confucianism he stressed the compatibility between the two ethical systems. For instance, like other Renaissance texts, in *De Amicitia* quotations from Seneca, Cicero, Plutarch, and Aristotle appear side by side with quotations from patristic writers like Augustine, Ambrosius, and Cyprianus, the authority of classical antiquity lending support to that of Christian antiquity.

Ricci was not only introducing Stoic thought to the Chinese, but also establishing a link between the European humanist tradition and the Confucian tradition. His writings offer a concrete example of how he transposed Western Stoic philosophy into a Chinese Confucian setting in order to clear the way for Christianity. For example, as has been shown by Spalatin, the *Twenty-Five Sayings* disclose the original thesis that Ricci looked on Confucianism as possibly a type of Chinese Stoicism. He saw these two moral philosophies as having a similar philosophical understanding of reality and a parallel moral

---

[27] Christopher A. Spalatin, 'Matteo's Ricci's Use of Epictetus' *Encheiridion*', *Gregorianum*, 56 (1975), 551–7.

[28] Pasquale d'Elia, 'Musica e canti Italiani a Pechino', *Rivista degli Studi Orientali* 30 (1955), 131–45. Cf. Spence, *Memory Palace*, 141–2. Spence is of the opinion that the classical references in *Ten Discourses by a Paradoxical Man* or the collection of songs for the Wanli emperor, as well as those in *On Friendship* or the *Twenty-Five Sayings*, were not direct translations from books, but that Ricci had learned numerous passages in school and carried them in his memory.

[29] Howard L. Goodman and Anthony Grafton, 'Ricci, the Chinese, and the toolkits of textualists', *Asia Major*, Third Series 3/2 (1991), 95–148, 106.

[30] Jill Kraye, 'Moral philosophy', in Charles Schmitt (ed.), *The Cambridge History of Renaissance Philosophy* (Cambridge, 1988), 367–8.

outlook on life. Following the model of Jesuit humanist education of the Renaissance, which used the pagan moral philosophy of Stoicism as a propaedeutic for Christianity, Ricci attempted to deploy the pagan moral philosophy of Confucianism as a preparation for the fullness of Christianity. The pagan classics, whether Greco-Roman or Chinese, were acceptable ways of human maturation and Christianization.[31]

In short, Ricci discerned Stoicism in ancient Confucianism. This had two implications: first, that Stoicism became a building block for entering into dialogue with Confucianism. Just as Ricci identified the other (Confucianism) with the familiar (Stoicism), the Chinese might recognize the other (Stoicism) as the familiar (Confucianism). The second step is that Stoicism was a building block for introducing Christianity, and that it was very often interpreted in a Christian way. Likewise Confucianism could become a corner stone, and indeed was also often interpreted in a Christian way by missionaries.

The transmission of Renaissance culture as realized by Ricci was to a large extent a case of spontaneous diffusion. Ricci did not leave Europe with a pre-formed project of translating Stoic or mathematics books for the Chinese. He was somewhat unprepared for this task, but gradually discovered his own way of dealing with the Chinese tradition and of responding to the demands of Chinese scholars by taking advantage of his broad humanist background and his specific mathematical training. To a certain extent, he was the right person in the right place, who – due to his Renaissance background – was able to respond to the requests and questions that were raised by his Chinese interlocutors and thus to transmit Renaissance culture in interaction with them.

TRANSLATION PROJECT (*c.* 1620–*c.* 1630s)

At the time of Ricci's death (1610) there were only sixteen Jesuits in China: eight European fathers and eight Chinese brothers, as reported by Niccolò Longobardo (1565–1655).[32] Longobardo would play a key role in Jesuit policy in the next two decades. Generally speaking, Longobardo transformed Ricci's spontaneous and almost individual transmission of Renaissance culture into a 'project' in terms of both planning and personnel. One of the reasons for this change came from Ricci himself. Near the end of his life, with the help of Sabatino De Ursis (1575–1620), Xu Guangqi, and Li Zhizao, Ricci had initiated a project of calendar reform with a plan for translations of related scientific works. He had written to Europe in order to obtain both the personnel and books for this purpose. Longobardo took over the idea

---

[31] Spalatin, 'Matteo's Ricci's use', 556; Rule, *K'ung-tzu*, 21.

[32] Tacchi Venturi, *Opere Storiche*, II, 488: Report by Longobardo to Cl. Acquaviva, 23 November 1610, in which he also asks for a library for each residence. He requests five copies of the bible, of the *Summa* and of Pedro de Ribadeneira, SJ (1527–1611), *Flos Sanctorum.*

and sent Nicolas Trigault (1577–1628) to Europe.[33] Besides solving the internal problems of the China mission, Trigault was supposed to make propaganda for the China mission, to obtain gifts for the emperor and *literati*, to gather a library, and to recruit new missionaries. The last two tasks were particularly important for the transmission of Renaissance culture.

The Trigault library

Trigault arrived in Rome at the end of 1614.[34] Already on 17 January 1615, the Jesuit General Claudio Acquaviva took action to have the aforementioned *De Christiana expeditione apud Sinas* by Ricci published in Augsburg. From 1615 till early 1616, Trigault was mainly in Rome arranging institutional affairs. In May 1616, he left Rome for good, embarking on a tour through Europe on which he was later joined by Johann Schreck (1576–1630), who would eventually travel with him to China. Via Florence, Milan, Lyon, Munich, and Ingolstadt, they arrived at Frankfurt, where they attended the annual book fair. They then went via Cologne to Brussels, where Trigault wrote a report to his fellow-Jesuits in China dated 2 January 1617.[35] From this report it already appears that the gathering of books was one of the most successful aspects of his trip.

When he sent Trigault on the journey, Longobardo had established a concrete plan for the process of collecting books: one should make a request to the pope for the principal library, destined for Beijing; in order to obtain his favour, one should dedicate the translation of Ricci's *De Christiana expeditione apud Sinas* to the pope (which was also done); in addition to this central library, which should be equivalent to the best Jesuit ones in Europe, there was also the need for more modest libraries for the Jesuit residences in other Chinese cities. Longobardo was of the opinion that the translation of these books was an excellent point of entry for propagation of the Gospel.

Paul V did not take long to answer Trigault's request favourably, and donated *c.* 500 volumes. In addition, the pope and the Jesuit General each donated 1000 ducats for further acquisitions. This money made it possible to have the books beautifully bound and marked with the papal insignia by the publisher Horace Cardon of Lyon.[36] The money was further spent in the major book centres of the time: Lyon, Frankfurt, and Cologne. In addition to purchases, there were multiple donations by authors and printing houses. They included not only the philosophical and theological books that could commonly be found in Jesuit libraries, but also books on medicine, canon

[33] Verhaeren, *Catalogue*, vii–viii.

[34] For a detailed report of Trigault's stay in Europe, see Edmond Lamalle, 'La propagande du P. N. Trigault en faveur des missions de Chine (1616)', *Archivum Historicum Societatis Iesu*, 9 (1940), 49–120.

[35] It is not impossible that Peter Paul Rubens's drawing of a Jesuit in Chinese dress was made with Trigault as model during his stay in Flanders; see Henri Bernard-Maître, 'Un portrait de Nicolas Trigault dessiné par Rubens?', *Archivum Historicum Societatis Iesu*, 22 (1953), 308–13; Hans Vlieghe, *Rubens Portraits of Identified Sitters Painted in Antwerp* (Leipzig, 1987), 191ff.

[36] Verhaeren, *Catalogue*, viii.

law, music, etc. By the time Trigault reached Brussels, he was nearly at the end of his propaganda tour – the Jesuit General having suggested to him not to go to the Low Countries, because these provinces were impoverished due to religious wars, nor to Spain, to avoid raising the suspicion of Philip III's government against his mission. This explains why there are no books in Spanish or Portuguese among the books in the Trigault collection still in Beijing, though there are some books by Spanish and Portuguese authors printed elsewhere. Trigault left Lisbon on 16 April 1618, and arrived in Macao on 22 July 1620. During his seven-year absence, the mission had been scattered by the anti-Christian incidents in Nanjing, which had caused the closure of the Beijing residence and the confiscation of the Nanjing residence (including the books).[37] It was not before 1623 that the Jesuits returned to Beijing and that books could be transported there.

The return of Trigault to China was, of course, quite different from the first journey by Ricci, who had left with hardly any information about China that could help him to prepare himself. Trigault, on the contrary, having already been in China, knew quite well what he had to bring with him. The only point that Trigault does not mention is how many books he collected. Contemporary Christian Chinese sources usually mention the round figure of 7000 volumes, but this has been considered an exaggerated rhetorical assessment. The librarian who compiled the modern catalogue of the library in Beijing is of the opinion that 757 works in 629 volumes had belonged to the collection brought by Trigault.[38] The number must have been higher, however, since we know of several works that had been translated at that time and yet are not to be found among the copies in the Beitang library today.[39]

The collection that has been identified as belonging to Trigault contains a wide variety of works.[40] Well-known Renaissance authors are represented. There are books of Nicholas of Cusa (1401–64), Paracelsus (Theophrast von Hohenheim: 1493–1541), Giovanni Pico della Mirandola (1463–94), Desiderius Erasmus (1466/9–1536), Girolamo Cardano (1501–76), Cesare Cremonini (1550–1631), Justus Lipsius (1547–1606), Petrus Ramus (1515–72), and John Case (*c.* 1546–1600).[41] Among the books that have been preserved,

[37] Ad Dudink, 'The inventories of the Jesuit house at Nanking, made up during the persecution of 1616–1617 (Shen Que, *Nangong shudu*, 1620)', in Federico Masini (ed.), *Western Humanistic Culture Presented to China by Jesuit Missionaries (XVII–XVIII Centuries): Proceedings of the Conference Held in Rome, October 25–27, 1993* (Rome, 1996), 119–57.

[38] Verhaeren, *Catalogue*, x–xii.

[39] See below: some works used for the *Chongzhen lishu* or *Qiqi tushuo.*

[40] André Rétif, 'Une bibliothèque de la renaissance en Chine', *Bulletin de l'Association Guillaume Budé*, 3 (1953), 113–25; for an extensive bibliography of the library, see Golvers, '1.2. Western primary sources', in Standaert, *Handbook of Christianity in China*, 209–11. The library has been virtually inaccessible since the 1950s; our knowledge is based on the catalogue compiled by Hubert Verhaeren (*Catalogue*) in 1949. In the following notes, the figures refer to the numbers in Verhaeren's *Catalogue*. The question mark indicates, that it is probably, but not certainly a book brought by Trigault.

[41] Cusa: 1410?; Paracelsus: 1146?, 3914; Pico della Mirandola: 2450; Erasmus: 4030, 4049–50; Cardano: 1204?, 1205, 1206; Cremonini: 1400, 1401; Lipsius: 2054; Ramus: 2540, 2541?; Case: 1225.

however, there are none to be found by Francis Bacon (1561–1626), Niccolò Machiavelli (1469–1527), or Giordano Bruno (1548–1600), nor by Martin Luther (1483–1546), Jean Calvin (1509–64), or Philip Melanchthon (1497–1560). The essential works of the different Renaissance theological schools are also available: from those who advocated the return to the sources (bible and patristics) to the great scholastics or authors who tried to adapt to the needs of modern thought. Besides ascetic and mystical theology (including Jan van Ruusbroec, 1293–1381),[42] there is moral theology and canon law. Important Jesuit theologians are also included: Sebastião Barradas (1542–1615), Pedro da Fonseca (1528–99), Benito Pereira (*c.* 1535–1610), Francisco Suárez (1548–1617), and Francisco Toledo (1532–96).[43] The library is especially rich in works on astronomy, technology, natural sciences, and medicine, but limited in literature.

Trigault not only carried books with him. On his return, he was accompanied by several missionaries, among them four who would play an influential role in the next decades. The aforementioned Johann Terrenz Schreck (1576–1630), a German from Constance in Swabia, was trained in medicine, mathematics, and philosophy at the universities of Paris, Montpellier, Bologna, and Padua. He had been named a member of the Academia de Lincei in 1611 (eight days after Galileo Galilei), before he joined the Society.[44] Giacomo Rho (1592–1638) was an Italian from near Milan, who had already excelled in mathematics as a student. He received his Jesuit training at the Roman College. Johann Adam Schall von Bell (1592–1666) had studied at the Jesuit school in his native town, Cologne, before joining the Society and continuing his studies at the Roman College as well. Francisco Furtado (1589–1653), from the Azores, entered the Society in Portugal, where he also received his training. With Trigault himself originating from the (then) Flemish Douai, the five of them represented a wide variety of Renaissance cultures.

The return of Trigault with his companions coincided closely with the end of a period of anti-Christian incidents during which communities such as Beijing had been closed and several missionaries had been expelled. To a certain extent, Trigault's seven-year absence was spent more fruitfully in Europe than if he had remained in China.[45] The political situation in China, however, was still quite turbulent in the 1620s. In the mid-1620s the central power was in the hands of eunuchs who forced many officials,

[42] Van Ruusbroec: 2639?

[43] Barradas: 939; Fonseca: 1620?; Pereira: 2403; Suárez: 2891, 2893?, 2894; Toledo: 2977?

[44] Giuseppe Gabrieli, 'Giovanni Schreck Linceo: Gesuita e missionario in Cina e le sue lettere dall'Asia', *Rendiconti della Reale Accademia Nazionale dei Lincei, Classe di Scienze morali, storiche e filologiche* ser. vi, 12/5–6 (1936), 462–514. Isaia Iannaccone, *Johann Schreck Terrentius: Le scienze rinascimentali e lo spirito dell'Accademia dei Lincei nella Cina dei Ming* (Naples, 1998).

[45] In the 1610s, Jesuits like S. De Ursis, D. de Pantoja and M. Dias Jr continued to translate some works, which were incorporated in the collection *Tianxue chuhan* (First Collectanea of Heavenly Studies), edited in 1626 by Li Zhizao. It includes Dias's *Tianwenlüe* (*Questions about Heaven*, 1615), known for its appendix, in which Galileo's invention of the telescope and the new observations he made with it were reported.

among them Christians, to retire. This had an unexpectedly positive effect on translation efforts since several of these *literati* collaborated closely with missionaries during their retirement: Xu Guangqi lived in retirement between 1622 and 1627; Li Zhizao retired in 1623 and Yang Tingyun (1562–1627) in 1625. After 1627, when the Tianqi emperor had died and the Chongzhen emperor had ascended to the throne, the climate changed favourably and Christian scholars were asked to collaborate on the reform of the calendar.

Several factors influenced the transmission of the Renaissance culture during this second period. The first is the background or specialization of a specific missionary or Chinese collaborator. Trigault, for instance, clearly had a keen interest in language and linguistics, which resulted in the fundamental syllabary (or phonetic dictionary) *Xiru ermuzi* (*An Aid to the Ear and the Eye of Western Scholars*, 1626), which he composed in collaboration with the convert Wang Zheng (1571–1644). There are no similar works of that quality by other missionaries, and Trigault himself did not excel in other scientific disciplines. He also translated some of Aesop's fables, which were edited as *Kuangyi* (*Appropriate Meaning Obtained through Comparison*, late 1620s) by the convert Zhang Geng (*c.* 1570–1646/7). This indicates the Jesuits' use of the *exemplum* literature which they inherited from the European tradition.[46]

A second factor is whether the translation was made at the request of Chinese collaborators or initiated by the missionaries themselves. As will appear subsequently, writings that fall under the first category had a wider spread or larger influence than the second.

The final factor is the location where the translation was made. It should be pointed out that from the European side the whole project was executed by less than ten Jesuits who were based in places separated from each other by more than 1000 kilometers. This not only impeded frequent communication but also hindered consultation of the available books.

In general, in this second period the Chinese were better informed about the wider context of the Renaissance educational system. Giulio Aleni (1582–1649), another Italian who had also studied under Clavius at the Collegium Romanum before he arrived in China in 1610, made efforts in this quarter. Besides some sections in *Zhifang waiji* (*Areas Outside the Concern of the Chinese Imperial Geographer*, 1623), he gave a detailed description of the curriculum of European universities including the Jesuit education centres in *Xixue fan* (*Summary of Western Learning*, 1623). In this work, the sciences are divided into six disciplines, arranged in the order as they appeared in the European educational system of the day: rhetoric, philosophy (in other words, logic,

---

[46] Li Sher-shiueh, 'Toward a missionary poetics in late Ming China: the Jesuit appropriation of "Greco-Roman" lore through the medieval tradition of European *Exempla*' (University of Chicago Ph.D. diss., 1999). Several of these fables were integrated in a collection of stories (*Wugan*) by the Chinese scholar Li Shixiong (1602–86).

physics, metaphysics, mathematics, and ethics), medicine, civil law, canon law, and theology.[47]

The transmission of Renaissance culture that took place in this second period can be divided in three broad categories: works related to the calendar reform, Aristotelianism, and the religious–devotional writings.[48]

The calendar reform

The main characteristic of the first project is that it was largely initiated and even led by Chinese converts to Christianity (Xu Guangqi and Li Zhizao). Their engagement in Western learning was not limited to scholarly pursuit only, but as officials they were also active in politics. The need for calendar reform had been felt among Chinese officials since the close of the sixteenth century, and several proposals and attempts had been made to that end.[49] The first proposal to entrust calendar reform to the Jesuits was put forward in 1613 by Li Zhizao, following the failure of imperial astronomers accurately to predict an eclipse. It took more than ten years, after another failure of official astronomers to make a correct prediction of an eclipse, before a proposal by Xu Guangqi to put the Jesuits to work on calendar reform was accepted in 1629. He had been given charge of establishing and supervising a new Calendar Office for that purpose. The specialized knowledge that had come with Trigault could now be used in an optimal way. Schreck and Schall – the former replaced by Rho, after his death in 1630 – began compiling an astronomical compendium, with the help of some twenty Chinese specialists. Instead of the Ptolemaic system used in earlier Jesuit writings, Schreck used as the basis for computing the calendar the Tychonic world system, which posits that the five planets orbit around the Sun, while the Sun and Moon orbit around the Earth, the latter being at rest at the centre of the Universe.

The result of this work, *Chongzhen lishu* (*Calendar Compendium of the Chongzhen Era*; the first set of writings were presented in 1631, the last in 1635), comprised twenty-two works in 137 volumes. Characteristic of this collection is that it included texts which were based on European documents of a very recent date. *Yuanjing shuo* (*Explanation of the Telescope*, 1626), by Schall, contained the first account of the Tychonic world system in Chinese,

---

[47] Bernard Luk Hung-kay, 'Aleni introduces the Western academic tradition to seventeenth-century China: a study of the *Xixue fan*', in Tiziana Lippiello and Roman Malek (eds), '*Scholar from the West': Giulio Aleni S. J. (1582–1649) and the Dialogue between Christianity and China* (Nettetal, 1997), 479–518; see also François de Dainville, *L'Éducation des jésuites (XVIe, XVIIe, XVIIIe siècles)* (Paris, 1978); Charles H. Lohr, 'Les jésuites et l'aristotélisme du XVIe siècle', in Luce Giard (ed.), *Les jésuites à la renaissance: système éducatif et production du savoir* (Paris, 1995), 79–91.

[48] For a systematic overview of the translations and a record of ancient booklists, see Henri Bernard, 'Les adaptations d'ouvrages européens: bibliographie chronologique depuis la venue des portugais à Canton jusqu'à la mission française de Pékin, 1514–1688', *Monumenta Serica*, 10 (1945), 1–57, 309–88.

[49] Keizo Hashimoto and Nicole Halsberghe, '4.2.2. Astronomy', in Standaert, *Handbook of Christianity in China*, 712ff. For a detailed analysis, see Keizo Hashimoto, *Hsü Kuang-ch'i and Astronomical Reform: The Process of the Chinese Acceptance of Western Astronomy 1629–1635* (Osaka, 1988).

and *Cetian yueshuo* (*Brief Explanation of the Measurement of the Heavens*, 1628) by Schreck, also discussed this system. Rho's *Wuwei lizhi* (*Astronomical Treatise on the Five Planets*, 1635) relied on a work by Christian Severin Longomontanus (1562–1647; a former assistant of Tycho Brahe), his *Astronomia Danica* (Amsterdam, 1622). This work, which proposed a slightly revised version of the Tychonic model, was used for several other treatises in the compendium. The last chapter of Rho's *Celiang quanyi* (Full Meaning of Mensuration, 1631), devoted to astronomical instruments, was based on Tycho Brahe's (1546–1601) *Mechanica*, as were the descriptions of instruments found in other parts of the compendium. Celestial atlases were also prepared. *Chidao nanbei liang zongxing tu* (General Star Map of the Southern and Northern Hemispheres Divided by the Equator, 1634) drew upon the star atlas by the Jesuit astronomer Christoph Grienberger (1580–1636; Schall's former teacher of mathematics), called the *Catalogus Veteres Affixarum Longitudines ac Latitudines Conferens cum Nouis* (Rome, 1612).

While mathematics did not appear as a distinct topic in *Chongzhen lishu*, it contained five works relevant to it:[50] Rho and Schall's *Chousuan* (*Calculating Rods*, 1628) was based on John Napier's *Rabdologiae, seu Numerationis per Virgula Libri Duo*, 1617; Rho and Schall's *Biligui jie* (*Explanation of the Proportional Compass*, 1630) on Galileo's (1564–1642) *Le operazioni del compasso geometrico e militare*, 1606. Schreck's *Da ce* (*Great Measurement*, 1631) had as its basis Bartholomaeus Pitiscus's (1561–1613) *Trigonometriae, sive de Dimensione Triangulorum Libri Quinque*, 1612, while Rho's *Celiang quanyi* (*Complete Meaning of Measurement*, 1631) was based on Clavius, *Geometria Practica* (1604). This makes it evident that information again travelled rapidly from Europe to China.

In terms of the dynamics of transmission, it can be pointed out that the translations fit well with the scientific qualities of the missionaries concerned. Another characteristic is that these translations were realized by a limited number of missionaries, who were primarily located in Beijing, close to the resources of the Trigault library.

As far as reception is concerned, in late Ming scholars' eyes, calendar reform was a contribution to the restoration of social order and the dynasty's strength. The result of the work done at the Calendar Office, however, only benefited the newly established Qing dynasty (beginning in 1644), to which Schall offered his service; the calendar promulgated in 1645 had been calculated 'according to the new Western method'. The compendium's title was changed accordingly to *Xiyang xinfa lishu* (*Calendar Compendium Following the New Western Method*), and a few works were added to it. Thereafter, Jesuits held official positions at the Astronomical Bureau. In the seventeenth

---

[50] Catherine Jami, 'Mathematics', in Standaert, *Handbook of Christianity in China*, 739ff; Catherine Jami, 'Mathematical knowledge in the *Chongzhen lishu*', in Roman Malek (ed.), *Western Learning and Christianity in China: The Contribution and Impact of Johann Adam Schall von Bell, S. J. (1592–1666)* (Nettetal, 1998), II, 661–74.

century, all Chinese preoccupied with astronomy or mathematics were aware of the works that had been translated in this project.[51]

Astronomy and mathematics, however, were not the only Renaissance sciences introduced by the missionaries. Two other significant fields should be mentioned here as well: technology and medicine. Noteworthy is *Qiqi tushuo* (*Illustrations and Explanations of Wonderful Machines*, 1627) compiled by Johann Schreck in collaboration with Wang Zheng. Based on works as diverse as Marcus Vitruvius Ollio's (first century BC) *De Architectura* (1567), Agostino Ramelli's (*c.* 1531–90) *Le diverse et artificiose machine* (1588), Jacques Besson's *Théâtre des instruments mathématiques et mécaniques* (1578), Faustus Verantius's *Machinae Novae* (1615), Vittorio Zonca's *Novo teatro di machini e edificii* (1607; 1621), and Heinrich Zeising's *Theatrum Machinarum* (1613), it explained the principles of Renaissance mechanics and contained an account of their applications by European engineers.[52] Agricola's (Georg Bauer, 1490–1555) *De Re Metallica* (1556) was the basis of *Kunyu gezhi* (*Exhaustive Investigation into [the Contents of] the Earth*, 1639), the result of collaboration between Li Tianjing (1579–1659) and Johann Adam Schall von Bell.[53]

The first work introducing Western medical knowledge, *Taixi renshen shuogai* (*Abstract of the Western Theory of the Human Body*, 1625 or shortly afterward), by Schreck, bears the influence of the discoveries by Andreas Vesalius (1514–64).[54] Giacomo Rho's *Renshen tushuo* (*Illustrated Explanation of the Human Body*, *c.* 1630), in the composition of which Schreck and Longobardo also took part, is a translation of the Latin version of Ambroise Paré's (1510–90) treatise on anatomy as contained in *Thesaurus chirurgiae* (Frankfurt, 1610).[55]

It must be pointed out, however, that these writings had only a limited reception. Due to different traditions in drawing techniques (for example, absence of geometrical perspective), the technological illustrations did not attain such quality that the instruments could be fabricated by an artisan. It remained a very bookish knowledge; and anatomy as a theoretical science was not initially oriented towards healing. Though some Chinese scholars were attracted by this theoretical approach, most were interested in practical medicine, and anatomy remained a curiosity. Another reason might be that these translations did not fall within a project initiated by Chinese scholars like the calendar reform.

[51] Catherine Jami, '4.2.1. General reception', in Standaert, *Handbook of Christianity in China*, 696ff.

[52] Joseph Needham *et al.* (eds.), *Science and Civilisation in China* (Cambridge, 1965), IV/2, 211ff.

[53] Peter J. Golas, '4.2.6. Technology', in Standaert, *Handbook of Christianity in China*, 780–1. S. De Ursis's *Taixi shuifa* (*Western Hydraulics*, 1612) was also based on *De Re Metallica*.

[54] Ursula Holler, '*Taixi renshen shuogai*: Ein anatomischer Text aus dem frühen 17. Jahrhundert in China' (Ludwig-Maximilians-Universität, Munich, MA thesis, 1993).

[55] Nicolas Standaert, 'A Chinese translation of Ambroise Paré's *Anatomy*', *Sino-Western Cultural Relations Journal*, 21 (1999), 9–33.

Aristotelian philosophy

A rather ambitious project, but a less successful one, was the effort of the
Jesuits to introduce Aristotelian philosophy in China.[56] In this case, the initiative
was mainly taken by Jesuits themselves, who, by emphasizing Aristotelianism,
attempted to reproduce what was the basis of their own education. Besides
the conviction that a good knowledge of this philosophy was required for
understanding Western thought and sciences, the Jesuits insisted on its
introduction for another reason. Though they expressed their appreciation
of Chinese (moral) philosophy, they observed a lack of logic and dialectics
in Chinese thought and therefore felt that acquainting Chinese with these
methods was needed.

There were two major translators of Aristotle: Francisco Furtado and
Alfonso Vagnone (1568/69–1640). Furtado collaborated with Li Zhizao after
the latter retired to his native town Hangzhou (and after Li's death with his
son Li Cibin). Furtado was Portuguese and took the well-known Coimbra
commentaries (*Commentarii Collegii Conimbricensis SJ*, 1592–1606) on Aristotelian philosophy as his primary source. They first translated the commentaries
on Aristotle's *De coelo* in *Huanyou quan* (1628, vols II–V). Even more difficult
was the translation of *Universa Dialectica Aristotelis* (Coimbra, 1606). This
resulted in a series of works: *Mingli tan* (first 5 vols, 1631) is a translation of
the introduction and of *Isagoge Porphyrii*;[57] the next five volumes (1639) are a
translation of *Categoriae*; the *Analytica Priora* was later included as *Litui zhi
zonglun* (5 vols) in *Qiongli xue* (see below). Furtado probably also translated
De Demonstratione.

The other person introducing Aristotelian philosophy was Vagnone. He
worked in collaboration with several Chinese converts of the Shanxi-Shaanxi
region, which was only opened as a new missionary area in the early 1620s.
His *Xiushen xixue* (*c.* 1631) is an adaptation of *Ethica Nicomachea*. Furthermore, the first volume of his *Kongji gezhi* (1633) includes elements of *De Coelo
et Mundo*, while the second volume is an adaptation of *Meteorologica*. Vagnone
also composed several other works that are based on Aristotelian philosophy,
but that are not necessarily adaptations of books by Aristotle: a compendium
on the philosophy of nature (*Feilu dahui*, 1636) and a series on ethics, composed around 1630 and dealing with politics (*Minzhi xixue* and *Xixue zhiping*),
the family (*Qijia xixue*), and the education of children and youth (*Tongyou
jiaoyu*). The sources of these writings have not yet been discovered. In terms

---

[56] Dudink and Standaert: '4.1.2. Apostolate through books', in Standaert, *Handbook of Christianity in China*,
606ff; Henri Bernard, *Sagesse chinoise et philosophie chrétienne: essais sur leurs relations historiques* (Tientsin, 1935;
repr. Paris and Leiden, 1951), 122. An example of an even less successful project is the translation of Thomas
Aquinas's *Summa Theologiae* (mainly *Pars Prima*), which was not started until 1645 by Lodovico Buglio (1606–
82) and published in 30 *juan* during the years 1654–78 (*Chaoxing xueyao*). It remained without influence and
was only rediscovered in the twentieth century.

[57] On this work, see also Robert Wardy, *Aristotle in China: Language, Categories and Translation* (Cambridge,
2000).

of Western libraries, the Shanxi-Shaanxi region was rather isolated. Keeping in mind that people tend to reproduce what they know best, and knowing that Vagnone had been a philosophy teacher in Milan for three years before his departure to China, it is quite probable that Vagnone took his own teaching notes as the basis for his Chinese writings. Vagnone is also known for his translations of general wisdom literature. For instance, his *Pixue* (1632, 1633) is a large collection of more than 700 short *sententiae*, each of which has the literary form of a 'comparison' (*pi*, comprising both metaphor and simile).[58] As in the aforementioned works by Ricci, the Christian element is almost non-existent in these examples. Vagnone also revised and edited with the Chinese convert Zhu Dinghan *Xiguo jifa* (1625), a work on the art of memory (*ars memorativa*) that was first compiled by Ricci.[59]

Aside from the writings of Furtado and Vagnone, Aristotelianism was also present in the writings of many other Jesuits. One of the most important themes was the question of the soul, as appears from several writings devoted to this subject. Francesco Sambiasi (1582–1649) and Xu Guangqi presented the theory of Aristotle's *De Anima* in *Lingyan lishao* (*Humble Attempt at Discussing Matters Pertaining to the Soul*, 1624). Aleni gave a synopsis of this work, and of *Parva Naturalia*, in *Xingxue cushu* (*Summary Exposition of the Science of the Psyche, c.* 1624).[60]

These writings on Aristotelianism reveal the complexity of cultural translation more clearly than certain scientific works.[61] There were three ways in which Western terms could be expressed in Chinese in these writings: (i) transliterated terms (for example, *fei-lu-suo-fei-ya* for philosophy); (ii) translation by choosing existing Chinese expressions that would correspond to the Western meaning; and (iii) the creation of new Chinese terms. The transliterated terms express the difference that existed between Western and Chinese traditions, while the translated terms indicate possible correspondence or parallelism. The new terms could be situated in between these two options. It is noteworthy that all these approaches appear in the texts simultaneously. This method appears for key-terms in many early texts of transmission of Renaissance culture. As for the translated words, one has to bear in mind a phenomenon that was rarely repeated later in the cultural exchange between China and the West, and that has become almost impossible now. The choice of the Jesuits and their collaborators to use common Chinese

---

[58] Erik Zürcher, 'Renaissance rhetoric in late Ming China: Alfonso Vagnoni's introduction to his *Science of Comparison*', in Masini (ed.), *Western Humanistic Culture*, 331–60.

[59] See Michael Lackner, *Das vergessene Gedächtnis: Die jesuitische mnemotechnische Abhandlung Xiguo jifa, Übersetzung und Kommentar* (Stuttgart, 1986). Spence's *Memory Palace* is inspired by *Xiguo jifa*.

[60] See also Zhang Qiong, 'Translation as cultural reform: Jesuit scholastic psychology in the transformation of the Confucian discourse on human nature', in John W. O'Malley, Gauvin Alexander Bailey, Steven J. Harris, and T. Frank Kennedy, *The Jesuits: Cultures, Sciences, and the Arts, 1540–1773* (Toronto, 1999), 364–79.

[61] Nicolas Standaert, 'The classification of sciences and the Jesuit mission in late Ming China', in Jan M. De Meyer and Peter M. Engelfriet (eds), *Linked Faiths: Essays on Chinese Religions and Traditional Culture in Honour of Kristofer Schipper* (Leiden, 1999), 287–317.

terms resulted in Aristotelian philosophy being explained in (neo-)Confucian terms. For instance, a neo-Confucian key-term *(gewu) qiongli* (investigation of things and fathoming of principles) had become a common term to explain 'philosophy', and Aleni and Vagnone described the major aspects of Western ethics in terms directly borrowed from the canonical writing *Daxue* (*Great Learning*): *xiu shen*, self-cultivation (*ethica*), *qi jia*, regulating the family (*oeconomica*), *zhi guo*, ordering the state (*politica*), and *ping tianxia*, bringing peace to the world.

Still, the dissemination of these works remained very limited. Several of them only circulated in manuscript and were not published until the twentieth century. This project, which was meant for a very broad intellectual readership, was mainly initiated by the missionaries themselves. At that time, however, Aristotelian philosophy did not correspond to the main streams in Chinese thought and was not accepted.

Religious–devotional writings

A number of works can be classified under the category of transmission of Renaissance religious–devotional writings. The catechetical, theological, and religious writings of the missionaries are numerous and represent the main currents of their time in Europe. Here I will only briefly enumerate some of the most significant.[62]

An important scientific enterprise of the Catholic Renaissance was the publication of the *Antwerp Polyglot*, printed at the famous publishing house of Plantin in eight volumes in 1569–72. A copy of this work arrived in Beijing as early as 1604, after Ricci had requested it. The polyglot was offered to him by the Cardinal of San Severino, Giulio Antonio Santori (d. 1602), and was beautifully bound and abundantly decorated with gold. It was exposed for the first time in the church on 15 August 1604, and is said to have attracted the admiration of many people.[63] Ricci also showed the bible to the Jewish scholar Ai during their encounter in 1605. When Ai saw the Hebrew characters, he recognized them without being able to read them.[64] The presence of this bible, however, did not lead to the publication of a translation. Although during his stay in Rome Trigault had obtained permission for a translation of the bible into Chinese in 1616, the Jesuits did not engage in such an enterprise, occupied as they were with the other projects, especially the reform of the calendar.[65] Still, biblical narratives are present in other writings. Giulio

---

[62] For an extensive overview, see Dudink and Standaert, '4.1.2. Apostolate through books', in Standaert, *Handbook of Christianity in China*, 608ff.

[63] d'Elia, *Fonti Ricciane*, II, 281–2; Spence, *Memory Palace*, 87–8.

[64] This event is not mentioned in d'Elia, *Fonti Ricciane*. It only appears in the Trigault version: Ricci and Trigault, *Journals*, 108, 444–5.

[65] For discussion of why the bible was not translated, see Nicolas Standaert, 'The bible in early seventeenth-century China', in I. Eber, S. K. Wan, and K. Walf (eds), *Bible in Modern China: The Literary and Intellectual Impact* (Nettetal, 1999), 31–54.

Aleni's *Tianzhu jiangsheng yanxing jilüe* (*Short Record of the Words and Deeds during God's Incarnation*, 1635) for instance, was based on the *Vita Christi*, a popular work by Ludolphus de Saxonia (*c.* 1300–78). Aleni also published an illustrated life of Jesus, *Tianzhu jiangsheng chuxiang jingjie* (*Annotated Images of God's Incarnation*, 1637). The illustrations were Chinese adaptations of the copper engravings of Jerónimo Nadal's (1507–80) *Evangelicae Historiae Imagines* (Antwerp, 1593). The illustrations in the latter had been made by the Wierx brothers of Antwerp, Johan (*c.* 1549–1615), Antoon (*c.* 1552–*c.* 1624), and Hieronymus (*c.* 1553–1619), who were among the most renowned engravers of the time.[66] Exegetical writings are rather rare. *Shengjing zhijie* (A Plain Explanation of the Holy Scripture, 1636–42) composed by Manuel Dias, Jr. (1574–1659) is noteworthy because it contains patristic explanations of the readings of each Sunday and the major religious feast days. Dias might have used *Commentaria in Concordiam et Historiam Evangelicam* (4 vols; vol. i, 1599), composed by Sebastião Barradas SJ, who was a teacher at the universities of Coimbra and Evora, as one of his sources. Dias also translated Thomas à Kempis's *Imitatio Christi* (*Qingshi jinshu* or *Contemptus Mundi* in the 'Granada' version). It was published posthumously, not by missionaries but by Chinese converts (*c.* 1680). Another work in the field of devotion and spiritual life was Theresa of Avila's spiritual admonitions translated by Rho (*Shengji baiyan*, 1632). An important work with texts for prayers was Niccolò Longobardo's *Tianzhu shengjiao nianjing zongdu*, which was based on Luís de Granada OP (1504–88), *Memorial de la Vida Christiana*. Many of these prayers have come down to the twentieth century without stylistic changes.[67] Noteworthy is Johann Adam Schall von Bell's *Zhuzhi qunzheng* (1636), which was based on Leonard Lessius's (1554–1623) *De providentia Numinis et animi immortalitate libri duo adversus Atheos et Politicos* (Antwerp, 1613).[68]

Contrary to the former category, which was meant for a broad public but eventually had a limited circulation, the writings of this category were intended for a confined, mainly inner-Church audience, in which context they had a relatively wide readership. Several were translated by authors who were also known for their translations of scientific works. This confirms how the 'religious' and 'scientific' sides of their activities formed an integrated whole.

[66] Jerónimo Nadal, *Evangelicae Historiae Imagines ex Ordine Evangeliorum, Quae Toto Anno in Missae Sacrificio Recitantur* (Antwerp, 1593); *idem.*, *Adnotationes et Meditationes in Evangelia Quae in Sacrosanctae Missae Sacrificio Toto Anno leguntur* (Antwerp, 1594). For studies of Nadal's works, see Maj-Brit Wadell, *Evangelicae Historiae Imagines: Entstehungs-geschichte und Vorlagen* (Göteburg, 1985); Pierre-Antoine Fabre, *Ignace de Loyola: le lieu de l'image* (Paris, 1992), esp. 163–296. For the Chinese versions, see Joseph Dehergne, 'Une vie illustrée de Notre-Seigneur au temps des Ming', *Neue Zeitschrift für Missionswissenschaft*, 14 (1958), 103–15; Paul Rheinbay, 'Nadal's religious iconography reinterpreted by Aleni for China', in Lippiello and Malek, *'Scholar from the West'*, 323–34.

[67] Paul Brunner, *L'Euchologe de la mission de Chine: editio princeps 1628 et développements jusqu'à nos jours (Contribution à l'histoire des livres des prières)* (Münster, 1964), 88–9.

[68] Ad Dudink, 'The religious works composed by Johann Adam Schall, especially his *Zhuzhi qunzheng* and his efforts to convert the last Ming emperor', in Malek, *Western Learning*, ii, 805–98.

THE AFTERMATH: THE FAILED ATTEMPT (1678–83)

The 1630s represent a major change in the China mission. As appears from the above account, the late 1620s and early 1630s were undoubtedly a climax in the production of translations. By the middle of the 1630s the situation gradually changed. There were a number of reasons for this. First, several of the high placed *literati* (Yang Tingyun [1627], Li Zhizao [1630], Xu Guangqi [1633]) and talented missionaries (Trigault [1628], Schreck [1630], Rho [1638]) had died by then. There was also a change in the Jesuit's missionary policy. After *c.* 1630, Jesuits made a double shift: in Beijing they mainly sought imperial protection and contacts with court officials, who became more important than the *literati*, while at the local level (for example, Fujian) they moved their attention to the lower levels of the *literati* and to commoners.[69] Finally, China itself was involved in internal and external wars which would lead up to the fall of the dynasty and the installation of a new dynasty in 1644. As for the number of missionaries, it was only in the 1620s that the number of Jesuits exceeded twenty. With the arrival of Franciscan and Dominican friars in the 1630s, and a slight increase of Jesuits in the same period, the number exceeded thirty. During the next fifty years, between *c.* 1630 and *c.* 1680 (except the years 1665–71, when, due to a serious conflict surrounding the introduction of the Western calendar, virtually all missionary activity was interrupted and most missionaries were expelled to Canton), the total number of foreign missionaries remained constant, at between thirty and forty. It was only at the end of the seventeenth century that the number increased considerably, reaching over 130 by 1701, which was the apex for the seventeenth and eighteenth centuries.

During the seventeenth century, changes in the European educational and scientific context also affected the type of missionaries sent abroad. This is best exemplified by the six French Jesuits sent to China by Louis XIV (r. 1643–1715) as 'the King's mathematicians', and the appointed correspondents of the French Académie Royale des Sciences.[70] These missionaries arrived in Beijing in 1688, just after Ferdinand Verbiest (1623–88) had died. In a sense, Verbiest can be considered the last introducer of Renaissance culture in China.

Verbiest's role is exemplified by an ambitious project which he initiated in 1678.[71] Seemingly at the suggestion of the Emperor, Verbiest began compiling a voluminous collection on Western dialectics and philosophy. Verbiest

[69] Dudink, '2.6.1. Sympathising *literati* and officials', in Standaert, *Handbook of Christianity in China*, 481.

[70] For an illustration of these changes in the field of mathematics, see Catherine Jami, 'From Euclid to Pardies: the geometry transmitted to China by Jesuits (1607–1723)', in Masini, *Western Humanistic Culture*, 175–99.

[71] For a detailed description, see Ad Dudink and Nicolas Standaert, 'Ferdinand Verbiest's *Qiongli xue* (1683)', and Noël Golvers, 'Verbiest's introduction of *Aristoteles Latinus* (Coimbra) in China: new Western evidence', in N. Golvers (ed.), *The Christian Mission of China in the Verbiest Era: Some Aspects of the Missionary* (Leuven, 1999), 11–31, 33–53.

considered the work as a propaedeutic for astronomy, but he was also of the opinion that it gave a better foundation for Christian teachings. In order to prevent the suspicion that the work would be considered too Christian, he left out the examples that referred to God directly. Moreover, he hoped that this philosophy would be adopted as part of the curriculum for the Chinese state examination system. Verbiest gave his collection the title *Qiongli xue* (Study of Fathoming Principles), for which he used, like his precursors, a neo-Confucian key-term to express the Western concept for 'philosophy'.

This project, however, was different from the previous ones in several regards. First, there seems to have been hardly any collaboration with Chinese *literati*. It was mainly a project of Verbiest's alone. Next, though Verbiest included some new texts which he himself translated, the main body of the collection consisted of texts that had been translated about fifty years earlier in the 1630s. There certainly had been an influx of new books, especially in the field of sciences, accompanying the new missionaries,[72] but since the Trigault mission, no similar project had been undertaken and the missionaries relied largely on the work by their precursors.

Verbiest's *Qiongli xue* has survived only in part (14 of *c.* 60 volumes). Yet, with the help of contemporary Western sources, we can reconstruct most of its contents. The collection included most of the aforementioned works on Aristotelian philosophy: the adapted version of Furtado's and Li Zhizao's translations of the *Conimbricenses*, some writings by Vagnone, Aleni's work on the soul, and Sambiasi's on the origin of all things, etc. In addition to these philosophical writings, there was also a considerable part devoted to the philosophy of nature or *physica*: mechanics, ballistics, meteorology, geography, etc. Here Verbiest had made selections from the aforementioned *Qiqi tushuo*, but also of his own work on astronomical instruments (*Yixiang zhi*, 1674, also partly based on *Qiqi tushuo*), and his explanation of his world map (*Kunyu tushuo*, 1674).[73] This clearly shows how *Qiongli xue* was a reflection of the traditional Renaissance course on philosophy which integrated dialectics, ethics, and psychology, as well as subjects in natural sciences like mechanics and ballistics. All these subjects were a preparation not only for theology, but also for the advanced courses in mathematics and astronomy, for the immediate purpose of which Verbiest had compiled the book. This curriculum

---

[72] For example, in 1652, Nikolaus Smogulecki (1610–56), in collaboration with Xue Fengzuo (1600–80), published an astrological work which was based on Cardano's commentary on Ptolemy's *Quadripartitum*; see N. Standaert, 'European astrology in early Qing China: Xue Fengzuo's and Smogulecki's translation of Cardano's commentaries on Ptolemy's *Tetrabiblos*', *Sino-Western Cultural Relations Journal*, XXIII (2001), 50–79. In 1678, Verbiest received a copy of *Opera mathematica* by his teacher Andreas Tacquet (1612–60); see Noël Golvers, *The Astronomia Europaea of Ferdinand Verbiest, S. J. (Dillingen, 1687): The Text, Translation, Notes and Commentaries* (Nettetal, 1993), 37.

[73] The original *Kunyu tushuo* contained illustrations that can be traced back to the writings of Konrad Gesner (1515–65); see Harmut Walravens, 'Konrad Gessner in chinesischem Gewand: Darstellungen fremder Tiere im *K'un-yü t'u-shuo* des P. Verbiest (1623–1688)', *Gesnerus*, 30/3–4 (1973), 87–98.

is clearly a mirror of the organization of studies as they were still taught in the middle of the seventeenth century at many European universities or Jesuit colleges, and which remained largely unaffected by the most recent scientific developments that had taken place outside the realm of their institutions.[74]

In October 1683, Verbiest officially presented his compilation to the throne with the request for imperial financial support and approval of its publication.[75] About two months later, Verbiest was informed of the negative response by the Emperor's advisers. The Emperor himself considered the style of the book 'perverse, erroneous and illogical', while the advisers pointed out that 'saying that man's knowledge and memory belong to his brains is in complete contradiction with the reality of the principle'.[76] In the eyes of Chinese scholars, knowledge and memory were not located in the brains but in the heart, which was considered the ruler of intelligence. With this response, his project failed definitively.

CONCLUSION

Verbiest's failed attempt symbolically closes the period of transmission of Renaissance culture to China. This article has paid only brief attention to the reception of the transmission that, as a whole, was very limited. I have tried to show that the transmission started as a spontaneous diffusion which fitted well with the aspirations of the transmitter as well as with the requests of the receiver. In the second period, the transmission became a project with varying success, depending on whether the initiative was taken by Chinese scholars, and on the audience for whom it was destined. In the last period, the transmission apparently no longer corresponded to the times, which is expressed not only by the negative reception but also by the limited participation of Chinese collaborators. Verbiest based his work on the solid Jesuit curriculum he himself had passed through; but the heyday of this system in Europe had already taken place. China had changed as well, and the new dominant intellectual currents which saw 'Western learning as originating in China' were no longer interested in the foundations of Western learning. Despite the efforts of the Jesuit missionaries at consciously or unconsciously introducing Renaissance culture, during this whole period the Chinese remained the principal actors: they ultimately decided whether they wanted to adopt it or not.

---

[74] See Jan Roegiers, 'The academic environment of the University of Louvain at the time of Ferdinand Verbiest', in John W. Witek (ed.), *Ferdinand Verbiest (1623–1688), Jesuit Missionary, Scientist, Engineer and Diplomat* (Nettetal, 1994), 31–44.

[75] For a translation of his memorial to the throne, see Golvers, 'Verbiest's introduction of *Aristoteles Latinus*', 38–9.

[76] For a translation of this response, see Dudink and Standaert, 'Ferdinand Verbiest's *Qiongli xue* (1683)', 17.

4

The widening of the world and the realm of history: early European approaches to the beginnings of Siamese history, c. 1500–1700

SVEN TRAKULHUN

The earliest European records on Siam were written during the first half of the sixteenth century, not long after Afonso de Albuquerque had sent Portuguese emissaries to Ayutthaya in 1511. At that time, Albuquerque occupied the Malay sultanate of Melaka (Malacca), over which the Siamese king had formerly claimed suzerainty.[1] However, due to the crown's wish to keep new discoveries secret, initial accounts of Siam and other Southeast Asian countries did not appear in print before the mid-sixteenth century.[2] Although some of the Portuguese historians at home showed considerable interest in Asia during this period, their attention was largely focused on current affairs and future projects in the East rather than on events that happened long before the Portuguese had gained a foothold in the East Indies. In addition, most Westerners in Asia were not primarily historians; accordingly, many eyewitness accounts written in the sixteenth century contain little history of Siam and neighbouring countries, but concentrate on the time after the arrival of the Portuguese in Southeast Asia. The extensive works written by João de Barros, Fernão Lopes Castanheda, Gaspar Correia, and Diogo do Couto were also primarily concerned with the history of the deeds of the Portuguese in Asia,

---

[1] See David K. Wyatt, 'The Thai "Palatine Law" and Malacca', in D. K. Wyatt, *Studies in Thai History: Collected Articles* (Chiang Mai, 1994), 82–8.

[2] There are, however, two exceptions that should be mentioned, though both authors refer only in passing to Siam; the first one is the account of the Venetian merchant Niccolò de Conti, who travelled through Asia in the fifteenth century and who probably had also touched the Siamese province of Mergui ('Macinus' – the Myanmar city of Tenasserim of today). After his return in 1444, he related his adventures to Poggio Bracciolini, secretary of Pope Eugene IV in Rome. An abridged Italian version of his report was printed in the first volume of Ramusio's *Navigatio et Viaggi*. The original Latin finally appeared in the fourth book of Bracciolini's treatise, *Historiae de Varietate Fortunae libri quatuor* (Paris, 1723), 126–52. The second account of Southeast Asia published at a very early date is Ludovico Varthema's *Itinerario*, which was first printed in Rome in 1510, shortly before the Portuguese captured Melaka. His book quickly became very popular in Europe, and was translated into other European languages and frequently reprinted until the seventeenth century.

and allusions to Siam's past before 1511 are scattered and fragmentary. Ecclesiastical histories like that of Fernão Guerreiro cover an even narrower field of Portuguese activities in the East.[3] Secular events seldom capture the author's attention. More often, the countries and peoples of Southeast Asia serve as a foil for the history of the spread of the Christian faith or for an account of the activities of a single Christian order in the East.

The emphasis of this essay will be on the early stages of the European discourse on the origin and early history of the kingdom of Siam. I begin by introducing initial European approaches to the history of Siam, which occurred in the second half of the sixteenth century. Secondly, I discuss the most important seventeenth-century European contribution to Siam's history, written by Jeremias van Vliet in 1640, and examine the development of European historiography as 'universal history' during this period. Finally, I consider how Siam was later relegated in Western eyes to the status of a second-rate civilization that possessed no history of its own.

The project of describing the evolution of Western historical thought against the background of European writings on Siam has a special importance to the extent that we can – wherever possible – uncover traces of native historical material through a close examination of these European accounts. This rather unusual way of recollecting indigenous sources is necessary because the official records of the kings of Ayutthaya[4] were almost entirely destroyed when the Burmese captured that city in 1767.[5] Thus the study of European records on Siam not only contributes to our knowledge of the perception of culturally distinct societies in early modern Europe; Western accounts on old Siam are also central to the study of Thai history.

I

In early modern Europe, the notion of 'Historia' was used in the sense Pliny the Elder had given to it in his *Historia naturalis* dating back to the first century AD. It included not only the narration of past events, but also covered disciplines such as geography, zoology, botany, and medicine,

[3] F. Guerreiro, *Relação annual das coisas que fizeram os Padres da Companhia de Jesus nas suas missões . . . nos anos de 1600–1609* [1603–11] (3 vols, Coimbra, 1930–42).

[4] According to a temporal scheme officially established in 1925, the history of Thailand is focused on the country's capitals and divided into three eras: the Sukhothai Era (1250–1350), the Ayutthaya Era (1350–1767), and the Bangkok Era (1768–present). See Thongchai Winichakul, *Siam Mapped: A History of the Geo-Body of a Nation* (Bangkok, 1994), 162.

[5] See W. A. R. Wood, *A History of Siam from the Earliest Times to the Year A. D. 1781, With a Supplement Dealing with More Recent Events* [1925] (Bangkok, 1994), 24. See also Damrong Rajanubhab: 'The story of the records of Siamese history', *Journal of the Siam Society*, XI/2 (1911), 79–98. The only royal chronicle (Phraratchapong-sawadan) of the Thai kings known to be compiled before 1767 is the Pongsawadan Luang Prasert, dating back to the seventeenth century AD. An English version was published in *Journal of the Siam Society*, VI (1909), 1–27. Another compilation of old Thai sources predating the destruction of Ayutthaya was prepared by Jeremias van Vliet in 1640 and will be discussed here in more detail in Section II.

or specialized works on the natural products of foreign countries.[6] The conception of the world as handed down from the Bible or classical Greek and Roman tradition was most influential throughout the sixteenth and seventeenth centuries, and the knowledge of the ancient world was also considered to be relevant for the present. Fable still vied with concrete information to form and visualize the European conception of the world beyond the old *oikumene*. Although the fifteen years between 1546 and 1560 witnessed the publication of some of the most important geographical books of the Renaissance, the more distant parts of the history of countries in the Far East remained unknown. Until the seventeenth century, even the most learned scholars discussed the historical origins of countries and peoples of Southeast Asia in terms and categories of the bible and classical antiquity rather than on the basis of more recent information. In his *Commentarius de Orphyra Regione* (Coimbra, 1561), the Portuguese scholar Gaspar Varrerius (in Portuguese, *Barreiros*) identified the kingdom of Pegu, the Malay Archipelago, Siam, and Sumatra with the biblical land of Ophir from which King Solomon ordered his sailors to fetch gold. And like many of his contemporaries, Varrerius used Ophir as a synonym for the 'Golden Chersonese'.[7] The 'land of gold' and presumably vast wealth was widely known from Ptolemaic geography and was also mentioned in the *Periplus Maris Erythraei*. This merchant handbook was originally written in Greek around AD 50; it describes India's coastal regions and gives a comprehensive picture of Rome's trade to India.[8] Other geographers constantly sought to identify Solomon's Golden Land with Arabia, Sri Lanka (Taprobane), or South Africa. However, most European writers on Southeast Asia were inclined to believe Varrerius's version.[9] One of the most popular sixteenth-century German books was the *Cosmographia* originally authored by the German Hebrew scholar Sebastian Münster (1488–1552). The last edition of the *Cosmographia* was published in 1628 by the Basel professors Johann Jacob Grasser and Wolfgang Meyer. On Siam they wrote:

In diesem Königreich von Siam ligt Aurea Regio, das guldene Landt Ptolemei / welches von Arriano *aurea continens* genennet wirdt. Zu

[6] J. Knape, *Historie in Mittelalter und früher Neuzeit: Begriffs- und gattungsgeschichtliche Untersuchungen im interdisziplinären Kontext* (Baden-Baden, 1984), 433–9.

[7] G. Varrerius, 'Commentarivs de Orphyra Regione . . . Gaspare Varrerio Lusitano auctore', in *De locis S. Scriptvrae Hebraicis Angeli Caninii Commentarivs . . . accessit Gasparis Varrerii Lusitani de Ophira Regione in Sacris litteris Disputatio. Antverpiae Anno MCD* (Coimbra, 1561), as reproduced in E. Schmitt (ed.), *Dokumente zur Geschichte der europäischen Expansion* (Munich, 1984), II, 20–8. Varrerius's book was reprinted several times (Antwerp, 1600; Rotterdam, 1616; Harderwijk, 1637) and was especially popular in the Netherlands.

[8] Compare D. F. Lach, *Asia in the Making of Europe, Vol. I: The Century of Discovery* (Chicago and London, 1965), Book 1, 14.

[9] See, for example, Pierre Du Jarric's commentaries in *Histoire des choses plus memorables advenues tant ez Indes Orientales . . .* (3 parts, Bordeaux, 1608–14), part 1, 619–29. An English translation of the text was published by A. Sauliére: 'The Jesuits on Pegu at the end of the XVIth century', *Bengal Past and Present*, 19 (1919), 16–80.

allernechst darbey ligt die Peninsel *Aurea Chersonesus*, welche mit einem
schmalen Halß an dem Landt hanget: Tremellius und Junius halten
darfür es seye eben das Land Ophyr / dahin Salomon seine Schiff
geschickt hatt.[10]

[In the kingdom of Siam there is the Aurea Regio, the Golden Land of
Ptolemy / which Arrian calls *aurea continens*. Next comes the peninsula *Aurea
Chersonesus*, having the figure of a slim neck: Tremellius and Junius believe
that it is the country of Ophir / to which Solomon had sent his ships.]

A similar interpretation is given by the Portuguese Renaissance poet Luis
de Camões, whose text may have served as model for the later, expanded
editions of *Cosmographia*. He wrote in his *Lusiads* of 1572:

> Olha Tavai cidade, onde começa
> De Sião largo o império tão comprido . . .
> Mais avante fareis que se conheça
> Malaca por empório ennobrecido
> Onde toda a província do Mar Grande
> Suas mercadorias ricas mande.
> Dizem que desta terra co as possantes
> Ondas o mar, entrado, dividiu
> A nobre ilha Samatra, que já d'antes
> Juntas ambas a gente antiga viu.
> Quersoneso foi dita; e das prestantes
> Veias d'ouro que a terra produziu,
> 'Aurea' por epitéto lhe ajuntaram;
> Alguns que fosse Ofir imaginaram.[11]

In Sir Richard Fanshawe's translation of the poem of 1655, these stanzas were
rendered as:

> Behold the City of Tavay, with which
> The spacious *Empire* of Sian begins! . . .
> Malacca see before, where *ye* shall pitch
> Your great Emporium, and your *Magazins*:
> The *Rendezvous* of all that Ocean round
> For *Merchandizes* rich that *there* abound.
> From this ('tis said) the Waves impetuous course,
> Breaking a passage through from Main to *main*,
> Samatra's noble *Isle* of old did force,

---

[10] S. Münster, *Cosmographia* (Basel, 1628), 1589. From 1544 to 1628, thirty-six complete editions and
reprints of the *Cosmographia* appeared, most of them after Münster's death. Later editions of the *Cosmographia*
were thoroughly revised and greatly enlarged; compared with the first edition, the last contains nearly twice the
amount of material. For details see Karl-Heinz Burmeister, *Sebastian Münster: Eine Bibliographie* (Wiesbaden, 1964).

[11] L. de Camões, *Os Lusíadas*, x, 123–4 [1572] (Lisbon, 1992), 278.

Which *then* a Neck of Land therewith did chain:
That *this* was Chersonese till that divorce,
And from the wealthy *mines,* that *there* remain,
The *Epithite* of Golden had annext:
Some think, it was the Ophyr in the *Text.*[12]

To this extent, it seems, the peoples of *India extra Gangem* were not regarded as completely unknown, because they already existed as part of the geographical knowledge of the classical world. During the fifteenth and sixteenth centuries, the recovery of antiquity not only brought to light almost forgotten manuscripts of Greek and Roman philosophers and historians; the study of ancient geographical literature and cross-comparison with new material could also help to incorporate Siam and Pegu (today's Lower Burma/Myanmar) into the horizon of ancient geography. The Roman and Greek tradition represented much more than simply an historical period. The canonization of various ancient authors established particular standards of historical truthfulness and veracity, which had a most pervasive effect on European conceptions of the world and a decisive function in shaping the experiences and perceptions of an educated sixteenth-century European mind.

Writing the history of the countries of Southeast Asia before the coming of the Portuguese was difficult and complicated. Very few chroniclers in sixteenth-century Europe, if any, were familiar with Asian languages, and most therefore remained unable to read the original sources. In addition, materials on the history of countries in Southeast Asia were sometimes difficult to gather. João de Barros tried to locate a chronicle of Melaka, but failed. In consequence he repeated the evidence of indigenous traditions. He gave a version of the *Paramesvara* story – the story of the Palembang prince Paramesvara, whose reign dates back to the fourteenth century AD – which he may have received (with other matters) from Tomé Pires.[13] As for China, he had in his possession at Lisbon a collection of Chinese books, together with a Chinese slave to read and abstract them for him.[14] As an official Portuguese historian, Barros probably saw more documents on his subject than anyone before or since. Other writers who were less well-equipped with written materials on the East depended upon second-hand information or had to draw on the knowledge of men who had served in the *Estado da Índia.*

In general, the Far East was not the centre of attention of European historians. Rather, they were interested in European regions or bordering

---

[12] Sir Richard Fanshawe (trans.), *The Lusiads* [1655], ed. Geoffrey Bullough (London, 1963), 329.

[13] See I. A. MacGregor, 'Some aspects of Portuguese historical writing of the sixteenth and seventeenth centuries on Southeast Asia', in D. G. E. Hall (ed.), *Historians of South East Asia* (London, 1961), 172–99, at 185. On Paramesvara and the Malay historical tradition see C. H. Wake, 'Melaka in the 15th century: Malay historical traditions and the politics of Islamization', in Kernial Singh Sandhu and Paul Wheatley (eds), *Melaka: The Transformation of a Malay Capital c. 1400–1980* (2 vols, Kuala Lumpur, 1983), I, 128–61.

[14] See C. R. Boxer, 'Three historians of Portuguese Asia (Barros, Couto and Bocarro)', *Instituto Português de Hongkong, Boletim,* 1 (1948), 18–24.

countries that were more familiar. Even though the Orient, whether India or China, was not *terra incognita*, it was still too far removed both physically and spiritually to stimulate an historian's curiosity when compared with regions already known in Europe since the Crusades, for example, Muslim North Africa, the Near East, or Southwestern Europe. In Siam and Southeast Asia there was no common ground of cultural or historical tradition and, as a result, European authors had very little preparation and only slight interest in Asian history or Asian learning.

Among the few exceptions, João de Barros was one of the first Europeans to inquire into the beginnings of Siamese history. He never got nearer to India than the coast of Guinea, but as a well-informed official historiographer, Barros had access to various kinds of written sources and oral testimonies. In his account of Siam of 1563, he declared that he received most of his information from Domingo de Seixas, who spent over twenty years in Ayutthaya and knew the country well. Seixas may also have reported on the rather unusual sexual practices observed among both the people of Siam and those of Pegu. Barros, however, knew nothing about the descent of these peoples. He therefore attempted to explain their origin from a common centre on the basis of similarities in their sexual behaviour. The men are said to wear little round bells in their sexual organs, inserted into the flesh of the foreskin. This practice of penile inserts was commonly called *bunkals* (Spanish: *buncales*), and apparently was widespread not only in Siam and Pegu but also in Cambodia, Ava, Tenasserim, Arakan, and Pattani from the fourteenth to the seventeenth century.[15] Many of the sixteenth-century writers ascribed this strange invention to an early Burmese queen who wanted to enlarge the *membrum virile* for the greater gratification of women and to 'rule out and render impossible the practising of venery in illicit parts of the body even with men'.[16] As an explanation, Barros links the description of these practices to a traditional native story according to which the people of Pegu are descended from the marriage of a Chinese woman and a dog. Finally, he offers an alternative argument based on European traditions in stating that the Burmese (as well as the Siamese) are descendants of expatriates from the Judea of King Solomon:

Este pouo de Pegú tem lingoa própria: differente dos Siames, Brammas, Arracam com que vezinha, por cada hum têr lingoa per si. Porem quanto á maneyra de sua religiám, templos, sacêrdótes, grandeza de jdolos & cerimonies de seus sacrificios, vso de comer toda inmudicia, & torpeza de trazer cascauêes soldádos no instrumento da gêraçam: conuem muyto com os Siames. E ainda dizem elles que os Siames proçedem da sua lin-

[15] See M. Smithies, 'Body ornamentation and penile implants in Siam and Pegu', *Journal of the Siam Society*, 82/1 (1994), 81–8.

[16] Francesco Carletti, *My Voyage around the World* [1606], as quoted in Smithies, 'Body ornamentation', 83.

hagem, & será assi: porque esta torpeza dos cascauêes em todas aquellas pártes nam se acha em outro pouo. Donde se póde crer ser verdáde o que elles contam q[ue] aquella têrra se pouoou do ajuntamêto de hum cam & hûa molher: pois que no aucto do ajuntamêto delles querem jmitar os câes, porque quem ô jmita delle deue proçeder. E a história desta sua gêraçam, ê que vindo têr a cósta daquelle reyno Pégu que ontam êram têrras her mas hum junco da China com tormenta se perdeo, de que somente escapou hûa molher & hum cam, com o qual ella teue copula de que ouue filhos que depois os ouuerâ della, com que a têrra se veo, a multiplicar, & por nam degenerarem do pay jnuentáram, os cascauêes: & daquy depois q[ue] a géte foy muyta se passou a Siam, dôde os daquelle reyno tem o mesmo cóstume, & porque em ambas estas pártes as molheres tem melhor pareçer que os homêes, dizem ellas que as femeas saem á primeyra mây & os machos ao pay. Outros dizem, que esta têrra & â de Arracam foy pouoáda de degradádos, & que o vso dos cascauêes foy remêdio contra aquelle nefando peccado contra natura. E ainda algûus judeus daquella regiam que sabem a lingoa, & antendem a escriptura delles: dizem, que estes degradádos êram enviados per el rey Salamam de Iudêa, no tempo que as suas náos nauegáuam aquellas pártes embusca douro que leuáuam de Offir que elles tem ser na jlha Samatrá, que naquelle tempo auiam ser têrra continua a esta. Seja como for, pois de tempos tam antigos nam temosescripturas: somente o que o pouo reçebe de pay a filho: & segundo o demónio naquelle te[m]po, & ainda agóra reyna em toda aquelle gentelidade, mais nefandos abusos, fora do pensamento nósso tem entresi.[17]

[The people from Pegu speak their own language, which differs from those of the neighbouring countries Siam, Brama, and Arracan. All of these peoples use their own idiom. But they resemble one another in the worship of their god, in the style of their temples, the appearance of the priests and the size of their idols, as well as in their sacrificial ceremonies. All these peoples eat anything and refuse almost nothing. Some of their soldiers also share the same despicable custom of wearing bells (cascauêes) in their sexual organ. The people of Siam are reportedly descendants from those of Pegu, which seems to be true since they are the only nations to observe this abominable custom. I'm therefore willing to accept as true a story that the Peguans are descendants from the marriage of a Chinese woman and a dog. Concerning the way they practice sexuality, they try to imitate the dogs and thus are likely to descend from a dog. The story of this people is the following: A Chinese junk was shipwrecked on the coast of the kingdom of Pegu (which was then uninhabited and

---

[17] J. de Barros, *Terceira Decada da Asia* (Lisbon, 1563), fol. 66[r-v]. Translations are my own unless otherwise indicated.

barren) and only a woman and a dog survived. They copulated and the woman bore children to whom she again made love. This is how this land was populated. And since the children are related to a dog they also use these bells. Later on, their population rose steadily and some of them migrated to Siam. Therefore, the people there have the same custom [like those in Pegu]. Because in both of these countries the women are more beautiful than the men are, they say that the former resemble their mother, while the latter resemble the father. Others say that sodomites (*degradádos*) inhabit this land and that of Arracan and that these bells are meant to prevent the men from this filthy and vile sin against nature. Some of the Jews who live in this area and speak the local language and script also reported on sodomy. They say that they are descendants of expatriates from the land of King Solomon, who were sent here at a time when their ships were searching for gold. Finally, they found it in Ophir and carried it off. During that period, the people placed the land of Ophir in Sumatra and thought that this island was not separated from neighbouring countries. However, since a long time has passed we have no written sources dating back to that period. We only have stories handed down from father to son. It is almost certain that the devil has reigned over this kingdom and still does, because things are happening here too terrible to imagine.]

Barros's explanation might also recall the medieval Alexander legend, which he may have combined with a traditional story current in the East. The *Romance of Alexander the Great* circulated in the whole of Europe throughout the Middle Ages and created the myth of Asia as a land of dog-headed monsters (in Greek: *kynokephal*) and other demons that slowly captured the popular imagination of medieval Europe.[18] It was not for many centuries after Marco Polo's time that the last of these fables disappeared from scientific and critical literature. Barros's legend of the mating of a woman and a dog to produce the people of Siam and Burma proved to be very durable, for it was quoted until the end of the sixteenth century in Portuguese and Spanish literature.[19]

Barros also investigated the religious beliefs of the Siamese and inquired into matters of chronology. Again, he presented to the reader what he had heard on the subject from his informant Domingo de Seixas:

Nestes saçerdótes está toda a doctrina: porq[ue] nam sômête estudâ nas cousas de sua religiã, mas ajnda na reuluçã do çeo & dos planetas, & nas cousas da filosophia natural. Tem q[ue] o mûdo teue principio, & q[ue]

---

[18] For details see P. Noble (ed.), *The Medieval Alexander Legend and Romance Epic: Essays in Honour of David J. A. Ross* (Millwood, NY, 1982).

[19] On this theme in literature see M. Chevalier, *L'Ariosto en Espagne (1530–1650)* (Bordeaux, 1966), 352–3.

ouue deluuio gêral & q[ue] o termo da duraçã do mûdo ê deoyto mil annos, de q[ue] já sam passados seis mil: & disto dáuã alguus doctos razão anno de mil & quinhêtos & quorêta, a hû Domingo de Seixas de q[ue] atras fizêmos mençã q[ue] lhe pergûtáua por estas cousas. Dizê que a fim do mûdo há de ser per fogo & q[ue] neste tépo se abrirâ no çeo sête olhos de sol, & q[ue] cada hú suciuaméte secára húa cousa, tê q[ue] aos cinquo secára o már, & q[ue] nos dous vltimos se queimára toda a terra: na cinza da qual ficárâ dous óuos, macho & femea, de q[ue] se tornárâ a produzir todallas cousas de q[ue] o mundo se tornárâ reformar. E q[ue] nam auera nelle már dagua falgada, se nã rios q[ue] reguê a terra: a qual será muy fêrtil & dará seus fructos sem trabalho dos homêes, com q[ue] elles viuã a seu prazer perpetuamente.[20]

[These priests are the possessors of all learning, because they not only study the matters of their religion but also the revolutions of the heavens and of the planets as well as affairs of natural philosophy. They hold that the world had a beginning, that there was a general deluge and that the world will last for eight thousand years of which six thousand have already passed. Some ascribed to Domingo de Seixas (who had already been mentioned and who enquired about these things) a reference to the year one thousand five hundred and forty. They say that the end of the World will be by fire and that when the fire comes, seven suns will appear in the heavens and that each one of these will burn up one thing, one after the other, and the fifth sun will dry up the sea, and that the last two will burn up all the earth. In the ashes will remain two eggs, a male and a female one, from which will be born all things again and from which the world will be re-made. They also believe that in this new world there will be no oceans of salt-water but that only rivers will water the earth. The land will be fertile and will produce its fruits without the labour of men, so that mankind will live in happiness forever after.]

At first sight, it seems as if Barros is here trying to trace the beliefs of the Siamese to those of the Christian tradition. His narration, it is true, contains various aspects that could easily be fitted into biblical accounts of Genesis and the Apocalypse, or the Christian idea of death and resurrection in a more general sense. In Siamese cosmography, it is assumed that a universal flood followed the creation of the world and that man will be born again in paradise. In fact, there were many folk tales or legends current in the region that tell of an enormous flood unloosed by the gods to punish man for his ingratitude to the Heavenly Spirit.[21] The conception of the world as an

---

[20] Barros, *Terceira Decada*, fol. 39ʳⁱ.

[21] See, for example, D. K. Wyatt, *Thailand – A Short History* (New Haven, 1984), 10–11, on the legend of *Khun Borom* that was told by the Lao and in neighbouring countries.

endless cycle of creation and destruction by fire and/or rain was a central element of Brahmanic as well as of Buddhist teachings.[22] This idea of a cyclical movement of history and being, however, was not entirely unknown to sixteenth-century scholars, because the motif had already been discussed among Stoic and Platonic philosophers and Pythagoreans in ancient Greece.[23]

Barros also reports that the Siamese monks declare that the world will last for 8000 years, 6000 of which have already passed. Most likely, this chronology derived from the *Khamhaikan Chao Krung Kao* (*Testimony of the Old City*), but interestingly enough, it also coincides with a calendar still current in sixteenth-century Europe, according to which the creation of the earth dates back to the year 5200 BC.[24] Barros seems to have been much inclined to *produce* similarities between Christianity and Buddhism (an argument implying the possibility of the conversion of the 'heathens'), but he actually recounts parts of the Theravada–Buddhist cosmology, *Traiphum Phra Ruang*. The *Traiphum* was reputedly first compiled in the Siamese language from the Pāli canon in 1345 and stood at the core of Siamese Buddhist belief for centuries, 'serving as an all-embracing statement of the world as seen through Siamese Buddhist eyes, as well as a primary instrument for educating subjects of the Siamese kings in Buddhist values'.[25] It contains a passage on the destruction of the *Mahakappa* (Great Era) that is almost identical with Barros's narrative and therefore must have been at least an indirect source of Domingo de Seixas's information.[26]

II

In Barros's view, the activity of the Portuguese in the East was, above all, a religious enterprise, its history a means of preaching Christianity.[27] In his *Décadas* he stressed the official theory of the Portuguese ethos in expansion as a model of religious zeal; the Christian religion was a major source for his sense of the relationship between past and present and for temporal change. History was part of theology and the moral sciences, and had specific didactic purpose. In the *Prologo* of his *Terceira Década* he declared:

---

[22] Compare W. Kirfel, 'Indische Parallelen zum Alten Testament', *Saeculum*, vii/4 (1956), 369–84, at 371.

[23] See P. Burke, 'Renaissance, reformation, revolution', in R. Koselleck and P. Widmer (eds), *Niedergang: Studien zu einem geschichtlichen Thema* (Stuttgart, 1980), 137–47, at 142 *et seq.*

[24] In 1485 the Portuguese Diogo Cão erected a *padrão* (memorial stone) at Cape Cross that carries the following epigraph: '6685 years have passed since the creation of the world. 1485 years have passed since Christ was born. The most noble King João II of Portugal has ordered Diogo Cão to erect this *padrão*'. Quoted in Schmitt, *Europäischen Expansion*, 72. On the *Khamhaikhan* compare Charnvit Kasetsiri, *The Rise of Ayudhya: A History of Siam in the Fourteenth and Fifteenth Centuries* (Kuala Lumpur, 1976), 6.

[25] See Craig J. Reynolds, 'Buddhist cosmography in Thai history. With special reference to 19th century culture change', *Journal of Asian Studies*, 35 (1975–6), 203–20, at 203.

[26] An English translation of the *Traiphum* was prepared by F. E. and M. B. Reynolds, *Three Worlds According to King Ruang* (Berkeley, 1982). The passage dealing with the destruction of the *Mahakappa* is on 307–11.

[27] MacGregor, 'Portuguese historical writing', 180.

E como a historia, he hum agro & cãpo onde está seme ad a toda a doctrina, divinal, moral, racional & instrumental: quem pastar o seu fructo, côuertello hâ em forças de jntedimento & memoria, pera vso de justa & perfecta vida, cô que apraz a Deos & aos homeês.[28]

[History is a field where is sown every divine, moral, rational and instrumental doctrine. Whoever feeds on its fruit will be furnished in understanding and memory for living the just and perfect life that pleases both God and mankind.]

A growing consciousness of the variety of the world and a rising interest in the history of the world outside Europe slowly emerged in late sixteenth-century Europe. Serious history, as opposed to 'curious history', responded to the opening of Asia during the last generation of the sixteenth century, when more detailed information on the Far East began to pour into Europe. Although most European historians at home continued to rely on biblical and antique authorities for the writing of their annals and chronicles, it became quite obvious, at least to some of them, that 'the Ancients were mistaken in many things relating to the knowledge of the earth'.[29] The accounts of the Castilian and Portuguese 'voyages' and the discovery of the New World challenged the authority of Greek and Roman tradition, and, at a later date, also gave way to 'heretical' ideas that also contested biblical narrative. The tendency of secular students of history to treat religion and the Church merely as historical developments subject to change stirred hostility among the orthodox. The first steps towards the writing of secular histories were already undertaken in late sixteenth-century France and Italy, where some historians had sought to examine the implications of the discoveries for historical thought. At that time neither France nor Italy were directly involved in trade and colonization in Asia, in contrast to sixteenth-century Portugal and Spain or seventeenth-century Holland, though the Portuguese kings were eager to retain the co-operation of Italy and the papacy, for it was on the basis of the line of demarcation drawn by Pope Alexander VI that the non-European world was given over exclusively to the Iberian powers.

A transition from divine to secular history was initiated by the French lawyer and political theorist Jean Bodin, who proposed in his *Methodus ad facilem historiarum cognitionem* (Paris, 1566) to study history as the past of *all* human societies. His *method* is an early call to study history in universal rather than in national terms in order to focus on problems of general import.[30] Unlike most other cosmographers and traditional historians of his day, Bodin

---

[28] Barros, *Terceira Decada*, prologo.
[29] The Italian historian Francesco Guicciardini in his *History of Italy* (Venice, 1567), as quoted in D. F. Lach, *Asia in the Making of Europe, Vol. II: A Century of Wonder* (Chicago and London, 1977), Book 2, 224.
[30] See Lach, *Asia in the Making of Europe, Vol. II*, 306–19.

is rigorous in excluding divine history from his considerations and therefore provoked attacks from the Catholic Church and the Jesuits, who sought to build intellectual defenses against the infiltration and dissemination of ideas deemed to be dangerous to the Church as a divine institution. In *Les six livres de la république* (Paris, 1576) Bodin employed travel accounts to show a relation between culture and geography, and argued on the basis of his readings that laws suitable to a people living in a northern climate were not suitable to peoples living in others:

> Therefore a wise governour of any Commonweale must know their humours, before he attempt any thing in the alteration of the state and lawes. For one of the greatest, and it may be the chiefest foundation of a Commonweale, is to accomomodate the estate to the humor of the citisens; and the lawes and ordinances to the nature of the place, persons, and time.[31]

The conviction had become firmly rooted among Renaissance thinkers that everything has a history, and that it is the function of history to provide knowledge of remote times and peoples to compare to the known present. In 1573 the Italian cosmographer Giovanni Lorenzo d'Anania (?1545–?1607) published in Naples his *L'universale fabrica del mondo*. He evidently combed the literature of antiquity and the Middle Ages, and also used, among other sources, Barros's first two *Décadas*, which appeared in Italian translation in 1562.[32] Anania was most interested in the religious practises observed in Ceylon, Siam, and Japan, and endeavoured to identify the history and origin of Buddhism. From the paintings in Japanese temples he concluded that the Japanese religion could be traced back to Siam:

> . . . entro è Amangucci città molto grande, ma con le case di legname, come sono gran parte di questa isola, quasi a cento miglia si troua Bungo capo del suo regno, & città grandissima, con un'ottimo porto a canto la marina, doue sono infiniti Christiani; leggendouisi l'Evangelio, & iui hor è fatto un Seminario, doue i nostri imparano la lingua Giupponese, & essi con la nostra legge, l'idioma Portoghese, & alcuni la lingua latina: all'intorno è Zuo, Mangati, Bungen, Chicungencachi, Iuma, Teimbo, & Deuchibozata, e dopo Rima, & Fianoiama molto notabile per la residenza, che vi fa il generale de i Bonsi: con questo nome chiamano i loro sacerdoti; i quali eßendo simili nella loro religione a i Bramini: dimostrano hauere il principio da loro per via di Siam: ilche si scorge in diuersi loro tempij dalla pittura, che gli è quasi la medesima . . .[33]

---

[31] Jean Bodin, *The Six Books of a Commonweale*, trans. R. Knolles (London, 1606), 663.

[32] *L'Asia del S. Giovanni di Barros*, published by Vincenzo Valgrisio (Venice, 1562).

[33] Quotations are taken from a later edition: Giovanni Lorenzo d'Anania, *L'Universale fabrica del mondo overo Cosmografia Dell'Ecc. Gio. Lorenzo d'Anania . . .* (Venice, 1582), 275 *et seq.*

[Amangucci [Japan] is a large city, which is built from wooden houses like most cities on this island. Bungo is the capital of the country, situated a hundred miles from here. It is a very large city with an excellent port where many Christians live. People read the Holy bible and there is a seminar where our people learn the Japanese language, while the others learn our laws, Portuguese, and some of them Latin. Not far from there is Zuo, Mangati etc and finally Rima and Fianoiama. The latter city is remarkable because it is the residence of the head of the Bonsi [Bonzes]. This is the native name of their priests whose religion resembles much that of the Brahmans. They have received their belief from Siam. This becomes evident from the paintings in their temples, which are similar to those [in Siam].]

Although Anania was far better informed about Asia than any of his Italian predecessors, his conception of the spread of Buddhism in Asia was still limited by the sources he used. But he was aware of the fact that Japanese Buddhism was but another form of the same religion existing in Southeast Asia.[34]

A common source of the religions practised in various countries of East and Southeast Asia was also assumed by the Spanish Franciscan Marcelo Ribadeneyra, who was one of the oath-taking friars who were driven out of Japan in 1597 because of their public preaching. He returned to Manila, where he prepared a work on Asia which he brought to Europe in 1600 and published at Barcelona the following year. In his account of Siam he relied on information he obtained from a handful of Franciscan missionaries who left the country in 1582 because of impending Pegu–Siamese wars. He relates that the Siamese religion is ancient and that the founder of Siam was the Buddha himself, who reportedly came from the vast desert of the kingdom of Cambodia a good 2000 years ago:

The religious who stayed in Siam had the opportunity of observing the religious rituals and ceremonies there, and of interviewing directly the priests and elders who led the people in the practise of their beliefs. This set of beliefs is ancient and goes back to the olden days when the first founder of Siam came all over the way from a vast desert in the kingdom of Cambodia . . . The educated men of Siam tell the legend of one of the first kings of the realm, and how he passed on this set of religious beliefs

---

[34] On the history of Japanese Buddhism, see Helmuth von Glasenapp, *Die fünf Weltreligionen: Hinduismus, Buddhismus, Chinesischer Universismus, Christentum, Islam* (Munich, 1996), 105–6. In Thailand, the basis of a Buddhist civilization was laid between the sixth and ninth centuries. During that period, there developed a distinctive Buddhist culture associated with a Mon-speaking population and a civilization often referred to as *Dvaravati*. The Thai form of Buddhism was overlaid with local traditions of Indian derivation, and at least during the eleventh century Hinduism was practised there as well as Buddhism. In the late thirteenth and early fourteenth centuries the Theravada form of Buddhism obtained exclusive royal support and ousted all rival religions; Wyatt, *Thailand – A Short History*, 21 *et seq.*; Barend J. Terwiel, *A Window on Thai History* (Bangkok, 1991), 54.

and practises to them – the priests. . . . While in China and Japan, the name of the great king who received these laws was Amida (Buddha), in Siam, he was called Perdeneab and various other derivations.[35]

However, only a few European historical writings on non-European countries exhibited a clearly expressed impartial, historical view. Most authors who had the time and inclination to tackle the chronologies of Asian kings were Jesuit missionaries, whose number in the East had grown rapidly and who by 1606 had taken over the leadership of the Christian mission from Goa to Nagasaki.[36] But only a relatively small number of Catholic priests settled in Siam before the 1660s, when Louis XIV and the friars of the French *Societé des Missions étrangères* discovered Siam as a worthwhile field for evangelization and for the expansion of French influence in the East Indies. Most of the Portuguese Dominicans who worked in Ayutthaya in the latter half of the sixteenth century were killed in the Burmese invasion of Ayutthaya in 1569, and most of the Spanish Franciscans who went there met a similar fate in the Burmese war of 1584 and the Cambodian war of 1594.

The majority of other European writings were intended to promote national overseas enterprise, to strengthen Europe's control of territory in the colonies, or to support the spread of the Christian faith. For the most part, historical research derived from religious and proselytizing considerations. For example, the sixteenth-century Spanish missionary Bernardino de Sahagún wrote an extensive history of Mexico based on local materials. He declared that profound knowledge of the history and religion of a foreign country was highly essential for effective missionary work: the study of the past was not undertaken out of intellectual curiosity but was a means to an end.[37]

The only European nation which maintained an almost continuous presence in Siam during the seventeenth century was the Netherlands. But the Dutch seem to have given little or no consideration to the possibility of spreading Protestantism outside Europe. Although there were Protestant *predikanten* (reformed ministers) in the Dutch overseas empire, they had to cope with several disadvantages when compared with their Catholic rivals, who were already firmly established in many parts of Southeast Asia, and were better skilled and far more numerous than their Dutch opponents. Most of the Dutch *predikanten* were recruited from the working class in the Netherlands, and only a few of them had more than a rudimentary theological training. Unlike the Roman Catholic missionaries in the East, they were often shifted at short notice from one place to another and thus had

---

[35] M. de Ribadeneyra, *Historia de las islas del archipiélago Filipino . . .* (new edn, Manila, 1970), 429–30.

[36] C. R. Boxer, 'Some aspects of Western historical writing on the Far East, 1500–1800', in W. G. Beasley and E. G. Pulleyblank (eds), *Historians of China and Japan* (London, 1961), 307–21.

[37] On Sahagún, see Tzvetan Todorov, 'The conquest as seen by the Aztects', in T. Todorov, *The Morals of History*, trans. Alyson Waters (Minneapolis and London, 1995), 17–33.

insufficient time to learn the local language. In addition, they were paid by the Dutch East India Company and not by the Church. As a result, the VOC (Vereenigde Oost-Indische Compagnie) officials regarded them as their salaried servants, 'and their order of precedence in the Company's official hierarchy was regulated accordingly, with the lay-readers at the bottom of the social ladder'.[38]

In the seventeenth century, Europe witnessed the publication of numerous travel accounts about the non-European world. Most printed reports came off the press of northern Europe – more from Dutch presses than from all the rest. Spain and Portugal continued to publish notices of victories in the East, though these became rarer by the latter half of the century. The centre of gravity in book production on the overseas world moved definitively to the Netherlands. In the first half of the sixteenth century the Portuguese jealously watched over every piece of information which might have led possible competitors to the sources of the spice trade, and as far as published accounts and maps are concerned, their policy of secrecy remained success-ful at least until 1550.[39] However, after Portugal's loss of control of informa-tion on the East Indies during the latter half of the sixteenth century, the number of publications on the countries of Asia constantly rose, and in the decades that followed the 'curious reader' could choose from a broad range of different travel collections published in Amsterdam, London, Paris, or Frankfurt.

Though the printers of the United Provinces flooded the market with accounts of Dutch voyages and expeditions to the Indies,[40] there were no Dutch counterparts to Portugal's official sixteenth-century chronicle writers, who had produced an outstanding series of historical records. An extended general account of the Lusitanian discoveries in India like Barros's *Décadas da Ásia*, or a poetic hymn of praise to the pioneering Portuguese like the *Lusiads* of Luis de Camões, was never written in the Netherlands. During the Dutch 'Golden Age', no one in Holland undertook the task of collecting the vast corpus of information about countries of the East to produce a comprehensive work on Asia and the history of the Dutch in the East Indies. A more systematic approach to the history of the countries of Asia and the activities of the Dutch in the East Indies did not appear in print before the eighteenth century, at a time when the Dutch empire in the East was already in decline; this was François Valentyn's 4800-page work, *Oud en Nieuw Oost Indiën* (*The Old and New East-Indies*).[41]

---

[38] See C. R. Boxer, *The Dutch Seaborne Empire 1600–1800* [1965] (London, 1990), 150.

[39] See Lach, *Asia in the Making of Europe, Vol. I*, 493 *et seq.*; on the geographical literature until 1600 see also B. Penrose, *Travel and Discovery in the Renaissance, 1420–1600* (Cambridge, MA, 1955), 275–326.

[40] For a general survey on the development of the printing of travel accounts on Asia during the seven-teenth century, see Donald F. Lach and Edwin Van Kley, *Asia in the Making of Europe, Vol. III. A Century of Advance* (Chicago and London, 1993), Book 1, 301–597.

[41] F. Valentyn, *Oud en Nieuw Oost-Indiën* . . . (5 vols, Dordrecht and Amsterdam, 1726); a chapter on Siam entitled 'Beschryvinge van Siam, en onsen handel aldaar' is included in the third book, 56–96.

The geographical literature published in seventeenth-century Europe was different in character, preferring the collection of voyages and maps to the Portuguese method of epic historico-geographical narrative. In 1646, Isaac Commelin published a four-volume compendium of voyages that also included Joost Schouten's description of Siam of 1638.[42] In Germany Levinus Hulsius and Theodor de Bry and his family produced a series of travel accounts on Asia and America in Latin and German, but these collections still paid little attention to Siam. The only exception is de Bry's publication in 1606 of an abridged version of Jacob van Neck's journey to the Siamese province of Pattani, which took place in 1601.[43] Melchisedech Thévenot began publishing at Paris in 1663 his *Relations de divers voyages curieux*.[44] However, only a few of the accounts he used came from manuscript sources, while a majority of his material was already available in print in other European languages. His collection was issued in many augmented editions 'so that the arrangement and collation of the copies vary enough to produce a bibliographical puzzlement'.[45] The most significant English contributions of the time to Europe's store of knowledge about Asia were those of Richard Hakluyt and Samuel Purchas.[46] Though at least Hakluyt's primary concern, as the title of his compilation indicates, was with 'English' voyages, both Hakluyt and Purchas not only collected information obtained from their countrymen, but also included translations from Portuguese, Spanish, Italian, French, and Dutch descriptions of Asia and other non-European countries.

Information on Asia was therefore more widely diffused than in the century before. Books and reports were published in all European languages, frequently reprinted and translated, and collected into large compilations of travel literature published during the seventeenth century. As a result, some descriptions of Siam (or parts of it) appeared in print in several different travel collections and languages, or were included in separately issued accounts of other authors. One of the most important of early Dutch descriptions of Asia, for example, was Jan Huygen van Linschoten's *Itinerario*, first

[42] I. Commelin (ed.), *Begin ende Voortgang vande Vereenigde Neederlandtsche Geoctroyeerde Oost-Indische Compagnie* (4 vols, Amsterdam, 1969), IV, 203–17.
[43] Theodor de Bry (ed.), *Achter Theil der Orientalische Indien, begreifend erßtlich ein historische Beschreibung der Schiffahrt/ So der Admiral Jacob van Neck . . . von Ann. 1600 bis an. 1603 gethan . . .* (Frankfurt, 1606), 1–40; the complete Dutch manuscript was first published as 'Journael van de tweede reys, gedaen by den Heer Admirael Naer Osst-Indien', in H. A. van Foreest and A. de Booy (eds), *De vierde Schipvaart der Nederlanders naar Oost-Indië onder Jacob Wilkens en Jacob van Neck (1599–1604)* (2 vols, 's-Gravenhage, 1980), I, 165–233; Levinus Hulsius, *Kurtze warhafftige Beschreibung der newen Reyse . . . in denn Orientalischen Indien . . .* (Nuremberg, 1598). For details on Hulsius's collection of voyages and travels see Adolph Asher, *Bibliographical Essay on the Collection of Voyages and Travels Edited and Published by Levinus Hulsius and His Successors at Nuremberg and Francfort from anno 1598 to 1660* [1839] (London and Belin, 1839).
[44] M. Thévenot (ed.), *Relations de divers voyages curieux* (4 vols, Paris, 1663–72).
[45] Lach and Van Kley, *Asia in the Making of Europe, Vol. III*, 410.
[46] Richard Hakluyt (ed.), *The Principal Navigations, Voyages, Traffiques, and Discoveries of the English Nation* [1598–1600] (12 vols, Glasgow, 1904); Samuel Purchas, *Hakluytus Posthumus or Purchas His Pilgrimes. Contayning a History of the World in Sea Voyages and Lande Travells by Englishmen and others* [1625] (20 vols, Glasgow, 1905).

published in 1595 and 1596.[47] He included in his book detailed sailing instructions that he had gathered from the Iberian 'routers', and in doing so provided a universal coast-pilot which soon became a standard part of the library carried by Dutch East India Company fleets. But his book was not exclusively based on his own experiences, and many passages in it were lifted from other accounts. Plagiarism, however, was not a serious literary crime then, and his description of Siam and Pegu was in fact almost entirely taken from an Italian account published in 1587 by the Venetian merchant Caesare Federici, who had travelled through Asia between 1563 and 1581.[48] Federici's report on Siam was also used by other contemporary commentators on Siam, such as Ralph Fitch,[49] Jacob van Neck, and Gasparo Balbi.[50]

Although all of these publications added much detail to the knowledge of the contemporary state of Siam and other nations of Southeast Asia, only a few authors inquired with any depth into the time before the coming of the Portuguese. However, a remarkable exception to this rule is a chronicle compiled in 1640 by a Dutch merchant (*koopman*). This ambitious man was Jeremias van Vliet. Unfortunately, however, his work was not published during his lifetime, though it was 'received with great thanks and praise' by the Governor-General and the Councils of the VOC.[51] It thus escaped the attention of interested seventeenth-century historians. Shortly after he had finished the 'Cort verhael van't . . . der Coningen van Siam' ('Short account of the kings of Siam'), the manuscript was dispatched to the archives of the VOC, where it remained untouched for more than 300 years. A complete transcription of the text with an English translation was not published until 1975.[52]

Van Vliet authored several other books and reports relating to Siam. In 1636, he wrote the *Beschrijving van het Koningryjk Siam* (*Description of the Kingdom of Siam*), which was printed in Leiden in 1692.[53] Subsequently he produced a detailed report of events that happened in 1636 in Ayutthaya, when a number of Dutch merchants were arrested by the Thai authorities.

[47] J. H. van Linschoten, *Itinerario. Voyage ofte Schipvaert van Jan Huygen van Linschoten naer Oost ofte Portugaels Indien 1579–1592*, ed. Hendrik Kern (2 vols, 's-Gravenhage, 1910).

[48] *Viaggio di M. Cesare de i Federici, nell'India Orientale, et oltra l'India* (Venice, 1587). T. Hickock's English translation was printed in 1588 in London. Parts of it were also included Hakluyt's and Purchas's collections of travels (Hakluyt, *The Principal Navigations*, v, 365–449; Purchas, *Hakluytus Posthumus*, x, 88–143).

[49] 'The Voyage of M. Ralph Fitch . . . begunne in the yeere of our Lord 1583, and ended 1591 . . .', in Hakluyt, *The Principal Navigations*, v, 463–505; his account is also published in Purchas, *Hakluytus Posthumus*, x, 165–204.

[50] G. Balbi, *Viaggio dell'Indie Orientali . . . Nel quale si contiene quanto egli in detto viaggio ha venduto por spatio di 9. Anni consumati in esso dal 1579, fino al 1588* (Venice, 1590). An abbreviated English version is published in Purchas, *Hakluytus Posthumus*, x, 143–65.

[51] Seiichi Iwao, 'Life of Jeremias van Vliet', in J. van Vliet, *Historiael verhael der sieckte ende doot van Pra Interra Tsia 22ᵉ coninck in Siam & den regherende Pra Onghsry 1640, door Jeremias van Vliet*, ed. S. Iwao (2 vols, Tokyo, 1956–8), i, viii.

[52] J. van Vliet, *The Short History of the Kings of Siam*, trans. Leonard Andaya, ed. D. K. Wyatt (Bangkok, 1975).

[53] Quotations in the text refer to the English translation: C. F. Ravenswaay (trans.), 'Description of the kingdom of Siam', *Journal of the Siam Society*, VII (1910), 1–105.

This account was included in the first two editions of Pelsaert's *Ongeluckige Voyagie*.[54] In 1640 he wrote two other more extensive works: the *Short History* already mentioned and another report that is also relevant to the writing of Thai history, *Historiael verhael der siechte ende doot van Pra Interra Tsia 22ᵉⁿ coninck in Siam & den regherende Pra Onghsry* (*Historical Account of the War of Succession Following the Death of King Pra Interajatsia, 22nd King of the Ayutthayan Dynasty*). The latter work was translated into French by Abraham de Wicquefort and published in Paris in 1663.[55]

Van Vliet did not have a great deal in common with his humanist predecessors such as João de Barros or Varrerius. In writing his reports and accounts he had other issues in mind than the blessings of pure research or historical learning, nor did he intend to celebrate or justify the deeds of his compatriots in Asia. His literary activities, it seems, were meant rather to promote his own career in the East. In his *Historiael Verhael* he frankly expressed his hopes of improving his position in the Dutch East India Company by writing his narrative.[56] Indeed, a number of careers in the East proved that demonstrating intimate knowledge of countries and places where the VOC had factories or agencies could open up a way to the highest posts in the Company's service. There were at least two examples that van Vliet could have had in mind. François Caron, who wrote the most authoritative seventeenth-century account of Japan, was soon afterwards made *opperhoofd* of the VOC's office in Hirado, Japan, and later given the post of a Director-General of Trade, an important position second only to that of Governor-General.[57] About the same time, the Dutch merchant in Ayutthaya, Joost Schouten, published a *Description of the Kingdom of Siam* (*Beschrijvinge van de Regeeringe, Macht, Religie, Costuymen, Traffijcquen ende andere remercquable saecken, des Coninghrijcks Siam*), which seems to have enjoyed great success for it was reprinted several times after its first publication in 1638. One year later, the VOC sent Schouten on several diplomatic missions in Southeast Asia. Meanwhile, van Vliet – who by then had already offered the manuscript of his own *Description of the Kingdom of*

---

[54] J. van Vliet, 'Verbael ende Historisch verhael van't gene des Vereenighde Nederlandtsche Geoctroijeerde Oost-Indische Companies Dienaers onder de directie van Jeremias van Vliet, in den Jaren 1636 ende 1637 . . .', in François Pelsaert, *Ongeluckige Voyagie, van't Schip Batavia, naer de Oost-Indien* (Amsterdam, 1647), 61–108. The same report was also published in the second edition under a different title: 'Een treur-blij ende Ongeluck, des Oost-Indische Compagnies Dienaers in't jaer 1636, wedervaren, in't Konincklijcke Hof van Siam, inde Stadt Judia, onder de directie van den E. Jeremias van Vliet' (Amsterdam, 1648), 40–71.

[55] J. van Vliet, *Relation Historique de la Maladie et de la Mort de Pra-Inter-Va-Tsia-Thiant-Siangh Pheevgk . . . escrit en l'an 1647 par Ieremie van Vliet* (Paris, 1663). An English translation was prepared by W. H. Mundie: *Van Vliet's Historical Account of Siam in the 17th Century* (Bangkok, 1904). This was reproduced in *Journal of the Siam Society*, xxx/2, 95–154. The complete Dutch text together with a facsimile edition of the original manuscript was edited by S. Iwao (see note 51).

[56] Van Vliet in Iwao, *Jeremias van Vliet*, i, 3–4.

[57] Until the eighteenth century, Caron's description of Japan was only excelled by Engelbert Kaempfer's *History of Japan*. Kaempfer's book was written around 1690 but not published until 1727, more than ten years after his death: E. Kaempfer, *The History of Japan Together with A Description of the Kingdom of Siam* (London, 1727).

Siam to the Director-General – succeeded him as chief merchant in Ayutthaya in 1638.

However, to stay alive and to remain successful, even the most capable and respected men in the East had to abide by certain seventeenth-century Dutch morals and customs. In July 1644 Schouten was accused of sodomy. He was found guilty, condemned to death by strangulation at the stake and then executed.[58] Van Vliet's subsequent career was also quite unlucky but ended in a less dramatic fashion. After his stay in Siam he was appointed to the governorship of Melaka. But he was charged with fraud while in office, and then sentenced to temporary suspension of his rank and salary. After his release he returned to Holland, where he died in 1663.

In the preamble to his manuscript chronicle, van Vliet addresses his superior, the 'noble, generous, wise, sober lord, the noble lord Antonio van Diemen', to satisfy his inclination for things worth remembering, and then stressed that the history of the Siamese kings is almost completely unknown in Europe.[59] As a good Protestant, he duly states his reason for writing: 'in order that the rest of the time would not be squandered in idleness, because idleness is the root of all evil, says Basilius'.[60] Unlike Barros and all other contemporary authors commenting on Siam, van Vliet was able to draw together native oral and written sources for the reconstruction of the kingdom's history. He lived in Ayutthaya from 1633 until 1642, which is a relatively long period of time when compared with other directors of the Dutch company's office in Ayutthaya, who rarely stayed longer than four or five years.[61] During the time of his residence, he is likely to have learned the Siamese language. As with most of his compatriots in Asia, he did not possess the gift of abstinence; he had a Siamese wife who bore him three children and probably assisted him in collecting and reading Thai manuscripts for the composition of his books.

Van Vliet's chronicle is a pioneering work since it was the first study of the history of a Southeast Asian country that was not based on travellers' reports, but was written exclusively by consulting a comparatively broad range of indigenous documents. In his chronicle, van Vliet is almost entirely concerned with the chronology, names, and great achievements of the Siamese dynasties, perhaps because of the nature of the Siamese histories from which he derived his materials. He recounts the deeds and reigns of the Siamese kings from the beginning of the kingdom up to his time, yet without giving exact dates. Some of his sources, he stated, were so intermingled with myth that it seemed impossible for him to extract anything true from them. He wanted to refer to real rather than imaginary events, and noted that the terminology of his source material is sometimes figurative, the tone pious,

---

[58] See J. Villiers, 'Introduction', in Caron and Schouten, *The Mighty Kingdoms of Japan and Siam (1671)* (Bangkok, 1986), unnumbered.

[59] Van Vliet, *Short History*, 53.

[60] *Ibid.*

[61] See George V. Smith, *The Dutch in Seventeenth Century Thailand* (DeKalb, IL, 1977), 142–7.

the epistemology mystical – all of the things he wished to expunge from his narrative. He therefore decided to omit the more 'incredulous' and 'fabulous' elements and bound together several sources of information into a chronological framework. Rather than an elaborated theory of historical truth, one may assume that he had in mind conventions in writing and composing travel accounts (*ars apodemica*), which were established on the basis of Renaissance learning during the sixteenth century.[62] Protestant cosmographers in Europe who used for the compilation of their books several ancient, medieval, and contemporary accounts of the non-European world had already rejected as fabulous several travel tales which had circulated in Europe since the Middle Ages, and had already raised doubts about the veracity of some of the earlier relations, especially those written by Catholic authors.[63] Truthfulness and novelty were major challenges required by the European public, and van Vliet had already obediently referred to this demand in his earlier work on Siam written in 1636:

> Only such information as I thought to be true, I have mentioned in this book and beg that the will may be taken for the deed and that these few lines may be received favourably which will in the near future encourage me to greater freedom.[64]

Nonetheless, he relates in some detail several stories which were current concerning the first king of Siam in ancient times, U Thong, and includes a nearly verbatim translation of parts of the Pāli chronicle *Sangitiyavamsa*, except for the last few reigns, where he added much material in his own words, deriving from his own knowledge of the more recent events.[65] He expressed his doubts about accounts he heard of the beginnings of the kingdom, 'because the Siameses are not curious enough to investigate events of ancient times and also because there are no relevant histories which have appeared publicly for posterity'.[66] But despite the care he took in preparing a faithful account, he inserted into his chronicle a Siamese folk story, albeit while being unconvinced about its veracity. He introduced this story with a puzzling excuse: 'Although the following . . . does not appear to be true, I have nevertheless decided to make note of it principally because with the

[62] Justin Stagl, 'Der wohlunterwiesene Passagier: Reisekunst und Gesellschaftsbeschreibung vom 16. bis zum 18. Jahrhundert', in B. I. Krasnobaev *et al.* (eds), *Reisen und Reisebeschreibungen im 18. und 19. Jahrhundert* (Essen, 1987), 353–84.

[63] See Wolfgang Neuber, *Fremde Welt im europäischen Horizont: Zur Topik der deutschen Amerika-Reiseberichte der Frühen Neuzeit* (Berlin, 1991), 225.

[64] Van Vliet, *Description*, 5. See also P. G. Adams, *Travelers and Travel Liars 1660–1800* (Berkeley and Los Angeles, 1962).

[65] Van Vliet, *Short History*, 53–5; the Pāli text of the *Sangitiyavamsa* was compiled in 1789, but is based on a tradition already written down at least as early as the first half of the seventeenth century. See Michael Vickery, 'Review of Jeremias van Vliet: *The Short History of the Kings of Siam*', *Journal of the Siam Society*, 64/2 (1976), 207–36, at 214 and 219.

[66] Van Vliet, *Short History*, 54.

Siamese as with us Evangelism is maintained.'[67] He then relates a curious legend of the envious king of Ramaradt, who tried to kill the Siamese king Ramathibodi II (r. 1491–1529) by using sorcery and 'devilish tricks'. After a number of attacks his efforts turned out to be fruitless due to the Siamese king's stronger supernatural power. Having learned about the greater strength of his counterpart, the king of Ramaradt finally gave in and decided to make peace with King Ramathibodi II.[68]

III

Among Asian cultures it was China that first attracted the attention of an academic European public. In 1585 Juan González Mendoza published an account of China, albeit a work of somewhat doubtful veracity.[69] Chinese history remained unknown; as far as the origin of the Chinese nation was concerned, he concluded by saying 'that there is opinion that the first that did inhabite this countrie, were the neuewes of Noe'.[70] Growing knowledge about the 'Mighty Kingdom' was later received from Matteo Ricci, who continually compiled accurate information on the kingdom. In 1615, the Jesuit Nicolas Trigault published a collection of Ricci's letters, reports, and diaries that contain little historical detail on early China. Yet it was not until 1658, nearly twenty years after van Vliet had written his chronicle, that the Jesuit Martino Martini composed a book on Chinese history based on indigenous sources.[71] With the publication of the succession of Chinese kings, the ground was prepared for the great discussions which soon developed in Europe on the antiquity of Chinese civilization and the relative reliability of Chinese and biblical chronology.

Western scholars commonly supposed that the people of Siam descended from the Chinese, or, at least, assumed that Siam and most neighbouring countries received a greater part of their cultural and scientific knowledge from China. In his *Description of the Kingdom of Siam*, written in 1636, van Vliet strengthened the argument that the Siamese descended from the Chinese by stating that a Chinese prince founded Siam 2000 years ago:

> More than two thousand years ago the country of Siam was an uninhabited wilderness. In a few places there lived some hermits and heathens (who had offered their bodies to the gods) and as we have heard from some reliable persons (yes, even from some old learned men) there was in China at that time an Emperor's son who attempted his father's life and

[67] Van Vliet, *Short History*, 65.
[68] *Ibid.* 65–9.
[69] J. G. Mendoza, *Historia . . . del gran Reyno de la China* (Rome, 1585). Parts of Mendoza's work were based on the *Relación* written by Fr. Martín de Rada in 1575; see Boxer, 'Western historical writing on the Far East', 309.
[70] Mendoza, as quoted in Lach, *Asia in the Making of Europe, Vol. I*, 2, 783.
[71] Martino Martini: *Sinicae Historia decas prima*, (Munich 1658).

to take the imperial crown, in which attempt however he did not succeed. The Emperor intended to have his rebellious son and his followers executed for this crime, but as he suspected that the nobility and the community had taken the side of his son (who was very intelligent and had many remarkable gifts of nature) his Majesty after many supplications was persuaded not to take the life of his son and his followers, provided that they all should leave China and that they should wander as outlaws and never return again.

These exiles tried to populate uninhabited countries and to extend their power. They travelled first through the land of Chiampa, after that Cambodia, from where they sailed with their boats to the Gulf of Siam. They first landed at the cape now called Cuy [Kuiburi], settled down there and built a town and to show their thankfulness to the gods erected a fine temple and many pyramids.[72]

In the eighteenth century, François Valentyn told a similar story in which he states that Siam was founded 2024 ago by a Chinese.[73] Van Vliet had also recorded this story in his chronicle of 1640, together with several other accounts which were current concerning the first king of Siam in ancient times, including the report by Ribadeneyra (as quoted above) claiming that Siam was founded by the Buddha (*Perdeneab*) himself.[74] Van Vliet, who evidently relied on oral sources for the origins of the kingdom, then proceeds by saying that after Buddha died, the kingdom 'went 713 years without a king and the kingdom decayed and nearly reverted to wilderness'.[75] To van Vliet, however, no satisfactory evidence had turned up to prove any of these stories. He therefore considered them 'unnecessary, since some are too fabulous and their veracity can not be determined by argument'.[76] He then relates that a long time later, about 300 years before his day, another son of a Chinese ruler, Chao Ui, arrived in Siam and became the Thao U Thong who founded Ayutthaya.

The notion of Siam as culturally dependent on China was affirmed by Gottfried Wilhelm Leibniz (1646–1716), whose enthusiasm for the Chinese appears in his attempt to create a chain of academies for cultural transmission between China and Europe. When he received a copy of a travel account on Siam by Simon de La Loubère, Louis XIV's envoy to to the country in 1687–8, Leibniz commented on a Siamese calendar discussed in the volume. Writing to the Jesuit missionary Philipp Grimaldi, Leibniz stated that the Siamese had received this almanac from the Chinese. But

[72] Van Vliet, *Description*, 6.

[73] Valentyn, *Oud en Nieuw Oost-Indiën*, 57.

[74] It should be noted, however, that in the Thai chronicles the name of the Buddha was also frequently used to refer to Thai kings; compare van Vliet, *Short History*, 55, note 4.

[75] Van Vliet, *Short History*, 55.

[76] *Ibid.*

in his view Siamese culture was among the gloomy examples of retrogression, and he denied that they were still capable of using it properly:

Lalovera [La Loubère] vir doctrina et judico egregius nuperque Regis Christianissimi [Louis XIV] ad Siamensium Regem Legatus, cujus relatio autoris beneficio ad me pervenit, inde attulit Cyclum quendam Astronomico-Chronologicum illis usitatum, cujus nodos mirabiles felicissime evolvit Cassinus, apparetque inventionem profectam olim a magno quodam viro supra praesentem captum gentis. Tanta rerum vicissitudum est. Nec dubito quin Te favente multo majora nostrae curiositatis alimenta prae-beant Sinensis, Magistri utique et Siamensium, et caeterorum vicinorum. Idem descriptionem Instrumenti Arithmetici Siamensis attulit. Didici nuper simile quiddam habere et Moschos fortasse Sinensibus doctoribus. Prae caeteris autem magni momenti esse judico, populorum situs et linguas exactius nosse, ut genera eorum et origines melius discerni possunt.[77]

[I have just received La Loubère's account as a present. He is a most distinguished and well educated man who recently travelled to Siam as plenipotentiary envoy appointed by the Most Christian King [Louis XIV]. He brought along with him an astronomical-chronological almanac com-monly used in Siam, the strange problems of which were solved extremely well by Cassini. This almanac must have been invented by a great man and goes beyond the present abilities of this people. This is how the times are changing. However, I do not doubt that through them our curiosity about the Chinese will be stimulated even more, because it is undeniable that they were the teachers of the Siamese as well as of all neighbouring countries. Furthermore, La Loubère described a Siamese calculator. I've learned recently, that there is a similar instrument used in Moscow, which might be of Chinese origin too. It is most important, I think, to learn more about the countries and languages of the peoples; this would enable us to distinguish between their origins and relationships.]

In the subsequent history of European reflection on Siam, two arguments were put forward in favour of Siam's exclusion from the rank of civilizations that possess a history worth studying. The first appears partly by implication in Leibniz's remark, namely that Siam possessed a rather stagnant, eventless, and therefore infinitely boring Oriental civilization.

The second argument cited the absence of any reliable sources dealing with Siam's history before the coming of the Portuguese, in other words, that their records were 'fabulous'.

---

[77] Leibniz, *Sämtliche Schriften und Briefe*, ed. by the Deutsche Akademie der Wissenschaften, erste Reihe (Berlin, 1964), 617–22, at 620.

Evidence of the latter view appears in La Loubère's account, which became one of the most famous seventeenth-century descriptions of the country, serving as a literary model for the writing of travel literature in Europe.[78] In fact, he stayed in Siam for only a short period of three months. At that time, the Thai King Narai (r. 1656–88) was much interested in other cultures, notably the French, and welcomed the missionaries and ambassadors so courteously that Louis XIV and the French Jesuits nurtured real hopes of converting the king to the Catholic faith. Yet the events that followed La Loubère's embassy led to anti-French and anti-Catholic feeling in Siam. After Narai fell seriously ill and died in 1688, Phetracha, who was one of the two heads of the Elephant department (Krom Chang), captured the Siamese throne, had the missionaries arrested, and forced the French garrisons to withdraw from Siam.

La Loubère himself was most sceptical as to the possibility of obtaining accurate knowledge on the Siamese's ancient history and chronology. Unlike many of his contemporaries, Leibniz among them, he remained unconvinced about the antiquity and superiority of Chinese culture. He was also unusual in that he did not share the views of many of the Jesuits who escorted him on his mission to Siam, and commented enthusiastically on the Siamese people and the personal abilities of their king.[79] But La Loubère doubted the reliability of stories he heard about the history of the Siamese nation:

> The *Siamese* History is full of fables. The books thereof are very scarce, by reason the *Siameses* have not the use of Printing; for upon other Accounts I doubt of the record, that they affect to conceal their History, seeing that the *Chineses*, whom in many things they imitate, are not so jealous of theirs. However that matter is, notwithstanding this pretended Jealousy of the *Siameses*, they who have attain'd to read anything of the History of *Siam*, assert that it ascends not very high with any character of truth.[80]

He assumed that their chronology, which claims that the foundation of their kingdom dates back to the Buddha's death, was arbitrary:

> . . . I am persuaded, that their most ancient *Epocha*, from which in this year 1689, they compute 2233 Years, has not been remarkable at *Siam* for any thing worthy of Memory, and that it proves not that the Kingdom of *Siam* is of that Antiquity. It is purely Astronomical, and serves as a Foundation to another way of calculating the places of the Planets. . . .[81]

[78] Simon de La Loubère, *Du royaume de Siam* (Paris, 1691). Quotations are taken from the English edition: *A New Historical Relation of the Kingdom of Siam* (London, 1693); see Dirk van der Cruysse, *Louis XIV et le Siam* (Paris, 1991).

[79] This is particularly true of the Jesuit diplomat and missionary Guy Tachard, who also published two accounts of Siam in 1688 and 1689.

[80] La Loubère, *A New Historical Relation*, 8.

[81] *Ibid.* 64.

To him, it is not clear whether the Siamese descended from the original inhabitants or from invading people who settled there over time. He also reflected on the possibility that the Siamese relate to the Sinic world because monosyllabic Siamese resembles the Chinese language:

> As for what concerns the Origine of the *Siameses*, it would be difficult to judge whether they are only a single People, directly descended from the first Men that inhabited the Countrey of *Siam*, or whether in process of time some other Nation has not also setled there, notwithstanding the first Inhabitants.
>
> The principal Reason of this Doubt proceeds from the *Siameses* understanding two languages, *viz.* the Vulgar, which is a simple Tongue, consisting almost wholly of Monosyllables, without Conjugation or Declension; and another Language which I have already spoken of, which to them is a dead Tongue, known only by the Learned, which is called the *Balie* Tongue [Pāli], and which is enricht with the inflexions of words, like the Languages we have in Europe.[82]

After all these speculations La Loubère concludes that 'it is certain that the *Siamese* blood is much mixed with foreign'.[83] To him, Siam has not achieved noteworthy spiritual or material progress over the past centuries, passing through one dynastic cycle after the next:

> Always the same manners amongst them, always the same Laws, the same Religion, the same Worship; as may be judged by comparing what the Ancient have writ concerning the *Indians*, with what we do now see.[84]

After the 1688 succession crisis and the usurpation of King Phetracha, Siam shifted from close contacts with the West back to a more traditional way of dealing with foreign nations, especially the Europeans.[85] Although this does not necessarily indicate a policy of self-imposed isolation comparable to the Tokugawa seclusion policy in Japan, a comparatively small number of Europeans remained in Ayutthaya, and only a few Western accounts of Siam were written until the reign of King Mongkut (Rama IV; r. 1851–68). Thus, contemporary Western accounts of Siam were scarce in the eighteenth century, and Siam played only a peripheral role in the European discourse on politics, society, and history. From time to time, earlier descriptions of the

---

[82] *Ibid.* 9.
[83] *Ibid.* 10.
[84] *Ibid.* 102.
[85] Compare Dhiravat Na Pombejra, 'Ayutthaya at the end of the seventeenth century: was there a shift to isolation?', in Anthony Reid (ed.), *Southeast Asia in the Early Modern Era: Trade, Power, and Belief* (Ithaca and London, 1993), 250–72.

country were used allegorically in order to illustrate philosophical interpretations of the history of humankind.

In 1771, the French historian François-Henri Turpin published in Paris a two-volume *Histoire Civile et naturelle du Royaume de Siam*. Unlike van Vliet's *Short History*, Turpin's *Histoire* was exclusively based on European accounts. In the book, he rejected as unnecessary all speculation on the beginnings of the kingdom; the question of the Siamese past before the arrival of the Europeans was left unanswered or even unasked:

> Je n'entreprendrai point de déchirer le voile qui couvre le berceau de cet Empire. Ce peuple n'a jamais connu l'art de l'Imprimerie, qui seul peut consacrer les vertus & les foiblesses de ceux qui président aux destinées publiques. Ses monumens historiques ne sont fondés que sur des fables grossieres & des traditions accréditées par l'imposture des Prêtres habiles à substituer le merveilleux à la vérité simple & nue. Les Siamois ne nous sont connus que depuis la découverte des Indes par les Portugais, & c'est à cette époque que nous devons fixer leur histoire.[86]

---

[86] François-Henri Turpin, *Histoire Civile et naturelle du Royaume de Siam, et des Révolutions qui lui ont bouleversé cet Empire jusqu'en 1770* (2 vols, Paris, 1771), II, 4.

5

The Spanish contribution to the ethnology of Asia in the sixteenth and seventeenth centuries

JOAN-PAU RUBIÉS

In his famous account of the first circumnavigation of the world led by Magellan, which inaugurated Castilian claims to the Spice Islands, Antonio Pigafetta described in minute detail the clove and nutmeg trees for his European audience. He also asserted, amongst many details relating to the physical aspects, customs, and even languages of the native inhabitants of the Spice Islands, that the 'gentiles' of Gilolo (modern Halmahera) worship each day 'the first thing they see in the morning when they go out of their houses', an observation meant to describe a kind of primitive 'natural' religion.[1] To the modern reader Pigafetta's statement, obviously superficial and misleading, is a characteristic example of how Europeans in these early encounters projected their own religious prejudices onto native cultural realities. In other words, they were willing to accept fantastic hearsay (even if often locally generated) without critical scrutiny, content to confirm when possible, rather than challenge, European mythologies. The statement can therefore be read alongside reported stories of an island inhabited only by women who 'get pregnant from the wind', and the like.[2] However, Pigafetta's careful descriptions of the highly valued clove and nutmeg plants as personally observed, and his accurate compilations of native vocabularies (Malay, Bisayan, Guarani, and Patagonian), attest to something very different too, namely the empirical bent of many European narratives. In this respect, Pigafetta's account can also stand as a characteristic example of Renaissance 'scientific curiosity'.

This apparent contradiction within Pigafetta's narrative invites reflection on the relation between prejudices and curiosity in the early literature of encounter, much of which was generated within the Spanish Pacific opened

[1] 'Li gentili non teneno tante donne ne viveno con tante superstitioni [as the Moors], ma adorano la prima cosa che vedeno la matina quando escono fora de casa, per tuto quel giorno'. Antonio Pigafetta, *La mia longa e pericolosa navigatione*, ed. L. Giovannini (Milan, 1989), 170.
[2] *Ibid.* 209. Here, as when reporting similar stories, Pigafetta specifies that his source was an 'old pilot' from 'Maluco' (the Moluccas), probably Malay-speaking. This is consistent with similar stories told by Marco Polo when travelling the same seas over 200 years earlier – he too was reporting local sailors' tales.

up by Magellan's expedition. The papal bulls and further bilateral treaties which, from Tordesillas in 1494 to Zaragoza in 1529, divided the world between the two Iberian monarchies for the purposes of exploration, trade, evangelization, and conquest awarded most of Asia to the Portuguese, and it is easy to forget not only the eventual colonization of the Philippines for the Crown of Castile in the 1560s on the back of the precedent established by Magellan a few decades earlier, but also the myriad of additional contacts in the Pacific islands, China, Japan, and Southeast Asia generated by that seemingly isolated colony. In this article I seek to assess the relative importance and peculiar conditions of the early Spanish historiography of Asia, and in particular its ethnographic and ethnological value. This, however, can only be done properly by acknowledging the problem of defining the scientific value of the early modern genres of travel writing and colonial historiography. As the example of Pigafetta testifies, the marvels reported by European travellers were not usually self-conscious fictions, but rather evidence by observation or hearsay of the exceptional and the exemplary in the world. Whilst Pigafetta's interest in the marvellous – as his fascination with sexual matters – can be explained in concrete terms as an expression of the popular humanism which permeated the aristocratic and patrician culture of the first decades of the sixteenth century (he was after all no more than a young adventurer seeking to entertain his audiences by describing heroic navigations and the world's natural diversities), it is also symptomatic of a wider issue, namely the extent to which humanist culture contributed to a scientific ideal within early descriptions of non-European societies.[3]

In effect, the literature of colonial encounter was mostly represented by a descriptive, practical genre such as the 'relation', and was only rarely formulated as an erudite, academic discourse. When the latter emerged, the concerns which dominated the analysis of cultural diversity were either theological or inscribed within a humanist historical discourse. And yet – I would like to argue – in the space of cultural tension between the ethnographic description written for practical aims and the ideologically more complex works by religious and humanist historians and cosmographers there grew concerns, theories, and methods which constituted the seeds for an ethnological science.[4] Whilst early modern assumptions about biblical history and chronology, and about Aristotelian natural philosophy were widely rejected by modern authors, the growing early modern concerns with empiricism, classification, comparison, and logical coherence can be seen as leading to modern methods and assumptions. In other words, the scientific aspect should be seen as central to the literature of encounter, but only as defined with reference to contemporary assumptions about what 'science'

[3] Notwithstanding a veneer of classical erudition, Pigafetta was an adventurer from the impoverished nobility seeking to sell his tale. He was not, as some modern commentators would have it, a humanist writer.

[4] For a detailed elaboration of this argument, see my *Travel and Ethnology in the Renaissance. South India through European Eyes 1250–1625* (Cambridge, 2000).

was, and through a careful classification of narrative sources according to various sub-genres.

Any assessment of the Spanish contribution to the ethnography and ethnology of Asia must consider the strength and constraints of Counter-Reformation culture. It was perfectly possible and legitimate to develop a rational analysis of observed phenomena, given that the distinction between a natural order governed by divine reason and the supernatural was fully developed within orthodox theology, especially after the Council of Trent made Thomas Aquinas its key 'modern' authority. The problem was less the legitimacy of empirical enquiry than institutional support for, and control of, discourse. Who wrote, and for whom, and what was allowed to be published conditioned the scientific horizons and ideological assumptions of much of what was produced. Royal, ecclesiastical, and aristocratic patronage were crucial. This can be illustrated by considering the various Spanish genres and sources about Asia, which, inevitably, closely followed the models for Spanish America and were not very different from those which operated in Portuguese Asia. Generally, authors can be divided between lay and religious: the former were usually participants in the colonial system of conquest, trade, and administration, the latter members of the missionary orders. Only rarely was the observer, lay or religious, operating in an independent capacity. There was room for disagreement on issues of interpretation because there was institutional support for such disagreement – with much controversy between lay and religious, or amongst the religious orders – but the debate was always conducted within the ideological assumptions of the Catholic monarchy and its peculiar form of religious–colonial imperialism.

In the following pages I seek to identify a number of conditions pertaining to sixteenth- and seventeenth-century Spanish historiography of Asia which determine the significance and value of a remarkably rich body of ethnographic sources. These conditions include the peculiar, highly peripheral colonial context which produced this literature; the roles of lay and religious institutions in the cultural system of the Catholic monarchy; the distinct historiographical genres and ideological agendas these institutions supported; the alternative, often opposing traditions represented by various missionary orders; the theological, humanistic, and scientific assumptions of the system of learning of the Counter-Reformation; and the pervasive tension between different national identities within the Spanish system of power, especially during the union of crowns with Portugal, which invites a reconsideration not only of what constituted 'science', but also what constituted 'national identity', in that context.

The Philippines, for obvious reasons, were the main focus of Spanish writing on Asia, and the principal reason why Spanish writing on Asian lands and peoples forms a significant and in some cases indispensable body of literature. The colony established in Manila in 1571, indirectly connected to Spain through Mexico, never attracted many Spaniards – around 2000 soldiers, sailors, merchants, priests, and bureaucrats by 1600 (there were around 600 households within the city, but the number of people fluctuated a great deal due to high mortality rates and the transient nature of many colonists). However, the settlement proved surprisingly stable, despite ferocious Dutch and English attacks throughout the seventeenth century. It ruled over a very substantial territory (including a few smaller Spanish towns) and a large number of superficially Hispanicized natives – about half a million. It soon became the most extensive and heavily populated country in the East under direct European rule, surpassing Portuguese colonies like Goa, Malacca (Melaka), and Macao, which never involved the annexation of large territories.[5] However, the archipelago's importance was also strategic, since it could be used as a platform from which China, Japan, the Moluccas, and other parts of Southeast Asia could be reached. Whilst access to the Spice Islands motivated the earliest Spanish expeditions, it was the Chinese commercial connection that rapidly became the key to Manila's economy, and Chinese settlers soon outnumbered the Spanish by about ten to one. Spanish interest and, occasionally, intervention in all those different parts of East Asia meant that Spanish writing on Asian peoples went far beyond the conquered Philippines.

What is perhaps more striking in the body of ethnographic literature generated by this colony is the overwhelming predominance of religious writers.[6] In the case of the Philippines, for example, there are many separate histories of the missions produced by the different orders, compared with one single major account of the islands by a layman, Antonio de Morga's famous *Sucesos de las Islas Filipinas* (Mexico, 1609).[7] Although the 'relations' of particular expeditions written by conquerors and ambassadors could be very informative – for example, Miguel de Loarca's account of the 1575–6 Spanish embassy to China, and Rodrigo de Vivero's description of his improvised negotiations in Japan in 1609–10 – these were few and far between, and

---

[5] For the Spanish colonization of the Philippines, see J. L. Phelan, *The Hispanization of the Philippines: Spanish Aims and Filipino Responses 1565–1700* (Madison, 1959); N. Cushner, *Spain in the Philippines. From Conquest to Revolution* (Manila, 1971). Still important is the work of the Jesuit Pablo Pastells, including his *Historia General de las Filipinas* (Barcelona, 1927), as well as *Catálogo de documentos relativos a las islas Filipinas* (9 vols, Barcelona, 1925–34). In English, many of the key sources were collected and translated by E. Blair and J. Robertson (eds), *The Philippine Islands 1493–1898* (55 vols, Cleveland, 1903–9). Before 1700 no part of Asia was colonized by Europeans in the same degree. In the seventeenth century the Portuguese embarked on the conquest of Ceylon, but before they could make much headway they lost it to the Dutch in 1650s, who were equally unsuccessful in subduing the independent kingdom of Kandy. The Dutch only conquered large parts of Java after the 1670s, and did not implement a policy of religious and cultural transformation comparable to that accomplished by the Spanish in the Northern and Central Philippines.

[6] For a brief survey, see C. R. Boxer, 'Some aspects of Spanish historical writing on the Philippines', in D. G. E. Hall (ed.), *Historians of South East Asia* (London, 1961), 200–12.

[7] I have used the excellent edition by W. E. Retana: A. Morga, *Sucesos de las Islas Filipinas* (Madrid, 1909), with a full documentary apparatus. There is a good English translation by J. S. Cummins: *Sucesos de las Islas Filipinas* (Cambridge, 1972), with a valuable introduction.

remarkably scarce for the Philippines.[8] In fact, crown officials often relied on religious writers for specialized knowledge, so that, for example, in 1589 the Governor Santiago de Vera requested an account of the system of government and customary law of the Tagalos, the dominant native group in central Luzon, from the Franciscan Juan de Plasencia, the rules of which were soon integrated by the *Audiencia* into the Spanish system of local justice for natives. Plasencia's observations were also consulted by Morga – himself a leading member of the *Audiencia* at the turn of the seventeenth century – in his own synthetic account, although it is clear that Morga did not borrow textually from the Franciscan.[9] Morga, like many of the governors and lawyers who staffed the Spanish administration, in reality had limited direct knowledge of native life outside Manila. Manila alone, with its stone architecture, felt something like a Spanish city, the debilitating climate notwithstanding. The crown itself sought to limit the contacts between Spaniards and Filipino Indians, hoping to avoid the patterns of brutal exploitation which had marred the conquest and evangelization of America. It was those missionaries living amongst the islanders in rural areas, learning their languages and presiding over their communal lives, who generated a specialized ethnography which went beyond the superficial observations of occasional visitors.

Beyond the issue of different kinds of experience, there is also a question of writing: in effect, the conditions in which a layman would feel prompted to write his experiences were more limited, and often involved a justification for personal services (this includes Vivero's relation and Morga's work). Here a comparison with Portuguese India seems apt. Although in the long run the Jesuit missionaries became the leading analysts of many Asian societies, and the only ones to research native religious (and thus literary) traditions in some depth, during the first decades of contact lay writers such as Duarte Barbosa or Tomé Pires had taken the lead in producing accounts of the customs and political systems of those Asian societies they met, material which was then incorporated by historians of Portuguese exploits such as Fernão Lopes de Castanheda and João de Barros.

The exceptional work of Morga notwithstanding, there is no Spanish equivalent to the ambitious geographical and ethnographic compilations of

---

[8] For Vivero, a high-ranking Mexican criollo and short-lived Governor in the Philippines, see Juan Gil, *Hidalgos y Samurais. España y Japón en los siglos XVI y XVII* (Madrid, 1990), 140–207. The old encomendero Loarca, whose account, surprisingly, remains unpublished, is rather exceptional in that he also wrote about the Filipino Indians. None of these writings by lay ambassadors (and spies) was published in the Habsburg period, unlike much of what the missionaries wrote – for example, the account by Martín de Rada, Loarca's companion, was incorporated in the histories and cosmographies by Juan González de Mendoza and by Jerónimo Román before the end of the sixteenth century.

[9] See Retana, *Sucesos*, 171*, and 471–5 for a transcription. The suggestion by Retana (taken up by Phelan, *Hispanization*, 179; Boxer, 'Some aspects', 202; and Cummins, *Sucesos*, 27) that Morga merely followed Plasencia is based on the opinion of another Franciscan missionary, Juan Francisco de San Antonio (1735). A close textual comparison makes it clear that Morga constructed his own independent discourse but may well have used Plasencia's information.

those petty colonial officials in Portuguese Asia. By contrast, the predominance of the religious is apparent from the beginning: the Augustinian Urdaneta accompanied the conqueror Legazpi in 1564, acting as cosmographer as well as missionary, discovering the return route across the Pacific, and stamping the future evangelization of the Philippines with an overwhelming Augustinian presence which the authorities later came to regret; other orders, especially the Jesuits, incorporated there in 1581, proved to be much more disciplined.

During the first official contacts with China in the mid-1570s, missionaries such as Martín de Rada – one of the better educated Augustinians – seemed more prominent than lay representatives such as Loarca, and after the new Governor Francisco Sande (1575–80), totally mismanaging diplomatic affairs, opted for a more aggressive approach, the Jesuit Alonso Sánchez emerged as the key proponent of the conquest of China at the court, a project which Philip II wisely dismissed. Similarly, in Japan it was the Franciscans, breaking from Manila the Macanese Portuguese-Jesuit missionary monopoly, who drew the Spanish authorities towards various (eventually frustrated) attempts to establish permanent commercial relations. Even in Cambodia the fantasies of permanent conquest entertained by Portuguese and Spanish mercenary adventurers, and occasionally supported by the governors of the Philippines, found their most eloquent defence in the writings of missionaries such as the Dominicans Diego Aduarte and Gabriel de San Antonio, again giving religious plausibility at the court of a pious monarch to far-fetched schemes which, when actually implemented by Manila, led to little more than half-hearted plundering expeditions, confused negotiations, and shipwrecks.[10] Finally, the exploration of the South Pacific from Peru in search of the *Terra Australis*, with the short-lived attempt to settle a colony, a 'New Jerusalem', in the New Hebrides (Vanuatu), was the scheme of an exalted missionary-navigator, Pedro Fernández de Quirós, a Portuguese pilot working with Franciscan friars who got the ear of Philip III – to the king's later regret, since the expedition in 1605–6, like those which had preceded it, accomplished nothing.[11]

---

[10] Gabriel de San Antonio had been sent in 1598 from Manila via Goa to the court in Spain to represent the affairs of Japan, the Solomon Islands, and Cambodia. His description of Cambodia, in his *Breve relación de los sucesos del reyno de Camboxa* (Valladolid, 1604), was largely based on hearsay, especially from the oral account of the Dominican Diego Aduarte, a direct participant. This, combined with the desire to produce an extreme thesis for further intervention, explains why it is often unreliable. Cristóbal Jacque de los Ríos and Pedro Sevil, veterans of Gallinato's expedition, had reached the court of Philip III and had already lobbied, unsuccessfully, for further intervention in Cambodia.

[11] Quirós followed the model of another layman taken by a religious passion, Álvaro de Mendaña, whose pilot he had been in the ill-fated 1595–6 expedition which failed to settle the Solomon islands (first discovered by Mendaña in 1568). There is a striking parallel in the way both expeditions were caught between exalted idealism and insuperable practical problems. For a lucid account in English, see O. H. K. Spate, *The Spanish Lake* (London, 1979). The material for Quirós's expedition was collected and analysed by Justo Zaragoza, *Historia del descubrimiento de las regiones austriales* (3 vols, Madrid, 1876–82), and re-examined by C. Kelly, *La Austrialia del Espíritu Santo* (2 vols, Cambridge, 1966). For an edition of the mass of futile memorials produced by Quirós on his return to Spain, see *Memoriales de las Indias Australes*, ed. O. Pinochet (Madrid, 1990).

This exaggerated religious influence in leading imperial expansion and shaping its writing is in some ways different from the American experience, where men such as Cortés narrated their own conquests, and lay historians such as Gonzalo Fernández de Oviedo took the lead in applying humanistic rhetoric to the description of the New World. It can be explained in part by considering the later chronology of Pacific expansion. By the time the Spanish conquered the Philippines, the Counter-Reformation was in full sway, and the whole educational emphasis and imperial ethos of the Catholic monarchy had become clericalized. But it would be an exaggeration to say that there was no room for a lay cosmographical discourse in the Spain of Philip II and his successors, where Juan López de Velasco, working for the Council of the Indies, systematically compiled materials for an ambitious geographical project, and the court writer Antonio de Herrera published the major historical synthesis about 'Castilian' overseas expansion. In fact, the predominance of religious discourse in Spanish Asia also had to do with the peculiar position of the Philippines at the periphery of the empire, a distant colony of a more important colony (as it was initially an offshoot of New Spain), in which the Spanish court had to take account of the different views of Lisbon, Macao, Seville, and Mexico before making any decision. The supply of American silver to Spain, and all the concomitant business surrounding it, was infinitely more important than exchanging some of that silver for Chinese silk, which was the basis for the economy of Spanish Manila. Other schemes for Asian intervention, involving either new discoveries, complicated alliances, or far-fetched conquests, were even more problematic. As a result, policies were often slow and vacillating.

The two expeditions to Cambodia are a case in point.[12] The Portuguese adventurer Diogo Veloso was active at the court of King Satha from the early 1580s and managed to attract the support of Dominican missionaries from Malacca. After 1593 Veloso was joined by some Spanish soldiers, including notably one Blas Ruiz, escapees from slavery in Champa (Southern Vietnam). The king of Cambodia patronized these Europeans because he sought commercial contacts with Malacca and military assistance against the Siamese, who eventually invaded the country. There was, at that dramatic point, direct support from the interim young governor of the Philippines, Luis Dasmariñas, who in 1596 sent a small expedition under Juan Juárez Gallinato and some Dominicans to establish a Spanish protectorate, only to find a new dynasty in power. Gallinato did not trust the high-handed approach of Veloso and Ruiz (actively supported by the Dominicans Jiménez and Aduarte), which led to an attack on Chinese traders and the murder of the new king, presumably in order to restore the old dynasty under Spanish influence; he thus abandoned the project. A second expedition in 1598 – a

---

[12] For a discussion of these expeditions, see L. P. Briggs, 'Spanish interventions in Cambodia, 1593–1603', *T'oung-Pao*, 39 (1949), 132–60; B. Groslier and C. Boxer, *Angkor et la Cambodge au XVIe siècle, d'après les sources portugaises et espagnoles* (Paris, 1958); C. R. Boxer, 'Portuguese and Spanish projects for the conquest of South-East Asia, 1580–1600', *Journal of Asian History*, 3 (1969), 118–36.

virtually private enterprise of former governor Dasmariñas, still under strong Dominican influence – was shipwrecked in China, whilst Veloso and Ruiz, who had continued to plot in Cambodia and helped a new king to power, ended up being killed by a rival 'Malay' faction; the Spanish were, quite reasonably, seen as a threat. Morga, who had been close to these events and discussed them in detail, was not alone in thinking that the priority of the Castilians should be to consolidate the Philippines and its trade, and perhaps to secure the Moluccas, rather than expend valuable men in far-fetched conquests. In this sense his views were contrary to those expressed by the Dominicans Diego Aduarte and Gabriel de San Antonio.[13]

The golden age of Spanish intervention in Asia coincides with the union of the Portuguese and other Spanish crowns between 1580 and 1640. The details of the interaction between the Portuguese and the Castilians in the East are remarkably complicated and would require – and are still awaiting – monographic treatment. Portuguese hostility was logical, since all Castilian claims in the East were based on opportunistic miscalculations of the demarcation lines agreed in 1494 and confirmed in 1529. Goa and Malacca could do nothing to stop the Spanish from settling the Philippines, but in those spheres where the Portuguese were active – including China, Japan, Cambodia, and the Moluccas – they resisted fiercely, and often came to blows. The Jesuits operating under Portuguese religious patronage in Japan and China similarly resisted any missionaries coming from Manila, and this easily fed into their traditional rivalry with Dominicans and Franciscans, who were strangely eager not only to fish for souls in the more civilized nations of the East, but also to find fault with Jesuit missionary methods; the Spanish Jesuits in the Philippines, with a few exceptions, wisely tried to stay away from a conflict which divided their loyalties.

The clashes that ensued had an enormously destructive impact on the missions. And yet, the union of crowns complicated matters further. The Portuguese agreed to share a king but not an imperial system, which meant that there was little co-operation and a great deal of simmering hostility. The crown struggled to keep a balance. This uneasy settlement was put under additional pressure when the Dutch and English turned up in the seventeenth century. The Portuguese soon discovered that quite often they needed Spanish help, for example to relieve Malacca from a siege, to defend the Moluccas, or to revive the fortunes of Macao after the closure of Japan. However, even when confronted with a common enemy, the tensions between the two nations persisted, and the combination of Castilian arrogance and Portuguese pettiness contributed to derail many efforts to reverse the decline of the Catholic empires in the East.

---

[13] Morga's sceptical views on expeditions to Vietnam, Cambodia, or Siam are documented by Retana (for example, *Sucesos*, 242). Although San Antonio had been sent to Spain by Governor Francisco Tello and by Morga on the return of Gallinato's expedition, his imperialist views were closer to those of the governor. Morga's circumspect published account of the affair of Cambodia is more trustworthy than San Antonio's, which relied heavily on Aduarte's militant account.

In sum, the whole Spanish experience in Asia, despite the many possibilities for profit and expansion that often suggested themselves, was never a straightforward economic, or even strategic, proposition: rather, it was an expensive enterprise caught in a complex diplomatic tangle between, on the one hand, the sensibilities of the Portuguese and the Jesuits – allies who considered Asia their exclusive terrain and who, after 1580, did not feel reassured by the incorporation of Portugal into the realms of Philip II – and on the other hand, the far from harmonious or consistent perceptions of the Spanish themselves. After 1600, the direct threat from the Dutch (heretics and rebels in Spanish eyes) and from other rival European powers only made things more dramatic. In this context, it was religious idealism alone which kept the problematic Asian empire of Castile–New Spain, and in particular the Spanish Philippines, alive. The millions of souls presumably saved there compensated for the enormous costs of the enterprise, and gave direction to imperial diplomacy when other considerations faltered. It is therefore not surprising that those missionaries who gave the Spanish empire its soul also gave it the eyes with which to perceive Asia. Unfortunately, whilst religion could inspire extraordinary efforts, it often created political obligations where prudence would have indicated a more cautious course.

The four dominant religious orders in the Philippines – the Augustinians, Franciscans (discalced), Jesuits, and Dominicans – produced their own histories of the missions, often combining a narrative of spiritual affairs with geographic and ethnographic information. Some of these accounts dealt specifically with the Philippines or one of its parts. Others were more general syntheses, often written in Spain on the basis of a wide range of primary material. The more general works were also more likely to reflect the split between the areas of Portuguese control, dominated by the Jesuits, and the attempts by the mendicant orders to penetrate them. The Franciscan Marcello de Ribadeneyra, for example, in his *Historia de las Islas del Archipiélago Filipino y Reinos de la Gran China, Tartaria, Cochinchina, Malaca, Sian, Camboxa y Jappón* (Barcelona, 1601; revised edition in 1613) bitterly expressed the trauma of his order's (and his own personal) fiasco in Japan in 1595–7, where so many of his colleagues were executed. However, he also dealt with areas such as the Philippines, China, Siam (Thailand), and Cochinchina (Vietnam), where the discalced Franciscans were active. His thesis, implicitly polemical against the Jesuits, was that the Franciscans killed in Japan had been genuine martyrs, that the Portuguese and the Castilians could all get along in Asia as Spaniards sharing identical religious aims, and that the Jesuits should welcome the Franciscans in Japan and China for their unique evangelical virtue of poverty rather than oppose their presence on the grounds that they were making a mess of a prosperous mission. However, besides the usual hagiographic material devoted to his own order, Ribadeneyra also offered informed, if rather succinct, descriptions of Japan,

Siam, and Cochinchina, complementing his own observations with written relations. (Unfortunately he was on rather unsafe ground when describing China according to the yet unpublished 'relation' by Fernão Mendes Pinto, copying uncritically his fictionalized accounts of encounters with Portuguese captives and Tartar kings.[14]) For its ambition to integrate ethnographic surveys into a history of his order's missions, Ribadeneyra's work can be usefully compared in tone and depth of coverage with Luis de Guzmán's impressive overview and apology for the Jesuit missions all over Asia published in the same year, *Historia de las missiones que han hecho los padres de la Compañía de Jesús . . . en la India Oriental y en los reynos de China y Japón* (Alcalá, 1601), which sought to transcend nationalist sentiment and defend the Society's success under Portuguese patronage (he said more about Japan than the Philippines).[15]

Within the same genre, some decades later the Dominican Diego Aduarte – the same individual who as a young man had been a protagonist in the armed expeditions in Cambodia – composed his *Historia de la Provincia del Sancto Rosario*, which dealt with the whole range of Dominican activities in East Asia from the Philippines to China, Japan, Cambodia, the Moluccas and even some Pacific islands. When posthumously published in Manila in 1640, this voluminous work created no little controversy, since it attacked in public for the first time the Jesuit missionary method of accommodation in China. The book in fact can be regarded as a milestone in the history of the rites controversy, which would explode after 1640. However, unlike Guzmán and Ribadeneyra, Aduarte failed to describe Asian countries and peoples in any detail, concentrating instead on the hagiographic narrative.[16]

---

[14] From an ethnographic perspective the more interesting parts of Ribadeneyra's *Historia* are book 2, dealing with China (chs 8–15), Cochinchina (chs 16 and 18), and Siam (chs 20–25), and book 4 for Japan (chs 1 and 15–18). There is also some treatment of the Franciscan missions in Luzon and the Camarines in book 1 (chs 9, 10, and 12), but the description of Tagalog customs and religion is relatively succinct. For the almost verbatim use of Mendes Pinto (but without acknowledging his name) compare book 2, chs 8 and 14, with Pinto, *Peregrinaçam* (Lisbon, 1614), chs 91, 116, 121 and 127.

[15] Guzmán's work was continued in a biannual series for the years 1600–9 by the Portuguese Fernão Guerreiro, who produced five volumes of his *Relaçam* (Lisbon, 1603–11). The first and fifth volumes were also published in Castilian. Another armchair synthesis was the *Historia General de la India Oriental* by the Benedictine Antonio de San Román y Rivadeneyra (Valladolid, 1603), based on an extensive selection of Portuguese material on Asia. Inspired by Barros, this was, however, a book almost exclusively concerned with providing a historical narrative of the Portuguese discoveries and conquests up to 1557, with a limited focus on the geography and ethnology of Asia (there were some descriptive chapters for China, Japan, Brazil, and the Moluccas, but only the material for China was substantial). In a different genre, and far more interesting as a formulation of a comparative analysis of social and political systems, is the wide-ranging cosmographical work by the Augustinian Jerónimo Román, *Repúblicas del mundo* (1575; 2nd expanded edn 1595), which, although originally biased towards biblical and classical 'gentile' sources also incorporated material in 1595 on the civilizations of the New World (from Las Casas) and China (from Rada).

[16] The *Historia de la Provincia del Sancto Rosario de la orden de predicadores en Philippinas, Japón y China* (Manila, 1640) was completed by the provincial Domingo González and published in the Dominican College of Saint Thomas with the approval (dated 1638) of Augustinian and Franciscan censors. However critical of the Jesuits, Aduarte was in his old age a resident bishop and more moderate than some of the younger members of his order, such as Diego Collado (who sought to extend Dominican activities in Japan and China despite the political complications) and Juan Bautista de Morales (who in 1640 launched the systematic attack on the Jesuits in Rome).

Without any doubt the most scientifically significant works – those which best met the contemporary aim of providing an empirically informed, analytically organized, and speculatively rationalized discourse – were based on decades of sustained contact with the natives of Luzon and the Bisayan islands. Thus, the Augustinian Gaspar de San Agustín published in 1698 the first volume of his retrospective *Conquista de las Islas Filipinas*, incorporating material from the sixteenth century to 1614 (a second volume, which remained in manuscript, carried the story through to his own times). The Franciscan Letona, similarly, produced a *Descripción de las islas Filippinas* (La Puebla de Mexico, 1662). But of all the ethnographic works written in the Philippines in the seventeenth century, the most impressive are the series of histories written by Jesuits. Even though the they had no monopoly on humanistic education, it is nevertheless interesting to note that they lived up to their reputation as the most modern and intellectually sophisticated Counter-Reformation order, and this despite having found themselves relegated to some of the more difficult islands. Beginning with Pedro Chirino's *Relación de las islas Filipinas* (Rome, 1604), which to a large extent consisted of an advance on his more elaborate *Historia de la Provincia de Filipinas de la Compañía de Jesús* (covering the period 1581–1606, but completed *c.* 1610), the tradition was maintained by the Catalan Francisco Colín, who edited Chirino's manuscript and brought the story up to 1632, in *Labor Evangélica de la Compañía de Jesús* (Madrid, 1663). Chirino and Colín were well grounded in classical learning, and the latter participated directly in the seventeenth-century's antiquarian project of a comparative history of ancient and gentile religions.[17]

It is interesting to note that this humanistic education did not always imply political prudence or a less aggressive imperialism: Chirino could combine perfectly an enormous sympathy for the figure of Alonso Sánchez, the great promoter of the conquest of China in the 1580s, with the intellectual influence of José de Acosta, one of the key critics of Sánchez within the order.[18] It was not their politics, but their rigorous training, based on institutional discipline and a careful choice of personnel, which made the Jesuits stand out. One might argue that Chirino's erudition was not matched by critical judgement or an orderly method of exposition – he is surprisingly credulous about 'marvellous' phenomena, and his random distribution of descriptive material is unfortunate. However, this cannot be said of the scholarly edition by Colín, nor of those works by Francisco Combés on Mindanao (published

[17] Colín's *India sacra* (Madrid, 1666), which sought to use new information about Asia to elucidate passages of the Old Testament, was published posthumously. For a wider European perspective on the birth of the history of religion in the seventeenth century, see the articles collected in *Archiv für religionsgeschichte*, 3 (2001).

[18] In his *Historia*, Chirino offers a very peculiar (or perhaps 'sanitized') version of the activities of Sánchez, highly encomiastic but hiding the main point about his commitment to the idea of the conquest of China, and the opposition which this generated. See the recent Catalan edition of Chirino's Castilian manuscript, *Història de la província de Filipines de la Companyia de Jesús 1581–1606*, ed. J. Górriz (Barcelona, 2000).

in 1667) and by Francisco Alzina on the Bisayan islands and its people (completed in 1668, but not published), both extremely impressive examples of natural, ethnographic and linguistic research.

Besides this body of literature centered on the Philippines, there were also important Spanish missionary contributions to knowledge of other parts of Asia, especially China and Japan. In fact, it was the literature on China which made the greatest impact through the influential synthesis of the Augustinian Juan González de Mendoza, *Historia de las cosas más notables, ritos y costumbres del gran reyno de la China* (Rome, 1585), soon translated into various European languages. Although at some point Mendoza had been appointed ambassador to China, in reality he never went beyond Mexico, and all his knowledge was based on the reports of other missionary writers. However, he quickly superseded another armchair synthesis, Bernardino de Escalante's *Discurso de la navegación que los Portuguese hacen a los reynos y provincias del Oriente, y de la noticia que se tiene de las grandezas del reyno de la China* (Seville, 1577), which included a detailed discussion of China based on the Portuguese writings by the historian João de Barros (his third decade, Lisbon, 1563) and, more important, by the Dominican Gaspar da Cruz (Evora, 1569), who, unlike the others, had actually been in Canton in 1556 and can be properly considered as the first European to have published a book on Ming China.[19]

Mendoza knew both Escalante's *Discurso* and the book by Gaspar da Cruz, but he also relied a great deal on writings by his fellow Augustinian Martín de Rada, the main protagonist of the embassy to China sent from Manila in 1575, and the most scholarly of these earlier observers. Mendoza also used the reports by Miguel de Loarca, Jesuit letters, and other sources. The importance of Mendoza's book is that it synthesized all this material and made a general and coherent picture available. This 'history' was published alongside three more particular narratives of missionary journeys to Canton in 1575–82, in effect constituting the key European authority on China until Trigault's version of Matteo Ricci's fundamental history was published in 1615.[20] From a scientific and ethnographic perspective the writings by Rada are far more important than Mendoza's book, but it was Mendoza who helped shape more directly the European imagination, despite the fact that Rada's material was also made known by his fellow Augustinian Jerónimo Román in the second

---

[19] On Gaspar da Cruz, see C. R. Boxer (ed.), *South China in the Sixteenth Century* (Cambridge, 1953). Boxer stresses the importance of the narrative of the Portuguese captive Galiote Pereira (1553) for Cruz and those who followed Cruz. R. d'Intino has edited the Portuguese originals of many of these sources, *Enformação das cousas da China* (Lisbon, 1989). For an extended analysis of the Portuguese image of China, see Rui Manuel Loureiro, 'A China na Cultura Portuguesa do Século XVI', unpublished Ph.D. dissertation, university of Lisbon (1995).

[20] For a rigorous discussion of Mendoza and his sources see Donald F. Lach, *Asia in the Making of Europe* (3 vols, Chicago, 1965–93), I, 742–51. Manuel Ollé, 'La invención de China. Mitos y escenarios de la imágen ibérica de China en el siglo XVI', *Revista Española del Pacífico*, 8 (1998), 541–68, argues that the Iberian image of China represented a coherent paradigm which was only replaced by the Jesuits after Ricci.

edition of his cosmographical synthesis *Repúblicas del Mundo*, published in Salamanca in 1595 (Román in fact was bitter about the way Mendoza had been singled out to write on the topic). The issue is not simply one of primacy of publication, but also of emphasis of interpretation: at a moment when there was a powerful lobby supporting the idea of the conquest of China from Manila, a group to which Rada himself belonged, the positive views of China as a well-ordered and powerful state which Mendoza made available under the direct patronage of Rome came to reinforce the more accommodationist views of peaceful and gradual evangelization that the Jesuit authorities proclaimed, with the support of the papacy and, eventually, Philip II.[21]

There were other Spanish contributions to knowledge of China in the seventeenth century, for example the manuscript treatise by the Manila-based Jesuit Adriano de las Cortes, but on the whole the Spanish were less expert than the Jesuits from other national origins entering China from Macao under Portuguese patronage.[22] In fact, the best writing on China by a Spaniard was the letter produced in Peking in 1602 by Diego de Pantoja (1571–1618), a former student of Luis de Guzmán and close collaborator of Ricci who operated totally within the 'Portuguese' (but in reality rather cosmopolitan) Jesuit system.[23] Thus, in determining the Spanish contribution to the early ethnography of Asia it is crucial to distinguish the Spanish as individuals, who could operate within the Portuguese-Jesuit system, from the Spanish imperial system as such, based in the Philippines. It was mainly in opposition to the Portuguese Jesuit system – that is, as instigators of the rites controversy – that some Spanish missionaries, such as the Franciscan Antonio Caballero and the Dominicans Juan Bautista de Morales and Domingo Fernández de Navarrete, made their mark in the second half of the seventeenth century. They could at times be well informed (as Navarrete's *Tratados históricos, políticos, éticos y religiosos de la monarchía de la China*, published in 1676 and influential in France and England, exemplifies), but violent theological polemics totally unbalanced the image of China they transmitted to Spain and Europe.[24]

---

[21] On Rada, see Boxer, *South China*, lxvii–xci. On Mendoza's agenda, see Lach's insightful comments on his peculiar editorial practices and on the negative reception of his work in some quarters: *Asia*, I, 791–4. On the fact that China was seen initially in a very positive light not only by Pereira, Cruz, and Mendoza, but also by the Jesuits based at Macao, one may consider the Latin dialogue compiled by Duarte de Sande and Alessandro Valignano (Macao, 1590) on the basis of Ricci's early reports, best known through Richard Hakluyt's translation in the second edition of his *Principal Navigations* (1598–1600). Later in his life Ricci and his companions would adopt more negative views, although by a different path than the Manila-based Rada and Sánchez had followed some years earlier.

[22] Adriano de las Cortes, *Viaje de la China*, ed. B. Moncó (Madrid, 1991).

[23] D. Pantoja, *Relación de la entrada* (Seville, 1605). Two partial versions had been previously circulated by F. Guerreiro in the first volume of his *Relaçam* (1603) and (more fully) by his Castilian translator (1604), the Jesuit Antonio Colaço, who obviously had access to the original.

[24] On Navarrete see especially the sympathetic account by Cummins, *A Question of Rites. Friar Domingo Navarrete and the Jesuits in China* (London, 1993). Another notable work on China (and similarly hostile to the Jesuits) was the *Historia de la conquista de la China por el Tártaro* (Paris, 1670) by the Aragonese bishop of Puebla, Juan de Palafox y Mendoza, a work based, like Mendoza's book a century earlier, on material collected in Mexico, where Palafox had been active in the 1640s.

Equally influenced by anti-Jesuit feeling (albeit here the issue was more
political than theological) was the contribution of Franciscan and Dominican friars to empirical knowledge of Japan. Besides the more general works
by Ribadeneyra and Aduarte, there were more particular writings, especially
those by the Valencian Jacinto Orfanell, a Dominican martyred in 1622, but
whose history covering the years 1602–20 was expanded and published by
Diego Collado as *Historia Ecclesiástica de los successos de la Christiandad de Japón*
(Madrid, 1633). Orfanell, however exact and informed, was (like Aduarte)
mostly concerned with providing an apology and glorification of Dominican
efforts to penetrate areas where the Jesuits claimed to hold a missionary
monopoly, and had little to offer by way of the ethnography of Japan, not
even the succinct treatment offered by the Franciscan Ribadeneyra twenty
years earlier. Above all Orfanell's narrative fails to compete with those produced (but often not published) by Jesuit writers (Portuguese and Italian)
such as Luís Fróis, Alessando Valignano, and João Rodrigues, whose analysis
of local cultural realities was less marked by the theme of martyrdom, and
reflected a more mature engagement with the Japanese.

This was a kind of engagement which the Spanish, despite their imperial
wishes, could only support institutionally in territories like the Philippines
(actually incorporated within the crown of Castile).[25] One interesting paradox
in this case is that the key initial contacts between the Jesuits and the Japanese
in the middle of the sixteenth century had in fact been led by two Spaniards,
the Navarrese Francis Xavier and the Valencian Cosme de Torres, whose role
was crucial to the establishment of a remarkably promising mission. They
also helped shape the early European image of Japan and of Buddhism. As
in other Asian missions, the arrival of the 'Castillas' in the Philippines and
the union of crowns in Spain had the negative effect of stimulating the more
nationalistic members of the Portuguese establishment in the 'Estado da
Índia' to exclude when possible the Spanish, and especially Castilians, from
leading positions.

The predominance of the religious in both the operational basis of the
Philippines colony and in the writings produced about Asian peoples also
had an impact in the generation of an imperial historiography at the Spanish
court. Thus Bartolomé Leonardo de Argensola, the best representative of
this tradition, praised in his *Conquista de la islas Malucas* (Madrid, 1609) the
determination of Philip II to dismiss the idea of abandoning the Philippines
by opposing the superior principles of religion and justice to mere economic
considerations. He finished his account of the successful Spanish intervention in Ternate under governor Pedro de Acuña against the alliance of
Muslim natives and heretical Dutch with a lapidary: 'The voice of the gospel

---

[25] Of course, a different issue is the extent to which the Jesuits managed to publicize their best research. In
reality much of what missionaries such as Fróis, Valignano, and Rodrigues wrote about Japan and their
missions was publicized only partially in the form of letters or indirectly through the armchair syntheses by
Maffei and Bartoli.

sounded again in the furthest ends of the earth'.[26] He was not in disagreement with his contemporary Morga, who made the point even more clearly in the preface of the *Sucesos*.

Awareness that the Spanish presence in Asia made sense only if one placed religion firmly in the centre, however, does not explain why so little was done in Madrid to develop the imperial historiographical tradition represented by Argensola, which (as we shall see) is the isolated product of a particular moment. For obvious reasons, the main emphasis of imperial historians working in Castile had been on the new world of the 'Western Indies', in a tradition that went back to Peter Martyr of Anghiera and Gonzalo Fernández de Oviedo. However, the incorporation of the Philippines within the crown in the 1570s logically fell within this discourse, in the same way that Spanish trade, navigation, and administration were all extended from Mexico to Asia, with their ultimate political origin in a single Council of the Indies. Thus Antonio de Herrera y Tordesillas, the court historian of the mature empire at the turn of the seventeenth century, naturally included the Philippines and nearby areas in the geographical survey preceding his *Historia general de los hechos de los castellanos* (Madrid, 1601–15), a work of synthesis largely conceived during the last decades of the rule of Philip II.

What proved more difficult was to integrate the separate historiographical tradition based on the Portuguese empire in Asia as a result of the union of crowns. Philip II and his successors could of course patronize, in Lisbon and Goa, Portuguese writers such as João Baptista Lavanha and Diogo do Couto, who continued the tradition of official historiography best represented by João de Barros in the middle of the sixteenth century. The fascinating example of Manuel de Faria y Souza (1590–1649), who wrote his impressive *Asia Portuguesa* (and similar works on Africa and America) from Madrid and in Castilian, but within an independent Portuguese-patriotic paradigm, reveals the continuous development of this humanistic learned tradition up to the war of separation, and suggests a possible future for the union of crowns which the centralizing policies of Olivares made impossible.

As the titles of the respective works by Herrera and Faria y Souza reveal, the historiographical visions of Castilians and Portuguese only met as rivals in what can be best described as a clash between two Spanish nationalisms – Spain being then still the whole Iberian peninsula, despite a growing tendency towards the Castilianization of the concept which would eventually circumscribe it politically. What the court at Madrid needed was its own integrated vision of Asia, the lay equivalent of Guzmán's Jesuit synthesis. This need became especially urgent after 1600, when the pressure of Dutch and English competition forced a closer imbrication of the two empires, administered separately but constantly touching, and clashing.

---

[26] Bartolomé Leonardo de Argensola, *Conquista de las Islas Malucas*, with a study by M. Mir (Zaragoza, 1891), 393.

Spanish intervention in the Moluccas brought the issues to a head, and it was precisely under the administration of the count of Lemos in the Council of the Indies (1603–10) that for a brief period the vision of a more integrated all-Spanish (or, in today's idiom, all-Iberian) action in Asia was proclaimed. The young count of Lemos, Pedro Fernández de Castro (1576–1622), promoter of an imperialist offensive to re-occupy the Moluccas (long lost by the beleaguered Portuguese) from the Philippines, was also patron of the poet Argensola, whose detailed narrative of Spanish involvement in the Moluccas and other parts of East Asia from Magellan to the conquest of Ternate in 1606 he actually commissioned. The work made clear the historical origins of Portuguese and Castilian involvement in the area, and proclaimed the heroic nature and higher purpose of the Spanish campaign against Dutch penetration. Reading between the lines, it is clear that Argensola (himself Aragonese) sought to present Castilians and Portuguese as members of a single Spanish multi-national community ('both Spanish nations', he would often write), serving the same king in a common religious cause. His vision thus sought to integrate different patriotisms within Spain in an alternative to the dominant Castilian-centred approach of court writers such as Antonio de Herrera – an important issue in the complicated system of identities sustaining the Monarchy.[27] Given the existence of two separate imperial administrations, Argensola's model of Hispanic unity was perhaps the least painful way of making Castilian involvement in Asia acceptable to the Portuguese.

From our perspective, the most interesting aspect of the remarkably informed and well-written (in a baroque style) *Conquista* is its depiction of Asia. It was part of Argensola's humanist understanding of his subject that he should provide a full geographical and ethnological context for his heroic narrative. However, whilst Argensola worked hard to read as much published material as was available in both Portuguese and Spanish – for example, the works by João de Barros, Diogo do Couto, and Gabriel de San Antonio – and to consult primary relations submitted to the Council of the Indies, including some of Morga's papers, he was often betrayed by his lack of direct experience of Asia, and in particular by his imperfect knowledge of its geography.[28] Perhaps his most disastrous error was the confusion of Cambay in Gujarat, India, with Cambodia, which he perpetrated when relating Spanish

---

[27] The tension between Castilian-centred and multinational views on the Spanish empire during the period of Lerma's *privanza* is a subject which requires further research, but I suspect that the apology for Bartolomé's account written by his brother Lupercio, which prefaced the book in 1609 and defended the *Conquista* against critics of its wide-ranging coverage and elaborate style, may have responded to a rather more complex factional agenda at the court (Lemos was a close ally of the Lerma and Borja families). The Aragonese writer may have been seen as an unwelcome intruder into a 'Castilian' imperial domain – a recurrent pattern (Zurita's *Anales de Aragón* had also been savaged by Castilian-minded writers). Herrera and the Argensolas would also clash in the lively historiographical debate about the Aragonese rebellion of 1591.

[28] Argensola also used Jesuit materials and even used some translations of published Dutch sources. For an identification of many further sources of Argensola, see John Villiers's contribution to this volume.

involvement in the latter kingdom – an adventure which was fresh in people's minds when he wrote.[29] Although Argensola could be penetrating in his understanding of some issues, as when noting the mixture of 'idolatrous' and Muslim elements in the royal traditions of the Moluccas, many of his ethnographic descriptions were not only judgemental, if pithy, but also derivative. For example, native royalty in the Moluccas is by definition 'tyrannical'. The natives 'are poor, and for this reason arrogant; and since this vice encompasses many others, ungrateful'. Moreover, 'Their laws are barbaric. They place no limit to the number they can marry . . . Robberies, however small, are never forgiven; adulteries easily.' Argensola seemed to adopt a more neutral tone when describing their costumes and apparel in detail, but only to conclude that 'Men and women show in their dress the natural arrogance of their temperament'.[30] The criticism, of course, also expressed Argensola's austere clerical moralism.

Argensola did not lack a concern with historical accuracy, nor (remarkably) was he beyond criticizing the European Christians themselves for their tyrannical treatment of natives, but his attempt to write in a comprehensive and orderly fashion about Spanish involvement in the Moluccas was really subject to an ideological programme – he was also writing about a 'mystical empire', in his own expression. His represented a momentary and, as it would turn out, ephemeral effort to think of Asia as an area for Spanish intervention, an effort, moreover, conducted from the peculiar sensibility of a moral poet from Aragon.[31] Above all, it lacked the sense of deep reflection and familiarity with the subject which Barros (the most obvious model) had offered, despite his never having been to Asia either.

Argensola's limitations seem to reflect a wider problem within Spanish court culture. One gets the feeling that despite the considerable correspondence generated by the Philippines, and the need experienced by the Habsburg kings also to come to terms with their obligations as rulers of Portuguese India, the geographical and ethnographic realities of Asia were never fully clear at the court of Madrid/Valladolid.[32] Its political and intellectual elites failed to create a powerful imperial perspective able to go beyond

---

[29] Argensola's confusion is noted by Villiers. Argensola's position on Cambodia was circumspect, knowing that the views of the Dominican lobby at court were extreme and had been superseded (thus it was easy to defend Gallinato's prudence in Cambodia, since he was one of the heroes of the war in Ternate). Lemos had obtained information from Gabriel de San Antonio and Diego Aduarte about the affairs of Cambodia when they arrived in Spain in 1603, but decided to prioritize an expedition to the Moluccas requested by Governor Acuña from Manila.

[30] Argensola, *Conquista*, 3–4, 11–12. For the Indonesian islands he followed various sources, in particular Gabriel Rebelo's unpublished 'História das Ilhas de Maluco' (1561).

[31] Aragon experienced a late humanist literary revival in this period, for which the Argensola brothers provided a distinctively Horatian model. Although the Aragonese had participated with the Catalans in the creation of a Mediterranean empire, the kingdom was in reality landlocked within Spain, and lacked the maritime traditions which alone could sustain a colonial empire. This makes the choice of Argensola by Lemos the more peculiar: his cosmopolitanism was purely bookish (although he would later accompany Lemos to Naples).

[32] Philip III moved the court to Valladolid in 1600–6.

the agenda-ridden views of missionaries and governors, to appreciate fully the multiple possibilities which the numerous reports and embassies received from Asia could have suggested. The writings submitted to the crown and Council of the Indies in the first four decades of the century by *arbitristas* such as Hernando Ríos Coronel, Duarte Gómez Solís, and Juan Grau y Monfalcón, concerned with consolidating the Spanish presence in the Philippines or exploiting its economic potential more fully, often suggest by their tone that the Catholic monarchy had other priorities in mind. As the Dutch and the English grew in power in Asia, and as Spain fatally moved towards a destructive war in Europe which would carry, as part of the price, the separation of Portugal, the vision proposed by Argensola was to be shattered, like so much else.

Spain also failed to produce in the sixteenth and seventeenth centuries any outstanding examples of the humanist as curious traveller, a new type which generated some of the most interesting accounts of the East in the period. We have some valuable ambassadorial reports, such as the commentaries on his journey to Persia by Don García de Silva y Figueroa, but no examples of the independent and educated spirit of European travellers such as Carletti, della Valle, Careri, Sandys, Thévenot, Bernier, and Chardin. There were, it is true, some prominent adventurous travel writers, most famously the Portuguese Fernão Mendes Pinto, author of the *Peregrinaçam* (Lisbon, 1614), whose impact was especially powerful through the Spanish translation by Canon Francisco de Herrera Maldonado published in 1620. However, whilst Pinto did not lack a satirical edge, from a scientific point of view his account is almost worthless, since – modern criticism has now recognized – it is largely fictional. It should be read as a not very honest autobiographical romance, certainly inspired by the realities of the Portuguese empire, but, alas, not driven by any concern to describe Asian realities accurately.[33] It is perhaps significant that some of the better read Spanish armchair orientalists of the period, such as Herrera Maldonado and Faria y Souza, came to the defence of Pinto's reliability for his account of China, mistaking his agreement with writers like Gaspar da Cruz for a proof of accuracy rather than as a sign of plagiarism.[34]

It is equally significant that the other main example of an independent Spanish curious traveller was another fake, Pedro Ordóñez de Ceballos, a cleric whose *Viage del Mundo* was published in Madrid in 1614 and was taken seriously by many. Here again the point is not that everything was invented, since Ceballos read Jesuit letters and other published sources to flesh out his descriptions, but that his claims to personal observation were largely false, either because he simply plagiarized existing accounts (such as the *Itinerario*

---

[33] However, many geographical and other details are accurate. For a fully annotated English translation, see *The Travels of Mendes Pinto*, trans. R. Catz (Chicago, 1989). I have discussed the value of Mendes Pinto in 'The oriental voices of Mendes Pinto, or the traveller as ethnologist in Portuguese India', *Portuguese Studies*, 10 (1994), 24–43.

[34] Herrera Maldonado was extremely well read about China, and composed an *Epítome Historial del Reyno de la China* (Madrid, 1620) based on published and unpublished (largely Jesuit) material.

of friar Martín Ignacio, published in 1585 by Juan González de Mendoza, which Ceballos followed very closely to describe his own journey) or because he invented romantic situations, for example in the sections dealing with his adventures with the queen of Vietnam. In the 1580s and early 1590s Ceballos had probably been in America as a soldier and priest, but I doubt that he ever crossed the Pacific to Asia.

It is clear that for examples of Spanish ethnography at its best one needs to skip writers like Argensola or Ceballos and consider the primary accounts of writers like Morga or Chirino. This does not eliminate ideological and institutional constraints, but maximizes the empirical element which, perhaps more than humanist erudition *per se*, defines the lasting scientific value of early modern travel accounts. How 'scientific' is the ethnographic practice of writers like Morga and Chirino? And how do these writers compare as religious and lay? Finally, how do they compare to writers working within the Portuguese 'Estado da Índia'?

The starting point for a discussion of these questions is assessing the roles of empiricism and systematic research within the scientific cultures of the Counter-Reformation. The distance that separates modern ideas of science from early modern assumptions could obscure that fact that Renaissance writers, writing before the onset of what we now term the 'scientific revolution', in reality often worked around a powerful idea of science. This was a comprehensive system of knowledge which applied to all areas (human as well as natural) and which, whilst related to a religious view of the world, also included a number of empirical and rational disciplines. Within the Catholic world, after the thirteenth century the theology of Thomas Aquinas in particular provided a powerful strategy by which a rational understanding of the natural world, and of man as a natural being, was made compatible with the higher mysteries of the faith.[35] Thus European late-medieval and Renaissance science found its central formulation in the natural philosophy of the scholastic tradition, against which, but also from which, the modern systems would rise.[36] Of course, medieval writers and their early modern successors

---

[35] Although reason was not allowed to interfere with revealed truth, medieval Latin Christian writers were on the whole passionate about the use of reason in philosophy, and were in no doubt about the existence of rational science. Reason was seen as an expression of God's will. See E. Grant, *God and Reason in the Middle Ages* (Cambridge, 2001). The bias was, however, towards logical speculation, unlike in the Renaissance, when empirical concerns became more relevant. In the Middle Ages the epistemological value of sensorial experiences was not questioned, but the actual practice of science was not geared towards observation.

[36] That is, whilst there were different late-medieval approaches to the relationship between natural philosophy and metaphysics, Augustinian, Nominalist, Averroist, and Thomist, of which the latter became the more influential in the neo-Scholasticism of the Counter-Reformation, they all shared the agenda set in the thirteenth century of either coping with, or fostering, natural science, one which humanist scientists only revived. The late humanist and post-sceptical 'modern' systems of the seventeenth century – from the neo-Epicureanism of Gassendi to the intuitive rationalism of Descartes – would take as a starting point the criticism of Aristotelian natural philosophy, still borrowing its disciplines of logic, ethics, and physics.

would take beliefs about divine creation and providence, the immortality of
the human soul, and the intervention of the devil to be rational, a position
which many writers after the seventeenth century would increasingly question. But what characterized the literature of the period, and very clearly so
the literature concerning the natural and human diversity of the world as
observed by Europeans in Africa, America, and Asia, was the assumption that
an increased empirical knowledge could be rationalized in ways fully compatible with orthodox theology. There was, one may argue, a Renaissance
'empirical turn', in that the medieval Aristotelian principle that knowledge
through the senses was fundamental – an idea which, however, was often *de
facto* confined within a logical paradigm of rational speculation – was now
extended to the increased use of actual observations to qualify and, if need
be, question the authority of the written text in scientific matters.

This empirical criticism of secular textual authority and pure abstract reason-
ing was not necessarily felt to be a threat to religious dogma, unless actual
heresies, touching on matters of faith, were produced, in which case it was not
observation, but the faulty use of reason, which was to blame. For example,
until the case of Galileo and his Copernican theories exploded in the seventeenth century, provoking a traumatic Roman decision to marry Aristotelian
physics and Ptolemaic astronomy to religious dogma, many Catholic scientists
(including Galileo himself) felt confident that scientific speculation supported
by observation could only lead to a firmer faith. This confidence is especially
relevant when considering Spanish writings about the peoples of Asia, given
that the vast majority of these writers were in fact members of the religious
orders engaged in missionary work. Whilst the integration of religious
assumptions and 'scientific' concerns was particularly urgent amongst these
writers, the same overall paradigm informed – sometimes by implication –
the writings produced by laymen.[37]

A highly influential example of how this synthesis operated was the *Natural
and Moral History of the Indies* by the Jesuit José de Acosta (1590), describing
the Americas as known to the Spanish. As the title announced, it was as
'history' that the empirical science, or knowledge, of the New World was
presented, both a natural history of the world and a moral history of man as
a rational being. Thus history here did not merely, nor even primarily, concern the deeds and passions of men in time: it was, more generally, a descriptive, organized, and, when relevant, speculative account of the geography,
flora, fauna, and ethnology of the Americas, set within a biblical framework
of sacred history, informed by direct experience and observation, and
assisted by the comparative and chronological perspectives provided by classical learning. Acosta conceived it as a 'new' kind of history in that it combined history proper with philosophy, searching for the 'causes and reason'

[37] In reality, similar assumptions concerning the compatibility of rational science and revealed religion
operated amongst Protestant writers, albeit within a theologically more fideistic paradigm.

for novel natural phenomena, and placing at the centre of enquiry 'the deeds and history of the Indians themselves, original inhabitants of the New World'.[38] The humanist and the theologian met to supersede the learning of antiquity on the basis of new observations. The unprecedented attention given to ethnological concerns led Acosta to develop a systematic classification of different kinds of 'barbarians' according to varying levels of civility. Similarly, the central question of the relation of the American Indians to the rest of mankind was ingeniously tackled through a combination of religious (biblical) assumptions – mankind must be one, all descended from Adam and Noah – and rational–empirical arguments – the American Indians must have travelled by land, since they did not enjoy the navigation techniques which would make an oceanic crossing possible. Acosta exploited the new evidence collected by the Jesuits working under Portuguese patronage, and by Spanish missionaries operating from the Philippines (much of which he obtained in Mexico), in order to set the Chinese as counterparts of the Mexican and Peruvian Indians in his critical assessment of the cultural achievements of non-European 'barbarians'.[39]

Within this broadly based historical discourse we may therefore distinguish an empirical element, or, in modern idiom, an ethnography of human diversity, and a more speculative one seeking to provide a rationale for this natural and historical diversity, for which 'ethnology' may be appropriate. In effect, these two elements were practised within genres which belonged to a variety of early-modern rhetorical traditions – letters, 'relations', histories, and cosmographies – and often responded to specific milieux. Antiquarian or historical scholarship for its own sake was rare before the seventeenth century, and particularly so within the Iberian peninsula, but humanist standards permeated much of court culture and, increasingly, religious culture. Classical learning and curiosity were an educational aspiration for both the court historian and the missionary, and even young conquerors writing independently – men such as Pedro Cieza de León in South America – took up these ideals. Thus, the scientific ideal emerged as a pervasive but diffuse force, conditioned by colonial motivations and theological assumptions.

Morga's widely praised account can stand as a model of a historical and geographical relation composed within this 'scientific' horizon. In effect, whilst the first seven chapters of the *Sucesos* are a straightforward (if sometimes rather concise) historical narrative of the Spanish conquest and administration of the Philippines, the eighth chapter, describing 'the islands and their natural inhabitants, antiquity, customs, and government, both at the time of their gentilism and after they were conquered by the Spaniards, with

[38] J. de Acosta, *Historia Natural y Moral de las Indias*, ed. J. Alcina Franch (Madrid, 1987), 57.
[39] Acosta's incidental views on Asian peoples are analysed by Fermín del Pino, 'El misionero español José de Acosta y la evangelización de las Indias Orientales', *Missionalia Hispánica*, 122 (1985), 275–98.

other particulars', constitutes an excellent specimen of the geographical relation as practised in the Renaissance. Two issues are of importance here: the
breadth and logical coherence of its thematic coverage, and the relative
accuracy and depth of the analysis – a more difficult point, which requires
addressing questions of cultural translation and mistranslation.

It is perhaps the thematic coverage of Morga's relation which is more
obviously striking. He begins with a geographical survey, distinguishing the
different islands and noting their position at the point where two different
navigational routes meet across the world (so that, with some appreciation
of relativism, they were 'Eastern islands' to the Portuguese and 'Western
islands' to the Castilians).[40] Morga also makes explicit their incorporation
within the crown of Castile, and emphasizes the fact that the ancients had
been wrong to consider all those regions uninhabitable. He goes on to
describe the climate, and then offers a very detailed discussion of the natives
of the various islands, distinguishing, for example, the 'barbarian', nomadic
'negritos' of the interior of Luzon from the dominant coastal peoples of
Malay origin, who are seen in a more positive light.

Ethnographic themes covered by Morga include native dress both before
and after the impact of the Spanish, hygiene (he notes, for example, with
obvious reservations, that bathing is for them a medicinal practice), and the
role of women. It is clear that this is one of the topics that fascinated him:
not only does he disapprove of female unchastity, and of the use of erotica
like *sagras* (penile implants, which he describes later) amongst the Bisayas
(Visayas), but he considers the killing of adulterous women to safeguard male
honour as a sign of Spanish influence. The description goes on to consider
food and drink. Morga then introduces native warfare and, in great detail, their
navigation. The continuity of this account of native technology and customs is
broken by a wider consideration of the natural products and economy of the
Philippines, revealing the intimate link which in Morga's mind (and in those
of many Renaissance writers) people had with their environment. Thus the
trees and fruits, agriculture, animals (wild and domestic), fish, drugs, metals,
textiles, etc. of the region are all covered exhaustively, emphasizing, when
relevant, the introduction of new products from Europe, Mexico, and China
– a dynamic understanding which also permeated the discussion of native
customs. It is only after this picture of the natural setting has been completed
that Morga returns to a more detailed discussion of the native civilization of
the dominant groups of the Philippines – the Tagalog and the Bisayas –
offering a further discussion of their languages, customs, houses, system of
writing, political order, sexual practices, laws, and religion. Amongst these
aspects, the customary law which regulated marriage, inheritance, criminal

[40] Acosta (*Historia*, III, 23) had also noted with perspicacity the relative time-gap between those travelling
westward from Mexico, across the Pacific, and those travelling eastward from Europe and India, who gained
an additional calendar day.

justice, and slavery is what attracts most of Morga's attention, probably because he was professionally interested in the topic.[41]

Morga did not seek to invent reasons to disparage the natives; for example, albeit unchaste, they were not sodomites – until influenced by foreigners such as the Spaniards and especially the Chinese. Nevertheless, he found much to criticize. He singled out excessive rates of interest and debt slavery as the marks of a lack of true justice according to European ideals of rational equity (whatever the reality). Thus, he commented negatively on native contracts and trade, since 'each one only paid attention to how he might best pursue his business and self-interest'.[42] However, this negative judgement was much more emphatic when addressing native religion, where the influence of the devil was seen as pervasive within a system of gentile idolatry, witchcraft, and divination. There was no hint here of a search for God according to natural reason, such as the Jesuits of the time sought to find in Chinese Confucianism: 'in things pertaining to their religion they proceeded more barbarously and blindly than in other things, for besides being gentiles and having no knowledge of the true God, they neither sought Him by the use of reason, nor had any one fixed deity'.[43]

Morga concluded with an account of the impact of the Spanish, who had driven out the Muslims, initiated a carefully balanced policy of conversion, created a few urban settlements, and implemented their own military–commercial system. Morga described this colonial system at some length, occasionally letting through some of his own ideas for reform, but toning down the criticisms which one finds in his correspondence with the Spanish authorities.

It is clear that this relation is remarkably comprehensive, even if somewhat disorderly, and that the ethnographic sections are quite systematic. The tone is not neutral, and Morga makes no effort to hide his own European and Christian moral ideals, which he of course considers to be of universal applicability, but this does not detract from an impressive thematic coverage. Moreover, there is no reason to doubt the empirical accuracy of the relation. Albeit often the information is second-hand – Morga was a man who read books and documents rather than someone who personally visited each site – his sources were fresh and varied, and he certainly sought to get it right. Morga is not, however, exceptional in his 'scientific' methods and ideals. Whilst not all contemporary observers were as lucid and clear-headed, there is no doubt that in this relation Morga does little more than exemplify the key strengths of Renaissance ethnography: reliance on empirical observation, or a well-documented synthesis of primary sources, organized topically according to a method, and described in plain language for a practical aim. What distinguished some relations from others was not only the quality of the personal

---

[41] Morga in Retana (ed.), *Sucesos*, 192–6. In these passages he probably relied on Friar Juan de Plasencia's report on the 'government and justice' and other civil laws of the Tagalos of Luzon.
[42] *Ibid.* 195.
[43] *Ibid.* 196.

experience of the writer or the quality of the sources he had available, but also
the capacity to organize information coherently and the degree of engagement
with a historical perspective rooted in classical and biblical sources. In this
last respect, Morga's learning seems to have relied more on modern writers
than on classical ones, in contrast with Jesuit writers such as Chirino.[44]

Morga represented in many ways the model of a learned bureaucrat, or
letrado, which Philip II was keen to promote and often inspired – a man
comfortable with the pen but also willing to take up the sword, capable of
rational discourse but also pious. (Later in his career he became a notorious
philanderer, but this is another matter.) As often in this period, Morga did
not publish his account from a simple desire to spread knowledge, and there
is good reason to believe that when he took that step in Mexico in 1609 he
was concerned with rescuing his reputation from the fracas of his personal
naval intervention against the incursion of the Dutch ships led by Oliver van
Noort in 1600.[45] It is, however, hard to resist the impression that the account
goes beyond a self-justificatory piece. It seems, from the testimony of some
friars, that the first draft of his relation already existed in 1598, and therefore
must have been written as much for Morga's own self-information as for
others. He had, of course, sent the relation to Philip III years before he
thought of publishing it.

One important issue which has been raised by commentators such as his
modern English editor J. S. Cummins is whether the apparent systematicity
of Morga's relation was influenced by the instructions issued by the Council
of the Indies under its president Juan de Ovando, most famously those questionnaires prepared in 1577 and 1584 by the royal cosmographer Juan López
de Velasco for the whole of Spanish America, which generated a variety of
actual geographical relations, many of them still of extraordinary value for
the historian.[46] These questionnaires – which had a number of precedents –
were inevitably familiar to a man like Morga, but close scrutiny makes it
highly unlikely that he followed them directly, since he does not use the
same order, nor the same exact categories. The parallels are notable – but
not exceptional – only in the natural–economic sections. It would be more
accurate to say that the concerns which guided the questionnaires simply

---

[44] This is confirmed by the library which Morga left at his death, which contained a large number of modern
historical and cosmographical books in Spanish, many of them acquired in Peru (not an easy location from
which to build such a collection), years after his stay in the Philippines. These included Argensola's *Conquista
de las Islas Malucas*, Mendoza's *Historia del gran reyno de la China*, Jerónimo Román's *Repúblicas del Mundo*,
Mendes Pinto's *Historia oriental* (Maldonado's Castilian edition of the *Peregrinaçam*), Ceballos's *Viage del Mundo*,
and Botero's *Relaciones*. See Retana, *Sucesos*, 159*.

[45] Morga's version of the event, struggling to explain how the Spanish managed to lose a battle they had
already won, is given in ch. 7 of the *Sucesos* in great detail, and as a reply to van Noort's own published version.
The issue of Morga's motives is discussed in Cummins, *Sucesos*, 18.

[46] Cummins in *ibid.* 26. For an introduction to the *Relaciones* see H. F. Cline, 'The Relaciones Geográficas
of the Spanish Indies, 1577–1586', *Hispanic American Historical Review*, 44 (1964), 341–74. The classic study
remains M. Jiménez de la Espada, available in 'Antecedentes' to *Relaciones Geográficas de Indias. Perú* (Madrid,
1965), 5–117.

made explicit a system of thematic categories, or ethnographic assumptions, common in the period, a system which to some extent preceded any formal questionnaires but which found a perfect expression in the more elaborate relations practised by humanist trained writers, be it Venetian ambassadors, Jesuit missionaries, or Spanish *letrados*. To that extent they expressed the late Renaissance emphasis and topical methods for organizing information, methods which can be seen as a key element in the transition from rhetorical organization of information to inductive science.[47] Thus the questionnaires prepared by Velasco were no more than one possible way of organizing geographical and ethnographic information, one which Morga need not have followed, since he was sufficiently well read and educated to be able to develop his own method.

If Morga offers an example of the historical and geographical relation at its best, Jesuit writers like Chirino can be used to measure the achievements of European missionaries as ethnographers. When compared with Morga, Chirino is more obviously erudite, often comparing modern and ancient customs – a tradition inaugurated in the sixteenth century by humanist arm-chair historians such as Barros and the Jesuit Maffei. Knowledge of native communities and customs is also more direct amongst many of the missionary writers, even though much of what is found in a work of synthesis like Chirino's is based on the relations of other writers (even laymen such as Morga). This superior depth of analysis is, of course, closely related to their knowledge of native languages and systems of writing, and writers such as Chirino or Alzina were quite willing to extol the excellencies of the Tagalog and Bisayan languages, even above Latin and Castilian.

Equally important, missionaries were for professional reasons more willing to elaborate on native religious beliefs, and their blanket condemnation of native traditional mythology and 'idolatrous' beliefs does not exclude a certain amount of description which is empirically valid at a superficial level. On the other hand, quite often this ethnographic material is buried within a hagiographic discourse composed in praise of the missionaries themselves, which distorts the image a reader can form of a native cultural system. Inevitably, the devil serves as explanation for many non-Christian religious beliefs (Chirino, for example, although condemning the lies and deceits of native priests, who prey on popular superstition to make a living, also described rituals in which actual demonic possessions take place).[48] Curiously, for all his classical learning (and in part because of it), Chirino was also willing to repeat stories about monstrous phenomena, a concern with the supernatural which also affected the work of other educated observers, such as the Valencian Jesuit Francisco Ignacio Alzina.

---

[47] On this topic see Rubiés, 'Instructions for travellers: teaching the eye to see', *History and Anthropology*, 9 (1996), 139–90.

[48] Chirino, *Relación* (1604), ch. 21; *Història*, II, 15 (with variations).

Alzina's notable *Historia de las islas e indios de Bisayas* (1668) reveals what humanist science could achieve at its most empirically informed. As he declared

> I do not follow (nor could I have possibly followed) any authorities ... Most of what I write I have witnessed myself, and not a few times in order to get to the truth of what I had heard or read; and when I follow hearsay I make this explicit, because in these things it is too easy to add or subtract something, and I do not consider all my informants equally trustworthy, although I have tried to repeat only that which deserves some credit.[49]

Grounded on years of direct experience and competence in local languages, together with a willingness to incorporate the evidence of oral traditions after careful scrutiny, it is a model ethnography in its systematic approach, depth of analysis, and sympathy towards the natives and their natural milieu. It covers more ethnographic categories and in more detail than Morga, from the 'liberal arts or sciences' practised by the Bisayans to their peculiar, and technically complex, marriage practices.

Although Alzina was inspired by Acosta's model of a natural and moral history, his work did not have the same speculative and synthetic value, nor was it as influential as Chirino's writing, since it dealt with the Bisayan islands rather than the more prosperous and more intensively colonized Luzon. Its strength was above all its coherence as a primary description, informed by an intimate interaction with native communities, and elevated by the skills of an accomplished philologist. Indeed, the extent to which Alzina's method of exposition relies on explaining native words and concepts, often compared with Spanish ones, is striking. For Alzina, the expressive power of Bisayan was such that any fundamental difference between natives and Europeans was clearly less one of intellectual capacity than one of education and training. It was the cultivation of the liberal arts that distinguished the civilized from the barbarian, but this depended more on political context than on anthropological categories (in this respect, he saw the Bisayans as comparable to the ancient Spanish before the Roman conquest of the peninsula). What the Bisayans had lacked was essentially 'republics', or proper 'politics', with independence from questions of faith or race.[50]

[49] F. Alzina, *Historia de las islas e indios de Bisayas*, 'proemio'. The first part of Alzina's manuscript is a natural and moral history, in four books, and the second part, which has survived incomplete, dealt with the missions. The complete text has been recently edited (for the first time) by Victoria Yepes in three volumes, as *Historia Natural de las islas Bisayas* (Madrid, 1996), books 1 and 2; *Una etnografía de los Indios Bisayas del siglo XVII* (Madrid, 1996), books 3 and 4; and *Historia sobrenatural de las Islas Bisayas* (Madrid, 1998), part II. Yepes's edition of the first part of Alzina's manuscript follows the eighteenth-century copy (1784) by the cosmographer Juan Bautista Muñoz, now in Biblioteca del Palacio Real, Madrid. There is also a good copy of books 1 and 2 in the Jesuit Archive of Sant Cugat (Catalonia). Both copies include illustrations.
[50] Yepes, *Una etnografía*, 16.

A reader of both Chirino's 1604 *Relación* and Morga's 1609 *Sucesos* seeking to acquire a 'scientific' understanding of the Philippines would have found the latter more useful as a synthesis, better organized and historically more balanced, but also less detailed on a number of points. He would not have found a substantially different idea of ethnographic practice: whilst Chirino and Morga may have disagreed about particular policies, such as the project of conquering China, they shared a fundamental understanding of cultural diversity. Accordingly, one could to some extent justify different civil customs as relative to place and climate provided one remained within common standards of rationality. This limited relativism did not apply to religion, which was always measured according to a single standard of truth. Catholic Christianity was an absolute. Different societies, on the other hand, as defined by the development of cities and the economy, arts and sciences, government and law, were ranked according to a scale ranging from the 'bárbaros' to the 'políticos' – from the barbarian to the civilized.[51] These were understood as two separate spheres: religion was a matter of revelation and faith, civility was a matter of reason and nature. Whilst a certain level of civilization was almost seen as a requisite for conversion to Christianity, one could be both civilized and damned.

How, then, are we to assess the Spanish contribution to the ethnography and ethnology of Asia from the perspective of a changing early modern understanding of science? Many of these writings were produced within a paradigm of humanist learning and applied empiricism, in a spirit not so much contrary to the Aristotelian systems of natural and anthropological science as novel in its willingness to place new observations at the centre of rational discourse, and to devise new methods of research and exposition.[52] From a qualitative perspective the greatest challenge is to measure the depth of knowledge of European accounts and their capacity to perceive cultural differences and reflect upon their implications. Observations were often superficial. There were a great number of cultural mistranslations, in some ways inevitable. Perhaps more important, there were strong ideological biases, no less pervasive for often being so obvious. Against this, one must consider that those very ideological biases, based on the Christian understanding of universal history combined with the humanist understanding of civilization, created the intellectual framework for a largely empirical, methodically sophisticated, and increasingly systematic research on world history. As I have

---

[51] Chirino, *Història*, 173, comparing the Tagalos favourably (as more 'civilized') with the Zanagas of West Africa as described by Cadamosto in the fifteenth century.

[52] This explains why the same Jesuits who valued new observations, mathematical research, and humanist rhetoric could simultaneously be reluctant to embrace a new mechanistic paradigm for physics which directly challenged Aristotelian natural philosophy and (perhaps more decisively) its support for certain theological positions.

argued elsewhere, it was in fact the tension between the principles of Christianity and civilization which conditioned the transformation of practical ethnography into antiquarian ethnology.[53]

The existence of this early modern ethnological turn is, however, a complex process in which the different colonial experiences and religious confessions of each European nation conditioned the emergence of distinct cultural spaces and intellectual styles. Even within the Hispanic imperial and Counter-Reformation system, there were interesting institutional differences between Portugal and Castile which affected their respective contributions to this ethnographic production and ethnological turn (the latter, in the Iberian peninsula, remained rather timid).

In fact, one interesting point that emerges is that the very definition of a 'Spanish' contribution requires a number of important qualifications. To begin with, whilst there was a Castilian imperial system in Asia distinct from the Portuguese, it is not strictly correct to define the former as 'Spanish', not so much because the two crowns were united in a crucial sixty-year period of ethnographic production and ethnological development (since, after all, the two empires remained essentially separate), but because by the standards of their own humanist culture the Portuguese were Spanish, and often declared themselves to be Spanish. From Góis through Camões to Faria y Souza – straddling the periods before and after the union of crowns – we find a consistent definition of Spain as a common geographical and historical, but not political, unit, a definition perfectly compatible with an obvious emphasis on Portuguese nationalist themes.[54] The effects of the rebellion of 1640 and later trends in the history of Spain, in which multinational realities have been eroded by a state-centred Castilianization, have tended to obscure this earlier perception. Living in a common geographical and multinational space known as Spain (Hispania) in both classical and medieval sources, the Portuguese opposed themselves, as a national community, to the threat of Castilianization, rather than Hispanicization. We would therefore need to redraw national definitions according to the Portuguese and Castilian (rather than Spanish) imperial systems. (The problem has an additional dimension in the Crown of Aragon, also obviously Spanish but legally and culturally equally non-Castilian. The participation of the crown of Aragon in the Castilian colonial system was not impossible, but remained marginal for both legal and practical reasons.)

---

[53] Rubiés, 'New worlds and Renaissance ethnology', *History and Anthropology*, VI (1993), 157–97.

[54] For example, the Portuguese humanist and historian Damião de Góis wrote his *Hispania* (Louvain, 1542) for his fellow humanist friends in Northern Europe in defence of the honour of the whole of Spain against the views of the cosmographers Sebastian Münster and Miguel Servet (paradoxically, himself Spanish, although working in France and under a pseudonym). Barros would also use the concept of Spain to include Portugal, though not implying any political unity. In his national epic of overseas discovery, Camões would make Portugal the crown of 'nobre Espanha' (not 'Iberia', as some modern translations anachronistically rephrase it).

Even if we handle these definitions carefully, a number of additional qualifications are needed. First, many Portuguese writers used the Castilian language whilst still writing within a distinctly Portuguese sphere of influence – for example, not only the historical syntheses of Manuel de Faria y Souza, but also the primary accounts of writers like the Augustinian Sebastião Manrique, author of an *Itinerario* (Rome, 1649) which is valuable for knowledge of Bengal and Arakan. Much of the literature about the activities of the adventurer Filipo de Brito Nicote in Pegu (Lower Burma/Myanmar) was also published in Castilian to reach a wider court audience, for example, Manuel de Abreu Mousinho's *Breve discurso en que se cuenta la conquista del Pegu* (Lisbon, 1617). Other works originally written in Portuguese made their greatest impact via their Castilian versions, including the important *Imperio de la China* (Madrid, 1642) by the Jesuit Álvarez Semedo, again published by the initiative of Faria y Souza. In cases such as that represented by Jacques de Coutre, a Flemish merchant traveller established in Goa in the early decades of the seventeenth century but then expelled to Spain (on the exaggerated suspicion that he may have spied for the Dutch), the partly Hispanicized foreigner could adopt the Portuguese language to write his personal recollections, although Jacques de Coutre's son – brought up amongst the Portuguese in India – then translated the book into Castilian to address it to the king in Madrid.[55] There were also cases, albeit rare, of Castilians participating in the Portuguese imperial system and writing about it, such as the early example of Martín Fernández de Figueroa, whose *Conquista de las Indias* (Salamanca, 1512) admittedly has little ethnographic value.

Of greatest importance is the fact that the single most relevant contribution to the production of a sophisticated ethnohistory of Asia in areas under the nominal jurisdiction of the Portuguese 'Estado da Índia' was made by a multinational, cosmopolitan, and highly centralized religious organization with headquarters in Rome, the Society of Jesus. The Jesuits in Asia had many Portuguese members but also a great number of extremely influential members from other nationalities: Spaniards from Castile or from the Crown of Aragon, many Italians, and a few Northern Europeans (such as the Flemish Nicolas Trigault). Later in the seventeenth century the French took a leading role in the missions of Siam, Vietnam, and China. Interestingly, there were also non-Castilian Spanish Jesuits active in the Philippines, some of them (for example, Alzina, Colín, and Combés, from Valencia, Catalonia, and Aragon respectively) outstanding writers.[56] It is possible to argue that the contribution of these 'foreign' nationals within the Jesuit order – especially

---

[55] The 'Vida de Jacques de Coutre' was only published recently: Jacques de Coutre, *Andanzas Asiáticas*, ed. E. Stols, B. Teensma, and J. Werberckmoes (Madrid, 1991). The existence of a previous Portuguese text is not fully clear. Estevan de Coutre, responsible for the Castilian text, may have taken down his father's oral recollections (see the discussion by E. Stols, *ibid.* 38).

[56] The Jesuits were not alone in welcoming subjects of the Crown of Aragon – for example, the Dominican Diego Aduarte was Aragonese – but were perhaps the most generous and cosmopolitan.

non-Portuguese in the Estado da Índia – accounts for a higher proportion of ethnohistorical writings than their actual numbers would suggest. Although the role of Italians is especially prominent as an intellectual elite in the mission fields of Asia, it was also mainly as Jesuits that many Spaniards made an important contribution to the history and ethnography of India, Japan, China, or Africa – for example, Cosme de Torres, Antoni Montserrat, Francesc Ros, Jerónimo Javier, Diego Pantoja, and Pedro Paez. In this context, use of language was pragmatic and did not always correspond to a national affiliation – hence the Catalan Montserrat wrote about India in Latin and Portuguese, the Italian Valignano wrote about Japan and China in Castilian, and the Castilian Paez wrote about Abyssinia in Portuguese.

Were Spanish–Castilian descriptions of Asia intrinsically different from Portuguese material? Whilst the genres used were almost identical and the ideological traditions followed very similar patterns, it may be argued that there were differences in levels of institutional support and development which are worth noting. There was no Portuguese equivalent to the *Relaciones Geográficas* commissioned by the Council of the Indies, as there was never the same need to administer colonies of settlement in Portuguese Asia as existed in Spanish America and the Philippines. For similar reasons, whilst in Spain there was an intense debate about the legitimacy of conquest which generated a great deal of ethnological speculation around the idea of natural law, lawyers and theologians in Portugal did not engage in an equivalent exercise – they produced no writers equivalent to Vitoria, Las Casas, or Acosta. However, the Portuguese did generate a lay colonial ethnography geared towards practical purposes, with minor crown officials such as Duarte Barbosa and Tomé Pires developing early on a remarkably accurate geographical genre which combined economic and ethnographic information. These early surveys were well supported by additional relations of particular areas, such as the description of China by Galiote Pereira, an account which had exceptional diffusion across Europe. Similarly, in a more epic vein, writers such as Castanheda, Barros, and Osório also produced a sophisticated national–monarchic historiography which propagated an ideology of providential Catholic imperialism. Whilst the Portuguese experience in Asia was more wide-ranging than the Castilian, it was mainly the cosmopolitan Jesuits who, as part of their missionary work, undertook the writing of the history of those areas where Portuguese colonial power was remote. In the Philippines, by contrast, the role of different religious orders was more balanced.

In assessing and comparing these materials, the transition from empirical ethnography to antiquarian ethnology is the crucial issue. Both the Portuguese and the Spanish excelled in empirical descriptions of cultural diversity rather than in the analysis of the coherence of alternative belief systems, and those descriptions which they produced were usually prompted by practical considerations devoid of higher scientific pretensions. In Asia the Portuguese developed a more assured grasp of empirical realities, and created a more solid historiographical tradition than Castilian writers, whose expertise was more focused on the Philippines. The Castilian contribution thus had a clear centre, and even a golden age, in the writings of missionaries working in the Philippines from 1570 to 1670 (although in many ways the key patterns were all established by 1630). This Spanish enterprise in Asia was weakened by lack of consistent metropolitan support, given the fact that the crown had more pressing priorities elsewhere, but despite the enormous distances involved, it was pursued with extraordinary energy.

Considering its wider scope, it is remarkable that the Portuguese practice of ethnography did not encourage more scientific speculation, with a few exceptions, such as the Jesuits, who in reality represented a more universal Counter-Reformation late humanist culture. It was at this humanist–missionary level that both Portuguese and Spanish writers made their most remarkable contributions to ethnology, with men such as Luis Fróis, João Rodrigues, and Francisco Colín working alongside Italians such as Roberto de Nobili and Matteo Ricci. The aim was usually to argue against the beliefs of the religious enemy, to distinguish elements of cultural difference which were compatible with Catholic Christianity from others which were not, and finally (but more rarely) to engage in a historical–antiquarian reconstruction of the more urbanized and literary native cultures of Asia in order to position Christianity within a local tradition whose prestige could not be challenged politically from outside. It was very rare for any of these writers to seek to question the European understanding of world history and European assumptions about what constituted rational behaviour on the basis of knowledge of Asian history and cultural diversity. Whilst Spanish writers provided much material for the ethnological speculations of a number of European humanist cosmographers and thinkers in the sixteenth and seventeenth centuries, it was only through the unintended consequences of missionary debates, such as those concerning the rational capacity of American Indians or the rites controversy, that Iberian ethnology came significantly to affect the direction of European thought towards the philosophical and scientific concerns of the Enlightenment.

6

'A truthful pen and an impartial spirit': Bartolomé Leonardo de Argensola and the Conquista de las Islas Malucas

JOHN VILLIERS

At first sight it may seem strange that the commission to write the history of the Spanish capture of the Moluccan spice island of Ternate in 1606, published under the title *Conquista de las Islas Malucas al Rey Felipe Tercero Nuestro Señor* three years later, should have been given to the Aragonese priest, Bartolomé Leonardo de Argensola.[1] Although he had already established a certain reputation as a historian by that date, he had no special knowledge or first-hand experience of the region, or of recent events that had taken place in it. Moreover, both he and his brother Lupercio were better known as poets, whose polished style and purity of language were to earn them the joint epithet of 'los Horacios españoles'.[2] Some critics, both in his lifetime and since, have questioned whether, even from a purely literary point of view, he was the most appropriate person to write the *Conquista*, maintaining that the smooth and often florid elegance of his prose style and the prolixity of his narrative, with its many digressions, contrasted unfavourably, for example, with Lupercio's more concise and simple prose-writing, and were attributes more

---

[1] The term 'Malucas' (Moluccas) is used in the title of the book, as it was used generally in both Spanish and Portuguese in the sixteenth century, to designate only the five clove-producing islands of Ternate, Tidore, Makian, Moti, and Bacan, together with the kingdom of Jailolo in Halmahera. I have therefore used 'Moluccas' in this essay to denote those islands in preference to the Indonesian 'Maluku', which is the name of the modern province of Indonesia. In addition to the five clove-producing islands, modern Maluku covers most of the other 'spice islands', including northern Halmahera, Morotai, Ambon, and Seram, as well as the Banda Islands, which in the sixteenth century were still the only known source of nutmeg and mace.

[2] P. Miguel Mir, 'Estudio literario sobre el Doctor Bartolomé Leonardo de Argensola', preface to *Conquista de las Islas Malucas al Rey Felipe Tercero Nuestro Señor* (Zaragoza, 1891), xx. Argensola himself (Conde de la Viñaza [ed.], *Obras sueltas de Lupercio y Bartolomé Leonardo de Argensola* (2 vols, Madrid, 1889), II, 301) recommended that:

> Si aspira al laurel, noble poeta
> La docta antigüedad tienes escrita,
> La de Virgilio y la de Horacio imita
> Que jugar del vocablo es triste seta.

suitable for a work of romantic fiction than for a political and military history.[3]

The choice of Bartolomé[4] may, however, be less surprising if we consider the circumstances surrounding the composition of the *Conquista*. At that time, most historical works were commissioned by royal or noble patrons anxious to ensure the justification and glorification of their deeds and achievements for posterity in fittingly heroic language. In such cases, it was not considered essential or even desirable for the historian to maintain the strict impartiality and accuracy that, especially if he were a classical scholar and a humanist, he would no doubt have wished to exercise, and it was tacitly accepted that some distortions of fact or at least a measure of economy with the truth would inevitably result. At the beginning of the seventeenth century, the important objective was still to produce a heroic narrative that, even if it were a work of actual history, a *historia verdadera*, and not cast in the guise of a historical romance or an epic poem, which were merely 'the pretence of history', nevertheless still had a moral and didactic purpose that was not always compatible with strict veracity or impartiality.[5] In such narratives it is sometimes difficult to tell where true historiography ends and propaganda begins. As the great Portuguese chronicler, João de Barros, whose *Décadas da Ásia* Argensola must certainly have read, put it in the prologue to the third *Década*, first published in 1563, 'history is a tilth and field in which is sown every divine, moral, rational and instrumental doctrine: whoever feeds on its fruit may convert it through the power of intellect and memory into a means to lead a just and perfect life pleasing to God and to men'. In this respect, the role of works of true history was the same as that of myths and fables, which 'explain the truth to the wise under a veil of poetic fiction', and among which Barros cites the works of Homer, Xenophon's *Cyropaedia*, Thomas More's *Utopia*, *The Golden Ass* of Apuleius, the Πιναξ attributed to Cebes, and the fables of Aesop. Any writings 'which do not have this benefit of instruction, besides wasting time, which is the most precious thing in life, corrupt the understanding and fill the mind with dross from the torrent of words and facts which they carry'.[6]

So when Argensola was commissioned by his powerful patron, the conde de Lemos, president of the Council of the Indies, to write a history of the successful expedition led by Don Pedro de Acuña, governor of the Spanish Philippines, to conquer Ternate, his task was not merely to glorify Acuña's achievements, but also and more importantly to demonstrate that the conquest was an act of enlightened statecraft and a blow struck against the heretical Dutch, whose hostile presence in Southeast Asian waters threatened

---

[3] See, for example, Joaquín Aznar Molina, *Los Argensola* (Zaragoza, 1939), 205. Molina contrasts Bartolomé's 'amenísimo estilo, más propio de la novela que de la historia' with 'el estilo conciso de Lupercio'.

[4] Where confusion might be caused in relation to his brother, I refer to Argensola as Bartolomé. Elsewhere in this essay he is referred to simply as Argensola.

[5] See Michael Murrin, *History and Warfare in Renaissance Epic* (Chicago, 1994), 13.

[6] João de Barros, *Terceira Decada da Asia* (Lisbon, 1563), fols v', vii', and viii'. All translations from Spanish and Portuguese in this essay are my own unless otherwise indicated.

the spread of the Catholic religion. His task was to show that Philip III, in this remote corner of the vast double empire he had ruled since his succession to the Portuguese and Spanish thrones in 1598, had taken on the role of defender of Catholic Christendom assumed by his grandfather, Charles V, as the successor of Charlemagne, and that he had established in an imperial context the principle of *cujus regio, ejus religio* laid down by the Peace of Augsburg in 1555, whereby every ruler had the authority to determine whether his realm should be Catholic or Protestant.

For both the Spanish and Portuguese, the debate on how morally to justify such enterprises and the physical subjugation that they entailed was complicated by the difficulty of applying the principle of a 'just war' to the imposition by force of their rule on the indigenous peoples of Africa, Asia or America. This was done on the somewhat specious grounds that in newly discovered lands Christian princes had assumed responsibility for the conversion of their inhabitants to the Catholic religion in return for the temporal authority delegated to them in those lands by successive popes, who in turn were deemed to have derived their temporal as well as their spiritual sovereignty throughout the world from Jesus Christ. The task of proselytizing the people of the Moluccas and the other islands of eastern Indonesia had already been entrusted by the papacy to the Portuguese under the terms of the *Padroado Real* almost twenty years before they actually arrived in Indonesian waters. The *Padroado* was a collection of rights and duties contained in a series of papal bulls issued between 1456 and 1514 and bestowed on the Crown of Portugal in its capacity as patron of the Catholic missions in lands that the Portuguese had discovered and of which they claimed to have taken possession. These bulls were paralleled by a similar series of bulls issued in favour of Spain that constituted the Spanish *Patronato Real*. The provisions of both were confirmed by the Treaty of Tordesillas of 1494, which established the line of demarcation between Spanish and Portuguese claims to possession of lands newly discovered and yet to be discovered throughout the world.

Ternate was one of the five clove-producing islands of the Moluccas on which the Portuguese had established fortresses and trading posts in the years following their first arrival in eastern Indonesia. In 1575, they had been driven out by the island's Muslim ruler, Sultan Baab Ullah, but their expulsion did not mean that they were no longer bound by the *Padroado Real* to continue their endeavours to convert the inhabitants to Catholicism, and the Jesuit missions in the Moluccas remained under Portuguese control until 1606. Bartolomé was therefore unable to justify the Spanish capture of Ternate on the grounds that it would bring about the conversion or reconversion of the islanders to the true Faith, and instead used the argument that it was necessary to counter the threat of Protestant heresy posed by the hostile presence in Indonesian waters of the Dutch, who only a year before, in 1605, had driven the Portuguese out of the neighbouring islands of Tidore and Ambon (Amboyna). Bartolomé also believed that the piratical activities of Francis Drake in the West Indies and South America, which he describes at some length in the *Conquista*, provided a related example in the New World of this struggle between Iberian Catholicism and northern European Protestantism.

It must have appeared to those who knew Argensola and his writings, not least to the conde de Lemos, that he could be guaranteed, without straying too far from the truth, to produce a heroic narrative on this lofty theme, using as his models the works of the great Greek and Latin writers of heroic prose and poetry and of their Renaissance descendants, chronicles such as Barros's *Décadas da Ásia*, the first three of which were published in Lisbon between 1552 and 1563 (the fourth did not appear until 1615); the eight *Décadas del Nuevo Mundo* of Pietro Martire d'Anghiera (Peter Martyr), first published in full in Alcalá de Henares in 1530; the *Hispania Victrix*, consisting of the *Historia General de las Indias* and the *Cronica della Conquista de Nueva-España*, of Francisco López de Gómara, produced in Zaragoza in 1552; and epic poems on imperial themes such as *La Araucana* of Alonso de Ercilla y Zuñiga, first published in full in Madrid in 1590, and *Os Lusíadas* of Luís Vaz de Camões, the first edition of which appeared in Lisbon in 1572. Moreover, as a priest he could be relied upon to lay due emphasis on the religious motives behind the conquest of Ternate while remaining faithful to the classical ideals of Greek and Roman historiography, and would thereby ensure that the name of Philip III would shine with ever greater lustre as the defender of the true Faith at the same time as he established the fame of Don Pedro de Acuña as a military hero.

There are interesting parallels between the *Conquista* and *La Araucana*, a long narrative poem about the Spanish conquest of Chile from 1569 to 1589, sometimes known as the Chilean Aeneid. Both are heroic narratives on an imperial subject, and *La Araucana*, although in verse, strives no less than the *Conquista* to be both a *historia verdadera* and a work of creative imagination. Like Argensola, Ercilla declares that his aim is to write 'the truth shorn of artifice', and he laments that consequently he has to confine himself to a single theme and is bound by 'the rigour of a single truth' to tread 'so lonely and sterile a path', unable to intermingle the historical narrative with any other subjects. But, again like Argensola in the *Conquista*, this does not prevent him from interpolating digressions and irrelevant or fictitious episodes. In this respect, Ercilla shares with Argensola, who was also a poet before he was a historian, and indeed with most Renaissance writers in all genres, including prose fiction, a reluctance to draw a rigid distinction between *historia verdadera* and *cuento* (tale), in other words, between history as the documented record of events and history as a creative literary form based on historical material but not bound by it. Both felt it necessary to interlard their 'truthful' accounts of historical events with dramatic and original stories, to combine credibility with creativity and artifice with instruction. This debate over the definition of truth had been engendered by the rediscovery in the Renaissance of the *Poetics* of Aristotle, which maintained that art, because it was concerned with universals, was a higher form of truth than mere fact. Likewise, in *Don Quixote* and the *Novelas ejemplares*, Cervantes is as anxious as his contemporary and friend Argensola to present his fictional work as a *historia verdadera* and to establish the credibility of his stories without reducing their dramatic effect or their qualities of novelty, suspense, or originality. At the same time, he makes Cide Hamete, the narrator in *Don Quixote*, declare that he felt constrained to confine himself to writing about Don Quixote and Sancho Panza, and dared not interpolate too many 'digressions or more weighty or more entertaining episodes'.[7]

II

Bartolomé Leonardo de Argensola (or Leonardo y Argensola) was born about 1562 in Barbastro, a small town in Aragon about sixty miles northeast of Zaragoza. He was a younger son of Juan Leonardo, whose family originated from Ravenna in Italy, while his mother belonged to the ancient Catalan family of Argensola. With his elder brother Lupercio, who was born about 1559, and a third brother, Pedro, who died young, he was educated at the University of Huesca, where all three boys studied under the celebrated Flemish scholar Andres Schotto. At that time, Juan Leonardo was secretary to the Emperor Maximilian II (r. 1564–76), who on several occasions before his election as emperor had acted as governor of Spain during the absences abroad of his uncle, Charles V. Consequently, Juan Leonardo had numerous influential friends and connections at the Spanish court, among them Don Fernando de Aragon, duque de Villahermosa, and his wife, Doña Juana de Ubernstain y Manrique, who, after Maximilian's death, had accompanied his widow, the Empress Maria, from Germany to Spain. It was through Juan Leonardo's friendship with the duke and duchess of Villahermosa that Lupercio, on completing his university studies, was appointed secretary to the duke, and that in 1588 Bartolomé became rector of Villahermosa, the 'obscure and remote town' in La Mancha from which the duke's family took its title.[8] As Lupercio wrote picturesquely in a poem of 1592, Bartolomé found himself in Villahermosa, 'among those harsh and rigid cloud-covered crags, of which the peaks are always shrouded with dark clouds, now reproving the people for their habits, now offering sacrifices for them on altars lit by sacred fires'.[9]

---

[7] '... por haber tomado entre manos una historia tan seca y tan limitada como esta de don Quijote, por parearle que siempre habia de hablar del y de Sancho, sin osar estenderse a otras digresiones y episodios mas graves y mas entretenidos': Vicente Gaos (ed.), *El Ingenioso Hidalgo Don Quijote de la Mancha* (4 vols, Madrid, 1967), part 2, ii, 557. On the conflicts between realism and creativity, imagination and veracity in the writings of Ercilla and Cervantes, see Diana de Armas Wilson, *Cervantes, the Novel and the New World* (Oxford, 2000), 161–71, and *passim*; Dominick Finello, *Cervantes: Essays on Social and Literary Politics* (London, 1998), 47–80; Joseph V. Ricapito, *Cervantes's Novelas Ejemplares: Between History and Creativity* (West Lafayette, IN, 1996), 4. For a detailed analysis of *La Araucana* as a historical epic, see Murrin, *History and Warfare*, 97–102.

[8] Mir, 'Estudio literario', xxxi.

[9] Viñaza, *Obras sueltas*, i, 17.

From Villahermosa, Bartolomé travelled frequently to Salamanca, to Valladolid, where Philip III had established his court, and to Madrid, where he first went as chaplain to the Empress Maria. The empress, widow of Maximilian II, daughter of Charles V and Isabella of Portugal, sister of Philip II, and mother of the Emperors Rudolf II and Matthias, and of Philip II's fourth wife, Anna of Austria, was a very great lady indeed: 'augusta la mayor da las augustas', as Bartolomé described her.[10] She lived in retirement in the convent of the Descalzes Reales, where one of her daughters, Doña Margerita de la Cruz, was a nun,[11] and where she died at the age of 74 on 26 August 1603.

During this time, Bartolomé's poetry was becoming known and highly esteemed among his contemporaries. Don Esteban Manuel de Villegas, who knew him well in Madrid, wrote in a verse letter to him: 'More than once, Bartolomé, I saw the finger of Madrid pointing you out and saying: "This is the Spanish paragon".'[12] Bartolomé's work was chiefly made known through meetings of the various literary juntas and academies that he joined, among them the Imitatoria, of which he became treasurer and which numbered among its members such distinguished contemporaries as Lope de Vega and Cervantes.

In Valladolid, Bartolomé met many leading courtiers and members of the nobility, including Don Fernández de Castro, marqués de Sarria, later conde de Lemos y de Andrade, a person of 'elevated and generous spirit and modest and honourable habits, resplendent with the loftiest titles of the Spanish aristocracy, having joined to his own inherited nobility, which was among the purest in the kingdom, that of his wife, daughter of the all-powerful duque de Lerma, favourite of King Philip III'.[13] In 1606, when Don Pedro de Acuña led a successful expedition from Manila to conquer Ternate, Lemos invited Bartolomé to Madrid and commissioned him to write a history of the event. The resulting book was completed in May 1609. Lupercio obliged with a preface. The work enjoyed an immediate success in Spain, but had to wait a hundred years before it was translated into any foreign languages: in 1706 a French translation entitled *Histoire de la conquête des Isles Moluques par les Espagnols, par les Portugues & par les Hollandois* was published in Amsterdam,[14] in 1708 John Stevens's translation into English appeared in London, and in 1710 a German translation under the title of *Beschreibung der Moluckischen Inseln,*

[10] Mir, 'Estudio literario', xli.
[11] *Ibid.* xxxvii. Doña Margarita was a person of such exceptional holiness that Pope Pius V, who was himself later to be canonized, once declared that she should have been canonized in her lifetime, if such a thing had been permitted.
[12] *Ibid.* xxxviii.
[13] *Ibid.* xxxix. On Lemos and the Argensola brothers, see also Alfonso Pardo Manuel de Villena, marqués de Rafal, *Un Mecenas Español de siglo XVII: El conde de Lemos noticia de su vida y de sus relaciones con Cervantes, Lope de Vega, los Argensola y demás literatos de su epoca* (Madrid, 1911).
[14] This edition is dedicated to the count of Kniphuisen, deputy of the States General of the United Provinces, and is in three volumes, the third of which was added by the translator and contains an account of the Dutch conquests in Asia.

und derer zwischen den Spanien, Portugiesen und Holländern darum geführten Kriege was published in Leipzig.[15]

Soon after the completion of the *Conquista*, Bartolomé, who had never found court life greatly to his taste, left Madrid and returned to Zaragoza. In an autobiographical poem, he wrote

> Today, Fabio, I retire from the court to delay for a few years in a village, if I can, the drawing of my last breath . . . How happy I am that from this moment I am giving up this office that is so repugnant to my inclinations . . . I am too dull-witted for the artificiality of our court, and the longer I continue, the clumsier and more inexpert I become . . . How can this court give me any pleasure when nowhere there do I have a quiet corner to which I can withdraw on my own?[16]

However, he was not yet to be given an opportunity to indulge his love of solitude and the simple life, for in 1610, Lemos was made viceroy of Naples and invited the two Argensola brothers to accompany him – Bartolomé as his companion, and Lupercio as his secretary. Lupercio accepted the post with enthusiasm, but Bartolomé with obvious reluctance, thereby causing some irritation to his friends, notably Cervantes, who had hoped to be chosen by Lemos to join the viceregal entourage.[17] Being half-Italian and half-Aragonese as well as extremely well-connected, Bartolomé had no difficulty in obtaining an entrée into Neapolitan literary and aristo-cratic circles.

In 1613, Lupercio died and was succeeded as secretary to the viceroy by his son, Don Gabriel Leonardo de Albion.[18] Shortly after, the conde de Lemos wrote to the *diputados* of the kingdom of Aragon asking them to appoint Bartolomé as official *cronista* (chronicler) of Aragon, a post that Lupercio had formerly occupied, and praising Bartolomé's learning, his knowledge of Latin and Spanish, and his great reputation in 'almost all the kingdoms of Europe'.[19] Meanwhile Bartolomé submitted to the *diputados* an account of how he saw the duties of an official historian, entitled *Discurso acerca de las cualidades que ha de tener un perfecto cronista.*

Two years later, in May 1615, Lemos's brother, Don Francisco de Castro, who was then Spanish ambassador in Rome, with the support of Cardinal Borghese, recommended Argensola[20] to Pope Paul V for a vacant canonry in the metropolitan cathedral of La Seo in Zaragoza. Lemos did not live to see his protégé become either the *cronista* of Aragon or a canon of La Seo, as he

---

[15] As Mir has pointed out, Spanish works of this genre were seldom translated at the time ('Estudio literario', cii), which may explain the long delay in the appearance of editions in English, French and German.

[16] Mir, 'Estudio literario', xliii.

[17] Villena, *Un Mecenas Español*, 101–9.

[18] Don Gabriel collected the poems of his father and uncle after the latter's death and published them under the title *Rimas de Lupercio, i del doctor Bartolome Leonardo de Argensola* (Zaragoza, 1634).

[19] D. José Maria Asensio y Toledo, *El Conde de Lemos Protector de Cervantes: Estudio histórico* (Madrid, 1880), 29.

[20] See note 4 above.

died, at the age of 42, on 19 October 1622, and neither appointment was confirmed until 1625. Argensola spent the last thirteen years of his life in Zaragoza, which was then a city with a vigorous intellectual life, its university 'at the summit of its glory' and famous for the excellence of its teaching, and its monasteries full of men 'noted for the sobriety of their lives and the abundance and soundness of their learning'.[21] There, on 26 February 1631, died the man whom Lope de Vega called the 'divine Aragonese'[22] and Fray Jeronimo de San José addressed as 'superior Leonardo',[23] whom Cervantes praised for his 'wit, elegance, style and generosity of spirit' ('su ingenio, gala, estilo y bizarria'),[24] and who, in the opinion of Fray Marcos de Guadalajara Xavierre, deserved 'the highest praise for his exceptional eloquence'.[25]

III

In a letter to Fray Jeronimo de San José, Argensola wrote that the historian must have 'a truthful pen, an impartial spirit and a free but restrained use of language'.[26] In his *Discurso* he enlarged on this theme of truthfulness and impartiality, declaring that 'the task of the perfect chronicler is to resist oblivion, taking out of its hands all that is worthy of memory and making an example from it full of truth and learning', that he should never indulge in unnecessary digressions or allow himself to be carried away by emotion, however righteous and legitimate this might seem, if in consequence the truth were diminished or discredited. The historian's task was to provide an image of reality obtained from the events that he recorded but corresponding with the ideal that he had formed in his mind.[27] One of his nineteenth-century biographers, Don Mario de la Sala, went so far as to assert in the *Almanaque del Diario de Avisos* of 1882 that Argensola 'never disturbed the harmony between the priest, the poet and historian', but always matched the moral rectitude and erudition that he demonstrated in his poetry with 'a priest's gravity and a historian's accuracy and thoroughness'.[28]

Certainly, in the *Conquista de las Islas Malucas*, Argensola successfully combined this 'free but restrained use of language' with the stylistic elegance that characterizes his poetry, and he did so again in the three substantial historical works that he wrote as official chronicler of Aragon – *Advertencias a la Historia de Felipe II*, *Alteraciones populares de Zaragoza en el año 1591*, and *Primera*

---

[21] Mir, 'Estudio literario', xxvii, lvi.

[22] *Filomena*, epistle 9.

[23] In a sonnet beginning 'Oh quien pudiera, superior Leonardo'. Fray Jeronimo (Don Jeronimo Ezquerra de Rozas) came from an ancient Aragonese noble family. He was born in Mallén in 1587, became a Discalced Carmelite in Zaragoza, and was one of Bartolomé's closest friends and most regular correspondents.

[24] *Viaje del Parnaso*, lib. VII.

[25] Fray Marcos de Guadalaxara y Xavierr, *Quinta Parte de la Historia Pontifical a la Magestad Catolica de Don Felipe Quarto Rey de las Españas y Nuevo Mundo* (Barcelona, 1603), ch. XVI, 50, A.

[26] Viñaza, *Obras sueltas*, II, 329.

[27] Mir, 'Estudio literario', xciii–xciv; Asensio y Toledo, *El Conde de Lemos*, 30.

[28] Mir, 'Estudio literario', cxxx.

*parte de los Anales de Aragón que prosigue los del secretario Jerónimo Zurita desde el
año 1516*, published in Zaragoza in 1630 – and that earned him the reputation of being a Spanish Tacitus or Livy, as well as a Spanish Horace.[29]

As for his truthfulness and impartiality, by the standards of the seventeenth
century, Argensola was undoubtedly a conscientious scholar, and his veracity
is only occasionally marred by serious inaccuracies or by a manifestly tall
story. Yet he makes no attempt to conceal the political and religious message
that the *Conquista* was intended to carry: in a long, defensive statement at the
beginning of the book and at several points thereafter he boldly declares that
his principal aim is to glorify the achievements of the Spanish in conquering
the Moluccas, thereby protecting the people of those islands from heresy and
bringing them back to the Catholic fold. In this opening statement he also
outlines the historiographical principles on which the composition of the
Conquista is based, and what he considers to be his qualifications for the task:

> I write of how Don Pedro de Acuña, governor of the Philippines and
> admiral of the Spanish fleet, brought the Moluccas back to their obedi-
> ence to Philip III, king of Spain, and their rulers to their former vassalage,
> which their predecessors had acknowledged. This was a victory worthy of
> the foresight of so pious a monarch, of the care of the grave ministers in
> his supreme council, and of the valour of our nation, not so much
> because of the extraordinary fertility of those lands as because it deprived
> the fleets of the northern nations of an important reason for sailing in
> Spanish waters and so prevented the purity of the faith newly received by
> the East Indians and the inhabitants of our colonies who trade with them
> [the Philippines] becoming infected with heresy. The short time which
> this action took does not diminish its glory; on the contrary, for that very
> reason it should properly occupy a place in more extensive accounts ['mas
> copiosas narraciones']. I am well aware of the risks I am running, but I am
> also confident that I shall not lack defenders. . . . The account that I am
> writing of the recovery of these kingdoms must pay no heed to the esteem
> or the contempt of others, for the prudent, who know how history is
> made, will esteem the part drawn from life, while others who, as they
> themselves admit, only read to pass the time, will consider it of little value,
> preferring some tale full of monsters or a weighty tome with the title of
> history, containing admirable numbers and many deaths and describing
> events, not as God makes them, but as they wish them to be.[30]

---

[29] *Ibid*, cxxix. Don Francisco Diego de Sayas wrote of Bartolomé in a sonnet:

> En él la fe de Tacito respira
> Y Livio en leche su elocuencia extiende.

[30] P. Miguel Mir (ed.), *Conquista de las Islas Malucas al Rey Felipe Tercero Nuestro Señor* (Zaragoza, 1891), Book
I, 2. All subsequent references in the notes to quotations from the *Conquista* are taken from this edition and
not from the 1609 edition.

In spite of these strictures against tales full of monsters and the recording of events as readers wish them to be, at many points in the *Conquista* Argensola seems as reluctant as Ercilla or Cervantes to draw a firm line between history and fiction. He also indulges in numerous digressions, which give the reader the impression that he may have believed a simple account of the Spanish conquest of Ternate would not have given him enough scope for the exercise of his literary skills or his imagination, and that he wished to show off the breadth of his vision and the depth of his scholarship. His shortcomings in this respect are charmingly excused by John Stevens in his preface to his 1708 translation of the *Conquista*. Stevens's reference to Spanish books and 'pleasing incidents' suggests that he was familiar with the *historia verdadera* debate and, no doubt, with the writings of Cervantes:

> Our author . . . was a Learned Clergyman, and as such employ'd by the President and Council of the *Indies* to Write this History. He calls it, *The Conquest of the Molucco Islands*, without Enlarging any further in his Title, tho' at the same time his Work contains their first Discovery, their Description, the Manners, Customs, Religion, Habit, and Political and Natural History; with all the Wars, and other Remarkable Accidents in those Parts, since they were first known to *Europeans*, till their Reduction under the Crown of Spain. In Speaking of them, he Occasionally runs out to give the same Account of the Philippine Islands, and of several others in those Eastern Seas. This is frequent in *Spanish* Books, wherein we generally find much more than the Titles promise, contrary to what is Practis'd with us, who strive to fill up a Title Page with abundance of Inviting Heads, the least part whereof is treated of in the Body of the Work, or at best so Superficially, that scarce any more can be made of them there, than was in the Frontispiece. . . . [He] Embelishes the whole with such variety of pleasing Incidents, that few Books of Travels afford so much Profitable Entertainment, with such good Authority.[31]

The chronicle begins with the story of the foundation of the ruling dynasties in Ternate and some other eastern Indonesian islands. Much of this appears to have been taken directly from the lost *História das Molucas* of António Galvão, of which the *Treatise on the Moluccas* of *c.* 1544, discovered in 1928 in the Archivo General de Indias in Seville, is thought to be a preliminary version.[32] Argensola relates how, according to 'a tradition among these people

---

[31] Stevens supplies this 'abundance of living heads' in the full title of his translation of the *Conquista*, which is *The Discovery and Conquest of the Molucco and Philippine Islands. Containing Their History, Ancient and Modern, Natural and Political: Their Description, Product, Religion, Government, Laws, Languages, Customs, Manners, Habits, Shape, and Inclinations of the Natives. With an Account of Many Other Adjacent Islands, and Several Remarkable Voyages Through the Streights of Magellan, and in Other Parts.*

[32] See Hubert Th. Th. M. Jacobs, SJ (trans. and ed.), *A Treatise on the Moluccas (c. 1544); Probably the Preliminary Version of António Galvão's lost História das Molucas* (Rome, 1970).

that is venerated as part of their religion', the Moluccas were governed in the most distant past by a prince called Bicocigara (Bikusagara), who was sailing one day along the coast of the island of Bacan and saw among the rocks some 'reeds of the kind they call *rotas* [rottan], which the people use to make ropes'. However, when he ordered his servants to go ashore to cut some and bring them to his boat, they returned saying that his eyes must have deceived him because they had not seen any reeds there. So Bicocigara went ashore himself, and at once they appeared before everybody's eyes. He ordered them to be cut, and blood began to flow from them. He then found four serpent's (*naga*) eggs among the reeds and heard a voice saying 'Keep those eggs, for from them four excellent rulers will be born'. He took the eggs home and, soon after, four humans were born from the yolks, three male and one female. The three males were the founders of the ruling dynasties of Bacan, Buton (Butung, off the east coast of Sulawesi), and the Papuan islands, while the female married Prince Lolodo (Loloda), 'who gave his name to a country in Batochina [Jailolo]'. From them 'thirteen idolatrous kings' were descended until the accession of Tidore Vongi, king of Ternate, who was the first ruler in the Moluccas to adopt Islam. Since then, 'idolatry . . . has become confused with the precepts of that abominable sect, thus creating divisions and doubts in people's minds'. Tidore Vongi was succeeded by his son, Kaicili (Prince) Boleife, who was ruler of Ternate when the Portuguese first arrived in the spice islands. He 'was no less superstitious' than his father and claimed to be able to foretell the future, a talent which Argensola dismisses in a characteristic phrase as merely 'a different kind of foolishness' ('otro género de vanidad'), but which earned him the reputation of a living oracle.[33]

Both at the beginning and at the end of this story, Argensola demonstrates his clear understanding of the nature of Southeast Asian kingship and the constant need for rulers, particularly if they were usurpers or had seized power by force, to establish their legitimacy by proving at least their spiritual, if not their genealogical, descent from a real or imaginary founder of the realm. At the same time, he demonstrates his credentials as a good Renaissance scholar and his respect for classical authority by comparing the story with similar stories in Greek mythology. He begins by saying:

> Of the fourteen most powerful rulers who have the title of king and hold sway over the Moluccas, those of Ternate and Tidore claim to be of divine origin, such liberty do humans usurp or ascribe to the most remote antiquity.[34]

He sums up by enlarging on this idea:

---

[33] Book I, 4.

[34] *Ibid.* 2. In a letter to Lemos, Argensola expressed the view that the Greeks and Romans were 'prodigious giants in all the arts and especially in history', and that since their time there had been 'very few who are not their imitators [arrendajos]'. (Viñaza, *Obras sueltas*, II, 301).

This fable has acquired so much authority that Bicocigara is honoured as a hero, the rocks are venerated and the four eggs are worshipped. The truth is that, by means of this prodigious superstition, that prudent man made his lineage sacred and so acquired kingdoms and veneration for his four children. In the same way, the Greeks believe or pretend to believe the story that Leda brought forth by the adulterous swan the eggs from which Castor, Pollux and Helen were born. In all these beginnings, proud Fortune persuades those whom she wishes to crown that, in order to introduce into people's minds the idea that they are divine, they should found their kingship on fables that imitate true mysteries, so that the royal race becomes exempt from the ordinary laws of birth.[35]

In this passage Argensola demonstrates how a ruler can exploit religious belief as an element of statecraft, without denying that the Portuguese had performed an essential task by first bringing the Catholic faith to the people of the Moluccas, or that the Spanish had performed an equally essential task in 1606 by protecting the same people from Protestant heresy, or that both had thereby earned the right to rule in the islands. He appears to be in agreement with the precept advanced by Machiavelli in his *Discorsi* that

The rulers of a republic or of a kingdom ... should uphold the basic principles of the religion which they practise in it, and, if this be done, it will be easy for them to keep their commonwealth religious, and, in consequence, good and united. They should also foster and encourage everything likely to be of help to this end, even though they be convinced that it is quite fallacious.[36]

A similar argument is to be found in the *Brief and True Report of the New Found Land of Virginia* of 1588 by the Elizabethan mathematician, cartographer, and astronomer, Thomas Harriot. Harriot describes the Algonquin Indians of Virginia as a simple and uncivilized people who had been coerced into adherence to their religion 'by the subtlety of priests to help instil obedience and respect for authority'. Harriot's account of the Algonquins, like Argensola's of the Moluccan islanders, appears to endorse the Machiavellian precept that a successful ruler should assert his authority and preserve social order not only by physical force, but also by the imposition upon his subjects of a set of religious beliefs. Moreover, like most of their European contemporaries, whether or not they held orthodox Christian beliefs themselves, both Harriot and Argensola extended Machiavelli's proposition to embrace the idea that the most effective means by which Europeans could win over

---

[35] Book I, 2–3.
[36] Niccolò Machiavelli, *The Discourses*, trans. Leslie Walker, rev. Brian Richardson, ed. Bernard Crick (Harmondsworth, 1970), 143. Quoted in Richard Mackenney, *Sixteenth Century Europe: Expansion and Conflict* (Basingstoke and London, 1993), 68.

the indigenous people they subjugated in new-found lands and maintain their authority over them thereafter was by converting them to Christianity.[37]

IV

Argensola turns next to a factual account of the Portuguese and Spanish voyages of exploration from the time of the Infante Dom Henrique (Henry the Navigator) to Vasco da Gama's discovery of the sea route to India. He deals with these in somewhat cursory fashion, and then describes the great voyage of Fernão de Magalhães (Magellan) across the Pacific, and of António de Abreu, Francisco Serrão, and their successors in the Moluccas. He discusses at some length the provisions of the Treaties of Tordesillas and Zaragoza, and the problems of demarcation to which these gave rise in the islands, as well as the rivalry between Boleife of Ternate and Almansur of Tidore at the time the Europeans first arrived, before giving a detailed account of the interminable internecine warfare that ensued in the region during the rest of the sixteenth century, in which the Portuguese and later the Spanish and the Dutch became inextricably involved. In all this he relies heavily, particularly for the earlier period, on the major Portuguese chroniclers, Barros, Castanheda, Couto, and Resende, on Galvão's 'História das Molucas', and on other local accounts, notably Gabriel Rebelo's 'História das Ilhas de Maluco' of 1561 and the same author's 'Informação das cousas de Maluco',[38] as well as making use of the papers of the Council of the Indies to which he had been given access.[39]

In all this, Argensola makes little attempt to defend the methods adopted by either the Portuguese or the Spanish in their struggles to gain political and commercial control in the eastern Indonesian islands. He considers that both 'exercised their power and conducted their trade with ambition and, as all the accounts say, with cruelty everywhere they went', and nowhere more so than in the Moluccas, which of all these theatres of war was 'the most blood-stained with perpetual tragedies'. He observes bitterly that, while the two Iberian nations were in armed conflict with each other in their empires, their kings in Europe conducted their quarrels by means of legal niceties and cosmography ('sutilezas de derecho y cosmografía').[40] He recounts with gloomy relish many lurid stories of Portuguese atrocities, and gives examples

[37] See Stephen Greenblatt, *Shakespearean Negotiations: The Circulation of Social Energy in Renaissance England* (Oxford, 1988), 21–65.
[38] Both of Rebelo's manuscript accounts are printed in Artur Basílio de Sá (ed.), *Documentação para a história das missões do Padroado Português do Oriente: Insulíndia* (5 vols, Lisbon, 1954–8), III, 193–344 and 345–508.
[39] A reliable recent history of Maluku is Leonard Y. Andaya, *The World of Maluku: Eastern Indonesia in the Early Modern Period* (Honolulu, 1993).
[40] Book I, 43. This is a reference to the prolonged dispute between Spain and Portugal in the first half of the sixteenth century over the line of demarcation between their spheres of influence, initially laid down at the Treaty of Tordesillas (1494), subsequently embodied in successive papal bulls, and supposedly clarified in the Treaty of Zaragoza (1529), particularly as it applied to the rival claims of the two powers over the Moluccas.

of the perfidy with which they abused the 'sacred laws of hospitality' and the affronts that they offered to the Muslim religion. He puts into the mouth of the sultan of Tidore a declaration that, by making themselves masters of the most fertile islands in Asia, the Portuguese had brought servitude and vassalage to the islanders, and converted the 'happy liberality of the heavens into tribute to feed the ambitions of the newly-arrived tyrants'.[41]

The authoritarianism, cruelty, and religious bigotry of which Argensola here accuses the Portuguese in this distant corner of their Asian empire were thought by many at the time, and later, to be equally, if not more, character-istic of Spanish rule in the New World. They gave rise to the so-called 'black legend', of which Bartolomé de Las Casas in his *Brevissima Relación de la destrucción de las Indias*, published in Seville in 1552, was the most famous exponent. In the *Conquista*, Argensola does not entirely exonerate the Span-ish either, no doubt because he was well aware that to do so would be a case of the Spanish pot calling the Portuguese kettle black.[42] At the same time, he repeatedly emphasizes the religious motives that determined much of what the Portuguese did in the region, as they did those of the Spanish. He observes, for example, that António Brito, who succeeded Francisco Serrão as captain of the Moluccas in 1522, dedicated the fortress of São João Bautista, which he had been instructed to build for the defence of Ternate, 'to the service of the Gospel and its ministers', and that he tried to have the *casis* (Muslim religious teacher) whom he found 'spreading the blasphemies of Mohammed' expelled from the kingdom as 'an obstacle to the truth'.[43] Later, when writing of events in the middle of the century, he says:

> At this time, the voice of the Gospel rang in the barbarous ears of the people of the archipelago through the preaching of the religious – Augus-tinian, Dominican and Franciscan – and through Father Francis Xavier and his companions. . . . There were some governors who, in addition to the care with which they set about propagating the Gospel and maintain-ing peace in those states, attracted the barbarians to a love of our ways, our mode of life, our conversation and affability, and gently inclined them towards our customs.[44]

---

[41] Book II, 59.
[42] See Charles Gibson (ed.), *The Black Legend: Anti-Spanish Attitudes in the Old World and the New* (New York, 1971), 18–25; William S. Maltby, *The Black Legend in England: The Development of Anti-Spanish Sentiment 1558– 1660* (Durham, NC, 1971), 12–28. The Portuguese black legend is associated primarily with the *Diálogo do Soldado Prático* of Diogo do Couto and is concerned almost exclusively with political corruption in the Estado da Índia. The *Soldado Prático* was not printed until 1790, so it is unlikely that Argensola knew of it, but Couto's views are corroborated by Linschoten, whose *Itinerario*, first published in Amsterdam in 1596, followed by English and German translations in 1598 and two Latin translations in 1599, Argensola may well have read. See George Davison Winius, *The Black Legend of Portuguese India: Diogo do Couto, His Contemporaries and the Soldado Prático: A Contribution to the Study of Political Corruption in the Empires of Early Modern Europe* (New Delhi, 1985).
[43] Book I, 15.
[44] *Ibid.* 47–8.

With remarkable perspicacity, Argensola goes on to point out that 'in some places this made the people think they were being treated as equals, whereas in reality it was a kind of servitude'. He demonstrates how, in Machiavellian fashion, in this process of acculturation the imposition of civil authority ('justicia') following military conquest went hand in hand with evangelization or spiritual conquest, and how together they brought about both 'inner happiness and political control'. However, 'since the ministers [missionaries] did not have the first, the populace lacked the second and so returned to their former blindness'.[45] Argensola seems here by implication to be contrasting the role of the missionaries of the *Padroado Real* in eastern Indonesia, both the Jesuits and the Mendicant Orders, with that of the friars in the Spanish Philippines. His contention appears to be that in eastern Indonesia the missionaries tried to create peace and a love of European ways exclusively by proclaiming the Gospel and by example, without attempting to establish direct political control in the region, so that ultimately their efforts at evangelization were doomed to failure, whereas in the Philippines the Spanish had already begun the process of ensuring both their political control and the permanent conversion of the indigenous population by imposing the system that came later to be known as the frailocracy, by which in almost every parish the Augustinian, Franciscan, or Dominican friars eventually came to control the civil government at the expense of the local *gobernadorcillo*.[46]

In this discussion of the different methods adopted by the Spanish and Portuguese in their overseas empires, the part played by both powers in the struggle for control of the spice trade in the Moluccas, and the activities of the missionaries working there under the terms of the *Padroado* or the *Patronato*, Argensola had to take account of the fact that since 1580 the crowns of Spain and Portugal had been united. This was by no means an unprecedented event in the history of the Iberian peninsula. The monarchies of Castile–Leon and Aragon–Valencia–Catalonia had themselves originally come into being largely as a result of a series of dynastic unions, and they in turn had been united to form the Spanish monarchy following the marriage in 1469 of Isabella of Castile and Ferdinand of Aragon. As for the kingdom of Portugal, had plans materialized for Isabella to marry the elderly Afonso V of Portugal instead of Ferdinand, the Spanish monarchy would have consisted of Castile and Portugal instead of Castile and Aragon. Again, in 1497, after the death of Don Juan, the only son of Ferdinand and Isabella, it seemed likely for a short time that there would be a Portuguese succession to the thrones of Castile and Aragon. In the event, it was the death in 1578 at the battle of Alcazar-el-Kebir of the young King Sebastião of Portugal, and the extinction of the line of Avis two years later with the death of his uncle,

[45] *Ibid.* 48.
[46] On the history of the first century of Spanish rule in the Philippines and the role of the friars in establishing it, see John Leddy Phelan, *The Hispanization of the Philippines: Spanish Aims and Filipino Responses 1565–1700* (Madison, 1959).

Cardinal Henrique, that led to the succession to the Portuguese throne of Philip II, whose mother was Isabella of Portugal, daughter of Manuel I.

Although his succession had only been secured by a Spanish invasion and military occupation of Portugal, Philip II made it abundantly clear at the Cortes of Tomar in April 1581, at which he was acclaimed king, that Portugal was not to be regarded as a conquest or a realm that he had annexed and could therefore govern in any way he wished. It was his legitimate inheritance as the eldest (and, as it happened, also the most powerful and geographically the nearest) male descendant of Manuel I, and that the union of the two crowns was a purely personal one similar to that which had been established between Castile and Aragon 100 years earlier by the marriage of Ferdinand and Isabella. Portugal thus simply became one more of the already large number of kingdoms that Philip II 'ruled and governed as if the king who holds them all together were king only of each one of them'.[47] The independent identity of Portugal was guaranteed, it retained its own laws and its own coinage, and the government of all its imperial possessions was to remain in Portuguese hands. Trade throughout the empire was to remain under Portuguese control, and all trade between Spanish and Portuguese in their overseas possessions was prohibited.

Although none of these arrangements did much to diminish the ancient rivalries that existed between the two Iberian kingdoms or to reduce Portuguese resentment at finding themselves under Castilian rule, they had numerous advantages for both sides. Portugal desperately needed Spanish manpower and Spanish silver to sustain its already crumbling and impoverished empire, while Spain gained an immensely valuable addition to its imperial possessions in Asia, Africa, and America, and, perhaps even more important from the point of view of those who, like Argensola, saw the Atlantic powers of northern Europe – England and the Netherlands – as the most serious threat to Spain's imperial power and the spread of the Catholic religion, a new seaboard on the Atlantic and with it a substantial increase in naval power in the form of ships, shipyards and seamen, as well as the still thriving port of Lisbon. Cardinal Granvelle, indeed, urged Philip II to make Lisbon his permanent capital in preference to Madrid.

In the event, the 'Babylonian captivity' of the Portuguese under the rule of the Spanish Habsburgs lasted for only sixty years, and long before the revolt of 1640 that brought it to an end, the Portuguese empire in Asia had entered a critical phase. In 1591, Philip II created a new Council of Finance composed of men chosen by himself to control the Portuguese *Casa da Índia* and the operations of the spice trade, and Spanish merchants in the Philippines began to take advantage of these changes to encroach upon Portuguese commercial activities in Asia. Meanwhile, the Dutch and, to a lesser extent, the

---

[47] Juan de Solórzano Pereira, *Política Indiana* [1647] (Madrid, 1930), Book IV, ch. XIX, §37. Quoted in J. H. Elliott, *The Revolt of the Catalans* (Cambridge, 1963), 8.

English, having already successfully challenged Portuguese mastery of the sea route to India by way of the Cape, began to compete with the Portuguese for control of the spice trade and, by thus attacking the Portuguese in their maritime empire, at the same time struck a blow against Spanish power.[48]

V

Thus far, we have observed Argensola carrying out more or less conscientiously his commission both to write a book justifying and glorifying the Spanish conquest of Ternate in 1606 and to supply the historical background for that event by recounting as impartially as possible the indigenous history of the Moluccas as it was then known and the consequences of the arrival of the Portuguese in Indonesian waters in the early sixteenth century. But his tendency to digress and, as Stevens put it, to 'Embelish . . . with . . . pleasing incidents' is never long suppressed, and nowhere is this more apparent than in the description in Book VI of Cambodia (Camboja) and of its abandoned former capital, Angkor Thom. However, although this account provides a striking example of how his capacity (or his willingness) to judge what was relevant to his main theme could sometimes entirely desert him, it also provides a good example of his historical method. It is clear that, in a praiseworthy attempt to achieve impartiality and veracity, he consulted a wide variety of recently published secondary sources as well as some eyewitness accounts, but that his own lack of direct knowledge of the country and its history rendered him unable to distinguish between first-hand testimony and hearsay report, and led him into some spectacular confusions and factual errors in his general description of Cambodia, at the same time as it gave him sufficient material for a surprisingly accurate account of Angkor.[49]

He begins by saying that Camboja is an island, which he then confuses with Cambay (Gujarat) and describes as one of the most fertile of the regions of India, sending an abundance of merchandise to other parts, and consequently frequented by Spanish, Persian, Arab, and Armenian merchants. He says that the king is a Muslim and that his subjects are 'Gujaratis and Banians, who follow the precepts of Pythagoras, perhaps without any knowledge of him', and are 'all sharp-witted and reputed to be the cleverest merchants in India'. He then compounds the confusion by saying that the city of Camboja has given its name to the whole country and is also called Champa (the name of the Indianized kingdom of the Chams in southern Vietnam).[50] He is correct in saying that Cambodia was an important source of calambac, an aromatic wood also known as lignum aloes or eaglewood, and perhaps also in maintaining that it grew in regions still

[48] See J. H. Elliott, 'The Spanish monarchy and the kingdom of Portugal, 1580–1640', in Mark Greengrass (ed.), *Conquest and Coalescence: The Shaping of the State in Early Modern Europe* (London, 1991), 48–68.

[49] Book VI, 212–14.

[50] Stevens does not correct this confusion in his translation, except to say that Camboxa is a city, not an island, 'which gives its name to all the country, and is also call'd Champa' (Book VI, 142–3).

so unknown that the living trees had never been seen (by Europeans), but then mentions that precious stones and rock crystal were products of the country, which would apply more readily to Gujarat than to Cambodia. He is on slightly firmer ground in his description of the River Mekong, which appears to be largely based on the work of Gaspar da Cruz.[51] He says that it is 'the first river in India', that it waters the whole kingdom and carries so much water in the summer that it floods the fields like the Nile. He says that it joins another, lesser ('menos caudaloso') river at a place called Chardemuco, and that the water in this lesser river runs backward. This is a fairly accurate description of the Tonle Sap or Great Lake, which is situated in the centre of the great alluvial plain that covers most of modern Cambodia and from which flows a tributary that joins the Mekong at Phnom Penh. During the wet season of the southwest monsoon, the Tonle Sap can quadruple in size as the floodwaters of the Mekong are diverted into the lake, and the ensuing flood provides abundant water for wet rice production and a rich harvest of fish. But Argensola, apparently still following Gaspar da Cruz, gives fantastic reasons for this phenomenon, saying that, because the Mekong flows through such flat country and the south winds are so violent for six months of the year, the estuary becomes choked with sand, and that this checks the water and finally reverses its flow until the dry season ('el tiempo mas benigno'), when the process is reversed and the rivers are restored to their normal courses. He compares the Mekong with the Tagus, which flows into the Atlantic, and the Guadalquivir, which flows into the Mediterranean, 'opposed by the superior force of the sea waves and the winds', a comparison he may have borrowed from the recently published account of Gabriel Quiroga de San Antonio.[52]

At this point, Argensola's awareness that much of his description was based largely on unreliable or garbled hearsay evidence seems to have reasserted itself, and with it his fear that he might thereby be damaging his reputation for historical veracity, by which he set so much store. In his account of the great Khmer capital of Angkor that follows, he candidly admits that the very existence of an abandoned city of such magnificence in the middle of the Cambodian jungle seemed quite improbable and inexplicable to him. So he takes special care to remind the reader that he is making use of relatively trustworthy sources of information at the same time as he emphasizes his original reluctance to write about Angkor at all lest he be accused of indulging in fantasy. His description confirms and at some points amplifies much of what can be found in other sixteenth- and early seventeenth-century Portuguese and Spanish accounts of Angkor, notably those of Diogo do Couto, Marcello de Ribadaneyra, San Antonio, and Christoval de Jaque, which must in turn have been partly based on the first-hand reports of Chinese, Indian,

---

[51] Gaspar da Cruz, *Tractado em que se contam muito por estenso as cousas da China* (Évora, 1569). English translation in C. R. Boxer (ed.), *South China in the Sixteenth Century* (London, 1953), 3–239.

[52] Fray Gabriel de S. Antonio, *Breve e verdadera relacion de los successos del Reyno de Camboxa al Rey Don Philipe nuestro Señor* (Valladolid, 1604).

Malay, Thai, or Japanese traders, Portuguese and Spanish missionaries, and such adventurers as the Portuguese Diogo Veloso, the Spaniards Blas Ruiz and Gregorio Vargas, who were in Cambodia in the 1590s, and perhaps also of members of the two Spanish military expeditions sent from Manila to Cambodia under Juan Xuarès Gallinato in 1596 and under Luis Pérez Dasmariñas in 1598. Argensola also says he that he obtained information from the reports of someone whom he describes as a man 'eminent for his learning' ('un hombre grave en letras'), and from Augustinian and Dominican missionaries. Unlike his wildly confused general account of Cambodia, many details of his description of Angkor, notably his remarks about the time and the manner of its rediscovery, the architecture, and the hydraulic works, are correct or at least bear some relation to the facts:

> About this time [i.e. when the first missionaries arrived in Cambodia in the mid-sixteenth century] in the remotest part of the country beyond impenetrable forests, not far from the kingdom of the Laos, was discovered a city of about six thousand houses, which is now called Angon. The edifices and streets are made of massive marble stones, skilfully worked and still as intact as if they had been modern works. The strong walls are scarped or sloped on their inner side in such a way that it is possible to go up at any point on to the battlements, which are all different and represent various animals: one shows the heads of lions and another the heads of elephants or tigers, and so on in continual variety. The moat is also of hewn stone and is large enough to admit ships. It has a magnificent bridge, its arches in the form of stone giants of a prodigious height. The aqueducts, although dry, are no less magnificent. . . . On one side of the city is a lake over thirty leagues in circumference [the Tonle Sap]. There are epitaphs, inscriptions and characters that have not yet been deciphered. . . . I confess that I was reluctant to write about this and that it seemed to me that it must be an imaginary city like Plato's Atlantis or the city of his *Republic.* But there is no wonderful thing or event that is not a source of great doubts. Today the city is inhabited and our serious and trustworthy Augustinian and Dominican religious who have preached in those parts testify to the truth of it. A man eminent for his learning conjectures that it was the work of the Emperor Trajan, but though he extended his empire further than his predecessors, I have never read that he reached as far as Cambodia. Were the histories of the Chinese as well known as ours, they would inform us why so great a place was abandoned. They would explain the inscriptions on the buildings and everything else that is unknown even to the natives themselves. I do not know how to account for such a beautiful city being forgotten or not known.[53]

[53] Book VI, 214–15. For a detailed discussion of Argensola's account of Cambodia and a comparison of it with other sixteenth-century Spanish and Portuguese accounts, see Bernard Philippe Groslier and C. R. Boxer,

Argensola's healthy degree of scepticism about the notion that Angkor had been built by the Emperor Trajan is in refreshing contrast to the credulity of many of his contemporaries, including Ribadaneyra and San Antonio, who were willing to believe that it was the work either of the Romans or of Alexander the Great or even of the Jews. On the other hand, he sometimes shows himself to be as credulous as any of them about the wonders and marvels of the Orient. He maintains, for example, that crocodiles with four eyes and a very small heart had been caught in the Moluccas,[54] that on the Isle of Swans, a small island off the coast of Madagascar, there were bats with heads as big as apes and huge tortoises, one of them so large that it could walk with four men sitting on its back, while ten men could dine off the back of another.[55] He describes among the 'infinite curiosities' to be found on Sulawesi (Celebes) a certain tree with wide-spreading branches which had the strange property that anyone who lay under it facing west obliterated the shadow if he turned over so as to face east, while the same shadow acted as an antidote to poison at a distance of four spans (*palmos*).[56]

Like most of his contemporaries, Argensola makes little attempt to understand the cultures of the various people about whom he is writing, and he adopts an unashamedly Eurocentric and superior attitude towards them. This is particularly true of the people of the eastern Indonesian islands, about whom he makes sweeping generalizations full of moral indignation at their barbarity and physical disgust at their appearance. Some of these are taken almost verbatim from Rebelo and other Portuguese commentators. In Book II he follows Rebelo in declaring that the inhabitants of Sulawesi (Celebes), which, perhaps in an attempt to strengthen Spanish claims in the region, he says incorrectly is an archipelago that includes the Visayas and Mindanao in the Spanish Philippines, are 'filthy and lewd in their habits' ('sucios y torpes en sus costumbres'), and that they frequent male brothels ('mancebias nefandas', picturesquely translated by Stevens as 'stews of sodomy').[57] He

---

Angkor et le Cambodge au XVIe siècle d'après les sources portugaises et espagnoles (Paris, 1958), 21, 79–81, 87–9, 98, 107, and 152–3. It is somewhat ironic that much of our present knowledge of early Angkor is derived from those same Chinese sources that Argensola, with unwitting prescience, regrets were so little known in his time.

[54] Book II, 57.

[55] Book VII, 236.

[56] Book II, 72. Rebelo in his *História* also describes a tree with a shadow that is poisonous when it is on the tree's western side and that acts as an antidote when it passes over to the eastern side. This is one of the milder if more fanciful of the many descriptions of poisonous trees in the Indonesian archipelago, ranging from Odoric of Pordenone in the early fourteenth century, the *Herbarium Amboinense* (1685) of Rumphius, and *The Loves of Plants* (1799) of Erasmus Darwin to Leschenault de la Tour and Thomas Horsfield in the early nineteenth. The tree that gave rise to the legend is probably *Antiaris toxicaria*, which grows chiefly in Java. In Java it is known as *ancar*, and in Sulawesi and the Philippines as *ipo*. See E. M. Beekman (trans. and ed.), *The Poison Tree: Selected Writings of Rumphius on the Natural History of the Indies* (Amherst, 1981), 127–39. On European accounts of the poison and experimentation with it by the Royal Society, see Daniel Carey's essay in this volume.

[57] Book II, 72. Stevens's translation, 49. Rebelo also mentions male brothels in 'some parts of the island of Celebes', which he describes as 'mancebias públicas de homens, que usão por cima e por baixo' (Sá, *Documentação*, III, 394), and numerous other sixteenth-century writers comment on the prevalence of homosexuality ('o pecado nefando') in Sulawesi. Many of the homosexuals seem to have been *bissus*, the male transvestite priests who were often married to other men and whose chief function was to act as shamanistic

declares that the people of Batochina (Jailolo) are 'savages, without law, without king, without towns, living in the wilderness',[58] that Moro (northwest Halmahera, Morotai, and Rau) produces 'false, brutish and pusillanimous people',[59] and that Papua, 'islands that are little frequented by the Portuguese because they are numerous, and full of shoals', is inhabited by people with 'thin, ugly faces' who are 'capable of any treachery' and sometimes suffer from albinism, adding the curious comment that many of them are deaf.[60] Even the Chinese he dismisses as afflicted with 'an insatiable lust for gold and silver' and 'passionately addicted to luxury and lasciviousness', a trait which he ascribes to their inordinate love of perfumes,[61] while he says almost nothing about the Japanese, who were considered by many sixteenth-century European commentators to be the most civilized and refined people in Asia, and were described by Francis Xavier, for example, as unsurpassed among the pagan nations, and 'a race of very fine manners'.[62] It goes without saying that he is violently hostile to the 'Mohammedan superstition' of the 'abominable sect', wherever it might be found.

It is not altogether surprising that Argensola, with his shaky command of geography, should follow Rebelo, Luís Fróis, and other sixteenth-century commentators in perpetuating the idea of a Terra Australis, the vast southern continent that Ptolemy had postulated to balance the continental land masses of the northern hemisphere. The world maps of such late sixteenth-century Venetian cartographers as Giacomo Gastaldi and Giovanni Francesco Camocio still show this southern continent, which they call 'Terra Incognita', thus demonstrating that, even 150 years after the first Portuguese voyages east of Melaka and Magellan's voyage across the Pacific, the conflict between the authority of classical antiquity as exemplified by Ptolemy's *Geography*, of which the earliest printed editions date from the 1470s, and the mounting volume of empirical evidence accumulated in the wake of the discoveries, had still not been finally resolved in favour of the latter. What is perhaps somewhat unexpected is that, again like Rebelo and Fróis, he should claim that the existence of this continent had actually been confirmed by the voyages of discovery. 'If we are to believe the accounts of Spanish pilots who have sailed that way', he writes,

intermediaries in the religious rites of the pre-Islamic Bugis people. There is an extensive literature on the subject: see, for example, Gilbert Hamonic, 'Les fausses-femmes du pays bugis (Celebes-sud)', *Objets et mondes*, 17/1 (1977); *idem*, 'Travestissement et bisexualité chez les *bissu* du pays Bugis', *Archipel*, 10 (1975), 121–35; H. Jacobs, 'The first locally demonstrable Christianity in Celebes, 1544', *Studia*, 17 (1966), 294; Fr Paulo da Trindade, *Conquista espiritual do Oriente* (3 vols, Lisbon, 1967), III, 492–3.

[58] Book II, 70.

[59] *Ibid.* 71.

[60] *Ibid.* 71.

[61] Book IV, 158.

[62] This estimate of the Japanese is contained in a letter written in November 1549 by Francis Xavier from Kagoshima to his brethren in Goa. Quoted in Georg Schurhammer, S.J., *Francis Xavier: His Life, His Times*, (4 vols, Rome, 1973–82), IV, 82–3.

'these islands run along a vast continent which terminates at the Straits of Magellan.'[63]

Argensola's narrative skills, his elegant prose style, and his poetic sensibility are shown at their best and his impartial spirit is most apparent when he is able to base his description of an event on what is clearly first-hand evidence, even though he has had no direct experience of it himself. A good example of this is his vivid account of the installation of Kaicili Baab Ullah as sultan of Ternate in 1570, which gives him an opportunity to show again how Islam and pre-Islamic pagan religion existed side by side in the Moluccas, particularly in the context of royal rituals. Here Argensola the poet and Argensola the historian are well matched. When the new sultan had been acclaimed,

> the people went out in procession to the principal mosque to offer sacrifice. A boy went in front leading a kid with little gilded horns, which was to be the sacrificial victim. The Koran forbids sacrifices, but these islanders receive the rites of Islam so confusedly that they retain with them those of their ancient idolatry and intermix their ceremonies ['confunden las ceremonias']. According to custom, the man who conducted the sacrifice was followed by some members of the royal guard with their pikes raised, and after them went one holding aloft a small gold pan full of burning coals into which they threw incense. After him came the king, over whose head was carried an umbrella made of feathers of several colours and hemispherical in shape. The king was surrounded by these guards, who are given to him by his subjects as a form of tribute, like Turkish janissaries. In this order they proceeded to the mosque, at the gates of which anyone about to enter can find kettles and jars full of water with which to wash their hands and feet before they go in. As soon as the king reached the threshold, the music played and, as is their custom, they spread snow-white carpets, on which they kneel and mutter their vain prayers, bowing their heads to the ground. . . . The profane sacrifice being ended, they conducted the new king to the harbour, where he boarded his *kora-kora* [double outrigger boat] with his family and the other *sengaji* [governors] and great men and many others. . . . He sat or lay on [a] rich bed, while his household servants stirred the air above his head with a great fan made of various coloured feathers of the birds that fly about his islands. Thus he coasted about, while the sea and the shore resounded with gunshots, shouts and barbaric instruments.[64]

---

[63] Book II, 71. In a letter sent from Melaka on 19 November 1556 to the Jesuits in Portugal, Luís Frois states that the coastline of this southern continent was 700 leagues long and reached almost as far as Mexico, 'according to some Castilians who had come from there'. His letter is printed in Hubert Jacobs, SJ (ed.), *Documenta Malucensia I (1542–1577)* (Rome, 1974), 191.

[64] Book II, 79–81.

Such descriptive passages are all too rare in the *Conquista*, although occasionally Argensola enlivens his narrative with a telling little detail evidently based on the personal observation of one of his informants, as, for example, when he describes Almansur of Tidore in November 1521 boarding the *Trinidad*, the flagship of Gonzalo Gomez de Espinosa, commander of what was left of Magellan's fleet, and holding his nose 'with his fingers, either because of the smell of our food or of the ship'.[65]

VI

At the beginning of Book IV, Argensola justifies his long digression in Book III about the activities of Francis Drake in the West Indies and South America, and of Sarmiento's pursuit of him, by linking it, in the most exalted language, to his primary purpose of recounting the achievements of the Spanish in bringing the Catholic religion to the remotest corners of their empire and preventing the introduction of Protestant heresies. He expresses the opinion that, had he not been checked, Drake would have opened the way for 'Huguenot, Lutheran and Calvinist sectarians' to bring in ships laden with 'heretical Bibles and other books of infected doctrine', thus poisoning the innocent souls of the people with this 'infernal novelty', which in his view was no less offensive to God than idolatry or the teachings of the Koran. However, divine providence had ensured that this did not happen and that the people remained 'in the shadow and darkness of ignorance until the pure Gospel could be sent to them'.[66] Argensola seems to have believed that the same thing might have happened in the Moluccas after Drake's successful visit to Ternate in 1579, had not the Spanish intervened so decisively in the affairs of the Moluccas after the union of the crowns of Spain and Portugal in the following year.

Argensola then delivers a peroration in which he sums up the main argument of the whole book and reiterates his view of the purpose of history and the duties of the historian:

The perfect history is the witness of the times, the light of truth, the life of memory and, in fine, the master of life. Therefore, to perform the duty that such lofty functions make incumbent upon it, one cannot be excused from making important digressions [for example, the description of Drake's activities in the Americas], still less when they only divert a little from the principal subject and may have some connection with it. In this matter, honour is due to a most prudent action of Philip II and his ministers. It demonstrates his Catholic indignation against the sectarians, his zeal to preserve the faithful of his Indies inviolate, and to increase

[65] Book I, 20.
[66] Book III, 107.

the disposition of idolatrous souls to apply themselves to the Faith. It shows how the world was bestirred by means of his captains to introduce the Faith in all its corners, and does credit to our vigilance in the service of this mystical empire, which now struggles to triumph. For this reason, it is essential not to decry the constancy of Sarmiento, nor to abandon him in those remote seas until he returned to Spain and we yield place to the Moluccas.[67]

In the very last sentence of the *Conquista*, Argensola returns to his principal argument and states again what he considers to be the true and most important outcome of the Spanish conquest of Ternate. 'The Moluccas being reduced', he writes, 'our ministers and preachers went thither and the voice of the Gospel resounded again in the uttermost ends of the earth.'[68] So the book closes as it begins, with a declaration from its author that the principal aim of the Spanish in trying to drive the Dutch out of the Moluccas was not so much to ensure their domination of the trade in cloves and nutmeg as to prevent the northern nations from infecting the islanders' newly won faith with heresy. In reality, while it is true that the desire of the missions in the Philippines to propagate the Catholic religion in the Indonesian archipelago and elsewhere in Southeast Asia was an important motive behind successive attempts by the Spanish to acquire a fortified base in the Moluccas (as it was behind their expeditions to Cambodia), no less important was their goal of participating directly in the spice trade, an ambition that they had entertained ever since the Portuguese loss of Ternate to Baab Ullah in 1575 and even more strongly since the union of the crowns in 1580; and there is no doubt that the presence of the Dutch in the region threatened from the outset to be a far greater impediment to the latter enterprise than to the former. In this connection, Argensola very appositely quotes a letter written from Tidore in July 1591 by the Venetian Fr António Marta, superior of the Society of Jesus in the Moluccas, to Don Gómez Pérez Dasmariñas, governor of the Philippines, in which he urges the Spanish to conquer the spice islands not only because they produce an inexhaustible supply of cloves, nutmeg, and mace, but also because

> Your Lordship will gain more than 200,000 souls for God, since all the inhabitants will become Christian as soon as the kingdom is subdued, with very little or no opposition, whereby Your Lordship will have a burning flambeau in this world to light and lead you to heaven . . . and it will ennoble and perpetuate your name with a title equal to that of such ancient Roman commanders as Germanicus, Africanus and others like them.[69]

---

[67] Book IV, 127–8.

[68] Book X, 393.

[69] Book V, 188. The full text of the Spanish translation of the lost Portuguese original of the letter is in Hubert Jacobs, SJ (ed.), *Documenta Malucensia II (1577–1606)* (Rome, 1980), 304–9.

Although the aim of converting 200,000 of the islanders to Christianity was no more nearly achieved than that of gaining an inexhaustible supply of spices, by 1640 such arguments as there still were in favour of the Spanish remaining in the spice islands were certainly more religious than commercial. The enormous expense and difficulty of maintaining the Spanish presence in the islands in the face of mounting hostility from the Dutch and their increasing domination of the spice trade was already proving too great a drain on the exiguous resources of the Spanish Philippines. This, together with the general eclipse of Portuguese power in the Indonesian archipelago, culminating in the Dutch conquest of Portuguese Melaka in January 1641, combined with the almost simultaneous Portuguese revolt against Spain, the dissolution of the union of the two crowns, and the accession of João IV to the Portuguese throne, even prompted some members of the Council of the Indies to advocate the total abandonment of the Spanish fortresses in the spice islands. As the Jesuit Fr Diego de Bobadilla declared bluntly in a report written about 1640, Spain now held on to her possessions in the Moluccas 'rather for the conservation there of the Faith . . . than for the profit that is derived from them'.[70] In the end, however, it was not Dutch hostility, but the threatened attack on Manila in 1662 by the Chinese condottiere Koxinga from his base in Formosa, that led the Spanish to withdraw their garrisons from Ternate and Tidore, and thus to nullify the achievements of a conquest that fifty years before Bartolomé Leonardo de Argensola had hailed as a notable victory of the true religion over Protestant heresy.

---

[70] An English translation of Bobadilla's report is in H. H. Blair and J. N. Robertson (eds), *The Philippine Islands, 1493–1898* (55 vols, Cleveland, 1903–9), XXIX, 309. Bobadilla became provincial of the Philippine province in 1646. See also John Villiers, 'Manila and Maluku: trade and warfare in the Eastern Archipelago, 1580–1640', *Philippine Studies*, 34 (1986), 146–61.

7

'Wherever profit leads us, to every sea and shore . . .':[1] the VOC, the WIC, and Dutch methods of globalization in the seventeenth century

CLAUDIA SCHNURMANN

The history of Dutch Atlantic expansion as embodied in the activities of the Vereenigde Westindische Compagnie (WIC) was for a long time over-shadowed by the 'glorious' deeds of the Dutch East India Company (VOC)[2] in the Asian and Pacific regions, and therefore largely neglected by the academic world.[3] On the rare occasions when the WIC was not ignored and the two companies were compared, the WIC was always described as a failure, while the VOC successes were noted and even celebrated.[4] It is the purpose of this paper to question these historical assumptions.

A new comparison of both companies, focused on their institutional frames, aims, ideas, and politics, should treat them as separate units. The

[1] The quotation from the poem by Joost van den Vondel (1587–1679) follows the English translation made by Donald Keene, *The Japanese Discovery of Europe* (London, 1952), 7; see C. R. Boxer, 'The Dutch East-Indiamen: their sailors, their navigators, and life on board, 1602–1795', in C. R. Boxer, *Dutch Merchants and Mariners in Asia, 1602–1795* (London, 1988), 81.

[2] The literature dealing with the VOC fills several shelves; see the references in Femme S. Gaastra, *De Geschiedenis van de VOC* (Zutphen, 1991); C. R. Boxer, *The Dutch Seaborne Empire* (London, 1965); *idem, Jan Compagnie in oorlog en vrede: Beknopte geschiedenis van de VOC* (Bussum, 1977); Eberhardt Schmitt, *Dokumente zur Geschichte der europäischen Expansion* (4 vols, Munich, 1986–8).

[3] On the history of the WIC, see for example: Boxer, *Dutch Seaborne Empire*; W. R. Menkman, *De Geschiedenis van de West Indische Compagnie* (Amsterdam, 1947); J. G. van Dillen, *Van Rijkdom en regenten: Handboek tot de economische en sociale geschiedenis van Nederland tijdens de Republiek* (The Hague, 1970); W. J. van Hoboken, 'The Dutch West Indian Company: the political background of its rise and decline', in J. S. Bromley and E. H. Kossmann (eds), *Britain and the Netherlands* (London, 1960), 41–61; Henk den Heijer, *De Geschiedenis van de WIC* (Zutphen, 1994); Ruud Spruit, *Zout en Slaven: De Geschiedenis van de Westindische Compagnie* (Houten, 1988).

[4] One of these rare birds, a direct comparison between both companies, was made by German historian Horst Lademacher, 'Ost- und Westindische Kompanie. Bemerkungen zum Aufbau eines Kolonialreiches', in Bernd Wilczek (ed.), with the assistance of Jos van Waterschoot, *Amsterdam 1585–1672: Morgenröte des bürgerlichen Kapitalismus* (Bühl-Moos, 1993), 42–59. On the importance of capital and know-how from the southern provinces (today's Belgium) to the companies' foundation, see E. Stols, 'De zuidelijke Nederlanden en de oprichting van de Oost- en Westindische Compagnieën', *Bijdragen en Mededelingen betreffende de Geschiedenis der Nederlanden*, 88 (1973).

companies' members and employees (whether civil servants, merchants, soldiers, or settlers) were endowed by the companies' founders – officially the Dutch Republic, unofficially citizens who covered the complete social scale of the Netherlands – with comparable authority, but how were they affected by their overseas experiences? Questions like this lead us to analyse structures that were transplanted from the Netherlands to non-European soil, with particular emphasis on how this transfer affected the territories and the lives of the people in colonized regions, how these changes affected the interdependencies of the colonized overseas regions, how they influenced the behaviour of European rivals in the Atlantic and Pacific worlds, and, finally, how they shaped these companies' importance, impact, and opportunities in the formative seventeenth century.

INSTITUTIONAL THEORIES AND INTERNATIONAL LAW 'TO EVERY SEA AND SHORE'

At the outset, both the VOC and the WIC had much in common, not only in respect of their personal and financial structures, but also in their ideological backgrounds. Both represented Dutch responses to long-standing Spanish and more recent English claims, challenges, and initiatives; even more importantly, the foundation of both companies has to be viewed within the context of the ongoing struggle between Habsburg Spain and the Netherlands (1566–1648). From the point of view of rivalry and competition between various mercantile interest groups within the Netherlands, the VOC, founded in 1602, gained the undisputed pole position, although within the wider European mercantile world the VOC's foundation followed the pattern set in part by London merchants in 1599/1600.

In the last decades of the sixteenth century, Dutch merchants and shippers from Holland and Zeeland finally gave up any inhibitions they might have harboured and began to intrude into the Iberian hemisphere created by Spanish and Portuguese monarchs with papal assistance in the last decade of the fifteenth century (papal charters of 1493, the Spanish–Portuguese treaty of Tordesillas of 1494).[5] Following Columbus's landfall in the West Indies in October 1492, the Spanish-born head of the Roman Catholic Church, Pope Alexander VI, had decided in 1493–4 to assign the monopoly for missionary work as well as trade in most of the New World, the Atlantic Ocean and its islands, and the American continent itself, to the monarchs of Castile and Aragon. Some months later, these monarchs went one step further. In the treaty of Tordesillas in 1494, an agreement was formed to divide the globe between them on their own terms; papal approval of the treaty was considered unnecessary. According to this treaty, the Spanish monarchs owned the western hemisphere

---

[5] Miguel Batllori, 'The papal division of the world and its consequences', in Fredi Chiappelli (ed.), *First Images of America. The Impact of the New World on the Old* (2 vols, Berkeley, 1976), I, 211–20.

except for part of the South American continent, later called Brazil, while the whole of Africa and Asia went to the Portuguese crown.[6]

At first, these events received little attention from the other European monarchs. This was to change after Europe had become divided into Protestant and Catholic countries. Anglican England under Elizabeth I (r. 1558–1603) and the mainly Calvinist Dutch Republic – which had established itself in the fight against its sovereign, the Most Catholic Spanish King Philip II (r. 1556–98), who had lost his subjects' loyalty finally in 1581 with the *acte van afzwering* – no longer tolerated Spanish and Portuguese monopolistic claims. Dutch citizens, merchants, craftsmen, and bankers alike set out to acquire their own share of this tempting global enterprise. In the last quarter of the sixteenth century the presence of a growing number of Dutch ships in Asia, together with a lively public debate in the Netherlands about the merits of founding trading companies as a means to advance Dutch interests in the region, awakened fears in England of losing out once more to Dutch competition. Thanks to their efforts, Dutch ships and middlemen controlled not only the continental trade in English cloth but the cross-continental exchange of goods from southern Europe, Middle Europe, and the Baltic Sea, having left the former dominant Hanseatic league far behind. As a result, the Anglo-Dutch alliance suffered its first fissures, an alliance formed in 1585 with the treaty of Nonsuch in response to Spanish threats to Dutch liberties and privileges, as well as to English security concerns in the Channel region and economic dependencies on the Dutch market.

Dutch and English privateers, with the backing of their governments, endeavoured to damage Spanish interests in their Asian and American possessions by destroying Spanish property and invading regions claimed under the papal bulls. Between 1580 and 1640 – when the Portuguese crown was involuntarily united with the Spanish crown – former Portuguese colonies in India and the Far East became additional targets of Dutch and English economic envy, depredations, and incursions, as well as ideological rancour. Of particular importance was the trade in spices, especially pepper, cloves, nutmeg, and cinnamon, which the Portuguese controlled as a result of their successful exploration and military fortification of the sea routes in the Indian Ocean, the Red Sea, and near the Cape of Good Hope.

Efforts in the second half of the sixteenth century to break Portuguese control of these sea routes through the establishment of alternatives had been blocked by the Turks' aggressive policies in the eastern parts of the Mediterranean. In particular, the pepper trade via Italy had been the domain of the London-based Levant Company, founded in 1592 by merging the Venice and Turkey

---

[6] See the documents in their original language with English translations in Frances G. Davenport (ed.), *European Treaties Bearing on the History of the United States and Its Dependencies* (4 vols, Gloucester, MA, 1967), I, *passim*. The different Iberian attitudes to colonialism are discussed in Claudia Schnurmann, *Europa trifft Amerika: Atlantische Wirtschaft in der Frühen Neuzeit 1492–1783* (Frankfurt-am-Main, 1998), 18–21.

companies. The predecessors as well as this newly founded Levant Company followed the organizational pattern of regulated companies. They worked on co-operative principles in which short-term associations of merchants aimed for quick profits. These companies received little support from their monarchs and were granted only limited rights. In a way, this type of company was a relic of the past; during the later Middle Ages and in the sixteenth century it had often been used by Hanseatic, Dutch, or Italian merchants.

Dutch merchants, eager to get a footing in Asian trade, had pooled financial and naval resources on a short term basis, authorizing individual journeys. In what is known as the 'Voorcompagnieën', these enterprises led to some forty ships being sent to Asia between 1595 and 1600, returning with profitable luxury goods in high demand from European customers.[7] As a result, English merchants trading to Russia, the Indian Ocean, or the Far East felt obliged to change their mercantile methods. On 16 October 1599, a remarkable meeting took place at Hampton Court Palace near London. Queen Elizabeth I welcomed leading representatives of the Levant Company; these merchants expressed their fear of losing the booming pepper trade to the Dutch. Dreading the loss of much needed taxes to the royal treasury, Elizabeth and the merchants agreed on the outlines of a charter that led in December 1600 to the foundation of a 'company of merchants of London trading into the east Indies'. It boasted over 200 members.[8]

In the charter, new and old principles of trade and commercial management were blended cleverly. On the one hand, it was normal to name a company by emphasizing its urban origins as well as the region in which the company was permitted to trade. These traditional features were matched by strikingly innovative ones that encompassed a series of new legal possibilities as well as important organizational innovations. The company, soon conveniently called the East India Company (EIC), was not only invested with mercantile privileges; the crown provided it with parts of its own jealously guarded rights of sovereignty. In the Asian trading regions assigned to the EIC, the newly chartered company could act as the crown's *alter ego*, with the capacity to form treaties, conclude international agreements, and take military action. The fact that the EIC was a joint stock company was particularly significant. This organizational form made more efficient use of its shareholders' investments by granting the company the quality of a corporate person. Until 1657, however, the 900 shareholders avoided long-term investments; thereafter the stockholders at last granted permission to use the company's finances for long-term trading purposes. This change significantly

---

[7] J. R. Bruijn, F. S. Gaastra, and I. Schöffer (eds), *Dutch–Asiatic Shipping in the 17th and 18th centuries* (3 vols, The Hague, 1979–87), *passim*; Gaastra, *Geschiedenis*.

[8] In 1698 the EIC was reformed in order to solve internal problems. An important sign of its prospective importance for the national economy and identity was its renaming. Its urban origin was forgotten, and instead it was titled 'The English company trading to the East Indies'.

improved the company's capacity for systematic planning and employment of sophisticated financial strategies.[9]

On the other side of the English Channel, in the Dutch provinces of Holland and Zeeland, merchants quickly learned their lesson. Pressed by the States General assembled in the Hague, by the influential politician Johan van Oldenbarnevelt (1547–1619), and by the impressive prince Maurits of Orange (1567–1625), the competing groups of merchants and towns in the leading maritime provinces gave up their infighting, dissolved newly established companies like the Vereenigde Zeeuwse Compagnie (Veere and Middelburg), the Nieuwe Brabantse Compagnie, or the Eerste Vereenigde Compagnie op Oost-Indië tot Amsterdam, and agreed to merge forces. In March 1602 a new, nationwide operating company, the Vereenigde Oost-Indische Compagnie (VOC), was created by a state's charter that imitated the example set in London two years earlier.

THE COMPANIES' ORGANIZATION, FINANCING, AND AGENDA: THE VOC AND THE WIC AT HOME

In many ways, the Dutch VOC operated as a copy of the London EIC; it was not only invested with the same monopolistic area, Asia, but it also belonged to the new type of progressive joint stock company; in addition, it enjoyed strong support from the Estates General, which granted it sovereign rights, as Elizabeth I had done in England. However, from the start, the VOC improved on the London prototype by daring to risk more money. The initial capital, from shareholders all over the Netherlands and from all classes and professions, totalled nearly 6.5 million Dutch guilders. Each citizen was allowed to get involved in the company, and many citizens, merchants, manual workers, academics, teachers, and clergymen became investors, making contributions from 50 to 85,000 guilders. In Amsterdam alone nearly 3.7 million guilders were raised; a high percentage of this money came from merchants who were immigrants from the Spanish Netherlands, which still belonged to the Habsburg empire. By fleeing Habsburg oppression, commercially innovative refugees brought expertise and capital alike to their new home in Holland.[10] Although many of the ordinary people who had not resisted the common craze for new riches soon got cold feet and sold their shares, reducing the number of stockholders to members of big

---

[9] K. H. Chaudhuri, *The English East India Company: The Study of an Early Joint Stock Company, 1600–1640* (London, 1965); *idem, The Trading World of Asia and the English East India Company, 1660–1760* (Cambridge, 1978); L. Blussé and Femme S. Gaastra (eds), *Companies and Trade: Essays on European Trading Companies during the Ancien Régime* (Leiden, 1981); Larry Neal, 'The Dutch and English East India Companies compared: evidence from the stock and foreign exchange markets', in James D. Tracy (ed.), *The Rise of Merchant Empires: Long-distance Trade in the Early Modern World, 1350–1750* (Cambridge, 1990), 195–223; Robert Brenner, *Merchants and Revolution: Commercial Change, Political Conflicts, and London's Overseas Traders, 1550–1653* (Cambridge, 1993).

[10] Lademacher, 'Ost- und Westindische Kompanie', 45; Gaastra, *Geschiedenis*, 26.

businesses, the VOC was able to retain a strong financial base that allowed it to pursue ambitious plans, grander than the English EIC's.

An important article of the charter granted by the States General stipulated that the use of capital was not restricted to one expedition only; instead, the company received permission from the States General to work with the shareholders' investments within a timeframe of ten years. While it is true that this stipulation weakened the shareholders' influence on the company's policy – robbing them of their ability to steer the company by withholding capital – it nevertheless strengthened the company in the long run.[11] Not only did the company reflect established urban interests in The Netherlands, its institutional frame also mirrored deeply rooted federal features of the Republic itself. The VOC's management was largely monopolized by the Dutch Republic, and its organization was dominated by the leading provinces of Holland and Zeeland, along with the metropolitan centres of Amsterdam, Rotterdam, and Middelburg.

The VOC was created by the state in cooperation with private capital as a national tool designed to fight against Spain and its satellite Portugal; yet at the same time, its organizational features were designed to satisfy the Dutch sense of particularism. It consisted of six chambers, located in Amsterdam, Middelburg (chamber Zeeland), Rotterdam, Delft, Hoorn, and Enkhuizen. Each chamber was ruled by a group of directors, the so-called *bewindhebbers*, who chose representatives for de Heren XVII, the supreme government of the VOC. From a superficial point of view this system seemed to be quite democratic; yet closer inspection reveals Amsterdam's dominance. Almost one-third (20–23) of the seventy-six *bewindhebbers* of the six chambers belonged to the Amsterdam chamber and eight of de Heren XVII had been former members of the Amsterdam chamber, so it is no wonder that Amsterdam became the usual seat of de Heren XVII.[12]

The VOC was founded at a time when the outcome of the Dutch fight against the Spanish monarchy still hung in the balance; its Atlantic pendant, the WIC, came into being in 1621 after the Spanish monarch had been forced to acknowledge indirectly his former subjects as forming an independent nation by agreeing on a twelve-year armistice in 1609. The truce ended in 1621, when the Dutch–Spanish war resumed (Spain did not formally recognize the Dutch Republic until 1648, when the treaty of Westphalia was signed, ending the Thirty Years' War [1618–48] and reorganizing the political landscape of Europe). Although the position of the Netherlands had improved before the settlement, the Dutch changed neither their attitude towards the Iberian powers nor their economic policies or strategies on how to achieve political and economic success. Once again, commerce,

---

[11] Femme S. Gaastra, 'Die Vereinigte Ostindische Compagnie der Niederlande – Ein Abriß ihrer Geschichte', in Eberhard Schmitt, Thomas Schleich, and Thomas Beck (eds), *Kaufleute als Kolonialherren: Die Handelswelt der Niederländer vom Kap der Guten Hoffnung bis Nagasaki 1600–1800* (Bamberg, 1988), 7.

[12] R. van Gelder and L. Wagenaar, *Sporen van de Compagnie: De VOC in Nederland* (Amsterdam, 1988).

capital, and state power worked hand in hand to produce another weapon in the struggle for Dutch independence, profit, and influence, and once again a company seemed to provide the proper and necessary means. The charter granted in June 1621 by the States General that led to the foundation of the WIC as the second semi-national company minced no words about its far-reaching purposes. Shortly after the deadline of the armistice had expired, the WIC was meant to weaken Spanish power by attacking its very lifeline, the most important resources of Spanish wealth, territorial riches, and military opportunities in the Atlantic world, especially the Americas.

Like the VOC, the WIC was granted rights and means to undertake military action, build forts, form international agreements, capture foreign ships, and confiscate cargoes, as well as conquer, exploit, and settle land given to the Iberian monarch by papal judgement. The forty-five articles of the charter discussed in detail all eventualities which might occur in the course of Dutch settlement and trade, and especially in Iberian–Dutch military clashes in the Atlantic. In essence, these stipulations of the charter copied the Catholic privileges granted by the pope in the 1490s. They imitated their Iberian rivals' worldview by claiming the Atlantic, West Africa down to the Cape of Good Hope, and the Americas, as Dutch-controlled spheres of law, possession, trade, and interests.[13] It was no surprise that in 1609 Hugo Grotius, the country's most prominent promoter of free trade and *mare liberum*, fell in line with traditional supporters of early mercantilist thinking and declared the view that exclusive possession of large regions – land as well as sea, people, and resources – was agreeable to international law.[14] It is clear that the WIC's highly ambitious aims were meant to be achieved by copying the institutional patterns and strategies of the VOC.

The WIC's organization, as with the VOC, was deeply rooted in Dutch urban culture. Under the guidance of Amsterdam – once more successful in controlling the new company's finances and management – the WIC copied the VOC's institutional structures as well as encompassing the entire range of Dutch society in its group of shareholders. Again, citizens from everywhere in the Netherlands and from all social classes were eager to invest their money in the newly founded company.[15] The internal administrative structure was changed in one small, yet significant aspect. Instead of the six chambers that formed the VOC, the WIC consisted of five chambers, leaving less commercially striving areas behind: the chambers of the WIC – Amsterdam, Zeeland, Maas, Stad en Lande, and Noorderkwartier – were, like in the VOC, governed by *bewindhebbers* and headed by de Heren XIX, a

[13] See the English translation of the first WIC charter in W. Keith Kavenagh (ed.), *Foundations of Colonial America: A Documentary History, vol. 2. Middle Atlantic Colonies* (New York, 1973), 739–45.

[14] Hugo Grotius, *De mare liberum*, 1609.

[15] Norbert H. Schneeloch, *Aktionäre der Westindischen Compagnie von 1674: Die Verschmelzung der alten Kapitalgebergruppen zu einer neuen Aktiengesellschaft* (Stuttgart, 1982).

body slimmed down to the Heren X in 1674 after the company's refoundation. The members assembled alternately in Amsterdam and Zeeland. After the first enthusiasm had faded, and hampered by financial setbacks, the chambers took some time to accumulate the necessary capital. Yet by 1623 the shareholders had invested around 7.1 million guilders, ready to be used for advancing the country's glory and individual profit.[16] Thus the framework of 1602 was recreated in 1621. Yet this was just the beginning. The real test the company faced lay in the new territories it was to discover, conquer, and exploit. This leads to some simple but crucially important questions: what happened to the mind-boggling claims, to the demands, interests, and ideas conceived in the safety of Dutch towns when they were transported to distant worlds and exposed to new and unknown realities? How did company officials, separated from their home country by distance and poor communication, motivated too by individual interests and fearful of the dangers of traffic and wars, cope with these difficulties and pursue the WIC's imperial designs?

THE VOC OUTSIDE OF EUROPE

In 1603 the VOC embarked on its first enterprise by sending twelve heavily armed ships to Africa and India. That fleet charted the path the VOC was to follow in its overseas enterprises, for not only was it supposed to engage in successful mercantile business, but it was also expected to attack and conquer Portuguese strongholds in Mozambique on the East African coast and Goa on India's Malabar coast. While trading in these regions was quite successful, in this and following years the military actions were failures. Nevertheless, a pattern had been established that in years to come would dominate the VOC's politics in Asian lands and waters.

The chronology and mixed fortunes of Dutch expansion in Asia are described at length by experts like Femme Gaastra, Kristof Glamann, and Niels Steensgaard.[17] Their painstaking and groundbreaking studies cannot be matched by this paper; instead, in the following pages I will emphasize the VOC's activities in Asia during the seventeenth century and the different methods the VOC adopted in relation to Asian trade, countries, territories, towns, people, their rulers, and European rivals. Apart from the fact that the arduous task of building an empire was not really characterized by continuity, strict planning, co-operation, or crystal-clear explicitness, four models can be distinguished of how the Dutch secured and maintained property, influence, power, and prestige.

---

[16] Heijer, *Geschiedenis*, 33.

[17] See references in Gaastra, *Geschiedenis*, 181–8; Niels Steensgaard, *The Asian Trade Revolution of the Seventeenth Century: The East India Companies and the Decline of the Caravan Trade* (Chicago and London, 1974); Kristof Glamann, *Dutch-Asiatic Trade 1620–1740* (2nd edn, The Hague, 1980); L. Blussé and J. de Moor, *Nederlanders oversee: De eerste vijftig jaar 1600–1650* (Franeker, 1983); M. A. P. Meilink-Roelofsz, *De VOC in Azië* (Bussum, 1976).

Model 1

Due to the self-imposed task of fighting Portuguese strongholds, the VOC turned to East Africa, the Indian Ocean, and Persia, but put special emphasis on the Indian subcontinent and Ceylon (Sri Lanka). Following the Portuguese example, the VOC conquered Portuguese trading posts (for example, Colombo in 1656) and successfully established factories as evidence of its presence. These were mostly placed on India's long coastlines on the periphery of local territories, and blended commercial interests and military action by hiding numerical weakness behind martial appearance. At first, military power was used to fight the Iberian monarchs; later the VOC's heavily armed vessels and soldiers were also employed against Asian rulers and rivals from France, Sweden, and Denmark, and, after 1620, from England. In short, the VOC not only assumed an active role in the transfer of European conflicts to Asia – for example, in the Ambon massacre of 1623[18] – but became profoundly entangled in internal Asian wars, too. In so doing, the company used internal disputes between local princes to strengthen its own position. Dutch merchants mostly lived in trading towns along the coastlines, once again imitating the Portuguese, who, as the saying went, preferred to live like crabs near the surf. Inhabiting the remote periphery of native states, the Dutch newcomers, like their Portuguese predecessors, were able to make contact with the local populations and adjust in some degree to local cultures, habits, and sophisticated fashions which were tempting and attractive to people not used to this level of luxury. Although indigenous rulers retained their power for much of the seventeenth, and in some cases even for a number of decades into the eighteenth century, their influence in the peripheries of their territories was so slight that European merchants ran little risk of incurring the rulers' displeasure when mixing with indigenous populations.[19]

Model 2

The second model fits the concept of informal colonialism; it was realized in Vietnam, Cambodia, and Thailand (Siam). After several failures, the VOC successfully established trading posts in these countries that were needed for

---

[18] In 1623 the conflict between Dutch and English rivals for the island's riches escalated; several English people were killed. Shocked by this experience, English forces for the time being were pulled back from the Pacific arena. Nevertheless the events in Ambon remained in public memory, evident whenever England tried to provoke the Netherlands or had to legitimize anti-Dutch policy. See Public Record Office SP 84/178 fols 58–9; M. A. P. Meilink-Roelofsz, 'Aspects of Dutch colonial development in Asia in the seventeenth century', in J. S. Bromley and E. H. Kossmann (eds), *Britain and the Netherlands in Europe and Asia* (London, 1968), 56–82; Herbert H. Rowen, *John de Witt, Grand Pensionary of Holland 1625–1672* (Princeton, 1978), 258.

[19] Gaastra, 'Vereinigte Ostindische Compagnie', 29; Holden Furber, *Rival Empires of Trade in the Orient, 1600–1800* (Minneapolis and London, 1976), 317ff.

the supply of goods for its internal Asian and Asian–European trading activities. The most important factory was founded in Siam in 1613; from 1688 onwards, only Dutch merchants had access to Thai trade and resources; they lost their privileged access to the Thai market in 1756. Another interesting place was Tonking in North Vietnam: it was Dutch-dominated from 1640 to 1699 and provided the VOC with silk necessary for the exchange with Japan. Model 1 and especially the trade-oriented model 2 came closest to de Heren XVII's idea of a maritime empire, especially in the light of their concern that military expenses not exceed commercial profits.[20]

Model 3

The third model forms an exception insofar as Dutch presence was based on local sufferance and local power, and depended solely on the native rulers' goodwill, for neither Dutch military power nor Dutch attempts to resort to the otherwise successful strategy of 'divide et impera' could be applied to China or Japan. Both empires were much too strong, too densely peopled, too remote from the mother country, and on far too high a cultural level for them to have bent to a handful of traders hailing from a distant continent considered by Chinese and Japanese rulers as lacking in cultural achievements. Compared with the Far East's progressive medicine, industry, and *savoir vivre*, even the Dutch, although highly sophisticated from a European perspective, at best measured up to what today would be considered 'third world' inhabitants in Asian eyes.[21]

Like the Portuguese before them, the Dutch could get a foot in the door only by remaining content to live in, and trade from, permitted restricted places. Even so, in China the Dutch residential presence was rather short-lived. Driven out of Macao by the Portuguese in 1622, the VOC founded Fort Zeelandia in Formosa (Taiwan) in 1624. This stronghold soon became quite important both from a commercial as well as a strategic perspective. In 1662 the company lost Formosa to China for good, as well as some smaller trading factories nearby. After several attempts by the VOC to regain Taiwan had failed, Dutch shipping to China stopped in 1690. Henceforth the VOC relied more and more on traditional Chinese junks to supply Dutch trading posts with Chinese goods in the Pacific region. While Dutch posts were lost and active Dutch–Chinese trade was reduced to occasional visits by Chinese junks and yearly expeditions of VOC merchants to Canton, the limited Dutch success nevertheless bestowed prestige on the VOC and evoked envy, especially in England, where less successful rivals in London nicknamed the

---

[20] Gaastra, *Geschiedenis*, 56ff.

[21] Frederic Mauro, 'Towards an "intercontinental model". European overseas expansion between 1500 and 1800', *Economic History Review*, 14 (1961), 1–17; Immanuel Wallerstein, *The Modern World System* (2 vols, New York, 1974–80).

Dutch 'the Chinese of Europe' because of their trade with the Far East, their importation of Chinese goods, and the Dutch craze for Chinese porcelain, lacquerwork, and other fancy household stuffs.[22]

Even more prestige, profit, and durability, but still less freedom, characterized Dutch trade with Japan. Replacing the Portuguese merchants as the only Europeans granted access to Japan, the VOC after 1641 was just a bird in a gilded Japanese cage. The Dutch merchants were restricted to the island of Deshima in Nagasaki harbour. There they lived in splendid isolation, enlivened only by the yearly journey to the emperor's court in Edo (Tokyo) or by visits from prostitutes procured through Japanese mediation in nearby Nagasaki. Offspring produced in this kind of intercultural contact were forbidden to leave the empire but had to stay with their indigenous mothers.[23]

Model 4

The last model fits the concept of formal colonialism best: by blending commercial and economic interests, territorial expansion, and permanent settlement in Java, from the turn of the seventeenth to the eighteenth century, the Dutch VOC managed to change from a trading company to one that also functioned as a territorial ruler. At the same time, Indonesia reflected the Dutch concept of maritime colonialism as formulated in the first years of the VOC's existence.[24] From 1619 Java provided the company with the strategically important harbour, Batavia, which made it possible to control vital seaways and remained accessible in all seasons – even the monsoon season. Batavia quickly emerged as the VOC's Asian centre.[25] Taking traditional Dutch sympathies for decentralization into account, this indeed implied an unusual decision; its status, however, was later to be challenged by sub-centres in Colombo and Melaka (Malacca). Both ports managed to circumvent Batavia by establishing direct sea-links with the home country.

The Governor-General resided in Batavia. Together with his council, the so-called Hoge Indianse Regering, they formed the highest body of the VOC outside the Netherlands. Batavia became the heart of Dutch trade within, from, and to Asia. All Dutch ships had to call at Batavia and all decisions taken by the governors, directors, or so-called *opperhoofden* in other Asian sites had to be confirmed with the Governor-General, who was responsible

---

[22] P. J. van Winter, *De Chinezen van Europa* (Groningen, 1965).

[23] Gaastra, *Geschiedenis*, 78.

[24] Gaastra, 'Vereinigte Ostindische Compagnie', 14; see P. J. A. N. Rietbergen (ed.), *De eerste Landvoogd Pieter Both (1568–1615), Gouverneur-generaal van Nederlands-Indië (1609–1614)* (2 vols, Zutphen, 1987).

[25] Batavia was to become an interesting mixture, blending Dutch urban architecture and Asian environment. On its social, economic, and political development, see J. G. Taylor, *The Social World of Batavia: European and Eurasian in Dutch Asia* (Madison, 1983); L. J. Blussé, *Strange Company. Chinese Settlers, Mestizo Women and the Dutch in VOC Batavia* (Dordrecht, 1986).

to de Heren XVII back home. This chain of command reflected a concept developed in Europe without any regard to overseas realities, regional
interests, and human behaviour. The concept had its pitfalls. Immense power
grew out of the charter's articles, granting the right to wage war and conclude peace, and to make other treaties. This, together with Batavia's commercial success – thanks to trade within Asia as well as to Asian–European
trade – could tempt an ambitious Governor-General to lose sight of the company's needs and instead try to supplement Dutch commercial activities with
the acquisition of territories; by doing so he would enlarge the Governor-
General's powers with the competences of a territorial ruler and improve his
position by controlling trade, production, and the indigenous labour force
through repression, slavery, and violence. Small wonder that the military
enthusiasm of some VOC officials annoyed de Heren XVII, who, as merchants
focused on personal gain and larger profits, loathed to lose control of the
company's purses to some faraway power-hungry company officials.

In 1614 Governor-General Jan Pietersz Coen wrote to de Heren XVII: 'Your
honorable Lords should know that the Asian trade has to be protected by arms;
these arms however have to be paid by profits from trade: that means in
Indonesia we cannot trade without war and we cannot wage war without trade.'[26]
Although it is true that personal ambitions as well as local opportunities
benefited from the length of time it took to communicate between Batavia
and the Netherlands, it is equally true that Coen was pointing out a simple
necessity. The administration on the spot had to make decisions at once; it
could not wait for the nine to twelve months a decision of de Heren XVII took
to arrive from Europe; on occasion the governors-general exploited the delay
in communication with de Heren XVII for their own purposes and made decisions which definitely did not please the moneylenders back home. In 1649
Cornelis van der Lijn bluntly declared that he could not wait for the decision
of de Heren XVII, who treated the colonial staff members like children.[27]

Although in the long run the administration in Batavia successfully
expanded its power across Indonesia and, untroubled by humanitarian
scruples, brought more and more land, people, and precious resources like
spices under its control,[28] this policy did not gain de Heren XVII's unquali-
fied support. However, this approach helped to create a regional power
base that did not depend on the establishment of European settlements
mirroring Dutch society. Yet the costs for this policy were high. After the
1690s it necessitated expensive military establishments that contributed to the

[26] My translation of the Dutch quotation in Lademacher, 'Ost- und Westindische Kompanie', 47.
[27] Gaastra, 'Vereinigte Ostindische Compagnie', 25.
[28] In several cases the local population of Pacific islands was forced to labour or migrate and even suffered
death when economic interests of the VOC seemed to be at stake. Nature itself was not exempt from Dutch
interventions: spice trees which needed many years before they produced the desired fruit were destroyed to
protect the companies' monopoly and price policy. See Gaastra, 'Vereinigte Ostindische Compagnie', 15ff.

Company's permanent financial troubles.[29] In a way, this colonial expansion, especially the massive financial investment necessary for becoming a commercial *and* a territorial power in Indonesia and on the other spice-producing Pacific isles like Ambon, Seram, and Banda, led to the Company's rapid decline in the eighteenth century and to its end in 1795.[30] The cost of administrative staff, mariners, and soldiers necessary to control native populations and European rivals was immense; the dangers and the high mortality rate of Dutch staff intensified the employees' wishes to return home, which again increased costs because it necessitated new replacements.[31]

Dutch expansion across Asia was not only the result of individual ambitions and co-operative energy, but to a great extent a reaction to urgent mercantile needs. Due to the fact that Asian consumers were not especially interested in goods made in underdeveloped Europe (with the exception, for example, of products like woollen cloth), the goods Europe needed had to be bought with Asian products and American precious metals, especially silver. This need for Asian products forced the Dutch to play a greater role in Asian markets and global commerce than they probably initially envisioned. Closer involvement with Asian markets forced colonial administrators and merchants to loosen their ties with their homeland, although de Heren XVII sustained internal Asian trade activities.[32] The VOC officials had to react to local conditions, but the tendency to autonomous action by VOC officials in Asia was neither foreseen nor applauded by company officials in the Netherlands.[33]

Actions and reactions, European demands, and Asian realities created a mixed bag of problems for the VOC. At home the VOC had its troubles and disputes; these were intensified by developments in Asia. Confronted with special conditions, the pretence of group solidarity slowly eroded. Varying regional conditions in Asia contributed to this process. Far away from the Netherlands, the VOC was less a monolithic colossus than something shaped by the many regional policies and conditions that developed under the institutional umbrella called the VOC.

---

[29] Gaastra, *Geschiedenis*, 132; Femme S. Gaastra, *Bewind en beleid bij de VOC: De financiële en commerciële politiek van de bewindhebbers, 1672–1702* (Zutphen, 1989), 283ff; J. P. De Korte, *De jaarlijkse financiële verantwoording in de VOC* (Leiden, 1984), *passim.*

[30] For detail on the VOC's development during the eighteenth century, see for example Gaastra, *Geschiedenis*; and especially Peter Harmen van der Brug, *Malaria en malaise: De VOC in Batavia in de achttiende eeuw* (Amsterdam, 1994).

[31] For the figures on the number of mariners, soldiers, and administrative staff, and the mortality rate, see Gaastra, 'Vereinigte Ostindische Compagnie', 14ff, 30ff; Gaastra, *Geschiedenis, passim*; Bruijn *et al.*, *Dutch-Asiatic Shipping*, I, 144.

[32] 'Seide aus China und Persien, Kupfer und Silber aus Japan, Reis aus Hinterindien, Textilien aus Vorderindien, Opium und Salpeter aus Bengalen, Zimt aus Ceylon, Tee und Porzellan aus China, Kaffee aus Mokka (und später Java), Edelhölzer, Farbhölzer, Gewürze und Drogen – alle diese Produkte transportierten holländische Schiffe. Der Gewinn aus diesem innerasiatischen Handel ermöglichte den europäisch-asiatischen ... Warenaustausch'. Ilja Mieck, *Europäische Geschichte der Frühen Neuzeit. Eine Einführung* (6th edn, Stuttgart, 1998), 248. See also Jonathan Israel, *Dutch Primacy in World Trade 1585–1740* (2nd edn, Oxford, 1991).

[33] Gaastra, *Geschiedenis, passim.*

THE WIC AND THE ATLANTIC STAGE

From the beginning, the WIC's tasks were clearly defined. Its field of operation was the Atlantic ocean, the whole American continent, and the western
half of Africa. The sphere of the VOC's influence started on Africa's southern tip, the Cape of Good Hope. There in 1652 the VOC had founded
a trading post that experienced and survived hard times.[34] The WIC's
operational tasks rested on three pillars of Dutch strength: expertise in mercantile
shipping and profitable commerce; experience in naval warfare, privateer-
ing, and land war; and the deeply rooted desire to found settlements and
towns.[35] All three pillars were incorporated into the WIC charter granted in
1621. The WIC wasted no time in pursuing its goals. Settlements, trade, and
war were all started simultaneously, with but different results and varying
long-term consequences.

The Dutch had to battle Portuguese and Spanish colonies and trading
posts all at once in the western hemisphere, due to the union of the two
countries in 1580. Since they were nearer to their home ports as well as to
the decision-making royal courts, and thanks as well to long-established
familiarity with the Atlantic arena since the fifteenth century, Spanish and
Portuguese colonists – officials, planters, merchants, and soldiers –
maintained a stronger position there than in Asia where they had to satisfy
themselves with trading-posts and temporary residences. A large part of the
treasures stored in Iberian coffers came from South American silver and gold
mines; new Spanish and Portuguese societies emerged in the New World.
The wide range of skin colours in Portuguese Brazil – creoles, mestizos,
and mulattos – testified to greater tolerance in Portuguese territories than
in Spanish American colonies like Cuba, Mexico, Peru, or Chile. Spanish
women who were willing to emigrate disapproved of the sexual morality
implied in this greater tolerance.[36]

Pillar 1: privateering, naval warfare, and territorial conquest

Direct confrontations were surprisingly rare given the fact that the Dutch–
Iberian war ended in 1648 with the treaty of Westphalia. Only then did the
Dutch Republic officially join the family of European nations. The charter of
the WIC had been packed with instructions about conquering territories,
building forts, and taking rich Iberian prizes. All these things were done.
But they lacked for the most part the breathtaking glory of the much
earlier Spanish exploits, although Johan de Laet, the promoter of the WIC's

[34] R. Elphick and H. B. Giliomee, *The Shaping of South African Society 1652–1820* (London, 1972).

[35] On the importance of urbanism and urban rulership in the Dutch Republic, see for example J. L. Price,
Holland and the Dutch Republic in the Seventeenth Century: The Politics of Particularism (Oxford, 1994).

[36] Renate Pieper, 'Hispanoamerika: Die demographische Entwicklung', in Walther L. Bernecker *et al.* (eds),
Handbuch der Geschichte Lateinamerikas (3 vols, Stuttgart, 1994–6), I, 313–28, Schnurmann, *Europa trifft Amerika*, 73.

aggressive course, counted nearly 600 ships that were captured from the enemy with goods worth more than 118 million guilders, enriching the coffers of Dutch shareholders.[37]

Prize-taking and Dutch aggression did not often come to public attention – with two exceptions in 1628 and in 1630. In September 1628 the Dutch admiral Piet de Heyn won eternal fame when he captured the *flota*, the Spanish silver fleet in Matanzas Bay off the Cuban shore, loaded with precious metals, coins, jewels, and colonial products like indigo, Asian silk, and hides, worth all in all more than eleven million guilders. 177,000 Amsterdam pounds of silver were worth about eight million guilders.[38] This event was celebrated in the Dutch press, praised by pamphlet writers, marvelled at in poems, and glorified in popular songs. They made Piet de Heyn a great national hero. These sudden riches not only improved the company's very strained financial situation, they gave prestige, self-confidence, and new energy as well. Provided with a welcome injection of fresh means, amounting to nearly seven million guilders, and a distribution of dividends of 3.5 million guilders to highly pleased shareholders, the WIC started anew on conquering the Portuguese sugar colony of Brazil. Earlier efforts in 1623–4 to attack Brazilian Bahia had miserably failed, draining the WIC's funds.[39]

In 1630 the Dutch fleet and soldiers were even more successful. Helped by Jewish residents of Brazil, who had been forced to hide their faith and opposed Portugal's Catholic government in Brazil, the Dutch managed to conquer the sugar centres of Olinda and Recife of Pernambuco. From 1636 to 1644 Johan Maurits van Nassau-Siegen (1604–79), an enlightened and capable nobleman, acted as governor of the Dutch colony in Brazil. Although the colony was retaken by the Portuguese in January 1654, when Lisbon exploited its English ally's war against the Dutch Republic (1652–4), Dutch possession of Brazil had its impact on Dutch art history as well as on the Netherlands' role in Atlantic history. It introduced new subjects and objects into Dutch art (now proudly exhibited, for example, in The Hague's Mauritzhuis). The Dutch intermezzo in Brazil, however, had less pleasant consequences, too: it brought the WIC into active contact with the African slave trade. Before conquering Brazil, Dutchmen had made their appearance on Africa's west coast. Here they took Portuguese posts like Sao Jorge da Mina in 1596, and in 1612 established Fort Nassau as well as other forts on the Gold Coast. Yet in these early days Dutch trade was restricted to the exchange of European consumer items for African goods; it did not include the acquisition of slaves. Only the possession of a colony whose sugar economy

---

[37] Heijer, *Geschiedenis*, 65.

[38] S. P. L'Honoré Naber and I. A. Wright (eds), *Piet Heyn en de zilvervloot, Bescheiden uit Nederlandsche en Spaansche archieven* (Utrecht, 1928); J. C. M. Warnsinck, *Drie zeventiende-eeuwsche admiraals: Piet Heyn, Witte de With, Jan Evertsen* (Amsterdam, 1943); Pieter Emmer *et al.* (eds), *Wirtschaft und Handel der Kolonialreiche* (Munich, 1988), 463–7.

[39] Heijer, *Geschiedenis*, 39.

was based on black slavery helped to destroy the few tender Dutch scruples against a trade that had not been mentioned in the charter of the WIC, but which would in years to come play an important role. Until the middle of the seventeenth century, the Dutch outdistanced their European rivals by conquering and establishing forts and trading posts on the West African coast.[40]

Pillar 2: settlement – the establishment of more durable colonies

Well before the WIC was founded, Dutch ships had made their way to the Americas, and Dutch capital had provided the means for other nations' enterprises. Funded by the VOC, the Englishman Henry Hudson had explored North America's east coast in 1609. During this expedition Hudson discovered what the VOC named Noord Rivier and which later was renamed the Hudson River. The WIC inherited the VOC's claim to the right of first discovery; in 1624 the company founded on the isle of Manhattan the nucleus of Nieuw Nederland, to be followed from 1634–6 by the foundation of Dutch settlements in the Caribbean (Sint Maarten 1630, Curaçao, Aruba and Bonaire, Sint Eustatius, 1636). Other colonies, like New Sweden on the Delaware in 1655 or Surinam in South America, were conquered in 1667. Those territories changed proprietors quite frequently; they were taken and retaken until they were finally lost by decisions made back home. As an example, the most important Dutch stronghold on the North American continent, Nieuw Nederland, was lost to England in a surprise attack during peace-time in 1664, which was confirmed by a diplomatic settlement in 1667. In 1673, during the third Anglo-Dutch War (1672–4), the territory was retaken by a Dutch force, only to be lost for good in 1674 in the treaty of Westminster. Nieuw Nederland mutated into New York. This is not the place to describe Nieuw Nederland's history at length. Scholars have written extensively on this topic; the rich texture of its history continues to be enlarged by new and exciting evidence.[41] However, it should be mentioned that Nieuw Nederland from its beginning was planned as a permanent settlement based on European agriculture, manufacture, and the fur trade with Indian peoples. At first, the colonial economy was monopolized by the WIC; after much haggling, the WIC then had to give up its overall monopoly and open the fur trade to colonists; in addition, the company in 1639 adopted a new land policy. In 1647 Pieter Stuyvesant became governor not only of a Nieuw

---

[40] See Johannes Postma, *The Dutch in the Atlantic Slave Trade 1600–1815* (Cambridge, 1990).

[41] See Oliver Rink, *Holland on the Hudson: An Economic and Social History of Dutch New York* (Ithaca, 1986); Charles Gehring and W. A. Starna (eds), *A Journey into Mohawk and Oneida Country, 1634–1635. The Journal of Harmen Meyndertsz van den Bogaert* (2nd edn, Syracuse, 1991); V. C. Bachman, *Peltries or Plantations: The Economic Policies of the Dutch West India Company in New Netherland 1633–1639* (Baltimore, 1969); Jaap Jacobs, *Een zegenrijk gewest: Nieuw-Nederland in de zeventiende eeuw* (Leiden, 1999), gives a broad overview of the most important literature regarding Nieuw Nederland.

Nederland shaken by an Indian war but also of Curaçao in the West Indies. Underlying this development was the WIC's intention to copy VOC strategy by binding its American colonies together, connecting the entrepôt Curaçao with Spanish American resources on the one hand and with demands of the self-sustaining settler-colony in the North on the other. As official policy this co-operation failed, but in the 1670s it proved successful when organized by private entrepreneurs from New York.[42] While the first Dutch colony in America was lost in the seventeenth century, other colonies like St Maarten, the ABC-isles (Aruba, Bonaire, and Curaçao), and Surinam remained in Dutch possession until well into the twentieth century.

Notwithstanding the colonies' fate, white settlers who came with the WIC's encouragement and permission to the New World left significant traces. Although they did not arrive in great numbers – and in contrast to the VOC settlement-efforts they frequently did not come from the Netherlands at all but from France, Belgium, and Germany – many of them stayed and made their impact on colonial society. An interesting example is the German Jacob Leisler (1640–91), who in 1689 staged with the so-called 'Leisler's rebellion', the New York version of England's Glorious Revolution (1688–9). Leisler, a New York merchant and leader of the local militia, convinced a majority of the colony to take the side of the Dutch-born Protestant, William of Orange, who had come to the throne by parliament's grace, ousting the Catholic James II (r. 1685–9) and ruling jointly with James's daughter Mary.[43] The Dutch colonial societies in the Americas consisted not only of men, who stayed for a short time, but mostly of families, who were determined to stay for good. Due to Dutch tradition, many women soon pursued their own vocation in the Atlantic economic world; they traded, owned ships, and acted on their husbands' behalf when the latter made business trips to Europe or travelled to other colonies.[44] Nieuw Nederlanders were busy as planters, farmers, merchants, labourers, clergymen, and soldiers, often pursuing all these professions simultaneously. In contrast to the VOC, where more and more soldiers had to be employed in order to stave off increasing English and French inroads, the WIC after 1648 emphasized the civil aspect of colonizing, although Indian wars, European attacks, and invasion fears were recurrent features that had to be dealt with.

---

[42] See Claudia Schnurmann, *Atlantische Welten. Engländer und Niederländer im amerikanisch-atlantischen Raum 1648–1713* (Cologne, 1998), *passim.*

[43] Jacob Leisler now is the subject of an international research project. Three work-groups in Göttingen, New York, and Penn State University are currently collaborating on a multi-volume edition of Leisler's documents trying to reconstruct his Atlantic network. See David W. Voorhees, 'The "Fervent Zeale" of Jacob Leisler', *William and Mary Quarterly*, 51 (1994), 447–72; Claudia Schnurmann, 'Die Rekonstruktion eines atlantischen Netzwerkes – das Beispiel Jakob Leisler, 1690–1691. Ein Editionsprojekt', *Jahrbuch für Europäische Überseegeschichte*, 2 (2002), 19–39.

[44] Schnurmann, *Atlantische Welten, passim.*

Pillar 3: trade

Recent research describes three types of trade the WIC tried to control in the seventeenth century:[45] (i) the trade between the Netherlands and America; (ii) the triangular trade between the Netherlands, Africa, and America; and (iii) the intercolonial trade, uniting Dutch, Spanish, French, Portuguese, and English colonies in a close-knit network that was outside WIC's influence. Of special importance is the already mentioned slave trade and its function in the relationship between the WIC, Curaçao, and Surinam.[46]

In 1674, the year Nieuw Nederland finally became New York, the WIC was re-established and began to adopt a new commercial and colonial strategy. Freed from the dangers stemming from English threats to its North American colony, the second WIC concentrated its efforts on those colonies it was left with. Of special importance became Curaçao, the hub of Dutch trade in the West Indies and an important bridgehead to Spanish America.[47] On a smaller scale, tiny Caribbean islands had strategic as well as commercial advantages, providing fish-exporters back home with salt or playing the part of a smuggler's eldorado.

Surinam, the sugar colony, had adopted the staple of Brazil. Taken from the English in 1667, this colony was owned by the Dutch province of Zeeland. Surinam experienced dire straits due to a lack of provisions, an inadequate animal labour force, and insufficient labourers desperately needed for the making of sugar. In the 1670s, several famines, natural catastrophes, and Indian wars ravaged the 1,000 settlers from the mother country and the British Isles; these ordeals widened the gap between the colonists' expectations and their diminishing respect for Zeeland's authority and efficiency.[48] In 1682 Zeeland had to give in; it sold the colony for 260,000 guilders to the WIC, which tried to make good for the loss of Brazil. Only one year later the WIC succumbed to its financial constraints. Unable to meet its obligations as sole proprietor of Surinam, it sought and found rich partners, like the city of Amsterdam and the important family of the van Sommelsdijck. In May 1683, the three founded the Societeit van Suriname.[49]

In dealing with both tropical colonies, Curaçao and Surinam, the company through the Societeit pursued different policies. Curaçao, the Dutch ticket to Spain's American riches, was granted more freedom and received more

---

[45] See, for example, Jacobs, *Een zegenrijk geweest*; Schnurmann, *Atlantische Welten*; Wim Klooster, *Illicit Riches: Dutch Trade in the Caribbean, 1648–1795* (Leiden, 1998).

[46] Schnurmann, *Atlantische Welten*, passim; Postma, *The Dutch in the Atlantic Slave Trade*.

[47] See Klooster, *Illicit Riches*.

[48] Victor Enthoven, 'Suriname and Zeeland. Fifteen years of Dutch misery on the Wild Coast, 1667–1682', in John Everaert and J. M. Parmentier (eds), *International Conference on Shipping, Factories and Colonization* (Brussels, 1996), 250–65.

[49] Schnurmann, *Atlantische Welten*, passim; Gerard Willem van der Meiden, *Betwist Bestuur: Een Eeuw strijd om de macht in Suriname, 1651–1753* (Amsterdam, 1986).

attention, soldiers and *predikanten* (reformed ministers). Surinam, on the other hand, was subjected to the darker aspects of the Societeit/WIC's mercantilist principles. The colony was forced to trade only with The Netherlands. Exportation of the country's colonial products, like refined sugar, raw sugar, molasses, and wood, was restricted to The Netherlands, while for the importation of food, household goods, luxuries, and especially black labour, the colony was expected to rely exclusively on the company's mediation – and with graceful acceptance of Dutch prices, although they could have been purchased much cheaper elsewhere in the West Indies.

In the seventeenth century, the WIC dominated the Atlantic slave trade; most of the kidnapped black Africans were sold via Curaçao to Spanish America; when legalized in 1662, this exchange increased in scale. The WIC again bought the *asiento*, the Spanish monopoly to supply Spanish America with black labour.[50] As a result, the WIC in 1674 changed its priorities, putting the slave trade first on the list of economic interests. This change of priorities was resented in Surinam; the colony's staple economy depended entirely on black slavery. When the newly founded Societeit van Suriname could not supply the necessary numbers of African slaves nor provide the colony with sufficient goods, more and more of Surinam's colonists – Dutch and English Christians, as well as Dutch and Sephardic Jews alike – turned to English colonies for help. They first approached Barbados, relying on familial, religious, and long-established connections; later, Surinam planters turned to North American colonies like New York, Massachusetts, Connecticut, Rhode Island, and Pennsylvania, creating their own intercolonial network while cheerfully ignoring the companies' mercantilist charters and Dutch demands.[51]

In the early eighteenth century two events finally lightened Surinam's burden. The WIC lost its role as the leading slave-trader in the Atlantic region to Great Britain and the Societeit gave in to some of Surinam's demands for a more liberal trade policy. As a result of intricate political dealings in 1713, Great Britain was granted the *asiento* in the treaty of Utrecht; nine years earlier, in 1704, the Societeit van Suriname had to legalize the colony's intercolonial trade on Surinam's terms.[52]

SUMMARY

Horst Lademacher summarizes a commonly held opinion when he calls the WIC the inferior sister of the VOC, because the WIC had been, he claims, far behind the VOC's economic and political achievements.[53] This statement

---

[50] Postma, *Dutch Atlantic Slave Trade*, 33ff.
[51] Schnurmann, *Atlantische Welten, passim.*
[52] Schnurmann, *Atlantische Welten*, 307–9.
[53] Horst Lademacher, *Geschichte der Niederlande: Politik, Verfassung, Wirtschaft* (Darmstadt, 1983), 147; Lademacher, 'Ost- und Westindische Kompanie', 58ff.

simplifies history because it does not clarify the criteria on which the interpretation is based. In this paper I have argued that various facts, events, and
structures have to be considered before one describes one company as a
success story and the other as a failure. The figures for short-term profit,
national income, imports, and exports are important, as are the numbers for
ships and capital, and, last but not least, the numbers of officials, settlers, and
goods involved in the activities of these companies.[54] But other questions are
even more significant: what kind of role did territorial property play, and
how important was the longevity of colonies or the impact of colonial products on Dutch culture and everyday life? What was more significant, short-
lived successes or policies that shaped developments for long periods? Taking
all this in account, it is not appropriate to put some aspects to the fore while
ignoring or neglecting others simply because they do not fit the prevailing
image.

I have taken another approach in this paper. Without doubt VOC and WIC
were the brain-children of one culture dominated by merchants, their capital, and their far-reaching commercial interests. Their origins, organization,
and institutional framework followed one concept; they were chartered to
function in comparable contexts. In the beginning, the conditions were
quite similar, having been generated from commercial enterprise and anti-
Spanish policy. But these similarities vanish as soon as the companies are
viewed in the context of the different overseas territories assigned to them.
For there, conditions varied dramatically, not only in relation to forms of
settlement, but also trading possibilities and markets, as well as labour supply.

The WIC representatives were initially confronted with indigenous people
only, but in the end had to bend to European rivals, too. While both companies in different fields had impressive (if sometimes short-lived) successes
and provided the young Dutch Republic with the remarkable status of a
commercial power that practised its own early modern version of globalization, in building up a permanent and lasting presence they had to act and
react to rapidly changing local and regional conditions. The Heren and the
governors-general of both companies opted for different approaches. Their
scale ranged from tolerance to violence, and from co-operation to suppression and inflexibility. There existed not one VOC nor one WIC operating
around the world and putting the Dutch Republic in the core of the early
modern globalization process, but many VOCs and WICs adopting different
attitudes, proceedings, and actions that paid tribute to Dutch individualism
and pluralism.

---

[54] Many figures are given in Rothermund, *Europa und Asien, passim.*

8

Riches, power, trade and religion: the Far East and the English imagination, 1600–1720

ROBERT MARKLEY

I

For many scholars, European relations with Asia in the seventeenth century remain an area of vague assumptions and misconceptions. Although there are obvious political differences between traditionalists, who celebrate the spreading of 'civilization' to the non-European world, and their revisionist critics, who decry the violence and ecological devastation of European imperialism, both camps share a fundamentally Eurocentric perception of early modern history. Both employ analytical models – colonialist or post-colonialist – which assume that the technological inferiority, economic backwardness, and political conservatism of oriental cultures spelled their inevitable defeat by European colonizers. This default view of European–Asian relations has been challenged vigorously in recent years by K.-N. Chaudhuri, J. M. Blaut, Frank Perlin, Paul Bairoch, R. Bin Wong, Andre Gunder Frank, and Kenneth Pomeranz, who argue – in different ways – that until 1800 an integrated world economy was dominated by India and China, and that our recognition of this domination requires a fundamental reassessment of both neoclassical and Marxian accounts of the economic 'rise' of the West.[1] In this essay, I draw on the work of these historians to challenge the theoretical values and historical assumptions that underlie Eurocentric accounts of global relations in the early modern period. In focusing on Peter Heylyn's *Cosmographie* (1652; eight editions before 1700), I argue that seventeenth-century

---

[1] K.-N. Chaudhuri, *Asia before Europe: Economy and Civilisation of the Indian Ocean from the Rise of Islam to 1750* (Cambridge, 1990); J. M. Blaut, *The Colonizer's Model of the World: Geographical Diffusionism and Eurocentric History* (New York, 1993); Frank Perlin, *'The Invisible City': Monetary, Administrative and Popular Infrastructure in Asia and Europe 1500–1900* (Aldershot, 1993); Paul Bairoch, *Economics and World History: Myths and Paradoxes* (Hemel Hempstead, 1993); R. Bin Wong, *China Transformed: Historical Change and the Limits of European Experience* (Ithaca, 1997); Andre Gunder Frank, *ReOrient: Global Economy in the Asian Age* (Berkeley and Los Angeles, 1997); and Kenneth Pomeranz, *The Great Divergence: China, Europe, and the Making of the Modern World Economy* (Princeton, 2000). In different ways, all of these historians challenge traditional accounts of a distinct period of European 'mercantilism' in the sixteenth and seventeenth centuries. On European perceptions of Asia, see Donald Lach, with Edwin J. Van Kley, *Asia in the Making of Europe* (3 vols, Chicago, 1965–93).

writers in England did not automatically assume the cultural, economic, or even religious superiority of Christendom.[2] Travel narratives, diplomatic correspondence, and geographies typically employed a compensatory rhetoric for what their authors feared was England's and Europe's marginalization within a world dominated economically by Asia. In short, influential but all too often ignored texts – such as Heylyn's massive historical atlas – tell a far more complicated tale about Europe, the Far East, and the course of world history than most traditional accounts of 'mercantilism' suggest.

The prospect for trade to the Far East between 1600 and 1750 became a crucial element in European economic thinking because it allowed writers to displace domestic problems – ranging from high tax rates, to environmental degradation, to lagging productivity in some sectors and unmarketable surpluses in others – onto the vision of a theologically sanctioned and enormously profitable commerce. For England, largely excluded from trade east of India, the Far East – China, Japan, and the Spice Islands – fulfilled two crucial and imaginary roles: as both an insatiable market for European goods and a vast, inexhaustible storehouse of spices, luxury goods (from tea to textiles), and raw materials. If China and India represented the apex of civilization – idealized embodiments of the sociopolitical order and cultural sophistication necessary to carry on an ever-expanding trade – the islands of the Indonesian archipelago and the imaginary continent, Terra Australis Incognita, offered visions of exotic realms where the East India Company could either gather commodities with little effort or strike good deals with co-operative natives.[3]

I begin my analysis with the first diplomatic letter that Elizabeth I sent to the king of Aceh (Achen) in western Sumatra in 1600 in order to examine the ideological presuppositions that structure a widespread faith in the benefits of trade. As Josiah Child, director of the English East India Company, put it later in the century, 'Foreign Trade produceth Riches, Riches Power, Power preserves our Trade and Religion; they mutually work one upon and for the preservation of each other'.[4] The crucial term in this logic is 'produceth'; like many of his contemporaries, Child assumes that trade itself can generate wealth in excess of the expenditures of labour and capital required

---

[2] According to his preface, Heylyn began *Cosmographie* as an updating of his popular *Microcosmos: or, A Little Description of the Great World* (Oxford, 1621; eight editions by 1639). The project grew, however, so that the later work greatly expands into an 1100-page folio what had been a short quarto volume.

[3] I have examined this ideology as it operates in different writers' perceptions of the Far East in Markley, '"So inexhaustible a treasure of gold": Defoe, credit, and the romance of the South Seas', *Eighteenth-Century Life*, 18 (1994), 148–67; idem., 'The destin'd walls/ of *Cambalu*: Milton, China, and the ambiguities of the Far East', in Balachandra Rajan and Elizabeth Sauer (eds), *Milton and the Imperial Vision* (Pittsburgh, 1999), 191–213; and idem., 'Civility, ceremony, and desire at Beijing: sensibility and the European quest for "free trade" with China in the late seventeenth century', in Maximilian E. Novak and Anne Mellor (eds), *Passionate Encounters in a Time of Sensibility* (Newark, 2000), 60–88. Additional primary and secondary sources on Europe and Asia in the early modern period are cited in notes in these articles.

[4] Sir Josiah Child, *A Treatise Wherein is Demonstrated . . . that the East-India Trade is the Most National of All Trades* (London, 1681), 29.

to man and provision ships for multi-year voyages, that it can be both mutually beneficial for all (civilized) parties concerned and yet always work to the economic advantage of England. This assumption of mutual enrichment dominates European defenses of trade in the seventeenth century. Elizabeth's diplomatic correspondence with Aceh, in this respect, reveals the promise that the Far East holds as both a producer of desirable commodities and an insatiable consumer of English goods, especially textiles. But Asian markets were also perceived as the sites of rags-or-riches competition with rival European powers, and chroniclers such as Samuel Purchas and Heylyn qualify this panglossian model. These writers follow Elizabeth's lead in trying to enlist various Asian nations as allies against commercial rivals, whether the Portuguese, Spanish, or Dutch; consequently, they employ exclusionary, triangular models of communication and trade to isolate these antagonists and to reassert and protect their ideological investment in the self-perpetuating logic of infinite riches, unchallenged power, expanding trade, and true religion.

The fantasy of infinite productivity and profit, however, requires a concomitant (and profoundly anti-ecological) faith in the existence of inexhaustible resources that can be endlessly exploited. In an important sense, the ideology of trade – reiterated throughout the sixteenth, seventeenth, and eighteenth centuries – is a response to crises of intensification. The widespread perception in the first half of the seventeenth century that England's resources were inadequate to support its population, or that nature itself had been corrupted by humankind's sins, placed the burden on international trade to solve complex ecological, demographic, and economic crises.[5] Recent work in historical ecology and related disciplines offers an eco-cultural approach to this 'general crisis' of the seventeenth century, calling into question the economistic premises of Eurocentric conceptions of modernity. Historians from Karl Marx on have read seventeenth-century European accounts selectively – if not ahistorically – in their quest to define an 'origin' for a 'modern' capitalist system and to contrast it to a 'primitive', Asiatic mode of production. The revisionist project of Jack Goldstone, Anne Osborne, and others, has profound implications for ecological, economic, and social history of Sino-European relations by challenging some fundamental assumptions about agricultural and proto-industrial productivity in the world economy of the seventeenth and eighteenth centuries.[6] If, as Frank

---

[5] See Andrew McRae, *God Speed the Plough: The Representation of Agrarian England, 1500–1660* (Cambridge, 1996).

[6] See Jack A. Goldstone, *Revolution and Rebellion in the Early Modern World* (Berkeley and Los Angeles, 1991); and the essays collected in Mark Elvin and Liu Ts'ui-jung (eds), *Sediments of Time: Environment and Society in Chinese History* (Cambridge, 1998): Anne Osborne, 'Highlands and lowlands: economic and ecological interactions in the Lower Yangzi region under the Qing', 203–34; Eduard B. Vermeer, 'Population and ecology along the frontier in Qing China', 235–79; Robert B. Marks, '"It never used to snow": climactic variability and harvest yields in late-imperial South China, 1650–1850', 411–46; Li Bozhong, 'Changes in climate, land, and human efforts: the production of wet-field rice in Jiangnan during the Ming and Qing dynasties', 447–85; and Helen Dunstan, 'Official thinking on environmental issues and the state's environmental roles in eighteenth-century China', 585–615.

and Pomeranz argue, there is no empirical evidence for the technological superiority and economic domination by western Europe before 1800, then seventeenth-century texts do not foreshadow an inevitable rise of modern notions of history, economics, and social theory, but register instead complex and often competing assessments of European relations with the Far East.

In this context, Heylyn's *Cosmographie*, arguably the most influential work of its kind published in English in the second half of the seventeenth century, transmutes first-hand accounts of voyages to the East into truisms about race, wealth, and civilization in the Orient. Instead of imposing orientalist assumptions on the Far East, Heylyn registers the complications of shifting alliances among European and Asian powers, internal conflicts within Asian and Pacific countries, and the changing patterns of trade that fascinated many of his sources.[7] But in reworking first-hand descriptions of Asia by East India Company merchants and Jesuit missionaries into encyclopedic overviews, Heylyn translates these complex interactions into a hierarchy of nations and peoples, an evaluative travelogue of non-Western cultures based on their perceived willingness to engage in a trade beneficial to England. In this respect, his attack on the Moluccans and Russians, his praise of upper-class Indians, and his ambivalence in describing the Japanese reveal the economic determinism that underwrites Renaissance perceptions of the Orient. Ultimately, then, the *Cosmographie* complicates conventional readings of travel literature and economic discourse before 1750 by forcing us to question the Eurocentric narratives of progress and power that underlie traditional notions of modernity. In its place, Heylyn describes global patterns of trade, cultural contact, and international rivalry that register England's comparatively marginal position in the seventeenth-century world.

II

In 1600, the first venture of the East India Company, under the command of Sir James Lancaster, carried a letter from Queen Elizabeth to the king of Aceh in Sumatra, England's first attempt to gain a foothold in the lucrative trade in Southeast Asia then dominated by Portugal. The letter, a small masterpiece of diplomacy, testifies to Elizabeth's sensitivity to a range of interrelated issues – political, theological, economic, and ecological – that structure European perceptions of Asia in the following century and a half. It begins with a ceremonious, and symbolically significant, greeting to a brother monarch, then immediately offers a theological justification for international trade:

---

[7] On the problems of imposing nineteenth-century conceptions of orientalism on the late medieval and early modern world, see Janet Abu-Lughod, *Before European Hegemony: The World System A. D. 1250–1350* (New York, 1989); and Bernadette Andrea, 'Columbus in Istanbul: Ottoman mapping of the "New World"', *Genre*, 30 (1997), 135–65.

ELIZABETH by the Grace of God, Queene of England, France, and Ireland, defendresse of the Christian Faith and Religion. To his great and mightie King of Achem, &c. in the Iland of Sumatra, our loving Brother, greeting. The Eternall God, of his divine knowledge and providence, hath so disposed his blessings, and good things of his Creation, for the use and nourishment of Mankind, in such sort: that notwithstanding they growe in divers Kingdomes and Regions of the World: yet, by the Industrie of Man (stirred up by the inspiration of the said omnipotent Creator) they are dispersed into the most remote places of the universall World. To the end, that even therein may appeare unto all Nations, his marvellous workes, hee having so ordained, that the one land may have need of the other. And thereby, not only breed intercourse and exchange of their Merchandise and Fruits, which doe superabound in some Countries, and want in others: but also ingender love and friendship betwixt all men, a thing naturally diuine.[8]

Elizabeth invokes a shared monotheistic religion to establish common cultural and philosophical grounds with an Islamic monarch thousands of miles away. This opening promotes a mutually profitable trade, 'a thing naturally diuine', as both a means to ensure 'love and friendship' between England and Aceh and an end for fulfilling God's plan for humankind. By exchanging goods 'which doe superabound' in their own realms for others they lack, both nations can compensate for their limited resources. Trade, at least in theory, can overcome the entwined evils of sin and scarcity that have plagued humankind since the expulsion from Eden. Materially as well as theologically, this 'exchange of . . . Merchandise and Fruits' can redeem a fallen world.

After staking out of a common religious ground, Elizabeth proceeds to the business of forging political and economic links between the two nations. To entice the king into allowing the East India Company to trade in Aceh, Elizabeth must construct for herself an authority that mirrors his. She employs the rhetoric of absolute monarchy – of regal brotherhood – to appeal to him, describing the Company's merchants as her 'subjects' and implying that she wields the same kind of power over them that he claims over his traders. But Elizabeth knew that this was not the case; the very articles which she was seeking to negotiate were intended to guarantee that English merchants in Aceh would retain control over their property, goods, and persons as guaranteed by English common law rather than being subject to an absolute monarch. In the Indonesian archipelago in the seventeenth century, as Jeyamalar Kathirithamby-Wells has demonstrated, control of trade and capital lay entirely in the hands of monarchs: strict controls existed on the sale and ownership of property, and there was no independent class of

---

[8] Samuel Purchas, *Hakluytus Posthumus or Purchas his Pilgrimes* (4 vols, London, 1625), Book ɪɪ, 154.

merchants or administrators, except for palace favourites. Consequently, foreign merchants – whether Chinese, Dutch, Portuguese, Spanish, Japanese, or English – were essential to the region's international trade.[9] In effect, then, Elizabeth required the king of Aceh to decree, with his absolute power, favourable trading conditions for her subjects, while downplaying the independence of the merchants of the East India Company, their *de facto* freedom at the end of lengthy chains of supply and communication, from her or her government's authority.

Elizabeth's chief rhetorical strategy in her letter, though, is to exploit the complicated structures of communication – and power – that exist among the English, the Portuguese and Spanish, and Indonesians. Religious differences between Christian and Muslim are elided to allow the queen to emphasize the theological, political, and economic enmity between Protestant England and Catholic Iberia, and to promote the common interests that she and the king share in frustrating Spanish and Portuguese designs in the East Indies:

> your Highnesse shall be very well served, and better contented, then you have heretofore beene with the Portugals and Spaniards, our Enemies: who only, and none else, of these Regions, have frequented those your, and the other Kingdomes of the East. Not suffering that the other Nations should doe it, pretending themselves to be Monarchs, and absolute Lords of all those Kingdomes and Provinces: as their owne Conquest and Inheritance, as appeareth by their loftie Title in their writings. The contrarie whereof, hath very lately appeared unto us, and that your Highnesse, and your royall Familie, Fathers, and Grandfathers, have (by the grace of GOD, and their Valour) knowne, not onely to defend your owne Kingdomes: but also to give Warres unto the Portugals, in the Lands which they possesse: as namely in Malaca, in the yeere of the Humane Redemption 1575 under the conduct of your valiant Captaine, Ragamacota, with their great losse, and the perpetuall honour of your Highnesse Crowne and Kingdome.[10]

Rather than an oppositional model that posits enmity between a European 'self' and non-European 'other', Elizabeth describes the discourse of trade in terms of triangular relationships – efforts to forge alliances with 'others' against a third disruptive or threatening force. Michel Serres argues that because the 'other' is a projection of the negative qualities of a solipsistic identity, no communication can take place without the presence of a

---

[9] Jeyamalar Kathirithamby-Wells, 'Restraints on the development of merchant capitalism in Southeast Asia before *c.* 1800', in Anthony Reid (ed.), *Southeast Asia in the Early Modern Era: Trade, Power, and Belief* (Ithaca, 1993), 123–48. See also Anthony Reid, *Southeast Asia in the Age of Commerce, 1450–1680. Volume II. Expansion and Crisis* (New Haven, 1993), 17–26.

[10] Purchas, *Hakluytus Posthumus*, Book II, 154.

'third man' or parasite who creates the noise against which – and only against which – meaning can emerge.[11] In this respect, the crucial dynamic in relations between England and Aceh may be understood, not as the clash of antagonistic cultures, but as efforts to exclude the 'third man', in this case, the Spanish and Portuguese, who are essential to English–Sumatran relations: they must be excluded as the basis for Elizabeth's overtures of friendship for her 'brother' monarch and her vision of a mutually profitable trade between the two countries.

This triangular (or Serrean) model of communication and politics was well understood by the king, who, according to Lancaster, 'seemed to be very well pleased' with the queen's letter. In his reply to Elizabeth (translated from the Arabic by William Bedwell, the foremost English translator of that language at the time), the king granted the East India Company merchants free entry and trade into Aceh; absolute control over their own property, including the ownership, sale, and inheriting of land, chattels, and inventories; 'stability of bargaines and orders of payment by [his] subjects'; and legal jurisdiction over all English citizens in his country. 'Our joy [is] increased and our societie confirmed', in this agreement, the king wrote to Elizabeth, because the English provide a bulwark against Portuguese and Spanish encroachment on Aceh's trade: the Iberians 'are our enemies in this world, and in the world to come: so that we shall cause them to die, in what place soever we shall meete them, a publicke death'.[12] Like the English queen, the king employs a transhistorical rhetoric: his nation's conflict with Spain and Portugal over the strategic port of Maleka (Malacca) will continue indefinitely, even into a monotheistic afterlife. Elizabeth's claim 'that this beginning shall be a perpetuall confirmation, of love betwixt our Subjects on both parts'[13] also suspends the mutability of historical time by envisioning unending cargoes from the East and an untroubled future of domestic production to supply the presumptive demands of Southeast Asian markets. Because it is constituted by bodily metaphors of integration, circulation, and order, this ongoing commerce can fail to produce the benefits that Elizabeth and the king describe only if it is disrupted by the machinations of malicious rivals.

In yoking theology and economics, Elizabeth assumes a shared perception of the moral and material world in England and Aceh, a shared conceptual vocabulary. Balance sheets, price increases, exchange rates, credit, moneylending, and the negotiating and honouring of contracts are embedded within a language of political values as well as theological imperatives. Their mutual distrust of the Spanish and Portuguese allows Elizabeth to play shrewdly on the king's fears that her European rivals represent threats to the king's political position as well as to Aceh's trade; she flatters him with her

---

[11] Michel Serres, *The Parasite*, trans. Lawrence Schehr (Baltimore, 1982).
[12] Purchas, *Hakluytus Posthumus*, Book II, 160.
[13] *Ibid.* 154.

knowledge of his victories, and appeals to the primal fear of absolute rulers –
usurpation. Elizabeth tars the Spanish and Portuguese with illegitimacy. Her
indictment of their false claims to sovereignty in Southeast Asia seems
intended to resonate with a monarch who must remain constantly vigilant
against foreign incursions and the intrigues of his own court. By emphasizing
the Catholic threat, the queen can gloss over the fact that the newly formed
East India Company is trying to insinuate itself into an established trade in
Southeast Asia that will compete with Sumatran as well as European shipping: English bullion and (she hopes) woollens to India; Indian goods to
Sumatra and the Moluccas; and, in return, pepper, nutmeg, mace, and cloves
from the Spice Islands that can be resold in Europe at a substantial profit.
While her protestations of friendship may be sincere, that sincerity can be
measured only as an expression of her country's desire for a 'perpetuall
trade', for mutually amicable relations that never deteriorate into the self-
interest, suspicion, and single-minded pursuit of profit that attend England's
commercial relations in Europe.

III

Trade between Europe and Asia throughout the seventeenth century was
defined by shipments of New World silver from Amsterdam, Lisbon, and
London to India and China in exchange for finished goods and luxury items,
often for textiles that competed directly with European products. The slave
trade between Africa, America, and western Europe, with its genocidal horrors, functioned as a cog in larger economic networks. To simplify: African
slaves mined precious metals in South America and produced cash crops
(tobacco, sugar) in the Caribbean and Carolinas that were sent to Europe in
exchange for manufactured goods of all sorts; gold and silver were shipped
from South and Central America to Spain to finance the cost of maintaining
a colonial empire, and then from Iberia to northern Europe to purchase
cloth, manufactured goods, raw materials, and more African slaves from
Dutch, French, and English traders. Silver also went west from Acapulco to
the Philippines to allow the Spanish and Portuguese to trade with mainland
China and Japan. Bullion from the Netherlands and England went east,
usually through the Ottoman empire and Persia, to India, where it allowed
the Europeans to enter the long-established and complex Asian market.
Indian cloth and manufactured goods were traded to Southeast Asia for
cloves, nutmeg, mace, and pepper; spices were shipped throughout Asia,
according to local and international surges in demand; Chinese commodities
(porcelain, tea, and silk) attracted much of the region's silver and copper;
and spices were imported to Europe, in large measure to finance the Dutch
seaborne empire. The propaganda of Child and other supporters of the
East India Company notwithstanding, England and the Netherlands paid
hard cash for what many considered luxury goods.

Seventeenth-century accounts of a world dominated by Chinese demands for silver provide an important context for discussions of European ventures to the Pacific, particularly the ascendancy of the Dutch East India Company (Vereenigde Oost-Indische Compagnie, VOC).[14] Child maintained that the preservation of the East India Company's trade was essential to England's economy. 'All other Foreign Trade in Europe', he declared, 'doth greatly depend upon *East-India* Commodities; and if we lose the Importation of them into *Europe*, we shall soon abate in all our other Foreign Trade and Navigation: and the Dutch will more then proportionably increase theirs.' Were the Dutch to monopolize this trade, 'the excess of price which they would make the *European* World pay for *East-India* Commodities more than they do now, would cause a disproportionable and greater increase of their Riches. The augmentation whereof would further enable them to over-ballance us and all others, in Trade, as well as in Naval strength.'[15] Child's characterization of the Dutch threat to English economic stability, especially its re-export trade to the Americas, is the product of a long-standing rivalry between the East India companies of the two nations.[16] During the first two decades of the seventeenth century, the Dutch consolidated their near-monopoly of the spice trade to Europe. They forced the Portuguese out of Ternate and Tidore, fought off incursions by Spanish vessels operating from the Philippines, and between 1619 and 1623 drove the English out of the lucrative market in cloves and nutmeg. The execution of English merchants on the island of Ambon in 1623 became a focus for English anxieties about national identity well into the eighteenth century.[17] In a crucial image in Book Two of *Paradise Lost*, John Milton compares Satan's 'solitary flight' from Hell to a Dutch merchant fleet 'Close sailing from *Bengala*, or the Isles/ Of

[14] Frank, *ReOrient*, 165–87. Joseph Needham's multivolume work, *Science and Civilization in China*, is a crucial resource for understanding the complex interactions among Eastern and Western technologies, and for appreciating the achievement of the Chinese in science, technology, and engineering. On shipbuilding, to take only one example, see Joseph Needham, with Wang Ling and Lu Gwei-Djen, *Science and Civilization in China* (Cambridge, 1971), iv/3, 433–695. See also Mark Elvin, *The Pattern of the Chinese Past* (Stanford, 1973); Timothy Brook, *The Confusions of Pleasure: A History of Ming China (1368–1644)* (Berkeley and Los Angeles, 1998); Joanna Waley-Cohen, *The Sextants of Beijing: Global Currents in Chinese History* (New York, 1999), 55–128; Pomeranz, *Great Divergence, passim*; and Ward Barrett, 'World bullion flows, 1450–1800', in James D. Tracy (ed.), *The Rise of Merchant Empires: Long-distance Trade in the Early Modern World 1350–1750* (Cambridge, 1990), 224–54.

[15] Child, *A Treatise*, 26, 27. On English perceptions of Dutch economic prowess, see Joyce Oldham Appleby, *Economic Thought and Ideology in Seventeenth-century England* (Princeton, 1978).

[16] On the English–Dutch rivalry in Southeast Asia, see Kristof Glamman, *Dutch–Asiatic Trade 1620–1740* [1958] ('s-Gravenhage, 1981); Holden Furber, *Rival Empires of Trade in the Orient, 1600–1800* (Minneapolis, 1976); O. H. K. Spate, *The Pacific Since Magellan. Volume II. Monopolists and Freebooters* (Minneapolis, 1983), 87–91; Jonathan I. Israel, *Dutch Primacy in World Trade, 1585–1740* (Oxford, 1989); Steven Pincus, *Protestantism and Patriotism: Ideologies and the Making of English Foreign Policy, 1650–1668* (Cambridge, 1996); Neils Steensgaard, 'The growth and composition of the long-distance trade of England and the Dutch Republic before 1750', in Tracy, *The Rise of Merchant Empires*, 102–52; and, in the same volume, Larry Neal, 'The Dutch and English East India Companies compared: evidence from the stock and foreign exchange markets', 195–223.

[17] See Robert Markley, 'Violence and profits on the Restoration stage: trade, nationalism, and insecurity in Dryden's *Amboyna*', *Eighteenth-Century Life*, 22 (1998), 2–17.

Ternate and *Tidore*', laden with 'spicy Drugs'.[18] The VOC imaged as 'the flying Fiend' traces a course of both conspicuous consumption identified with Dutch economic power and of frustrated English desires for a share of that trade.

The Dutch role in Southeast Asia, however, was not that of a colonial power dictating terms to vanquished indigenes. Before 1600, nutmeg and mace were grown solely on the Banda Islands, six islands south of Seram that total only seventeen square miles. Ternate and Tidore, 'minuscule volcanic islands' off the west coast of Halmahera, were the principal commercial source of cloves in Asia, and the rival sultanates on each of these islands used their strategic control of these commodities to extend their influence in the sixteenth century across the widely dispersed islands in the region.[19] One thousand miles east of Java, these sultanates governed by dynastic alliances, trading networks, and tribute obligations rather than by military force. As Oskar Spate notes, however, the arrival of one or two well-armed ships could and did wreak havoc on small islands and isolated ports in the Pacific, and seaborne invasions occurred with regularity in the Spice Islands.[20] The Dutch seized Banda in 1621, turning the islands into slave plantations; they then used the profits from their control of nutmeg and mace to increase their naval presence in the region. In 1656, the VOC destroyed the clove crop on Ternate and Tidore in order to monopolize production in areas that they controlled directly on Ambon. In both cases, the Dutch reaped significant economic benefits by strategic military actions on small islands that could not muster large-scale defensive forces.[21] While the Dutch fleet in Southeast Asia significantly outnumbered English ships, the VOC comprised only a small fraction of the regional carrying trade: all European vessels in Southeast Asia were outnumbered ten-to-one by Chinese junks with roughly similar cargo capacities; the eight Dutch ships that docked in Japan every year after 1638 were far less significant than the eighty Chinese junks which regularly plied the waters between China and Japan.[22]

Rather than employing hierarchical models of imperial conquest, seventeenth-century English accounts of the Spice Islands emphasize the uncertain and multi-dimensional nature of conflicts (and alliances) among Europeans and indigenous peoples. John Saris, the captain of an East India Company trading voyage in 1611–12, notes in his narrative that Ternate and

---

[18] John Milton, *Paradise Lost*, ed. Merritt Y. Hughes (New York, 1962), Book ii, 638–40, 643.

[19] Lynda Norene Shaffer, *Maritime Southeast Asia to 1500* (London, 1996), 32–3.

[20] Spate, *Monopolists and Freebooters*, 90.

[21] On the Dutch in Southeast Asia, see Philip D. Curtin, *Cross-cultural Trade in World History* (Cambridge, 1984), 158–66; C. R. Boxer, *The Dutch Seaborne Empire 1600–1800* [1965] (London, 1977); Leonard Andaya, 'Interactions with the outside world and adaptation in Southeast Asian society, 1500–1800', in Nicholas Tarling (ed.), *The Cambridge History of Southeast Asia. Volume I. From Early Times to c. 1800* (Cambridge, 1992), 345–401; in the same volume, Anthony Reid, 'Economic and social change, c. 1400–1800', 460–507; and Jan M. Pluvier, *Historical Atlas of South-East Asia* (Leiden, 1995), 25–7.

[22] Frank, *ReOrient*, 165.

Tidore – the linchpin of the Dutch monopoly of the spice trade – had been wasted by decades of civil war prior to the arrival of Europeans:

> The *Portugall* at his first discoverie of [these islands in the sixteenth century], found fierce warres betwixt the King of *Ternate* and *Tydore*, under which two Kings all the other Ilands are either subiected or confederated with one of them. The *Portugall* for the better settling of himselfe, took part with neither of them, but politikely carrying himselfe kept both to bee his friends, and so fortified upon the Ilands of *Ternate* and *Tydore*, where, to the *Portugals* great advantage, having the whole Trade of *Cloves* in their owne hands, they domineered and bore chiefest sway untill the yeare 1605 wherein the *Flemming* by force displaced them, and planted himselfe: but so weakly and unprovided for future danger, that the next yeere the *Spaniard*, (who whilest the *Portugall* remayned there, was ordered both by the Pope and the King of *Spaine* not to meddle with them) came from the *Philippinas*, beat the *Flemmings* out of both Ilands, tooke the King of *Ternate* Prisoner, sent him to the *Philippinas*, and kept *Ternate* and *Tydore* under their command. The *Flemming* since that time hath gotten footing there againe, and at my being there had built him [several] Forts. . . . These Civill Warres have so wasted the *Nationals*, that a great quantitie of Cloves perish, and rot upon the ground for want of gathering.[23]

Saris's account reveals the limitations of European power in the region and the strategies that the Portuguese, Spanish, and Dutch employed in contending for the clove trade. Expeditions of a ship or two with approximately 100 or 150 men each are enough to constitute beach-head forces on small islands where the Europeans' overriding goal was to insinuate themselves 'politikely' in order to play one side off against the other in a dynastic dispute and civil conflict. The forts that the Europeans erected could not withstand blockade or bombardment. The communities of merchants, administrators, and soldiers in the Spice Islands during the early seventeenth century usually numbered in the dozens, although larger forces, such as the Spanish expeditionary force, could be mustered for one-shot naval operations. What European powers could do was to intervene strategically, currying favour by paying higher prices for cloves on Ternate and Tidore, or, as Saris did when he arrived at Bantam (Banten), paying 'thrice the value [for seven hundred sacks of pepper] of what they were bought for'.[24] Even though he was well aware of this 'great (though sudden) alteration in the prices of commodities' and was warned by the Dutch against trading in the Moluccas, Saris willingly paid a steep price to try to buy England's way into the lucrative markets of the Far East.

---

[23] Purchas, *Hakluytus Posthumus*, Book ii, 363.
[24] *Ibid.* 353.

The Europeans' strategic intervention, both economic and military, in Southeast Asia, in this respect, should not be interpreted as ironclad evidence of technological superiority in shipbuilding, cannon, or trading practices. Frequently in the seventeenth century, the Dutch gained entry into markets by providing currency or its equivalent to cash-strapped parties in internal conflicts. It is significant, in this regard, that Saris paid for pepper in Bantam with silver coins; he did not offload the pepper in Ternate where cloves lay rotting on the ground because he lacked the military and financial resources to insinuate himself into a Dutch-dominated trade or to challenge the VOC. The Dutch in 1612 could not compel outgunned natives to harvest the cloves; they were not (yet) an imperial power that governed Ternate and Tidore, but a trading monopoly enforcing its 'perpetuall contract with [the Moluccans] for all their Cloves'[25] at a fixed price. Backed by huge invest ments of men and ships from the Netherlands, the VOC was intent on maximizing profits and had already begun to develop the strategies that led to its *de facto* and finally colonial control of much of the Indonesian archi- pelago by the late eighteenth century: it used force when necessary, often hiring local mercenaries; intervened in dynastic conflicts to secure alliances favourable to their shipping; and attacked their European rivals to ensure their control of production, price, and shipping. Even at the height of their commercial empire in 1688 the Dutch had fewer than 5000 troops stationed in their principal possessions in Southeast Asia and another 1900 seamen, artisans, merchants, and traders; the garrisons on Ternate and Tidore were manned by fewer than 300 soldiers.[26] Dutch successes in the Far East, as Saris recognizes, result from picking their fights, and their trading alliances, very carefully.

IV

As the most popular historical geography of the second half of the seven- teenth century, Heylyn's *Cosmographie* offers a compendium of English atti- tudes toward other cultures, a measure of the complex tensions and desires that characterize descriptions of the Far East. It is hardly an original work; although Heylyn claims to have written it after Commonwealth officials had seized his library, whole pages are lifted from prior works such as Pierre d'Avity's *Estates, Empires, & Principalities of the World* and Giovanni Botero's *The Travelers Breviat*; sections from Hakluyt and Purchas are condensed and rephrased.[27] This redactive, intertextual quality of the *Cosmographie* is char- acteristic of a genre – the universal geography – that recycles and recombines

[25] *Ibid.* 360.

[26] Jonathan Israel, *The Dutch Republic: Its Rise, Greatness, and Fall 1477–1806* [1995] (Oxford, 1998), 939–43.

[27] Pierre d'Avity, *The Estates, Empires, & Principalities of the World*, trans. Edward Grimstone (London, 1615); Giovanni Botero, *The Travelers Breviat, or an Historicall Description of the Most Famous Kingdomes* (London, 1601; five editions by 1626).

eyewitness accounts, such as the writings of the Jesuit Matteo Ricci on China (condensed and included by Purchas in his *Pilgrimmes*), in order to provide snapshot views of a world potentially open to ever-expanding trade. A significant market existed for such compendia, and the ideology of trade that motivated writers as radically different as John Milton (who planned a one-volume redaction of Purchas) and Peter Heylyn testifies to the ways in which the appeal of the Far East cut across the divisions of partisan politics in mid-seventeenth-century England.[28]

At first glance, Heylyn seems an unlikely author of a manifesto that places geographical knowledge firmly within an expansionist trade policy. A prominent royalist and Anglican clergyman, he served as Archbishop Laud's right-hand man in the 1630s, and wrote a celebratory biography of his benefactor after Laud was executed. The author of controversial works, Heylyn was ejected from his living in 1642 and was – according to his own account – literally on the run for several years, hiding with various royalist families and churning out anti-Commonwealth propaganda. His decision in the late 1640s 'to review my *Geographie* [*Microcosmos*]; to make it more complete and usefull to an English Reader',[29] may have been, in part, a financial one, but Heylyn thoroughly transforms what had been a pocket guide into a full-fledged historical geography, enlarging and updating entries to reflect three decades of English dealings with the peoples of the world.

Heylyn's preface is tub-thumpingly patriotic, asserting that as an Englishman and a divine he has 'apprehended every modest occasion, of recording the heroic Acts of my native Soil, and filing on the Registers of perpetual Fame the Gallantry and brave atchievements of the People of *England*' (A3ʳ). Elizabeth's image of a fallen world that can be redeemed through trade is one which Heylyn seizes on as a crucial principle to reaffirm a heroic national identity that transcends the 'Tragedies of blood and death' (B1ʳ) which have disfigured recent English politics. While barely concealing his ardent royalism, Heylyn reasserts a familiar theological argument for prosperity through trade: 'Nothing more sets forth the Power and Wisdome of Almighty God', he declares, 'than that most admirable intermixture of Want with Plenty, whereby he hath united all the Parts of the World in a continuall Traffique and Commerce with one another' (4). For Heylyn, as for Elizabeth, such 'continuall Traffique' is essential if humankind is to overcome the defects of poslapsarian nature. An inclusive ideology of trade, moreover, offers the hope in 1652, on the eve of the first Anglo-Dutch war, of putting

---

[28] See D. S. Proudfoot and D. Deslandres, 'Samuel Purchas and the date of Milton's *Moscovia*', *Philological Quarterly*, 64 (1985), 260–5. On the popularity of accounts of China in the seventeenth century, see Lach, *Asia in the Making of Europe*, I, 730–821.

[29] Peter Heylyn, *Cosmographie* (2nd edn, London, 1657), A2ʳ. All quotations are from this edition. For the circumstances of Heylyn's revision, see the rival biographies of Heylyn, by George Vernon, *The Life of the Learned and Reverend Dr. Peter Heylyn* (London, 1682), and John Barnard, *Theologico-Historicus, or the True Life of the Most Reverend Divine, and Excellent Historian Peter Heylyn* (London, 1683).

aside (or papering over) the antagonisms of the Civil War by unifying the English against the threats of the Dutch, French, and Spanish. The structure of the *Cosmographie* suggests where Heylyn's interests lie in rendering his efforts 'usefull' to this commercial project. In a one-volume work divided into four books (one each for Europe, the Americas, Asia, and Africa), the countries of Asia receive as many pages as those of Europe and three times as many as the Americas. While his entries on Asia testify to his and his readers' fascination with the possibility of trade to the Far East, he must define the 'brave atchievements of the People of *England*' very carefully in a region of the world where trade has yet to make good on its promises of peace and prosperity.

Throughout the *Cosmographie*, Heylyn's responses to the peoples he describes are governed not by skin colour, religion, or geographical proximity to England, but by an archaeology of European desire. He offers few original judgements on the major trading nations of the Far East, preferring instead to appeal to what he presumes his readers want to hear about the possibilities of trade to Asia. China, for example, was almost universally admired in the sixteenth and seventeenth centuries for the unprecedented opportunities that it would offer to European merchants; as the sink for New World and Japanese silver, it was the ultimate goal for generations of Dutch, Russian, Portuguese, Spanish, Persian, Turkish, French, and English merchants who realized that their silver bullion would purchase more in Chinese ports and boost their profit margins considerably. Echoing Jesuit accounts which had themselves been reprinted, translated, and redacted many times, Heylyn lavishes praise on the Chinese for 'their natural industry, and their proficiencie in Manufactures and Mechanick Arts', and reiterates the widespread view that, because China enjoys the 'abundance of all things necessary to life', it is a bastion of political stability and economic prosperity.[30] Since English efforts to open trade to China had met with little success, Heylyn has no 'brave atchievements' to report, and no tragedies like the one in Amboyna to explain away. Consequently, his entry on China is measured, even pedestrian, a derivative encyclopedia piece on a land that remains an idealized manifestation of Europeans' desire for trade.

The Dutch domination in the Spice Islands, in contrast, offers profound challenges to the *Cosmographie*'s mercantilist ideology. Although Heylyn praises the Dutch for their industry and navigation, he cannot bring himself to voice the logical conclusion that the VOC has bested England at its own game. He does not mention that in 1620 Dutch vessels in Southeast Asia had outnumbered English ships eight to one, and instead scapegoats the Moluccans for the English failure to crack the Dutch monopoly of the spice trade.

[30] Heylyn, *Cosmographie*, 865–6. On the royalist use of China as a model for England, see Rachel Ramsey, 'China and the ideal of order in John Webb's *An Historical Essay* . . .', *Journal of the History of Ideas*, 62/3 (2001), 483–503.

Racial qualities, national identities, and moral fitness become functions of
what Southeast Asians have to offer English merchants. Without their spices,
the people of these islands are described as

> *Idolaters* . . . [of] severall *Originals*, and different languages, but all in
> general fraudulent, perfidious, treacherous, inhumane, and of noted
> wickednesse. Few of them clothed, nor much caring to hide their shame.
> Not civilized by cohabitation of more modest and civill Nations.[31]

Heylyn's terse, almost telegraphic style lends a journalistic authority to what
is at best a second-hand account. No sources are cited. The history of triangular rivalries, civil war, and European competition offered by Saris is sub-
sumed into essentialist judgements of national character. The same islanders
who had been visited by Sir Francis Drake in 1579 and who had petitioned
James I to come to their aid against the Portuguese are denigrated by a
logic that registers their subservience to the VOC as an intrinsic moral
failure. The Moluccans seem beyond the pale of morality and civilization
because, in Heylyn's eyes, they have allowed themselves to be dominated by
the Dutch.

Another Asian country with a population of '*Idolaters*' ruled by Muslims
receives much more favourable treatment. Heylyn carefully includes the East
India Company's chief trading partner – the Mughal empire – within the
circuits of civilization. South Asians accordingly are described as

> tall of stature, strong of body, and of complexion inclining to that of the
> *Negroes*: of manners Civill, and ingenuous, free from fraud in their deal-
> ings, and exact keepers of their words. The Common sort but meanly clad,
> for the most part naked, content with no more covering than to hide their
> shame. But those of greater estates, and fortunes (as they have amongst
> them many antient and Noble families) observe a majesty in both Sexes,
> both in their Attendants and Apparel; sweetning the last with oils, and
> perfumes, and adorning themselves with Jewels, Petals, and other Orna-
> ments befitting. They eat no flesh, but live on Barley, Rice, Milk, Honey,
> and other things without life. . . . Originally descended from the Sons of
> *Noah*, before they left these Eastern parts to go towards the unfortunate
> valley of *Shinaart*.[32]

Indians are spared the calumny directed at the Moluccans because the English have crucial trading interests in the Mughal empire; India supplies the
bulk of the goods that are re-exported from England to markets in Europe
and the Americas. As significantly, South Asians can be assimilated within a

[31] Heylyn, *Cosmographie*, 918.
[32] *Ibid.* 881.

biblical history that works in their favour: the Indians are descended from those virtuous sons of Noah who remained in the East when their wicked brethren journeyed to Shinaar to build the Tower of Babel. Heylyn, in this instance, follows Sir Walter Ralegh in implying that India was resettled after the Flood by those who preserve a Noachian virtue.[33] If nakedness is *de facto* evidence of depravity in the Moluccas, it is simply a characteristic of the lower classes in India that can be passed over quickly in order to praise the 'majesty' of the elite orders. Skin colour, religious differences, and seemingly odd customs such as vegetarianism can be encompassed by a class-specific notion of trans-cultural civilization: upper-class Indians (both Hindu and Muslim, as Heylyn makes clear elsewhere) exhibit the civility, honesty, and even aesthetic sensibilities that mirror an idealized self-image of English virtues. This identification of Indian and English sensibilities enacts the civilizing function that Heylyn attributes to the activity of trade itself. Trade civilizes: it both produces and reaffirms a like-minded compatibility between English desires and South Asian interests.

In identifying trade with civilized morality, Heylyn's *Cosmographie* breaks down as many distinctions between Europe and the Far East as it establishes. While Heylyn invokes racial hierarchies, defends European technology, rails against the impediments to trade enforced by Chinese and Indian bureauc-racies, and repeatedly denounces 'heathen' religious practices, his most vit-riolic attacks are aimed at other Europeans who either compete with English trade or frustrate English ambitions to access the markets of Japan and China. In this regard, he follows his sources, notably Botero and d'Avity, by abusing the Russians at length.[34] By the mid-seventeenth century, efforts to use Russia as a conduit to the riches of the Orient had proved fruitless. Trade between England and the tsar was particularly vexed, and Heylyn includes a litany of complaints: the Russians competed with English merchants in the Baltic; they repeatedly sought to drive prices for their timber and fur exports as high as they could, demanding silver in return; and they persisted in trying to open an overland trade route to China.[35] The result is a third- or fourth-hand account of Russian perfidy that marks the tsar's subjects – though 'white' and Christian – as thoroughly 'other':

> [They] are very perfidious, crafty, and deceitful in all their bargains, false-dealers with all they have to do with, making no reckoning of their prom-

---

[33] Ramsey, 'China', and Markley, 'Newton, corruption, and the tradition of universal history', in James E. Force and Richard Popkin (eds), *Newton and Religion* (Dordrecht, 1999), 121–43. See also Chaudhuri, *Asia before Europe*, Sinnappah Arasaratnam, *Maritime Trade, Society and the European Influence in Southern Asia, 1600–1800* (Aldershot, 1995); and Shankar Raman, *Framing 'India': The Colonial Imaginary in Early Modern Culture* (Stanford, 2001).

[34] See d'Avity, *Estates, Empires, & Principalities of the World*, 690–1. In *Microcosmos*, Heylyn's description of Russia (183) is glossed in the margins as derived from Botero's *Travelers Breviat*. As a rule, Heylyn modifies passages in which Botero and d'Avity highlight the successes of Italy and France respectively in order to emphasize the 'glory' of England.

[35] See Mark Mancall, *Russia and China: Their Diplomatic Relations to 1728* (Cambridge, 1971).

ises, and studying nothing more than ways to evade their Contracts. Vices so generally known, and noted in them, that when they are to deal with strangers, they dissemble their Country, and pretend to be of other Nations, for fear lest no body should trust them. Destitute of humane affections, and so unnatural, that the Father insults on his Son, and he again over his Father and Mother: So malitious one towards an other, that you shall have a man hide some of his own goods in the house of some man whom he hateth, and then accuse him for the stealth of them.[36]

Heylyn borrows from Botero and d'Avity the example of neighbours staging robberies and then charging each other with theft; he generalizes this story into ethnic characteristics of dishonesty and malice. Familial disorder and – horror of horrors – dishonesty in trade define a violent and tyrannical state. Heylyn's condemnation of the Russians, in one respect, harks back to the misunderstandings and distrust which accompanied the decline of the Muscovy Company's fortunes in the late sixteenth century, when merchants began to encounter the difficulties of trading to a country that demanded silver for raw materials and provided no easy access to the Far East. Renaissance commentators were explicit about what they expected from the forays of the Muscovy Company. Purchas, for example, describes the 'intent' of the Company's first voyage in 1553 as 'the discouerie of *Cathay*, and diuers other Regions, Dominions, Ilands, and places vnknowne';[37] Robert Parke, the translator of González de Mendoza's *Historie of China*, notes in his dedication that the Muscovy Company's attempt at 'the discouerie of *Cathaia* and *China*' was motivated 'partly of desire that the good young king [Edward VI] had to enlarge the Christian faith, and partlie to finde out some where in those regions ample vent of the cloth of England.'[38] Heylyn's description of the Russians is redolent of the disappointments that a century later confronted English merchants who had to compete with German, Dutch, Hungarian, Swedish, Danish, Polish, Turkish, Persian, and Central Asian traders in Russia, as well as trying to placate a court that tried to keep strict control over much of the country's international trade. For Heylyn, as for Botero and d'Avity, civilization is defined by a language of 'promises' and 'contracts', by the ties of nation, family, friendship, and profit. The Russians fall beyond the pale of civilized behaviour because their deceit in trade is emblematic of a lack of moral self-consciousness and industry. They are the antithesis of the Indians, even as they reinforce the same values and assumptions that inform the ideology of trade: skin colour, clothing, customs, and even religion are not the ultimate markers of civilized behaviour – trade is.

---

[36] Heylyn, *Cosmographie*, 511.
[37] Purchas, *Hakluytus Posthumus*, Book III, 212.
[38] González de Mendoza, *The Historie of the Great and Mightie Kingdome of China*, trans. R. Parke (London, 1588), ¶2ᵛ.

Ternate, Tidore, India, and Russia present comparatively few problems for a mid-seventeenth-century cosmographer because European views of these nations had remained more or less static since the late sixteenth century: eyewitness accounts were reprinted and summarized, and all could be situated within the narrative structures of a divinely sanctioned trade. In writing about Japan, however, Heylyn confronted a recent history of failure – the expulsion of Catholic missionaries and the restrictions placed on European trade – that challenged his vision of nations unified by 'a continuall Traffique and commerce with one another'. In the late sixteenth century, missionaries had converted hundreds of thousands of Japanese of all social classes and established dozens of churches across Japan. Beginning in 1587, however, the shogunate issued edict after edict to control the activities of Christians; intensifying repression followed, and the missionaries were finally expelled and the indigenous Christian population massacred during an unsuccessful rebellion in 1637–8 in Shimabara. A once burgeoning trade with the Spanish and Portuguese was curtailed; after 1638 only the Dutch and Chinese were allowed to do business in restricted ports.[39] Because Heylyn cannot simply summarize the views of earlier commentators who celebrated the inroads of Christianity and the opportunities for trade, his description of Japan testifies to the ambiguities of European responses to the Far East when ideological expectations meet brutal experience: the dream of an infinitely profitable commerce remains, but history cannot be ignored.

After John Saris left the Spice Islands with his cargo of pepper, he sailed northward to Japan, both 'for a triall there' of trading possibilities and in response to letters from Will Adams that had arrived at the VOC factory in Batavia, a port then open to English ships.[40] Adams, the English pilot of a Dutch ship, had been detained in Japan for several years. His letters, reprinted by Purchas, both endorse and counter Jesuit descriptions of Japan by downplaying the significance of the Catholic missions and emphasizing the possibility that the English East India Company might extend its trading ventures to Hirado. Distrusted by the Jesuits, who urged the shogunate to imprison or execute Adams and his Dutch shipmates, the Englishman presents himself in his letters as a spokesman for English trade: 'We were a People', he tells the emperor, 'that sought all friendship with all Nations, and to have trade of Merchandize in all Countries . . . through which our Countreys on both side[s] were inriched'.[41] His portrait of Japan, intended for East India Company officials who might stop in Batavia, is equally encouraging. According to Adams,

---

[39] See C. R. Boxer, *The Christian Century in Japan, 1549–1650* (Berkeley and Los Angeles, 1951), and Michael Cooper, SJ, *Rodrigues the Interpreter: An Early Jesuit in Japan and China* (New York, 1974).

[40] Purchas, *Hakluytus Posthumus*, Book II, 353.

[41] *Ibid.* 127.

The People of this Iland of *Iapan* are good of nature, curteous above measure, and valiant in warre: their Iustice is severely executed without any partialitie upon transgressors of the Law. They are governed in great Civilitie, I thinke, no Land better governed in the world by civill Policie.[42]

Adams's letter is clearly designed to hasten his rescue by idealizing the Japanese as potential trading partners. The Japanese, though militaristic, are 'curteous', 'civill', and rigorous in the impartial application of the law. The government functions both efficiently and with 'Civilitie'; in effect, the people of Japan, like the Indian elite in Heylyn's description, embody the characteristics that the English see in themselves and identify with civilized behaviour. Adams is explicit about his conflicts with Catholic missionaries at court, and the opportunities that the shogunate's suspicion of the Spanish and Portuguese offer the English. The emperor, he tells us, 'asked much concerning the warres betweene the Spaniards and Portugals, and us, and the reasons: the particulars of all which I gave him to understand, who seemed to be very glad to heare it'.[43] In Adams's account, both English seaman and the Japanese emperor are seeking a 'third man' to counter the influence of the Spanish and Portuguese. For Saris and the East India Company, then, the lure of a well-governed nation, lying far enough north to offer a prospective market for English woollens, and apparently willing to entertain a potential trading partner at odds with Catholic Iberia, proved irresistible.

After arriving in Hirado, Saris gave permission for a group of Japanese women to come aboard his ship, then realized that his cabin featured an immodest painting of Venus and Cupid that he feared might scandalize his visitors. The scene that he describes discloses the complex problems of cultural translation that the ideology of trade glosses over in its eagerness to project Western ideas of commerce and religion onto potential trading partners:

> I gave leave to divers women of the better sort to come into my Cabbin, where the Picture of *Venus*, with her sonne *Cupid*, did hang somewhat wantonly set out in a large frame, they thinking it to bee our Ladie and her Sonne, fell downe, and worshipped it, with shewes of great devotion, telling men in a whispering manner (that some of their owne companions which were not so, might not heare) that they were *Christians*: whereby we perceived them to be *Christians*, converted by the *Portugall* Iesuits.[44]

This passage suggests that religious conversion has political and socioeconomic implications as well as spiritual significance. The Japanese women

[42] *Ibid.* 128.
[43] *Ibid.* 127.
[44] *Ibid.* 367.

translate a Christian conception of divinity into their own semiotic systems and moral codes: the wantonness of Venus and Cupid (both presumably nude) does not signify for them as it does for the English captain. The brazen lack of 'shame' that Heylyn attributes to scantily clad Moluccans is not inconsistent with these Japanese women's religious beliefs: the proximity of mother and child – whatever the setting, boudoir or manger, and whatever their postures – represents a spiritual authority that transcends the obligations of patriarchal and feudal obedience.

While many commentators have assumed that Christianity posed a significant threat to the Tokugawa shogunate as 'a type of fifth column', a potential wedge for Spanish and Portuguese military intervention, such an interpretation exaggerates both European naval capabilities and the ability of Christian ritual and institutions to transform Japanese society.[45] The persecution of Christians in Japan, such as the martyrdom of twenty-three Franciscans and three Jesuits in Nagasaki in 1597, seems best understood as a response to anxieties – even the paranoid obsession of subversion from within – about peasant rebellion, the unruliness of disaffected *ronin* (masterless *samurai*), and the threat that a rhetoric of obedience to a higher authority posed to a feudal system of loyalty.[46] The Christian women on Saris's ship worship an image of fair-haired divinity, but their kneeling to Venus and Cupid reveals two threats to Western conceptions of religious belief – from external persecution and from the destabilizing nature of accommodation itself. If the Jesuits, led by Matteo Ricci, actively promulgated a policy of accommodation that sought to recast Chinese Confucianism in the image of Western theology, Saris's account of the women's shipboard visit suggests that Christianity itself was accommodated reciprocally to a cultural semiotics that redefined cultural systems of belief.[47] The women whisper not because Christianity poses a spiritual threat to indigenous beliefs but because signs of obedience or deference to any authority besides one's master was politically dangerous in Tokugawa Japan.

While Saris's account is emblematic of the complex history of European contact with Japan, it is also indicative of the problems that face Heylyn in writing about a nation that is characterized in his sources by its civilized morality, good government, and rigorous adherence to the rule of law, and yet that has recently rejected Christianity and cut off trade to all foreigners except the Dutch and Chinese. If the extirpation of Catholicism can be rendered comprehensible by implicit appeals to his readers' Protestant loyalties, the frightening prospect of a Dutch–Japanese alliance has to be dealt

---

[45] Cooper, *Rodrigues the Interpreter*, 160; Boxer, *Christian Century in Japan*, 338.

[46] On the class-specific nature of anti-Christian edicts between 1587 and 1642, see Ohashi Yukihiro, 'New perspectives on the early Tokugawa persecution', trans. Bill Garrad, in John Breen and Mark Williams (eds), *Japan and Christianity: Impacts and Responses* (New York, 1996), 46–62.

[47] See Lionel M. Jensen, *Manufacturing Confucianism: Chinese Traditions and Universal Civilization* (Durham, NC, 1997).

with carefully. Although the Shimabara rebellion halted plans for a joint Dutch–Japanese invasion of the Philippines, the Dutch had sent a ship to help crush the Christian-inspired uprising in 1638; consequently the VOC was allowed, with restrictions, to trade for Japanese silver, a crucial privilege at a time when silver mining had declined in South America.[48] The Dutch monopoly on European trade to Japan rankled with the English, who, as always, were seeking a market for their cloth. Child complained that the Dutch East India Company 'industriously avoid[s] introducing our English Cloth [to Japan]. Which Country being exceeding large, rich and populous, and lying in such a Northern Latitude, might vent as much of our English Manufactures, as *Spain* or *Portugal,* if we could gain a footing into that Trade: in the endeavor whereof the Company have [*sic*] already lost above Fifty thousand pounds *Sterling.*'[49] An investment of this magnitude, the desperate effort to sell English woollens to a country north of the tropical islands of Southeast Asia, can be justified only if trade in Japan is perceived as essential to the nation's prosperity as well as the East India Company's financial well-being. The prospect of the Japanese trading silver to the VOC, then, poses as many difficulties for Heylyn as the persecution of the Christians.

Japan, quite simply, is too enticing a potential trading partner to be condemned outright, and has too rocky a history with Western merchants and missionaries to be idealized as a nation of like-minded merchants. As an object of intense speculation and desire, Japan cannot be easily located on a hierarchy of civilized (commercial) nations, and Heylyn therefore must find a rhetorical strategy to convey the ambiguity of European perceptions of a people who resist being pigeonholed. The Japanese, he tells his readers, are

> of good understanding, apt to learn, and of able memories; cunning and subtile in their dealings. Of body vigorous and strong, accustomed to bear Arms untill 60 years old. Their complexion of an Olive-Colour, their beards thin, and the half of the hair of their heads shaved off. Patient they are of Pain, ambitious of glory, uncapable of suffering wrong, but can withall dissemble their resentments of it till opportunity of revenge. They reproach no man for his poverty, so it come not by his own untruthfulness, for which cause they detest all kinds of gaming, as the wayes of ill-husbandry and generally abhor Slandering, Theft, and Swearing.... The very Antipodes of our world in customs, though not in site: and the true type or Figure of the old English Puritan, opposite the Papists in things fit and decent, though made ridiculous many times by that opposition.[50]

[48] See Conrad Totman, *Early Modern Japan* (Berkeley and Los Angeles, 1993), 114–16.
[49] Child, *A Treatise,* 9.
[50] Heylyn, *Cosmographie,* 915.

Heylyn's description rests on two modes of triangulation: the Japanese are opposed to 'Papists' and identified with 'the old English Puritan', not the regicide of the 1640s but a 'ridiculous' figure closer to the stage-caricatures of the Jacobean theatre, such as Ben Jonson's Zeal-of-the-Land Busy. These images allow the non-puritan reader to judge 'objectively' the strengths and weaknesses of the Japanese – identifying with them against Catholics, and holding them at arm's length when they are identified with the pride, rigidity, moralistic self-denial, and economic aggrandizement of the puritans. But these two triangular comparisons fail to resolve the problem of a people who offer a radical alternative to Western ideas of a mutually profitable trade. If the Japanese are 'cunning and subtile in their dealings', they are also 'ambitious of glory' in a manner that resonates with Heylyn's praise of the 'heroic Acts' of the English. In both respects, they are motivated by a self-interest that mirrors and opposes the self-image of the nation. The Emperor's questions to Adams, in this regard, indicate that his subjects are not passive counters in the religious and political conflicts between England and Iberia but active constructors of their own modes of triangulation that play Protestants against Catholics, Dutch against Portuguese, silver miners against pepper merchants. Like the woman worshipping Venus and Cupid, Heylyn's Japanese translate into their own terms English desires for a 'mutual' trade; rather than conforming to European theocentrism, 'their dealings' serve their own ends in 'cunning and subtile' ways. If they are 'the very Antipodes of [Europe] in customs', their rejection of gambling, swearing, and prodigality (the venal sins of a profligate European aristocracy) mark them as worthy antagonists, policing conceptual boundaries that European merchants, and readers, cannot easily cross. Heylyn's analogies, then, ultimately confront the limitations of a world-view that cannot force into signification the prospect of a wealthy and virtuous nation that has rejected the commercial and religious bases of European self-definition.

VI

In Act IV of William Wycherley's *The Country Wife* (1674), Horner and Lady Fidget exit to his China closet to rut among the porcelain wares he has collected, while her husband remains oblivious to his cuckolding. No critic has asked why Horner has a room devoted to China; most assume that this collection is a mark of his gentlemanly status, an indication of his good taste and disposable income. Seen in this light, Horner's China closet can be treated as an early example of *chinoiserie*, a fad for things Chinese in the long eighteenth century that marks, for most scholars, the advent of European imperialism in the Far East. The sexual pun on China, however, has another dimension. China itself is precisely what the English went whoring after in their largely unsuccessful efforts to open trade to the Far East. The English exported silver and brought back in return earthenware and porcelain that was produced specifically for export.[51] Horner does not own the seventeenth-century porcelain equivalent of the Elgin Marbles pillaged by unequal treaties from oriental 'others'; the collection in his closet may be the stuff of a knock-off trade: cheaply produced and marked up for red-haired barbarians. His escapade with Lady Fidget assumes different connotations if it takes place among tacky souvenirs rather than among priceless foreign treasures.

At the margins of such canonical works as *The Country Wife* and *Paradise Lost*, then, lie brief references to the economic ties between Europe and Asia, subtle indications perhaps of a cultural awareness that Eurocentrism could be subject to qualification – Christianity rejected, overtures of friendship ignored. Pronouncements about the glories of English trade served a variety of rhetorical purposes for seventeenth-century writers, but behind the promises of infinite wealth generated by the East Asian trade lies the recognition that no market of consequence in the Far East existed for European goods. In his final novel, *A New Voyage Round the World* (1724), Daniel Defoe sums up more than a century of opposition to the Far Eastern trade, reiterating an argument that he makes almost obsessively in his economic writings. The 'necessary or useful things' brought back to England by the East India trade ('pepper, salt-petre, dyeing-woods and dyeing-earths, drugs, . . . shellac, . . . diamonds, . . . some pearl, and raw silk') are much less important than such 'trifling and unnecessary' imports as 'china ware, coffee, tea, japan works, pictures, fans, screens, &c.' and 'returns that are injurious to [Britain's] manufactures': 'printed calicoes, chintz, wrought silks, stuffs of herbs and barks, block tin, cotton, arrack, copper, indigo'. 'For all these', he declares, 'we carry nothing or very little but money, the innumerable nations of the Indies, China, &c., despising our manufactures and filling us with their own.'[52] Long before Defoe, Elizabeth I, Saris, Heylyn, and Child deal with the prospect of nations that 'despis[e]' European goods by projecting onto their peoples the ideological values that inform the ventures of the Dutch and English East India Companies. But this fascination – a middleman's eagerness for a share of the carriage trade – cannot contain the fear of an alterity that threatens to remind readers of England's marginalization in a worldwide economy dominated by the markets of the Far East. To move beyond the seventeenth century and to explain the decline of Asia after 1800 is to recast a familiar narrative of imperialism, to explore the implications of our self-congratulatory fictions of Eurocentrism. This new cosmography has only begun to take shape.

[51] On Chinese porcelain in eighteenth-century Europe, see Lydia H. Liu, 'Robinson Crusoe's earthenware pot', *Critical Inquiry*, 25 (1999), 728–57.

[52] Daniel Defoe, *A New Voyage Round the World by a Course Never Sailed Before*, ed. George A. Aitkin (London, 1902), 155–6.

9

The political economy of poison: the kingdom of Makassar and the early Royal Society[1]

Daniel Carey

One of the earliest European accounts of the Indonesian archipelago came from the fourteenth-century Franciscan friar Odoric of Pordenone, who travelled in Sumatra and Java, among other islands in the region, in the 1320s. In the midst of an account of Eastern marvels, which ranged from the exotic spices of clove, nutmeg, and mace, to the wealth of local potentates whose palaces glittered in jewels and gold, he took occasion to note a remarkable tree in the country of 'Panten',[2] which produced a poison 'the most deadly that existeth in the world'. In one of the many manuscript versions of his travels, Odoric explained that the country's warriors used this poison in military engagements. They armed themselves with hollow canes of a fathom ('braccio') in length which they loaded with darts dipped in the lethal substance. His report continued: 'and when they blow into the cane, the bodkin flieth and striketh whom they list, and those who are thus stricken incontinently die'.[3] The virulence of the poison was such that only one remedy existed, a particularly odious one, namely to imbibe a mixture of human excrement diluted with water and thereby to induce a violent purgation.

Although the country in question is unclear from his account, Odoric describes a poison that became indelibly associated in the early modern period with Makassar. This important kingdom, located in South Sulawesi (Celebes), became a focal point of European trade and conflict in Southeast

---

[1] I am grateful to a number of friends and colleagues for their help in conducting my research: E. M. Beekman, William Cummings, Doreen Innes, Jacinta Matos, Hermann Rasche, David Richardson, and Karen Vandevelde. This essay is dedicated to the memory of Norman Bisset.

[2] 'The travels of Friar Odoric', in Sir Henry Yule (trans., ed.), *Cathay and the Way Thither* (4 vols, London, 1913–16), II, 155. He also calls it 'Thalamasyn'. Neither name has been identified authoritatively with any country in the region. See Yule, *Cathay*, II, 155n. On Odoric's journey and Franciscan missionary activity, see J. R. S. Philipps, *The Medieval Expansion of Europe*, 2nd ed. (Oxford, 1998), ch. 5.

[3] Yule, *Cathay*, II, 158. This passage appears in the Palatine manuscript. Odoric's text became one of the sources for the travels of Sir John Mandeville. In the Egerton manuscript, Mandeville adapts the description of the poison tree by saying that the only remedy is to drink a mixture of the tree's crushed leaves and water. The poison is harvested by piercing the bark with a hatchet and allowing the 'liquor' to seep out. Mandeville adds that he discovered a plot by the Jews to poison 'all Christendom' with this venom. *Mandeville's Travels*, ed. Malcolm Letts (2 vols, London, 1953), I, 134.

Asia in the seventeenth century. Numerous travellers, soldiers, naturalists, and other authors returned again and again to the subject of this horrifying and pernicious poison, describing its effects and attempting to discover its toxicity, how it was harvested, and any antidotes that might spare its victims. There was some urgency in this case because *Ipo*, as the poison was known in Makassar, played a part in resistance to Dutch commercial hegemony in the country. As the Dutch consolidated their position they increasingly concentrated on subduing the threat of Makassar, and their growing conflict meant they faced the prospect not only of artillery and firearms but also of poisoned spears and darts blown from *sumpitans* in any land battle. Indeed, Georg Rumphius, the great naturalist who worked for the Dutch East India Company, claimed that Dutch soldiers were more afraid of the poison than they were of 'Canon or Musket'.[4]

An investigation of the substantial literature devoted to Makassar poison forms part of a larger history of toxic encounters in the era of early modern European expansion and trade. Poisons in general constituted an area of extensive concern because of the potentially fatal threat they posed to explorers in unfamiliar terrain, especially if the substances in question had a military application.[5] In this essay, I examine the array of accounts devoted to arrow poison in Makassar, but I also look at the impact of these reports in Europe. In particular, the Royal Society of London dedicated considerable effort in the 1660s to experimenting with samples they acquired from various correspondents in Southeast Asia. Their relative lack of success in testing them highlights the difficulty of obtaining correct material in the first place and the problem of standardizing such experiments. But their efforts also reveal a new dimension of seventeenth-century political economy. Obtaining knowledge of the effects and antidotes of the poison potentially strengthened the position of the English against their key rivals, the Dutch, with whom they were fighting a virtually global war for trade.

I

The attention given to Makassar poison in the seventeenth century testifies to its destructive effects and the sometimes extravagant rumours surrounding its operation. But these accounts proliferated for another reason, namely the importance of the Makassar sultanate in the period and its role in international trade. The position it occupied led to a series of military conflicts that culminated in the Makassar war with the Dutch, ending with the fall of the royal citadel of Sombaopu in 1669. The kingdom of Makassar (which consisted of the twinned monarchies of Gowa and Talloq) achieved an increasingly

---

[4] *The Poison Tree: Selected Writings of Rumphius on the Natural History of the Indies*, ed. and trans. E. M. Beekman (Amherst, 1981), 127.

[5] On South America, see Norman G. Bisset, 'War and hunting poisons of the New World. Part 1. Notes on the early history of curare', *Journal of Ethnopharmacology*, 36 (1992), 1–26.

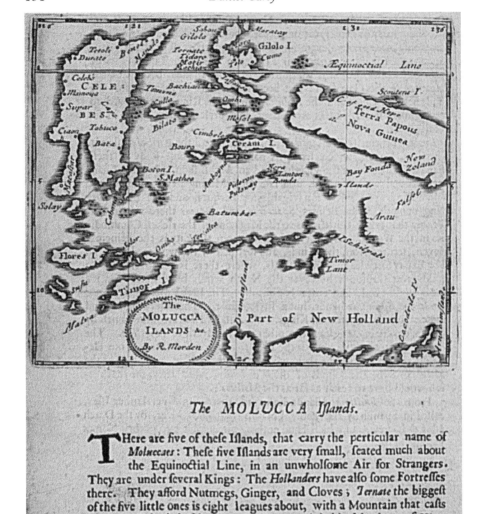

The *MOLUCCA Iſlands.*

THere are five of theſe Iſlands, that carry the perticular name of *Moluccaes*: Theſe five Iſlands are very ſmall, ſeated much about the Equinoctial Line, in an unwholſome Air for Strangers. They are under ſeveral Kings: The *Hollanders* have alſo ſome Fortreſſes there. They afford Nutmegs, Ginger, and Cloves ; *Ternate* the biggeſt of the five little ones is eight leagues about, with a Mountain that caſts out fire. It hath beſides ſeveral Villages uninhabited in times of War,
three

Map of the Moluccas and the kingdom of Makassar in Celebes. From Robert Morden, *Geography Rectified: or, A Description of the World* (London, 1680), 314. Reproduced by permission of the Bodleian Library, University of Oxford (shelfmark Don e. 440).

dominant position in South Sulawesi after the middle of the sixteenth century. The determination to extend the kingdom's influence and overlordship of various territories on the island was strengthened by the adoption of Islam in the early years of the seventeenth century.[6] The Makassarese successfully

[6] J. Noorduyn, 'De islamisering van Makassar', *Bijdragen tot de Taal-, Land- en Volkenkunde*, 112 (1956), 247–66; Anthony Reid, 'A great seventeenth century Indonesian family: Matoaya and Pattingalloang of Makassar',

overcame the Bugis population in the kingdom of Bone, their rivals based in the western part of the peninsula, and they extended their reach to include some of the Lesser Sunda Islands and the east coast of Borneo (Kalimantan).[7] Their economic strength depended on the vitality of the port-city of Makassar, which served as a key entrepôt for trade in cloves, nutmeg, mace, sandalwood, Indian textiles, tortoiseshell, benzoin, pepper, slaves, and a variety of other lucrative commodities, creating a network of trade that linked them with Macao, Manila, Cambodia, Timor, the Spice Islands, Aceh, and India.[8] Javanese, Indian, Malay, and Chinese traders all frequented the city and many settled there, while a series of European nations established factories and appointed commercial agents – the Portuguese, Dutch, English, Spanish, French, and Danes.[9] Indeed, after the fall of Melaka (Malacca) in 1641, the Portuguese made it their principal port, receiving encouragement for their continued trade with the Spice Islands and Timor (the source of the best sandalwood). The strategic location of the port, at a midpoint between the Spice Islands and the Straits of Melaka, strengthened its trading position, together with a substantial export market in rice and their own finished good of cotton cloth.[10] This economic activity, complemented by the 'gifts' expected by the country's rulers and their ability to fix prices at which they made purchases,[11] made the kingdom rich, allowing it to develop extensive fortifications and naval resources. At the same time, the Makassarese continued their own voyages to the Spice Islands (especially outlying Seram and Buru) and sold the valuable cargo to European traders. However, all of this was dependent on encouraging unrestricted trade, provided that their

Masyarakat Indonesia, 8/1 (1981), 13–19. Reprinted in Reid, *Charting the Shape of Early Modern Southeast Asia* (Chiang Mai, 1999), ch. 7. The first Muslim ruler of Makassar was Sultan Alauddin (r. 1593–1639). A series of 'Islamic Wars' on the island took place in the early seventeenth century leading to the successful forced conversion of the Bugis Kingdom of Bone. See Leonard Y. Andaya, *The Heritage of Arung Palakka: A History of South Sulawesi (Celebes) in the Seventeenth Century* (The Hague, 1981).

[7] The fullest account is Andaya, *Arung Palakka*.

[8] See Anthony Reid, 'The rise of Makassar', *Review of Indonesian and Malayan Affairs*, 17 (1983), 117–60, reprinted in Reid, *Charting the Shape*, ch. 6; Anthony Reid, *Southeast Asia in the Age of Commerce, 1450–1680* (2 vols, New Haven, 1988–93); John Villiers, 'Makassar: the rise and fall of an East Indonesian maritime trading state, 1512–1669', in J. Kathirithamby-Wells and John Villiers (eds), *The Southeast Asian Port and Polity* (Singapore, 1990), 143–59; Roderich Ptak, 'Der Handel zwischen Macau und Makassar, 1640–1667', *Zeitschrift der Deutschen Morgenlandischen Gesellschaft*, 139 (1989), 208–26. Earlier, Makassar had benefited from the Portuguese conquest of Melaka in 1511, which resulted in increased trade through its port by Javanese and Malay traders; it also benefited from the decline of the Javanese coastal states. See E. S. De Klerck, *History of the Netherlands East Indies* (2 vols, Amsterdam, 1975), I, 257; Bernard H. M. Vlekke, *Nusantara: A History of the East Indian Archipelago* (Cambridge, MA, 1945), 113.

[9] The Dutch established a factory in 1603, the English in 1613, and the Danes in 1618, while traders from Spain and China began to appear from 1615 and 1619 respectively. On the trading activities of Makassar and the European presence in kingdom, see note 8, and C. R. Boxer, *Francisco Vieira de Figueiredo: A Portuguese Merchant-adventurer in South East Asia, 1624–1667* ('s-Gravenhage, 1967); John Villiers, 'One of the especiallest flowers in our garden: the English factory at Makassar, 1613–1667', *Archipel*, 39 (1990), 159–78; D. K. Bassett, 'English trade in Celebes, 1613–1667', *Journal of the Malayan Branch of the Royal Asiatic Society*, 31/1 (1958), 1–39.

[10] Reid, 'Rise of Makassar', 138–9.

[11] Villiers, 'English factory', 168–70. This took the form principally of munitions – for example, cannon and gunpowder – which intensified during the growing conflict with the Dutch.

overlordship was respected,[12] a policy that set them on a collision course with the Dutch.

From its base in Batavia (former Jacatra), the Vereenigde Oost-Indische Compagnie (VOC) consolidated its position as the dominant European force in the archipelago in the seventeenth century, after repeated conflicts with the Portuguese, Spanish, and English. Their principal objective was to capture the spice trade, particularly in cloves, nutmeg, and mace, which focused their attentions on the Moluccas, Ambon, and the Banda Islands. If the Dutch company controlled production and supply of these goods, it would also control their price in Asian and European markets, but this monopolistic strategy required an attack on any trading powers that attempted to establish direct connections with the Spice Islands. Aggressive pursuit of this policy led to frequent skirmishes with the English (including the famous 'Amboyna Massacre' of 1623), a long-term blockade of the Portuguese stronghold of Melaka (1633–41), and the eventual occupation of Spanish forts at Tidore. An alliance with the Sultan of Ternate gave the Dutch political leverage in the territories under his influence, but this too had to be enforced. By 1657, partly through the destruction of trees in areas both within and beyond its direct control, the Dutch succeeded in making an arrangement in which the cultivation of cloves would be confined to Ambon and nutmeg to Banda. However, the adverse economic impact of the Dutch policy and the complex network of political alliances in the region resulted in a series of insurrections by Indonesian states, sometimes with the support of the Makassarese themselves.[13]

Initially the Dutch attempted to negotiate with the Makassarese in order to secure their position. They asked the sultan to refrain from trading with the Spice Islands, but his refusal led to a Dutch blockade. The conflict continued until 1637, when Anthony van Diemen persuaded Makassar to recognize the VOC's interests, but the terms of the treaty were not respected and the Dutch again attempted to obtain the necessary assurances, this time in the person of Arnold de Vlamingh van Oudshoorn, in 1653. The Makassarese once more refused, and reasserted their right to trade with Seram and Ambon, which was then in revolt. This rebuff resulted in a declaration of war by the Dutch in October 1653 in which they repeated the blockade of Makassar's harbour. Throughout this period the Makassarese were known to be providing support for resistance to the Dutch from various quarters, especially in Ambon, Buton, and Seram. Another treaty was signed, but mounting Dutch dissatisfaction led to a military expedition in 1660, which resulted in a treaty guaranteeing the eventual expulsion of the Portuguese from the island. After a series of further conflicts, a full-scale war began in November

---

[12] For an important clarification of what the *mare liberum* principle meant in a Makassar context, and the tribute they expected from vassal states, see Andaya, *Arung Palakka*, 46–7.

[13] For historical discussion in English, see Vlekke, *Nusantara*; De Klerck, *History of the Netherlands East Indies*; and D. G. E. Hall, *A History of South-East Asia* (London, 1955); in Dutch, see F. W. Stapel *et al.*, *Geschiedenis van Nederlandsch Indië* (5 vols, Amsterdam, 1938–40), III.

1666, when Cornelis Speelman led a fleet of twenty-one ships against Makassar. This was the first campaign in the Makassar war in which the Dutch allied with Arung Palakka, the exiled Bugis leader. Dutch supremacy in the region was finally attained in 1669 with the submission of the Makassarese.[14]

II

This background helps to explain the amount of attention given to Makassar and its poison by commentators of different nationalities in the period, including a range of traders, soldiers, naturalists, and VOC personnel. The poison tree, *Antiaris toxicaria*,[15] is part of the Moraceae plant family, found over a wide area of Southeast Asia, including Sulawesi, Sumatra, Java, Kalimantan, Myanmar (Burma), Thailand, and the Philippines.[16] The poison derives from the highly toxic latex of the tree.[17] This milky substance – usually described in early accounts as a sap – hardens to a dark brown colour. The exudate was acquired by jabbing the trunk with a grooved pole and allowing the liquid to seep down the tube. At this point it was carefully worked into a waxy accretion and transported in cloths. The method of preparing the poison, which was used for hunting as well as military purposes, varied between regions and individuals, and often included other plant-based substances, some of them containing strychnine, but the common ingredient remained *Antiaris*, which was more than sufficient in terms of toxicity. Warriors who used it for their darts and arrows were adept at judging the most poisonous examples according to colour and consistency, which they reconstituted by boiling and then applied to sharks' teeth or other sharp objects.[18] When they struck with these weapons, the poison entered the victim's bloodstream with rapid and usually fatal results. This is due to the presence of a complex mixture of cardiac glycosides in the poison, causing the heart to contract so severely that the muscle stops beating in

[14] See Andaya, *Arung Palakka*; De Klerck, *History of the Netherlands East Indies*, I, 255–9, 275–7; F. W. Stapel, *Het Bongaais Verdrag* (Groningen and The Hague, 1922).

[15] On this subject the major sources are: Thomas Horsfield, *Plantae Javanicae Rariores* (London, 1838), 52–63; Henry Yule and A. C. Burnell extended this account in their entry on 'Upas' in *Hobson-Jobson: The Anglo-Indian Dictionary* [1886] (Ware, 1996), 952–9; I. H. Burkill, *A Dictionary of the Economic Products of the Malay Peninsula* (2 vols, London, 1935), I, 174–84; see also John Bastin, 'New Light on J. N. Foersch and the Celebrated Poison Tree of Java', *Journal of the Malayan Branch of the Royal Asiatic Society*, 58/2 (1985), 25–44.

[16] On the geographical distribution of the tree, see N. G. Bisset, 'The arrow and dart poisons of South-East Asia, with particular reference to the *Strychnos* species used in them. Part I. Indonesia, Borneo, Philippines, Hainan, and Indo-China', *Lloydia*, 29/1 (1966), 1–18; N. G. Bisset and M. C. Woods, 'The arrow and dart poisons of South-East Asia, with particular reference to the *Strychnos* species used in them. Part II. Burma, Thailand, and Malaya', *Lloydia*, 29/3 (1966), 172–95. See also Paul Geiger, *Beitrag zur Kenntnis der Ipoh-Pfeilgifte* (Berlin, 1901), 37–41.

[17] On the chemistry of the poison, see references in Timila Shrestha, Brigitte Kopp, and Norman G. Bisset, 'The Moraceae-based dart poisons of South America: cardiac glycosides of *Maquira* and *Naucleopsis* species', *Journal of Ethnopharmacology*, 37 (1992), 129–43.

[18] Geiger's account includes illustrations of the technique of harvesting the poisonous latex and photographs of materials used in transporting it. See also H. van der Veen, 'Aanteekeningen van Dr. H. van der Veen over blaasroer, schild en pijl en boog bij de Sa'dan- en Binoeang-Toradja's', *Tijdschrift voor Indische Taal-, Land- en Volkenkunde*, 63 (1924), 368–73.

systole.[19] To this day, no adequate remedy against it has been found, with the effects dependent on levels of concentration in the dosage and how quickly the dart is removed. There is no question about its toxicity, but a series of legendary stories accrued around its effects and antidotes, sometimes drawn from local tradition but elsewhere embellished on the basis of fear and uncertainty.

During the period of European trade and colonization in Indonesia, the earliest accounts of arrow poison in the region came from the Portuguese, the dominant presence in the archipelago in the sixteenth century. In fact, Afonso De Albuquerque, who led the conquest of Maleka in 1511, described a series of battles in which many of his men were wounded and killed by poisoned weapons.[20] As far as Makassar was concerned, with which the Portuguese had little contact at this time, the information was less specific. Tomé Pires, author of the extensive *Suma Oriental* (composed between 1512 and 1515), had originally travelled to India as a factor of spices in 1511. From there he was sent to the Moluccas by Albuquerque and he made at least one trip to Java, but his information regarding Makassar was limited. According to Pires, the Makassarese were 'all heathens, robust and great warriors'. He noted that they were feared with good reason because 'They carry a great deal of poison[ed weapons] and shoot with them'.[21] However, he had no information on the source of the poison or techniques of production.

Subsequent Portuguese accounts were even more cryptic. Diogo do Couto's *Década Quarta da Ásia* (1602) contained a brief report on the island of Celebes, based on a manuscript from the 1560s by Gabriel Rebelo, who had spent thirteen years as a factor in the Moluccas. Couto's somewhat enhanced version of his source mentioned a dangerous tree located on the island:

> Ha n'estas ilhas muitas monstuosidades, de que não falamos, e antre ellas hua arvore, que quem se poem à sombra do ponente mata logo, se não vão buscar a sombre do levante, que he seu antidoto.[22]

---

[19] Chemically this is related to the operation of digitalis. For a report on a recent death that occurred after ingestion of *Antiaris toxicaria* latex, see L. M. Ho, I. Cheong, and H. A. Jalil, 'Rhabdomyolysis and acute renal failure following blowpipe dart poisoning', *Nephron*, 72 (1996), 676–8. This case is peculiar because the poison is not active through the gastro-intestinal tract, but the victim may have had a puncture in the stomach lining which allowed it to enter the blood stream.

[20] *The Commentaries of the Great Afonso Dalboquerque*, ed. and trans. Walter de Gray Birch (4 vols, London, 1875–84), iii, 104, 108–9, 121, 127. The first edition of the *Commentaries* was published in 1557, the second in 1576.

[21] *The Suma Oriental of Tomé Pires*, ed. and trans. Armando Cortesão (2 vols, London, 1944), i, 226, 227.

[22] 'There are in these islands many monstrous things, of which we haven't spoken, and among them a tree, which kills those who stand in its shade on the western side, but standing on the eastern side serves as an antidote.' Diogo do Couto, *Década Quarta da Ásia*, ed. M. Augusta Lima Cruz (2 vols, Lisbon, 1999), i, 386. There are three surviving manuscripts of Gabriel Rebelo's *Informação das Molucas* (dating between 1561 and 1569), the first two printed in vol. iii of *Documentação para a História das Missões do Padroado Português do Oriente – Insulíndia*, ed. Artur Basílio de Sá (Lisbon, 1955) and the third in vol. vi (Lisbon, 1988). In the latter, Rebelo's more restricted statement reads: '*Tem* arvores, cuja sombra e fina peçonha da banda do ponente, quando por ela pasão, mas cura-se este dano com a do levante' (202). 'There are trees whose shade is a delicate venom on the western side, when you pass by them, but the sickness can be cured by the shade on the eastern side.' On Couto's borrowings, see António Coimbra Martins, *Em Torno de Diogo do Couto* (Coimbra, 1985), 133–5.

However brief, Couto's account is significant because it frames this mysterious work of nature within the discourse of the monstrous. To that extent, he participates in a rhetorical tradition identifying the productions of the East as marvels, although in this case they create something closer to terror than to wonder. We shall see that this narrative approach, evident in the medieval travels of Odoric, had a long continuance in the developing response to Makassar poison. Bartolomé Leonardo de Argensola continued the pattern in his historical account of the *Conquista de las Islas Malucas* (1609). Argensola had never travelled in Southeast Asia and relied on Couto, among others, for his narrative sources. When it came to 'las islas Celebes', he elaborated on Couto's text by suggesting that they produced 'infinitas monstruosidades'. He included a similar account of the mysterious tree, concentrating on the fatal effect of its shade, which was remedied only by moving from the western side to the eastern at a distance of 'cuatro palmos'.[23] Clearly such a cure was not much help to anyone struck by a poisoned arrow. In any case, Rebelo, Couto, and Argensola seem not to have possessed information on the poisonous sap or latex of the tree and its military application.

Within Makassarese society itself, blowpipes and poisons played an important role. In the sixteenth century, royally sponsored blowpipe makers were established during the reign of Tunipalangga (1548–66).[24] The Gowa Chronicle, which described the history of the kingdom's rise and dominance, traced this power to the capture of a sacred blowpipe, called I Buqle, which originally protected a rival people, killing hundreds of Gowa warriors with its unfailing direction of fatal darts. Once Gowa obtained it, their overlordship was ensured.[25] The use of poison was not restricted to military occasions, however. It was also employed in judicial executions, with an acute awareness that its disturbing power exerted considerable social control.[26]

When we enter the seventeenth century – a period of increasing direct European contact with Makassar for trading purposes – a fuller account begins to emerge in Western sources. In 1603, Herman de Bree, a Dutch traveller, reported knowledgeably on the country's commercial networks. He commented on the 'outstanding humaneness' ('singulari humanitate') of the Makassarese, at this early stage of Dutch contact, and wrote with high expectations of a hospitable reception in the kingdom. At the same time he

---

[23] *Conquista de las Islas Malucas* [1609] (Madrid, 1992), 75. As Argensola's English translator rendered this passage: 'One of these [Monstrous Productions] is a Tree bearing a vast Head, the shade whereof kills any Man that lyes down under it on the West-side, unless he immediately lye down on the East-side; the same shade at only a Yard distance being an Antidote against its opposite Malignity.' *The Discovery and Conquest of the Molucco and Philippine Islands*, trans. John Stevens (London, 1708), 49. Here, malignancy becomes a kind of active principle. On Argensola's text, see John Villiers's essay in this volume.

[24] Anthony Reid, 'Pluralism and progress in seventeenth-century Makassar', *Bijdragen Tot de Taal-, Land- en Volkenkunde*, 156 (2000), 447.

[25] William Cummings, *Making Blood White: Historical Transformations in Early Modern Makassar* (Honolulu, 2002), 131–3.

[26] *Ibid.* 183–5.

noted their bravery in war and their use of arrows with sharp fishbone tips, 'so deeply dipped in poison that men wounded and struck by them cannot escape death' ('veneno adeo infectis, ut illis vulnerati & percussi mortem euitare non possint').[27] He added that the Dutch had received several quivers filled with these arrows, an unusually generous gift.

The earliest published report in English was written by Thomas Herbert, whose journey east began in 1626, initially as part of a diplomatic mission to the Persian court of Shah Abbas.[28] After the death of Sir Dodmore Cotton, who had led the embassy, Herbert continued his travels in India and elsewhere. His short discussion of Makassar begins with the lax sexual customs of local women and their habit of smoking tobacco, before turning to an observation 'which is rarest, yet very true'. He notes that the country's warriors employ 'long Canes (they call them *Sempitans*)' from which they blow a 'little pricking piercing quill'. If they draw any blood, the victim either dies immediately or within the hour. He then recorded a disturbing (if fabulous) feature of the poison's operation which exerted a considerable fascination among writers on the subject:

> All the wounded body (by the virulent strength of the venome) in that small space [of time] rots and consumes most rufully and not without much wonder.[29]

Herbert could not identify the source of the material itself but concentrated on its wondrous effects. As a result, the mystery surrounding the poison deepened in his disturbing tale.[30]

Around the time that Herbert was visiting Makassar, the Dutch naturalist and expert on tropical medicine Jacobus Bontius (Jacob De Bondt, 1592–1631) produced a similarly worrying – and highly influential – account of Makassar poison, although his version did not appear in print until 1658.[31]

---

[27] De Bree's account appeared in a Latin translation by Gotardo Arthus in a series produced by the De Bry brothers, *Indiae Orientalis Pars Octava* (Frankfurt, 1607), LI'.

[28] Herbert's published journal, which appeared originally in 1634, went through an elaborate series of expansions over the course of his life before his final edition in 1677. Herbert supported the parliamentary cause and attended Charles I in his captivity. He was eventually appointed groom of the bedchamber and became Charles's sole attendant in the final months of his life. Throughout the account of his travels, Herbert records his observations in an eccentric, digressive style, interlarding the text with classical comparisons and encountering human difference with an unusual mixture of liberality and dismay. On Herbert, who was given a baronetcy in 1660, see *DNB* and Boies Penrose, *Urbane Travelers, 1591–1635* (Philadelphia, 1942), 174–214.

[29] Thomas Herbert, *A Relation of Some Yeares Travaile, Begunne Anno 1626* (London, 1634), 199.

[30] This notion is probably behind Samuel Butler's simile drawn in his character of 'The Glutton': 'His Entrails are like the *Sarcophagus*, that devours dead Bodies in a small Space, or the *Indian Zampatan*, that consumes Flesh in a Moment', in A. R. Waller (ed.), *Characters and Passages from Note-Books* (Cambridge, 1908), 191–2.

[31] Bontius trained in medicine at the university of Leiden, receiving his degree in 1614. After starting a practice in the city, he opted to enter the service of the VOC as a doctor, apothecary, and surgical inspector, sailing with his family for Batavia in 1627. He died there just four years later. His time was productive in literary terms, and he achieved a posthumous fame with the publication of *De Medicina Indorum* in 1642. A further two books of this appeared in 1658 in the Elzevier edition of Willem Piso's *De Indiae utriusque re naturali et medica*, which contained Piso's natural history of Brazil, written in collaboration with Georg Marcgraff.

Bontius describes some 'marvelous works of nature' found throughout the East, including the vast stones expelled by Java's volcanoes, naphtha which burns in water and on one occasion consumed a Portuguese ship, and an early account of acupuncture in Japan. In this context Bontius remarks on the king of Makassar's poison. He describes the effect of the poison as immediate, causing death 'quicker than a sword'. He then elaborates on the phenomenon identified by Herbert: 'in half an hour the flesh putrefies by this obnoxious poison in such a way, that it may be torn [by the hands] from the bones like slime' ('carnes intro dimidiae horae spatium a septico hoc veneno, ita computrescent, ut tanquam mucus a subjectis ossibus manibus avelli queant'). The miraculous force of the poison did not end there, however. Bontius went on to report that if someone was wounded above the waist, and the trickling blood was touched with a poison arrow, the force of the venom was such that it 'ascends to the wound with the speed of the storm and the life of the patient is cut off in the same way'.[32] He insisted that these accounts were true, not fairy tales ('nugae'), and that they had been experienced not only by the Dutch but also the Danes and English in Makassar.

Not long after the accounts of Herbert and Bontius were composed, a fuller report of Makassar was given by Seyger van Rechteren, who visited the territory in March 1632 as part of a mission to exchange Dutch and Portuguese prisoners. He noted the enmity between the Dutch and Makassarese because the former had curtailed their trade with Ambon, but he took part nonetheless in a visit to the royal palace, where they were received by Sultan Alauddin. He describes the impressive interior of the building in some detail, the meal they were served, the royal concubines, as well as an exchange between himself and one of the princes in which he discussed the 'reformed religion' and provided him with a Malay translation of the Psalms. Like Herbert, van Rechteren remarks on the dress of local women which was sufficiently capacious to allow men to get inside it at night 'to observe the work of Venus'; sodomy, meanwhile, was very common and did not carry any punishment. He was impressed by the beautifully crafted ships in the king's navy and claimed that the sovereign could raise an army of 100,000 men in six hours. The soldiers' weaponry consisted mainly of their poisoned spears ('piecken'), which they were adept in handling. If someone committed an offence, such as theft – even for a sum as small as a 'styver' – the king would order a servant to shoot him with a poisoned arrow, using a blowpipe, wherever he might be at the time, even if he was lying with his wife ('op sijn Vrouw leggende').[33]

[32] Jacobus Bontius, *De Arte Medica*, trans. [books 5 and 6] A. Querido (Amsterdam, 1931), 287.

[33] Seyger van Rechteren's account, originally published in 1635, was reprinted (with interpolations) in the Dutch compendium edited by Isaac Commelin, *Begin ende Voortgangh van de Vereenighde Nederlantsche Oost-Indische Compagnie* [1645] (4 vols, Amsterdam, 1969), IV, sig. Eee4ʳ. For a brief summary of his work see Donald F. Lach and Edwin J. Van Kley, *Asia in the Making of Europe. Volume 3. A Century of Advance. Book 3. Southeast Asia* (Chicago, 1993), 1444–5.

The use of Makassar poison in a judicial context as mentioned by van Rechteren recurs in a number of seventeenth-century European accounts. John Jourdain, who established the English factory at Makassar in 1613, remarked on the same phenomenon in an unpublished report for the East India Company. He suggested that the king was able to judge the dosage of poison according to whether he wanted the prisoner to die on the spot or to allow him sufficient time to return home, where it would then take effect.[34] On the basis of other reports, it appears that the Makassar kings deliberately staged judicial events of this kind in order to emphasize their power, often for the benefit of foreign visitors.[35] By doing so they dramatically alerted their audience to the kind of military and judicial potency of the commodity they possessed. The earliest printed story to this effect appears in the *Itinerario de Las Missiones* (1646) by the Portuguese Augustinian Sebastião Manrique. Manrique, who had visited Makassar himself in 1640, told the story of a Portuguese nobleman who took refuge at Makassar during a trip from China to Goa. The good relations between the two countries meant that this gentleman was received with hospitality, and a gift exchange took place in which he received a 'very special' present, a certain root called Lucerrage, which provided an antidote to the force of Makassar poison. Clearly this was a valuable gift indeed. To demonstrate its usefulness, the king conducted an experiment on two convicts. Both were pricked with a poisoned dart, 'dipped in a most virulent' ('muy resinado') poison:

> The moment the sumpita touched him and a few drops of blood had fallen, the patient commenced to foam at the mouth and within half an hour fell prostrate on the floor, foaming at the mouth and writhing in the agonies of death. He was given a drink made of this pounded root in water and at once ceased to foam at the mouth, and in less than half an hour he was once more on his feet. The sentence was then carried out by another dose from the sumpita and within an hour he was removed for burial.[36]

Manrique concluded with a laconic remark: 'Such was the experiment usually carried out on such occasions by the King of Macassar'. His comment suggests that this kind of event was a regular occurrence staged for the benefit of visiting dignitaries. Support for this view can be found in later travel journals. Jean Baptiste Tavernier stated that his brother Daniel was 'much beloved by the King, who invited him to take part in all his amusements, and especially when drinking was in question'. On one occasion Tavernier was invited to witness the execution of an Englishman who had

---

[34] William Foster (ed.), *The Journal of John Jourdain, 1608–1617* (Cambridge, 1905), 295.

[35] See, for example, Nicolas Gervaise, *An Historical Description of the Kingdom of Macassar in the East-Indies* [1688] (London, 1701), 99.

[36] C. Eckford Luard (ed.), *Travels of Fray Sebastien Manrique 1629–1643* (2 vols, Oxford, 1927), II, 167.

committed murder. The king demonstrated the force of the poison by allowing Tavernier's brother to name the part of the body he wished him to strike. He suggested the right big toe. Two surgeons were present, both European, ready to make an immediate amputation, 'but they were unable to accomplish it so skilfully but that the poison, more rapid, had reached the heart, and the Englishman died at the same moment'.[37]

Among seventeenth-century authors, an important if disagreeable dimension to the story surrounding Makassar poison emerged in the work of Johann Jacob Saar, namely the consumption of ordure as the only available antidote.[38] Saar was a German soldier who joined the VOC at the age of nineteen and served with the company for fifteen years, between 1644 and 1659. His *Ost-Indianische fünfzehen-jährige Kriegs-Dienste* appeared in Nuremberg, his native city, in 1662, and recounted his military adventures in numerous conflicts in Banda, Ceylon, and elsewhere. Saar reported that

A tree grows on Makassar, a coastal area on the isle of Celebes, that is highly poisonous so that, if someone only gets struck in one of his limbs, and if this limb is not cut off immediately, the poison quickly reaches the heart and kills, unless – and this is the only antidote – he uses his own excrement, as fresh as it goes from him ['so warm als er von Ihm gehet'].[39]

Saar went on to describe an unfortunate incident in which two colleagues were shot with poisoned arrows during a fight with Bandanese warriors, one of them a carpenter and the other a sailor. Both managed to get back to the ship, where the sailor saved his life by consuming 'his own despicable medicine' ('Seine abscheuliche Medicin'), but the carpenter was unable to produce any excrement and died in short order.[40] Alas, this unfortunate cure would never have been efficacious, since *antiarin* operates through the

---

[37] Jean Baptiste Tavernier, *Travels in India* [1676], ed. and trans. V. Ball (2 vols, London, 1889), II, 299. Georg Rumphius also reported that the Makassar kings 'experimented' with the poison on criminals. *Het Amboinsche Kruid-Boek* (7 vols, Amsterdam, The Hague, and Utrecht, 1741–55), II, 269. Samuel Butler turned this information to satirical effect. In his character of a schoolmaster, he described the figure as having 'Absolute Dominion in his Territories and (like the King of Macassa) is Party Judge and Executioner Himselfe'. Hugh de Quehen (ed.), *Prose Observations* (Oxford, 1979), 265.

[38] Odoric of Pordenone's account of this 'cure' appeared in print in Latin and English in the second volume of Hakluyt's *Principal Navigations* (1598–1600). See Richard Hakluyt, *The Principal Navigations, Voyages, Traffiques & Discoveries of the English Nation* (12 vols, Glasgow, 1904), IV, 387, 417.

[39] Johann Jacob Saar, *Reise nach Java, Banda, Ceylon und Persien 1644–1660*, ed. S. P. L'Honoré Naber (The Hague, 1930), 56. On Saar see *Allgemeine Deutche Biographie* and the forward to The Hague edition by L'Honoré Naber. Saar noted that Bandanese women also caused considerable damage with the poison. They sat in trees and smeared their 'Fischgeräht' (57; possibly *sic*: Fischgräte) with poison and then blew the darts from small wooden pipes.

[40] Saar, *Reise nach Java, Banda, Ceylon und Persien*, 57. The Swiss VOC soldier Albrecht Herport told a similar story about Java in his travel account, dating from *c.* 1659, *Eine kurtze Ost-Indianische Reiss-Beschreibung* (Bern, 1669). Reprinted as S. P. L'Honoré Naber (ed.), *Reise nach Java, Formosa, Vorder-Indien und Ceylon 1659–1668* (The Hague, 1930), 29. See also Johan Nieuhof, another German-born author who served with the Dutch, who discussed the poison and its alleged cure in 1682 in *Zee en Lant-Reize, door verscheide gewesten van Oostindien*, translated as *Voyages and Travels to the East Indies 1653–1670* (Oxford, 1988), 278.

blood stream, with effects dependent on dosage, concentration, and the length of time the weapon remains in the wound.

The escalation of military conflict with the Makassarese in the 1660s meant that the Dutch faced an increasing threat from poisoned weapons of various kinds. Describing the campaign to subdue the country in 1660, Wouter Schouten narrated the capture of an important fort, Pa'nakkukang, which was immediately surrounded by hostile forces who attacked with 'uncommon fury', firing thousands of arrows and poisoned assagays.[41] The Dutch later allied with the Bugis, under the command of Arung Palakka, waging the 'Makassar war', which ended in 1669. Accounts of the numerous battles in the war indicate that the Dutch and Bugis concentrated on firing at their enemies from ships along the coast, as well as conducting night-time raids, burning villages, and using various explosive devices. Despite their precautions, during an attack on a small village in October 1667, three men were killed by 'spatten' and Palakka himself was injured, but his life was saved by taking an unnamed counterpoison (*tegen-gift*).[42] A contemporary Dutch engraving, celebrating the eventual victory over Makassar, pictures an extended landscape with an array of ongoing skirmishes. In the foreground Makassarese warriors with spears and blowpipes attack Dutch forces mounted on horse.[43]

The Dutch were led in this war by Admiral Cornelis Speelman. He had much at stake in obtaining accurate information about Makassar poison, although his opportunity to do so seems to have come only after the war was over. In an account published in 1685 in a German learned journal, Speelman noted that several obstacles existed to securing a full report. The Makassar princes were bound by oath not to divulge anything about their weapons or poisons. Furthermore, the 'choicest' poison on the island was obtained from the 'Loradia' (the Toraja), who inhabited a remote and mountainous inland territory.[44] Despite these difficulties, Speelman was able to construct an extensive account. Various princes supplied him with testimony, abandoning their oath, and indicated that around the poison tree itself nothing else would grow for a considerable expanse. The poisonous liquid was obtained by making a lesion in the bark of the tree with a long bamboo reed fixed with a sharp iron tip. The 'violent wounding' allowed the sap to emerge and gather in the reed, hardening to a black or dark-red colour. Speelman indicated that excessive heat and cold proved harmful to the poison and it had to be preserved with care, bound in numerous layers of cloth, which had to

[41] 'Bij duysende van Spatten / Pijlen / en vergifte Assagayen / vloogen door de lucht / en vielen in *Panakoke* neder.' Wouter Schouten, *Oost-Indische Voyagie* (Amsterdam, 1676), 90.

[42] *Vermeerdert Journael of Kort Verhael van 't Begin Voortgangh en Eynde des Oorloghs tusschen den Koningh en verdere Regeeringe van Macassar* (Amsterdam, 1670?), 7. The same report mentions the capture of numerous sumpitans, daggers (*kris*), and 'piecken' in various raids.

[43] Reproduced in Stapel, *Het Bongaais Verdrag*.

[44] On the Toraja, see Hetty Nooy-Palm, *The Sa'Dan-Toraja: A Study of Their Social Life and Religion* (2 vols, The Hague, 1979–86). On their use of the poison see I, 227–8; H. van der Veen, 'Aanteekeningen'; and H. van der Veen, *The Merok Feast of the Sa'Dan Toraadja* ('s-Gravenhage, 1965), 89, 91.

be changed regularly. In this fashion the poison was transported in 'granules or globules' and delivered to the Makassar princes.

The power of individual samples could not be determined by sight alone but was tested by placing some part of it in water. The more intense the bubbling, the stronger was the poison. When they were ready to apply the poison to the tips of their weapons – made from the teeth of a 'Lamian' fish – they would place it in water which was treated with a certain bitter herb, called Lampojang or Lampaya.[45] If properly handled, treated weapons retained their potency for two years, although other samples lasted only for a month or two. He noted that many antidotes were in use among the Makassarese and Bugis, and that a 'popular remedy' was human excrement. Yet none of them could overcome the strongest of the poisons, which led to instant death. What was more, anyone wounded by the poison who managed to survive would find that one, two, or three years afterwards they would succumb, especially 'those who mingle with and have intercourse with women and those who eat fungi and tubers in the ground' ('qui cum mulieribus sese miscent ac conversantur, fungosque & tubera terrae comedunt').[46]

By far the fullest description of the poison tree in the seventeenth century, building on the information of Speelman and others, was provided by Rumphius, the German-born naturalist who resided in Ambon between 1653 and 1702 while in the service of the VOC. Rumphius's remarkable seven-volume work, *Het Amboinsche Kruid-Boek*, did not appear in print until 1741–55, but the research and writing had begun in the 1660s.[47] Rumphius's report contains a mixture of fact with the fabulous, which suggests that understanding of the poison was still structured to some extent by the discourse of marvels, whether European or local in origin. At the time he was writing, Makassar had come under the control of the Dutch following Speelman's successful campaigns. This provided an opportunity for closer study of the poison tree but did not dispel the range of rumours and legendary stories concerning the poison's operation. According to Rumphius, the tree was so noxious that neither grass nor any foliage grew beneath it, and the ground below was 'russet, and as if scorched'.[48] Birds that landed on the branches would fall to the ground dead, and anything touched by wind that passed through it would perish. In a splendid elaboration of the mythology associated

---

[45] Identified as *Zingiber zerumbet* (L.) Sm. See E. D. Merrill, *An Interpretation of Rumphius's Herbarium Amboinense* (Manila, 1917), 151–3.

[46] *Miscellanea Curiosa, sive Ephemeridum Medico-Physicarum Germanicarum Academiae Naturae Curiosorum, Dec. II. Annus Tertius* (Nuremberg, 1685), 130. The text was reprinted in a section entitled 'India Literata' as part of Michaelis Bernhardi Valentini, *Historia Simplicium* (Frankfurt, 1716), 434–5.

[47] Rumphius went blind in 1670 and began composing the text anew in Dutch. The first six books were complete by 1690, two more by 1696, and three final books by 1697 (with an augmentation in 1701). On Rumphius see E. M. Beekman, 'Introduction' to Georgius Everhardus Rumphius, *The Ambonese Curiosity Cabinet* (New Haven, 1999), xxxv–lxxxiii; E. M. Beekman, *Troubled Pleasures: Dutch Colonial Literature from the East Indies, 1600–1950* (Oxford, 1996), ch. 5; H. C. D. de Wit (ed.), *Rumphius Memorial Volume* (Baarn, 1959).

[48] *Poison Tree*, 129.

with the tree, Rumphius reported that only one creature could abide to live beneath it: a 'horned snake that cackles like a hen, or as others are wont to say, crows like a cock, and by night has fiery eyes'.[49] Stories of this basilisk seem to have come from local sources, but whatever their provenance, they would have given pause to anyone contemplating a mission to secure their own sample. These and other accounts ensured that control of the substance was likely to remain in native hands.

The manner of harvesting it was perilous indeed, merely confirming the dangers associated with any near approach. It was necessary to cover the body with a series of cloths to avoid any direct contact. If any drops of sap touched the skin, the body would swell up. Even a branch sent to Rumphius in Ambon was still powerful enough, he commented, to create a tingling sensation if one stuck a hand into the container.

What made this inquiry more than purely academic, of course, was the use the Makassarese made of the poison in military conflict. Rumphius's chapter was framed by this concern. He began by noting the fear the poison had inspired in Dutch soldiers, but he was now confident that greater information on its 'nature and antidotes' meant that they had less to worry about. He closed the chapter with a discussion of military expeditions in which the poison had figured. During what he called the 'Madjerasensian War', when the Makassarese joined forces with Ambonese rebels, the Dutch took a variety of steps to combat their poisoned arrows, resorting to anti-poisons of several kinds and a number of other measures. Officers, who could afford to do so, dressed themselves in loose-fitting leather garments over their regular attire, ensuring that if they were struck with an arrow it would not penetrate. The sailors and 'grenadeers', of more modest means, used sailcloth to achieve the same effect. He continued:

> We also had to heed the Blow-pipes themselves, because those warriors in the front ranks of the enemy had fastened them with iron blades, like spears, and smeared these with poison. And with these they invaded our ranks, wherefore these spears were especially good.[50]

The Dutch responded by improvising their own form of bayonet, attaching spears onto their flintlocks. For those who had been hit, the danger did not subside even if they survived the immediate onslaught of the poison. Rumphius noted the case of a soldier, identified as a kinsman of Rumphius's who fought with VOC forces in Seram, who was shot in the chest with a dart in 1654. Three years later 'he felt a burning in the same spot, followed by a raging fever that killed him'.[51]

---

[49] *Ibid.*

[50] *Ibid.* 134.

[51] Rumphius, *Amboinsche Kruid-Boek*, II, 270 [book 3, ch. 46]. I am indebted to Professor E. M. Beekman for providing me with a copy of his translation of this chapter, part of his planned complete edition of the work.

'Makassarese poison blow-pipes'. From Johan Nieuhof, *Zee en lant-Reize, door verscheide gewesten van Oostindien* (Amsterdam, 1682). Reproduced by permission of the Bodleian Library, University of Oxford (shelfmark Mason T 123).

Rumphius devoted an entire chapter to the subject of antidotes. The most famous was the ordure cure, the only one that was known during the Ambonese wars. If a victim could not 'produce' himself, he would ask a colleague, the point being to cause severe vomiting. In fact, Rumphius noted the case of a valiant captain who saved himself by this means despite being hit by four or five darts. Rumphius's trust in this method is curious because he recognized correctly that the 'Ipo cannot exercise its power if it is not in contact with living blood'.[52] However, he concluded that this means of counteraction 'seems to break the power of the venom and expel it from the body'.[53] But things were looking up as far as antidotes were concerned, and he listed a host of herbal methods which had been discovered from the local people 'by coaxing or by force',[54] all of them predicated on inducing severe vomiting.

III

Makassar poison was the subject of ongoing discussion among an array of travellers, factors, soldiers, and naturalists resident in eastern Indonesia over the course of the seventeenth century. Their reports, based on a mixture of rumour, observation, myth, and local tradition, enhanced the reputation of the poison of *Antiaris toxicaria* as a highly lethal substance and a valuable possession of the Makassar kings. But what kind of impact did these stories have in Europe, and what importance was ascribed to this toxic entity? Evidence from the activities of the Royal Society of London in the 1660s indicates that the impact was substantial. Minutes of the Society's meetings reveal an extended engagement with Makassar poison, in an attempt to ascertain its effects and possible antidotes. These efforts complemented the project of natural history, but the evidence also provides the basis for a different perspective on European rivalries, and the political economy of seventeenth-century trade and colonial expansion.

Drawing on individual and collective initiatives, the Royal Society sent inquiries to English factors resident in Southeast Asia regarding Makassar poison, contacted returned travellers and agents of the East India Company for reports, and eventually obtained samples enabling them to conduct a series of experiments to establish its efficacy. Yet their research was much more than an attempt to document a curiosity of nature: it formed part of a larger commitment to support English enterprises of trade and colonial

---

[52] Rumphius, *Amboinsche Kruid-Boek*, II, 269.

[53] *Ibid.*

[54] *Ibid.* In Engelbert Kaempfer's report on Makassar poison, compiled during a ten-year Eastern journey from 1683 to 1693, he makes it clear that torture was employed to extract this information. See his *Amœnitatum exoticarum politico-physico-medicarum fasciculi V, quibus continentur variæ relationes, observationes, & descriptiones rerum Persicarum & ulterioris Asiæ* (Lemgo, 1712). For a translation of the relevant chapter, see Engelbert Kaempfer, *Exotic Pleasures Fascicle III Curious Scientific and Medical Observations*, trans. Robert W. Carrubba (Carbondale and Edwardsville, 1996), 96–107.

settlement around the globe.[55] In this regard, possession of accurate detail on the workings of Makassar poison was of potential benefit for several reasons: as long as the Dutch remained dominant in the East Indies, knowledge of a poison they could do little to combat was very valuable; English factors understood all too well the critical position of Makassar as a place of open trade, and the poison represented an unusual resource in local opposition to Dutch insurgence, something of potentially great use. Of course, depending on changes of fortune in the region, the English themselves might become subject to this component of the Makassarese arsenal.

At the same time, the struggle for lucrative spices and access to markets took place in a much larger context than Makassar or Southeast Asia alone. The three Anglo-Dutch wars between 1652 and 1674 occurred as much because of conflict over trade and colonial territory – whether on the African coast, the Americas, or the East Indies – as they did because of shifting political alliances in Europe. The Royal Society's investigations are significant in this respect because they took place just prior to and during the second Anglo-Dutch war (1664–7).

Yet the Royal Society's effort to understand Makassar poison also intersects with their wider concern with poisonous entities encountered around the globe by travellers and traders. Such phenomena had the potential to yield significant medical insights, but securing further knowledge of toxicity and counter-poisons related in the first instance to the needs of explorers who pursued English and European interests in very dangerous conditions. Finally, the possession of a potent poison, quick in operation and difficult to defend against, might have proved beneficial nearer to home in European political and courtly intrigue. Charles II, who gave the Society its royal status, may also have been the person who stood to gain, in this case, from its investigations.

The group that became the Royal Society was established on a formal basis at the Restoration, meeting on a weekly basis at Gresham College in London. As early as May 1661, the minutes of the Society indicate that the subject of poison had arisen. During the discussion, various poisons were mentioned, including *nux vomica* (strychnine) and viper poison, important in the making of theriac. Two Fellows, Dr Finch and Dr Baines, were requested to 'inquire after poisons' when they travelled next to Italy,[56] while Thomas Povey was asked to write to Bantam (Banten), in western Java, where the English had their largest Indonesian base, for information on that poison 'which is

---

[55] On the formulation by the Royal Society of inquiries for travellers to various countries, and the relationship between travel, colonialism and natural history generally, see Daniel Carey, 'Compiling nature's history: travellers and travel narratives in the early Royal Society', *Annals of Science*, 54 (1997), 269–92.

[56] Thomas Birch, *The History of the Royal Society* [1756–7] (4 vols, Hildesheim, 1968), I, 24. See Archibald Malloch, *Finch and Baines: A Seventeenth Century Friendship* (Cambridge, 1917), ch. 6.

related to be so quick, as to turn a man's blood suddenly into jelly'.[57] Evidently the Society had taken note of the disturbing narrative of Makassar poison delivered in Bontius's account of the marvels of the region, published three years earlier in 1658. In the meantime, Cornelius Vermuyden, recently elected to the Society, produced a poisonous arrow for testing in June of that year, but as John Evelyn reported, the trial conducted on a dog did not succeed.[58]

Two years later the matter came to their attention again when Sir Robert Moray, an active member of the Society and a courtier with close connections to Charles II, produced a 'poisoned dagger presented to his majesty from an Indian king by the captain of the ship Truro, lately returned from the East Indies'.[59] We cannot be sure whether the poison in question came from Makassar, nor whether Charles II's intention was for the Society to test it on his behalf. This supposition is not unreasonable, however, since the minutes for a subsequent meeting are more explicit in stating that the king requested tests on another deleterious poison, oil of tobacco, known as the 'Duke of Florence's poison'.[60] In any case, an experiment was performed on the day by warming the dagger and pricking a kitten to ascertain the poison's effects. The test was inconclusive, as the cat did not expire during the time of the meeting. The minutes of the subsequent gathering, on 1 April, state the 'The kitten wounded at the last meeting with the poisoned dagger, sent from the East Indies, was produced alive'.[61]

In October 1663, further information at last arrived from contacts in the East Indies. Daniel Colwall reported that he had received answers to inquiries he had sent there, dated 12 November 1662, from Bantam. He had asked for information on betel, camphor, edible birds' nests, rhinoceros horn, which was deemed 'antidotal', and ambergris, among other topics. The response on the subject of Makassar poison was intriguing. The correspondent stated that the 'famous' poison came from the island of Celebes and was made by the mountain people known as the 'Traia' (the Toraja), to whom Speelman and Rumphius later referred. He could not ascertain the precise ingredients of the poison and stated nothing about its origin in tree sap. However, he observed that 'such is the effect, that a small arrow being imbued with it, giveth a fatal wound, if it draw blood in any place, and is incurable'. The best available antidote was 'human ordure, which being crammed down the throat, enforceth so strong a vomit, that it often cureth'.[62] He went on to explain that Dutch army officers commanded their troops to carry their own excrement with them when they engaged in battle with the enemy. Otherwise he could report only that the

---

[57] Birch, *The History of the Royal Society*, I, 24.

[58] *Ibid.* 31; E. S. de Beer (ed.), *The Diary of John Evelyn* (6 vols, Oxford, 1955), III, 290.

[59] Birch, *The History of the Royal Society*, I, 214.

[60] At a meeting of 19 April 1665. See Birch, *The History of the Royal Society*, II, 31.

[61] Birch, *The History of the Royal Society*, I, 215.

[62] *Ibid.* 318.

natives preserved the poison by wrapping it in an 'incredible' number of warm cloths to protect it from the air. Despite its obvious toxicity, some paradoxes remained. He had seen a Malayan swallow down pills of the substance, 'pretending it antidotal', a point that Rumphius later confirmed,[63] while a Torajan man had consumed a bird, wounded with the poison, by taking no further precaution than cutting out 'a little of the surrounding flesh'.[64] The latter information was correct: since *antiarin* is not active through the gastro-intestinal tract, consumption of prey killed with it is not toxic, making it valuable for hunting purposes. Clearly there was much that remained to be investigated about this peculiar poison. The account as a whole was deemed sufficiently significant to be entered in the Society's register book.

In July 1664, as the second Anglo-Dutch war was getting underway, the Society made contact with an important correspondent based in Batavia, the seat of Dutch operations in the East Indies, Sir Philiberto Vernatti. Little is known of Vernatti, who was apparently born in England and educated at the university of Leiden. At some point he seems to have joined the VOC, becoming an agent of the company in Java.[65] During his time in Holland, Vernatti met Sir Robert Moray, who eventually wrote to him with the Society's East India inquiries. Vernatti responded to them at length and became an important correspondent, sending a number of boxes of curiosities for the Society's repository. On 27 July, the first of these, a wooden case containing the 'East-India present', was opened. At the same time, his answers to the inquiries were received with great interest and duly registered. Furthermore, they were to be communicated to other members of the Society with the request that they 'press for more particular answers upon these inquiries'.[66] When Thomas Sprat published his *History of the Royal Society* in 1667, he included Vernatti's responses as evidence of the organization's achievement. On the matter of Makassar, the question he answered was this:

What Poyson is it the King of *Macassar* in *Colebees* is said to have particular to himself, which not only kills a man immediately, that hath received the slightest Wound by a Dart dipt therein, but also within half an hours time, make [*sic*] the flesh, touched with it, so rotten, that it will fall like Snivel from the Bones, and whose poysonous Steam will soon fly up to a Wound made with an unpoysoned Dart, if the Blood be only in the slightest manner touch'd with a Dart infected with the Poyson? What certainty there is of this Relation?[67]

[63] Rumphius, *Amboinsche Kruid-Boek*, 2: 269.
[64] Birch, *The History of the Royal Society*, I, 319.
[65] W. Ph. Coolhaas refers to him as 'advocaat-fiscaal' in Batavia. See W. Ph. Coolhaas (ed.), *Generale Missiven van Gouverneurs-Generaal en Raden aan Heren XVII der Verenigde Oostindische Compagnie* ('s-Gravenhage, 1968), III, 663.
[66] Birch, *The History of the Royal Society*, I, 454.
[67] Thomas Sprat, *History of the Royal Society* [1670], ed. Jackson I. Cope and Harold Whitmore Jones (St Louis, 1959), 164.

The Society seems to have been thinking especially of Bontius's rather gothic tale of flesh that turned to slime on the bones as a result of the poison's action, a narrative twist that Herbert had also supplied. The concluding thought suggested a degree of doubt hovering over the extraordinary accounts of the poison.

Vernatti confirmed the existence of the poison, but admitted, 'what it is, no *Christian* hitherto ever knew right'. In a somewhat cryptic comment, he added, 'By the Government of Arnold de Flamminge Van Outshorn divers have been tortured; yea, killed'.[68] He refers here to the VOC governor, van Oudshoorn, renowned for his ruthless suppression of local opposition. What Vernatti seems to acknowledge is the fact that Van Oudshoorn tortured and killed various Makassarese in order to obtain information on the poison they possessed.[69] The Dutch had learned that the roots of the *Antiaris* tree supposedly provided an antidote, but 'our People', as he called the Dutch, 'found no Antidote like to their own or others Excrements' when they encountered the poison in their war with Makassar. On being hit, they 'instantly took a dose of this same', which led them to vomit, freeing 'the Noble parts from further Infection'.[70] The provenance of the poison remained uncertain, some affirming that it derived from the 'Gall of a Venemous Fish', while others traced it to a poisonous tree. Convicts condemned to die were commanded to fetch the poison, but its force was so great that 'not one of an hundred scape death' in doing so.

On the question of how a wound made by an *un*poisoned weapon could become fatally infected with *Ipo*, Vernatti was emphatic. The question he was asked again derived from Bontius's report. Bontius had claimed that blood trickling from a wound which subsequently came in contact with the poison would immediately become infected, causing the victim's death by ascending into the body with great speed. Vernatti found this account wholly persuasive. Those who studied the phenomenon of 'sympathy' understood the process all too well, and 'set belief in that much renowned Sympathetical Powder of Sir *Kenelme Digby*'. Vernatti referred here to the medical theories of a colourful Fellow of the Society and medical virtuoso, Sir Kenelm Digby. In 1658, he had published a *Discours . . . touchant la guerison des playes, par la poudre de sympathie*, originally delivered before a distinguished gathering at Montpellier. The work was translated into English in the same year, and described a cure achieved without direct contact with the wound itself. Instead, Digby's powder, basically copper sulphate, was combined with something that had made contact with the wound – a bandage, for example. As Digby explained the process, atoms of blood from the bandage sought out their place of origin, the wound itself, 'and so reenter into their naturall

---

[68] *Ibid.*
[69] For corroboration of this reading, see note 54 above.
[70] Sprat, *History of the Royal Society*, 165.

beds, and primitive receptacles'. Having mingled with the sympathetic powder, these atoms returned invisibly to the blood, where they 'joyntly imbibe
together within all the corners, fibres, and orifices of the veines which lye
open about the wound of the party hurt, which herby are comforted, and in
fine imperceptibly cured'.[71]

Several factors made Vernatti's invocation of the sympathetic powder apt.
First, the invisible operation of sympathy explained how a poisoned weapon,
making contact with blood outside the body, might have an immediate
impact internally. The victim's blood simply communicated with its point of
origin, carrying poisoned atoms along with it. Secondly, Digby's powder constituted a variation on the weapon salve: he suggested that the cure could
also take place by applying the compound to the blade which had made the
wound in the first place.[72] Hence a pernicious poisoning rather than a cure
could operate in the same way. Finally, Digby explained that the secret of the
powder had come from a Carmelite of his acquaintance, a man who had
travelled in Persia, China, and the Indies before arriving in the Medici
court at Florence. When pressed by the reigning duke, this individual
had answered 'That it was a secret which he had learnt in the oriental
parts'.[73] Even if the cure had become widely known, this fact suggested that
Eastern medicine possessed its own array of mysteries. As far as Makassar
poison was concerned, Vernatti came to a worrying conclusion: 'Yet such
Effects of the *Macassars* Arts are unknown to us'.[74]

Three months after Vernatti's responses were received, William Croone
provided a further update to the Society in October 1664. He had met
with a long-time resident at the court of Makassar who confirmed most of
the stories that had circulated about 'their strange poisons'.[75] This witness
had personally seen hundreds of people killed by them. No European
physicians could discover any way of preventing the effects of the poison
by surgery, even if they immediately cut out the wound inflicted by the
poisoned weapon. Field hospitals were thus of no use. In a short time anyone
hit by an arrow would 'fall down stone dead'. As for their flesh turning to

---

[71] Sir Kenelm Digby, *A Late Discourse Made in a Solemne Assembly of Nobles and Learned Men at Montpellier in France . . . Touching the Cure of Wounds by the Powder of Sympathy*, trans. R. White (London, 1658), 135–6.

[72] See Allen G. Debus, 'Robert Fludd and the use of Gilbert's *De Magnete* in the weapon-salve controversy', *Journal of the History of Medicine and Allied Sciences*, 19/4 (1965), 389–417, especially 416.

[73] Digby, *A Late Discourse*, 12. On Digby's powder and other exponents of it, see Lynn Thorndike, *A History of Magic and Experimental Science* (8 vols, New York, 1923–58), VII, 503–9. Robert Boyle remarked: 'Wherefore that the sympathetick powder and the weapon-salve are never of any efficacy at all, I dare not affirm; but that they constantly perform what is promised of them, I must leave others to believe'. *The Works*, ed. Thomas Birch (6 vols, Hildesheim, 1965–6), I, 346. See also *Some Considerations Touching the Usefulnesse of Experimental Naturall Philosophy* (1663), in *The Works of Robert Boyle*, ed. Michael Hunter and Edward B. Davis (14 vols, London, 1999–2000), III, 367, 430–1.

[74] Sprat, *History of the Royal Society*, 165.

[75] Birch, *The History of the Royal Society*, I, 478. Croone was professor of rhetoric at Gresham College and an active Fellow of the Society with interests in physiology. See *Dictionary of Scientific Biography*.

jelly, he could not affirm this account, as he had never seen the effect himself.[76]

It was not until 1665 that the Society secured further samples of the poison with which the Fellows could conduct experiments. John Graunt, the London draper and observer of 'bills of mortality', had received an account of Makassar poison and its effects which, as a meeting of March was informed, rectified the 'common stories made thereof'.[77] More importantly, he had also obtained some of the poison, which he intended to demonstrate. On 8 March, he produced his 'Makassar powder', but the test was reserved for the following meeting. On that occasion, a dog was injected with some of the poison, 'so famous for its suddaine operation', as Evelyn observed in his diary, but, in Samuel Pepys's words, 'it had no effect all the time we sat there'.[78] At this gathering something of a commotion was caused when it was discovered that the physician Walter Charleton had taken the poison home with him after the previous meeting, contrary to the Society's rules. Charleton, an eager experimenter with poisons, was apparently unable to control his excitement and was called to account for his actions. The incident made its way into a contemporary satire by Samuel Butler.[79]

Two months later, the Society received its fullest and most accurate narrative account of the poison, delivered to them by the nobleman Charles Howard. He had received it from someone who had lived in Makassar for four years but had now returned to England. According to his report, the poison was called 'Ippo' in the Makassar and Malay languages, and it was described as 'the gum of a certain tree, shining, brittle, black, and every way like stone-pitch'.[80] It was found in the upland area of the island, gathered by the 'savage' mountain people, the 'Teragias', with whom the Makassarese had some correspondence. No foreigner had ever seen it collected. The Torajas harvested it cautiously, remaining on the windward side of the tree and collecting the

---

[76] Robert Hooke summarized this report in a letter to Robert Boyle of late October 1664. See *The Correspondence of Robert Boyle*, ed. Michael Hunter, Antonio Clericuzio, and Lawrence M. Principe (6 vols, London, 2001), II, 370.

[77] Birch, *The History of the Royal Society*, II, 20.

[78] *Ibid.* 23; Evelyn, *Diary*, III, 403; *The Diary of Samuel Pepys*, ed. Robert Latham and William Matthews (10 vols, London, 1970–83), VI, 57.

[79] 'An occasional reflection on Dr. Charlton's feeling a dog's pulse at Gresham College. By R. B. Esq.', in René Lamar (ed.), *Satires and Miscellaneous Poetry and Prose* (Cambridge, 1928), 341–3, a parody of Robert Boyle; the original appeared in R. Thyer (ed.), *The Genuine Remains in Verse and Prose of Mr. Samuel Butler* (2 vols, London, 1759), I, 405–10. The relevant passage reads: 'Nor is the diligent and solert Dr. less proper for this Administration, as having so natural a Propensity to this Kind of venenous Operations, that it is not long since (as you well remember) when the King of *Macassar's* Poison was sent hither, the Dr. was so impatient to try the Experiment solitary, that, rather than attend the Pleasure of the *Royal-Society*, he adventured (though at the Price of their Displeasure) to invade it by Surreption and Involation, and secretly deprived the *Hint-Keeper* of it; for which he received, I will not say whether condign Punishment, or severe Castigation, from the learned and honourable *President*, in a grave and weighty Oration pronounced by his Lordship before this celebrious and renowned Assembly' (341–2). For some discussion, see Marjorie Hope Nicolson, *Pepys' Diary and the New Science* (Charlottesville, 1965), 67–8, 153–7.

[80] Birch, *The History of the Royal Society*, II, 43.

gum in hollow bamboo canes for transportation. They delivered it to Makassarese hunters and warriors, who carried long hollow trunks called a 'Sampitans' of six or seven feet in length, 'very accurately bored', into which they inserted a small arrow. At the bottom end of the arrow they affixed a piece of soft wood, similar to cork, which perfectly fit the bore of the sumpitan, allowing the air pressure to build when warriors blew into the tube. At the far end, they affixed a small fish tooth or piece of wood 'the bigness of the point of a lancet', which they 'anointed' with poison. The most powerful instances of the poison were owned only by the king and 'persons of quality'. Their samples, if carefully preserved, retained their force for two or three years. He added a local belief, a variation of which Rumphius subsequently reported, that no live crab should be 'burnt alive under the same roof' where the poison was being kept because this would destroy the efficacy of the poison.[81] The correspondent had not, however, had a chance to test this experimentally. 'Divers great persons' in Makassar told him that despite many efforts to find an antidote, nothing had been discovered that prevented its effects.

He described the manner of preparing the arrows in some detail. The local people scraped some poison into a turtle shell and added the juice of a grated 'galangal-root'. Using a stick, they would 'anoint' the fish tooth or blade and then lay it in the sun for two hours in order to bake it on. Afterwards, the treated arrows were placed inside hollow bamboos, where they would retain their 'virtue' for a month's time. On this basis, the witness explained why the samples sent to England had proved so disappointing. The time required to ship them to England would nullify their effect. The reaction to this testimony was notable. His authority was such that he was invited to attend a subsequent meeting in person and to offer an opinion on the sample supplied by Graunt. When he did so, the traveller made the disappointing announcement that the poison they had tested was not in fact from Makassar, 'nor at all like it'.[82]

This episode indicates some of the vagaries of early scientific experimentation. In this case, the Society could not be confident that it was testing the proper substance. They waited another three years before an opportunity arose to try once again. After a long interruption of its meetings caused by the plague in London, the Society convened in October 1668 and took delivery of another shipment of curiosities from Sir Philiberto Vernatti. His friend Sir Robert Moray presented 'Three small cans filled with Macassar poison, together with a description of its use upon arrows. For the trial of which poison a dog or cat was again ordered to be provided against the next meeting.'[83] When they returned to the subject on 5 November, a dog was

---

[81] *Ibid.* 44. See Rumphius, *Poison Tree,* 133.
[82] Birch, *The History of the Royal Society,* II, 47.
[83] *Ibid.* 314.

readied for the occasion. The poison was 'mingled' with lemon juice and applied to point of a knife, which was then 'struck into the fleshy part of one of the dog's hind legs'. By the time the meeting broke up, however, the animal appeared quite unaffected.[84]

The Society faced undoubted difficulties in pursuing the matter, as we have seen. Even accepting that they had located authentic samples, they encountered the problem of transporting them with sufficient speed and skill to ensure that they had not deteriorated in the process. The testimony of contacts in Makassar continually emphasized the care necessary to preserve the poison, the varying durability of it, and its susceptibility to extreme heat and cold.[85] They then had an insuperable challenge of standardizing dosages. The potential for making progress in experiment and understanding was therefore limited. This explains their heavy dependence on narrative accounts, which had the advantage of being closer to the source, although in practice they often included a mixture of rumour, legend, and fable as much as eyewitness experience.

The famed Italian naturalist and physician Francesco Redi was undeterred. Redi, who experimented extensively with poisons, especially from vipers, delivered his thoughts on the subject of Makassar poison in 1670, and they were subsequently translated into English and published by the Royal Society's printer in 1673. Redi questioned the veracity of existing reports which claimed that the substance had the power to kill 'in that very moment he receiveth the slightest wound thereby' and that the victim's flesh would putrefy in half an hour, falling 'from the bones in many pieces, whence do exhale such virulent streams, that if they light upon any ordinary and not envenomed wound, they mortally infect it, and without fail kill the Patient'.[86] Once again, Bontius's report proved durable in its impact. But Redi regarded it as a fable on the basis of his own experiments. In Tuscany the material had no such 'fierce and malignant a nature'. He wounded various dogs and some of them died in six hours, others seven, and others still in twenty-four hours. Certainly their flesh did not fall off and putrefy, nor did the wound infect other animals. He made the accurate suggestion that the effectiveness of the poisoned arrows depended on how long they stuck in the wound, and he conjectured that the native 'savages' deliberately designed the weapon tips to break off and remain in the incision. He even went so far as to suggest that the arrows in Makassar might have been treated with the poison of vipers or other serpents in the region, 'of a more maligne nature because of the diversity of the Climate'.[87] He had nothing to say, perhaps wisely, on the subject of cures.

---

[84] *Ibid.* 318.

[85] For example, Rumphius, *Poison Tree*, 132.

[86] *A Letter of Francesco Redi Concerning Some Objections made upon his Observations about Vipers* (London, 1673), 20.

[87] *Ibid.* 16. The question arises of how Redi 'sourced' the poison. He was head physician in the Medici court and superintendent of the ducal pharmacy. He may have been supplied by Cosimo III.

Redi may have undermined the belief of Bontius, Vernatti, and others in Makassar poison's ability to act at a distance, but questions still remained about the true origin and nature of the substance. In 1704, John Ray, a leading plant taxonomist and Fellow of the Society, included a report on the tree in his *Historia Plantarum* from Joseph Camello, a Jesuit based in Manila who attempted to sort out the confusion. If anything, this communication placed the inquiry right back where it began. Camello repeated the incorrect statement that the *Ipo* tree killed everything in its shade, adding that the bones of dead men and animals were often found in the ambit of its shadow. Birds who landed on its branches also succumbed unless they consumed *nux vomica*, and even then they still suffered a loss of feathers ('sed defluvium patiuntur plumarum'). Various groups, hostile to the Spaniards, made use of the poison, for which no remedy was known, overcoming all other antidotes except human excrement ('irremediabile venenum, omnibus aliis alexipharmacis superius, praeterquam stercore human propinato').[88] In his effort to identify the tree, Camello speculated on various connections with prior reports, including the cryptic statement of Argensola, who reported, as already mentioned, on the mysterious tree with heavy foliage whose western shade proved fatal, while its eastern shade was antidotal.

The phenomenon of Makassar poison engaged the attention of a wide array of travellers, soldiers, and naturalists in the sixteenth and seventeenth centuries, intent on discovering the nature of a substance surrounded in mystery. However gothic the tales of its effects and antidotes, recounted in narratives that thrived on the exotic and curious, the poison also indicates some of the dangers encountered in European expansion in Southeast Asia. At the same time, the keen efforts to learn more about its operation draw attention to the rivalry between the Dutch and their competitors, especially the English, who harnessed the new science to the project of trade and colonial development. For them, little could deter Dutch hegemony, it seemed, but some hope may have rested on Makassar poison, with its power to inflict instant death and inspire fear.

The place of this substance in contemporary political economy was predicated, in the first instance, on its deployment as a weapon in wars settling the trading status of a nation that refused to submit to Dutch control. But the poison also played the part of a commodity in a number of intriguing circumstances,[89] in which it was harvested, 'produced', and exchanged for

who made two trips to Holland between 1667 and 1669. The other leading possibility is the Royal Society's Fellows Dr Finch and Dr Baines, who were asked in 1661 to inquire into the subject of poisons by the Society during their upcoming trip to Italy (see note 56 above). They remained for two-and-a-half years in Florence, where Finch was 'in high favour with the Grand Duke of Tuscany' (Malloch, *Finch and Baines*, 40). In 1665, Finch returned to Florence as Charles II's Resident at the ducal court and stayed there until 1670.

[88] John Ray, *Historia Plantarum* (London, 1704), iii, L4r (Appendix, p. 87). The report was originally sent to Ray's collaborator, James Pettiver, in 1701.

[89] See Jay H. Bernstein, 'Poisons and antidotes among the Taman of West Kalimantan, Indonesia', *Bijdragen Tot de Taal-, Land- en Volkenkunde*, 149/1 (1993), 17–19.

local usage. As a form of tribute, gift, weaponry, and display, the poison assumed different roles in South Sulawesi, but it entered a new phase of its 'career'[90] when it was obtained by English traders (whether by barter, exchange, as a gift, or in payment of debts is unclear) and made its way to London. There it became a gift once again, donated to the Society for experimental purposes, and joined the company of other 'curiosities'. Investigation of it potentially extended the domain of natural knowledge, but also complemented English rivalry with the Dutch, who faced it on the ground but had little recourse against its mysterious force. If the long-sought-after reversal of fortune had occurred, with the English supplanting the Dutch and gaining an upper hand in the spice trade through Makassar, then they themselves would have faced the same difficult predicament.

[90] Arjun Appadurai, 'Introduction: commodities and the politics of value', in Arjun Appadurai (ed.), *The Social Life of Things: Commodities in Cultural Perspective* (Cambridge, 1986), 15.

Obituary

Professor C. R. Boxer (1904–2000)

Charles Boxer died on 27 April 2000, aged 96. He had been active as a scholar until well into his nineties, only the loss of his eyesight eventually putting an end to one of the most remarkable academic careers of modern times. Boxer was very much a Renaissance man, as Burckhardt understood the term. He was a soldier, a skilled sportsman, a scholar, a prolific author, the creator of one of the greatest private libraries of his time, a linguist, and a man who cultivated the arts of society and conversation. It was the breadth and richness of his experience as well as his academic achievement that made him such a magisterial figure among twentieth-century historians.[1]

Many scholars have been described as having 'dominated their field', but few have had so many fields to dominate or have dominated them for quite so long. The first articles written by Captain C. R. Boxer began to appear in 1926, when he was 22 years old.[2] It would have been an early age for an academic to be publishing, but at that time Boxer was not an academic and had never been to university. He was born in March 1904 at Sandown in the Isle of Wight, the son of Major Hugh Boxer of the Lincolnshire regiment. His father had been wounded in Kitchener's Sudan campaign in 1898 and was killed on the western front in 1915. Through their maternal grand-mother, the Boxers came to own a country house, Conygar, in Dorset, where Charles learned to ride and hunt, before being sent to public school at Wellington. From Wellington, where he apparently left almost no trace of his stay, he went on to Sandhurst and in 1923 was commissioned in the Lincoln-shires. He remained in the army until 1947, when, at the age of 43, he retired with the rank of major – an apparently run-of-the-mill career for a

---

[1] A biography of Charles Boxer has been written by Professor Dauril Alden, *Charles R. Boxer: an Uncommon Life* (Lisbon, 2001). The most complete bibliography of Boxer's writings to date is 'The Charles Boxer Bibliography', *Portuguese Studies*, 17 (2001), 246–76. This is based on two previous bibliographies, *Homen-agem ao Professor Charles Ralph Boxer. A Tribute to Charles Ralph Boxer* (Figueira do Foz, 1999) and S. George West, *A List of the Writings of Charles Ralph Boxer Published between 1926 and 1984* (London, 1984). See also M. D. D. Newitt, *Charles Ralph Boxer 1904–2000* (London, 2000) and M. D. D. Newitt, 'Biographical memoirs of Fellows, 1. Charles Ralph Boxer 1904–2000', *Proceedings of the British Academy*, 115 (2002), 74–99. Essays on Boxer's work and tributes paid to him at the memorial meeting held at King's College London, 11 July 2000 can be found on the College website at http://www.kcl.ac.uk/pobrst/chasb.html.

[2] His first published article was 'O 24 de Junho. Uma Façanha dos Portugueses', *Boletim da Agência Geral das Colónias*, 2 (1926), 117–28.

220 *Obituary*

public school-educated younger son of the minor gentry during the heyday of the British Empire.

However, Boxer's military career was far from ordinary. While still at school he had become interested in languages, and as a subaltern pursued the study of Portuguese, Dutch, and Japanese. This combination of languages led him to the relatively unexplored field of the history of the early European contacts with the Far East, and his first articles, which appeared in *The Mariner's Mirror* and *Transactions of the Japan Society of London*, were on this topic.[3]

Meanwhile Boxer served with his regiment in Ireland and was then seconded to the Far East as a language officer, spending some time before the war as a liaison officer with the 38th Japanese infantry regiment. By the time he was posted to the Far East he had published thirteen articles, and had prepared editions of *The Journal of Maarten Harpertszoon Tromp* and the *Commentaries of Ruy Freyre de Andrade*.[4] The story associated with the second of these is that Edgar Prestage, the professor of Portuguese at London University, had been working on an edition of the *Commentaries* for the Haklyut Society when he heard that Captain Boxer was also preparing a translation. Prestage was so impressed with Boxer's work that he stood aside to let the young army officer's edition appear as part of the Broadway Travellers Library.

Boxer's time in the Far East was a period of exceptional activity and excitement. In Japan he not only perfected his knowledge of the language, interpreting for the emperor on one occasion, but he also became an expert in kendo and came to know many Japanese officers and a great deal about the Japanese military. He travelled widely, from Manchuria and Siberia in the north to Indonesia in the south, where he made many acquaintances among the Dutch officers serving in the colony. It was during this time that he built up his great collection of rare books and manuscripts, and in 1937 published a catalogue of his private library in Macao.[5] Meanwhile he continued to produce a stream of scholarly publications. In 1936 appeared his first monograph, *Jan Compagnie in Japan*,[6] and in the year 1938 he published no less than ten articles on scholarly topics.

Boxer was by this time working for military intelligence in Hong Kong and it was here that he met the American writer, Emily Hahn, who had acquired some notoriety by her lone travels in the Congo and in war-torn China. There she had made the acquaintance of the Soong sisters, one of whom was married to Chiang Kai-shek, and had written their biographies. Emily had contracted into some kind of a marriage to a Chinese poet in Shanghai,

---

[3] For example, 'The siege of Fort Zeelandia and the capture of Formosa from the Dutch, 1661–1662', *Transactions and Proceedings of the Japan Society of London*, 24 (1927), 15–47.

[4] *The Journal of Maarten Harpertszoon Tromp, Anno 1639* (Cambridge, 1930); and *Commentaries of Ruy Freyre de Andrade* (London, 1930).

[5] *Biblioteca Boxeriana: Being a Short Title Catalogue of the Books and Manuscripts in the Library of Captain C. R. Boxer (March 1937)* (Macao, 1937).

[6] *Jan Compagnie in Japan (1600–1859)* (The Hague, 1936).

but she and Boxer (who was also by this time married) began an affair which resulted in the birth of their first daughter just before the outbreak of war.

Charles and Emily were in Hong Kong when the Japanese invasion occurred in December 1941 and Charles was seriously wounded in one of the few actions fought to defend the island. His injured shoulder never properly healed, and for the rest of his life he was left with a useless left arm and hand. Charles spent the war in a Japanese prison camp and experienced very harsh conditions, including torture, solitary confinement, and at one time was under sentence of death. Emily, meanwhile, having evaded internment through being technically married to a Chinese, was eventually evacuated with her daughter to the USA, where she wrote an extraordinary autobiography, *China to Me*, a chronicle of her life in China and her relationship with Charles Boxer.[7] Emily's portrait of Charles during these years is of an officer carrying out his military duties, going on excursions, and spending the evening in the endless social round of colonial Hong Kong. He was deeply sceptical of the capacity of the British Empire in the East to survive. 'Hong Kong is the dumping ground for duds . . . including me', he said on one occasion, and on another, 'the day of the white man is done out here . . . we're finished and we know it. All this is exactly like the merriment of Rome before the great fall.'[8] His experience of the fall of Hong Kong, which held out for only a few days against the Japanese, was later to colour his view of the determination and courage with which the Portuguese defended and held onto their eastern empire in the seventeenth century during the darkest days of the wars with the Dutch.

Although Boxer's scholarly output virtually dried up during the war years – not surprisingly, since his remarkable private library had been removed to Japan and he had no access to scholarly resources – he was already acknowledged as an expert on Dutch and Portuguese naval history, and on the relations of the two countries with Japan. Boxer's scholarship at this time was focused on the late sixteenth and early seventeenth centuries, and he wrote a series of studies of Dutch naval expeditions and Portuguese embassies, as well as numerous books and articles on the history of Macao and its commercial empire in the China Sea. Although much of his early work was concentrated on military and diplomatic records, he had undertaken the detailed study of the great contemporary Portuguese and Dutch chroniclers and historians, and had begun editing and translating Dutch and Portuguese texts of the period.

After Boxer's release at the end of the war, he and Emily married in New York, their reunion featuring on the front cover of *Life*, and then returned

---

[7] Emily Hahn, *China to Me* (New York, 1944); for Emily Hahn's life, see the biography by Ken Cuthbertson, *Nobody Said Not to Go* (Boston and London, 1998). Emily died on 18 February 1997, aged 91.

[8] Hahn, *China to Me*, 209.

to England, where Emily wrote a second book about her life with Charles, *England to Me*, describing England after the war through the saga of opening up and reoccupying their country house in rural Dorset.[9] Boxer was still on the army roll in 1947 when he was approached by Edgar Prestage to apply for the chair of Portuguese at London University.

Major Boxer's appointment to the Camões Chair of Portuguese at King's College was an extraordinary thing for a university to do, even in those days. The new professor had no degree, had never been to a university, and was at least as well known as a scholar of Dutch and Japanese as he was for his work with old Portuguese. However, in 1947 he resigned from the army and took up his chair, which he held, with a short break in 1951–3, until he retired in 1967.

The age of forty-three is unusually late for anyone to start an academic career, but the next thirty years were to see a remarkable outpouring of major academic works which confirmed Charles Boxer as one of the leading historians of the twentieth century. First there were his monographs on colonial history: *Fidalgos in the Far East* (1948), *The Christian Century in Japan* (1951), *Salvador Correa da Sá* (1952), *The Dutch in Brazil* (1957), *The Great Ship from Amaçon* (1959), and *The Golden Age of Brazil* (1962).[10] Some of these built on his twenty years' study of the Far East but the Brazilian volumes marked an excursion into a new area of Portuguese and Dutch history. Then there were the great translations of original texts, *South China in the Sixteenth Century* (1953) and the two volumes of extracts from *The Tragic History of the Sea* (1959 and 1968),[11] works which among other things demonstrated his encyclopaedic bibliographical knowledge – the introductions to these volumes being *tours de force* of bibliographical scholarship. Towards the end of his time at King's, Boxer worked on the two textbooks for Hutchinson which were to become classics of their kind, *The Dutch Seaborne Empire* (1965) and *The Portuguese Seaborne Empire* (1969).[12] Finally there were the lecture series, usually delivered as a visiting lecturer at some other university, and which he continued to give into his late seventies. These were published as

[9] Emily Hahn, *England to Me* (London, 1950).

[10] *Fidalgos in the Far East, 1550–1770. Fact and Fancy in the History of Macao* (The Hague, 1948); *The Christian Century in Japan (1549–1650)* (Berkeley, 1951); *Salvador Correa da Sá and the Struggle for Brazil and Angola (1602–1686)* (London, 1952); *The Dutch in Brazil 1624–1654* (Oxford, 1957); *The Great Ship from Amaçon. Annals of Macao and the Old Japan Trade, 1555–1640* (Lisbon, 1959); and *The Golden Age of Brazil 1695–1750. Growing Pains of a Colonial Society* (Berkeley, 1962).

[11] *South China in the Sixteenth Century: Being the Narratives of Galeote Pereira, Fr Gaspar da Cruz OP, Fr Martin de Rada OESA (1550–1575)* (London, 1953); *The Tragic History of the Sea, 1589–1622: Narratives of the Shipwrecks of the Portuguese East Indiamen São Thomé (1589), Santo Alberto (1593), São João Baptista (1622) and the Journeys of the Survivors in South East Africa* (Cambridge, 1959); *Further Selections from 'The Tragic History of the Sea 1559–1565': Narratives of the Shipwrecks of the Portuguese East Indiamen 'Águia' and 'Garça' (1559), 'São Paulo' (1561) and the Misadventures of the Brazil-ship 'Santo António' (1565)* (Cambridge, 1968).

[12] *The Dutch Seaborne Empire (1600–1800)* (London, 1965); and *The Portuguese Seaborne Empire, 1415–1825* (London, 1969).

thematically linked essays, and form some of his most stimulating and original work.[13]

As these works appeared, Boxer's stature in the scholarly world grew. The extraordinary awe in which he was, and still is, held by those who work in the same academic field perhaps needs some explanation. Boxer had a prodigious knowledge of, and scholarly expertise in, languages. He not only commanded old Dutch, Portuguese, and Japanese, but worked freely in Spanish and French as well. His work was always firmly anchored in original sources and detailed archival research, and he acquired an unparalleled knowledge of the printed sources of his subject that made him an outstanding bibliographer. His enthusiasm for bibliographical scholarship derived in large part from his work in building up his own library. In 1963 he produced a short pamphlet for the Canning House series Diamante on the Portuguese medical scientist Garcia d'Orta. The pamphlet mostly made use of other people's research and was designed to popularize the work of this great Portuguese scientist of the sixteenth century. But at the back was appended a note on the original edition of Garcia d'Orta's *Colloquios*. In this, Boxer traced every single known copy of the book and listed their whereabouts – not surprisingly, one of the twenty-four copies known to survive was listed as being in the library of 'C. R. Boxer'.[14] His essays always made liberal use of quotations from rare and previously unused sources, and frequently the preface to his books contains the sentence, 'This book has been written mainly from the resources of my own library'.[15]

The range of Boxer's scholarly output remained exceptional – over twenty years between 1947 and 1967 he produced 128 publications, including sixteen major books. As well as his main areas of interest, he published significant work on Portuguese missionaries, on the early history of the English East India Company, and on seventeenth- and eighteenth-century Portugal, and produced pioneering essays on writers such as João de Barros, Diogo do Couto, António Vieira, Garcia d'Orta, and many other intellectuals of the period.

However, Boxer's place among the great historians of the twentieth century remains problematic. He has sometimes been criticized for not having any overall vision or theoretical understanding of the periods about which he wrote. His long career covered nearly the whole of the period of the communist ascendancy, when intellectual Marxism invaded and nearly took over academic history writing; he was the contemporary of the great *annaliste*

---

[13] Boxer's main published lecture series are: *Four Centuries of Portuguese Expansion, 1415–1825: A Succinct Survey* (Johannesburg, 1961); *Race Relations in the Portuguese Colonial Empire 1415–1825* (Oxford, 1963); *Mary and Misogyny. Women in Iberian Expansion Overseas (1415–1815). Some Facts, Fancies and Personalities* (London, 1975); *The Church Militant and Iberian Expansion, 1440–1770* (Baltimore, 1978); and *Portuguese India in the Mid-Seventeenth Century* (Bombay, 1980).

[14] *Two Pioneers of Tropical Medicine: Garcia d'Orta and Nicolás Monardes* (London, 1963).

[15] For example, *The Dutch Seaborne Empire*, v.

French historians and their imitators; he lived through the decolonization of Asia and Africa, and was surrounded by the sometimes strident debates over development and underdevelopment and feminist historiography, as well as the more narrowly focused discussions affecting his period of specialism – the rise of the gentry, religion and capitalism, the general crisis of the seventeenth century, the military revolution, etc. With his massive knowledge of the primary and secondary sources in these fields, he was, of course, well aware of these debates, but contributed little directly to them. He seldom wrote for the mainline historical journals, tending to publish either in popular journals with a wide readership or local history journals or archival publications. His skill and motivation as a scholar, not to speak of his own predilection for collecting books and manuscripts, was directed towards exploring hitherto unused sources and bringing to life half-forgotten episodes of history through researches into the archives.

Nowhere is this clearer than in his selections from the *História Trágico-Marítima*. Although many of these shipwreck narratives had already appeared in English translation, it was Boxer's scholarly translations of six of them that really brought them to the attention of the English-speaking world. Boxer's expert translations were enhanced by bibliographical research into the texts, the biographies of their authors, and a disquisition on ship construction and the naval policy of the Estado da Índia. Yet the accounts that make up the *História* are more than just a collection of sea stories. They form an immensely rich and fascinating cultural document bearing on religious thought, social relations, and ethnography, while the narratives of the wrecks are themselves powerful metaphors for the human condition, and the parlous state of the empire and body politic of Portugal. Boxer studiously avoided exploring the aspects of the *História*, carefully observing the scholarly demarcation he had set himself. His expertise was in bibliography, biography, ship-building, and naval history and translation; he left to others the consideration of language, imagery, metaphor, and social and religious values.

Boxer's writing style was lucid and highly readable, and he abhorred historical jargon. When it came to the need to generalize or to make judgements he often made use of well-worn phrases and established clichés – 'If trade followed the flag in the development of the British Empire, the missionary was close behind the merchant in the expansion of the Portuguese Empire'[16] or 'the close connection between God and Mammon which characterised the trade of Macao and Japan from its romantic inception to its tragic end'[17] – using them partly ironically and partly to establish some common ground with the reader. Although there is no escaping his distaste for academic controversy or the often impassioned debates by historians on current political issues, there is one notable exception – the well-known

---

[16] Introduction to *Portuguese Merchants and Missionaries in Feudal Japan* (London, 1986).
[17] *The Great Ship from Amaçon*, 1.

volume of essays that he published on *Race Relations in the Portuguese Colonial Empire.*[18] This volume, with its sharp references to the writings of Gilberto Freyre and its still more pointed comments on contemporary Portuguese politics, plunged Boxer into the thick of contemporary controversy. He was denounced in the Lisbon press, and his work was widely quoted in the political debates raging at the time. Yet Boxer appears to have been both surprised and dismayed by this reaction. Although the text of the book clearly shows that he was aware that this was sensitive political territory, once he had published the lectures he backed off from further controversy of the kind and is even on record as expressing regret for what he had done.[19]

One possible explanation for his avoidance of academic controversy is that he was sensitive to the fact that he had no formal academic training. This may appear absurd to outsiders, dazzled by the range of his intellectual skills and the lucidity with which he could write, but there is plenty of evidence that Boxer was uncomfortable with his position. When he took the chair at King's he insisted that a separate appointment be made to look after the teaching of Portuguese language, which he was not qualified to undertake, and in 1951 he resigned to take the chair of Asian History offered to him by the School of Oriental and African Studies (SOAS). He remained at SOAS for less than two years, resigning this chair also, saying that his lack of knowledge of Chinese made it inappropriate for him to hold it. He returned to King's and remained there until 1967. He had in the meantime been offered yet another chair in yet another subject, University College offering him the chair of Dutch History and Institutions in 1958. Although he refused this appointment and stayed at King's, his early retirement at the age of 63 may partly have been the result of the continuous suggestions that reached him that the tenure of the Portuguese chair by a historian with no academic training was in some way inappropriate. He is on record as having said that at formal academic occasions, when he had to process wearing only his lounge suit (as he had no degrees), visitors probably thought he was the 'man who had come to see about the gas'. Such sensitivities do not seem to have been entirely allayed by the award of six honorary degrees, the Fellowship of the British Academy, two Portuguese decorations, a papal knighthood and, after he left King's, the appointment to the chair of European Expansion Overseas at Yale.

Boxer was aware that his work might be seen to lack theoretical underpinning. In 1970 he contributed a series of essays entitled *Mary and Misogyny* on the subject of women in the Iberian empires. In the introduction to this he wrote 'since the published documentation on women in the Iberian colonial world is sufficient neither in quantity nor in quality to provide adequate material for "structures", "models", and other fashionable inter-disciplinary

---

[18] *Race Relations in the Portuguese Colonial Empire 1415–1825* (Oxford, 1963).
[19] Personal communication from Professor Luís de Sousa Rebello.

paraphernalia, this tentative essay does not presume to be anything more than what is explicitly indicated in the subtitle'.[20] In spite of this admission, his essays raised a range of issues concerning the role of women and their status in the Iberian world which makes them still highly readable and very relevant today. And here perhaps is the clue to the importance of Boxer as a historian.

Charles Boxer had had an extraordinarily varied and active life: his travels in Asia, his life in the army, his Japanese experiences, intelligence work in Hong Kong, love affairs, war, wounds, prison camp, torture, and solitary confinement – all experiences built onto the social foundations of the minor military gentry of imperial England. He had seen the British Empire in inexorable decline. His personality was strongly marked by these experiences and he deeply admired the *Meditations of Marcus Aurelius*, keeping an annotated personal copy of this work with him until the end. His writings came to reflect his personal beliefs and his profoundly humanistic outlook on life. However, this did not take the form of theorizing or of making self-conscious statements of a philosophical or political position. Boxer was highly suspicious of ideologies, whether these were the imperial ideologies of the seventeenth or the twentieth centuries, the religious ideologies of the churches, or the academic ideologies of his colleagues. It was not that he discounted the power of ideas in human affairs, and he always accepted that even at their most violent and rapacious the Portuguese of the seventeenth century were deeply moved by their faith and the desire to spread it throughout the world, but he preferred to see human beings as motivated by a confused, complex mixture of high ideals and more mundane considerations – God and Mammon.

He was determined that what he wrote would be readable and accessible to a wide audience. He wrote with great narrative flair, never passing up a good story and punctuating his work with witty asides and a barely concealed delight in the absurdities of the human condition. While he was able to address the scholarly community and command its respect through his powerful bibliographical essays and his excursions into unpublished archival material, his books were designed to be free from jargon, theorizing, or obscure argumentation. His interpretations of the human condition and his ideas about the motors of history emerged through the course of the narrative.

Boxer did in fact address the great themes of his time, but deftly and often with a light touch that leaves the reader almost unaware of what he is doing. Take, for example, a short article entitled '"Christians and Spices"; Portuguese Missionaries in Ceylon, 1515–1658', which he wrote for *History Today*. This is typical of his work, a lightweight piece skating briefly over the history of Portuguese missionary enterprise and quoting in passing four or five less-well-known Portuguese writers. However, it is also a piece with a serious

[20] *Mary and Misogyny*, 10.

purpose. The article has a curious, unattributed text at its head which reads '*The methods used, or alleged to have been used, by Portuguese proselytisers more than three hundred years ago, remain a "living issue in Ceylon politics"*'. The article suggests that, contrary to the claims of some Sri Lankan politicians, 'the Portuguese did not seek to impose Christianity at the point of the sword . . . but they did seek to foster their religion through coercive and discriminatory legislation . . . since it is admittedly the evil rather than the good which men do that lives after them, this helps to account for the rather strident and nationalistic tone which is sometimes observable in the statements of contemporary Sinhalese Buddhists'.[21]

Another example would be the question of race relations. Before his famous lectures on the subject which caused such a furore, he had written a number of other articles bearing on the issue in a more subtle manner. In 'Fidalgos Portuguêses e Bailadeiras Indianas', which appeared in 1961, he had briefly mentioned the current theories about the colour blindness of the Portuguese and had gone on to publish a series of documents showing how the Portuguese authorities in eighteenth-century India had tried to check the mixing of the races and the sexual relations between Portuguese and Indian women.[22] Publishing original documents was a way of making a new contribution to a debate while at the same time drawing some of the venom from heated controversy. He used this device again in 1964, publishing a translation of an eighteenth-century pamphlet in which the issue of negro slavery was debated in the form of a dialogue.[23]

The British society in which Boxer grew up did not hold a very high opinion of Portuguese imperialism. The Portuguese were widely considered to have become decadent and to have lost their empire through cowardice, lack of enterprise, and general effeminacy resulting from miscegenation. To Boxer these judgements were cruel travesties of the truth, and his writings were designed to show the strength and resilience of the Portuguese during their struggle with the Dutch. In the introduction to his book *The Great Ship from Amaçon* he reflects on the passing of the Dutch, British, Spanish, and French empires, and concludes: 'The reasons which have enabled Macao to celebrate her fourth centenary are many and various, and not least among them is the indomitable resilience of her native sons'.[24]

Boxer's influence among his contemporaries came not only from his scholarship but also from his tireless travelling; the friends he made around the world and the hospitality he provided at his home in Hertfordshire; his appearance at conferences and symposia, always armed with a meticulously prepared and original academic paper; and the advice he generously gave to generations of scholars. After he left King's he took chairs at Indiana and

[21] ' "Christians and spices". Portuguese missionaries in Ceylon, 1515–1658', *History Today* (May 1958), 346–54.
[22] 'Fidalgos Portuguêses e Bailadeiras Indianas', *Revista de História (São Paulo)*, no. 45 (1961), 83–105.
[23] 'Negro slavery in Brazil. A Portuguese pamphlet of 1764', *Race*, 5 (1964), 38–47.
[24] *The Great Ship from Amaçon*, 19.

Yale. He sold his great book collection to the Lilly Library in Indiana and at once started on the building of a second collection. Meanwhile his lecture series appeared in volumes of essays which can still astonish with their erudition, which are phrased in a language rich with conscious and unconscious irony, and which are built around Boxer's deeply humanistic values. A final evaluation of his seventy active years of scholarship and writing can never be made because specialist scholars continually return to plunder his works for archival and bibliographical references or for the original materials he published either in translation or in their original language, while non-specialist historians and generations of undergraduates still find in his general histories, his monographs, and his essays the most lucid accounts of the period of the 1550s to 1650s that he made particularly his own.

MALYN NEWITT

Index

Printed and bound by CPI Group (UK) Ltd, Croydon, CR0 4YY

09/06/2025

14686137-0002